CADOGAN

London
Amsterdam

Cadogan Guides
West End House, 11 Hills Place, London W1R 1AG
becky.kendall@morrispub.co.uk

The Globe Pequot Press
246 Goose Lane, PO Box 480, Guilford,
Connecticut 06437–0480

Copyright © Andrew Gumbel & Rodney Bolt 2000

Updated by: Vanessa Letts, Jacqueline Chnéour, Gareth Mealing, Kate Paice, Dominique Shead, Mary-Ann Gallagher and Catherine Charles (London); Gerard van Vuuren (Amsterdam)

Book and cover design by Animage
Cover photographs © Kicca Tommasi

Chapter title pages designed by Kicca Tommasi from photographs by Kicca Tommasi, Antony Mason, Linda McQueen, Catherine Charles, Jacqueline Chnéour, Mary-Ann Gallagher and Gerard Van Vuuren.

Maps © Cadogan Guides, drawn by Map Creation Ltd

Editorial Director: Vicki Ingle
Series Editor: Linda McQueen

Editor: Matthew Tanner
Proofreading: Susannah Wight
Indexing: Isobel McLean
Production: Book Production Services

A catalogue record for this book is available from the British Library
ISBN 1 86011-985-9

Printed and bound by Cambridge University Press

About the Authors

Andrew Gumbel was born in a distant corner of that great anonymous expanse, the London suburbs. He first decided he loved London at the age of 10, and has been trying to make sense of it ever since. A journalist as well as a travel writer, he has returned to London periodically between lengthy periods abroad as a foreign correspondent for The *Guardian* and *The Independent*. He also wrote the Cadogan guide to Berlin. He currently lives in Los Angeles.

Rodney Bolt is seldom happier than when rattling along the canals of Amsterdam on his Miss Marple Dutch bicycle, or burrowing through papers in the Municipal Archive. Having lived in Greece, South Africa, Britain and Germany, he arrived in Amsterdam in 1991, and now nothing can convince him to leave. He has also written Cadogan guides to Germany, Bavaria and Madeira, as well as other books and numerous articles on the Netherlands. In 1994 he won the German National Tourist Office's 'Travel Writer of the Year' award.

Please help us to keep this guide up to date

We have done our best to ensure that the information in this guide is correct at the time of going to press. But places and facilities are constantly changing, and standards and prices in hotels and restaurants fluctuate. We would be delighted to receive any comments concerning existing entries or omissions, as well as suggestions for new features. Authors of the most helpful letters may be offered a copy of the Cadogan guide of their choice.

Contents

A Guide to the Guide

This guide is aimed at those of you who haven't much time to spend in these two great capitals of Europe. Getting from one to the other couldn't be easier. The **Travel** chapter will tell you how to get to London and to Amsterdam, move between the two, and get around efficiently.

Each half of the book launches with a few **practical tips**, then gets right to the heart of the matter with an alphabetical list of **Essential Sights**. This is followed with a chapter (or two) describing the city's key **Neighbourhoods**, or *Kwartiers*—places which may not be full of museums but which have a distinct atmosphere. But if museums are your passion, you can find what you want in the **Museums** chapter. **Shopping** points you towards the best areas in which to stock up on gifts while **Food and Drink, Where to Stay** and bang-up-to-date **Entertainment and Nightlife** listings ensure you get the best out of these two cities. **Gay Amsterdam** and a section on Dutch **language** conclude the guide.

Travel

TAXI

1

By Air to London

London is the spaghetti junction of the world's airways, with no fewer than five airports (at the last count) and planes from every conceivable airline zipping in from virtually every major city around the world. There should be no trouble finding a flight, even at the last moment, and you should be able to pick up a cheap deal without too much trouble. Shop around at several travel agents, and be prepared to consider Third World airlines as well as big names like British Airways, Qantas and the big North American carriers. North Americans wanting cheap flights to Europe can consult the worldwide web on: *www.travelocity.com*, or *www.lastminute.com*.

Travel times for direct flights are as follows: New York or Montreal 6 hours, Los Angeles 9 hours. The choice of airports is as follows:

Heathrow (✆ (020) 8759 4321), the largest of London's airports with four passenger terminals, is about 15 miles west of the centre. Terminal 1 is mainly for short-haul British Airways flights; Terminal 2 for the European services of non-British airlines; Terminal 3 for non-British long-haul services; and Terminal 4 for British Airways intercontinental flights and Concorde.

Gatwick (✆ (01293) 535353), with two terminals, is about 20 miles south of London and handles a lot of charter flights and the less prestigious airlines.

Stansted (✆ (01279) 680500) is the furthest from London, about 35 miles to the northeast, but in compensation is far and away the most pleasant. Only a few airlines, mostly arriving from continental Europe, use it for now, but it is likely to expand as pressure on Heathrow and Gatwick increases. Norman Foster's converted aircraft hangar design is pleasing to the eye and very efficient.

London City Airport (✆ (020) 7646 0000), about nine miles east of the centre, serves mainly business passengers arriving from continental Europe. It too is modern and pleasant.

Luton (✆ (01582) 405 100): Luton airport has recently undergone a thorough makeover, with a second terminal added to absorb some of the crowds. It mostly provides charter flights for British tourists heading for the sun, and is the base for the popular discount airline, easyJet.

By Air to Amsterdam

Schiphol enjoys a reputation as one of the world's most user-friendly airports and serves direct flights from London, Manchester, New York, Los Angeles, Toronto, Vancouver and Sydney as well as many other airports around the UK and Americas.

Flights from London take about 45 minutes, from New York about 8 hours. Prices direct from New York start at about $200 for special deals and go up to around $800 for more conventional fares. American travellers thinking of stopping over in London might find it cheaper to buy a ticket to Amsterdam in the UK.

KLM, the Dutch national airline, operates in partnership with the American company Northwest Airlines. Together they offer a service that takes in most major US cities, including New York, Baltimore, Los Angeles and Miami. KLM also flies to a number of Canadian cities, including Vancouver, Toronto and Montreal.

Airline Numbers

Schiphol Airport	(General Info)	✆ (0900) 0141
Air UK	UK	✆ (0345) 666 777
American Airlines	USA	✆ (1 800) 433 7300
British Airways	UK	✆ (0345) 222 111
British Midland	UK	✆ (0345) 554 554
Canadian Airlines	Canada	✆ (416) 798 2211 (Toronto)
	UK	✆ (020) 7745 5000
KLM	UK	✆ (08705) 074 074
	USA	✆ (1 800) 3 747 747
Transavia	UK	✆ (01293) 596 650
TWA	UK	✆ (020) 8814 0707
	USA	✆ (1 800) 892 4141

Between the Two Cities: London–Amsterdam–London

By Air

A browse through the travel ads in the British press (such as *Time Out* or the *London Evening Standard*) will divulge any number of return flights priced below £100, even on scheduled airlines. Among the most useful companies now operating from the UK are Air UK, British Airways, British Midland, KLM, Transvania and TWA. Travellers under 26 or students under 32 can pick up discounts at Campus Travel, ✆ (020) 7730 3402 or STA, ✆ (020) 7361 6161.

By Rail

Although there are plans to extend the **Eurostar** service to Amsterdam, for the moment you will have to take the Eurostar train to Brussels and make a platform change for a local train to Amsterdam. Fares start at £79 for a standard return and £159 for a first class return (if you book a week in advance). Eurostar information and booking: ✆ (0990) 186 186 or in person at Waterloo station. There are two **long-stay car parks** at Waterloo: ✆ (020) 7620 0357 or ✆ (020) 7582 9944.

By Bus

National Express/Eurolines (✆ (01582) 404 511) offer two options from London daily. On the morning departure you cross the Channel by hovercraft. The overnight trip involves the ferry and takes two hours longer. The current return price for either is £44, under-26/over-60 £39.

By Car

To bring your car into the Netherlands you'll need a valid insurance document (such as the EU 'green card'), current registration and road safety test certificates, an international identification disc and an EU or international driving licence. The shortest ferry crossing is Harwich–Hook of Holland (Stena Line, ✆ (01255) 243 333)—though, depending on where you're setting off from, you might find other lines more convenient.

Arriving by Air in London

Heathrow: There is an excellent new direct **train** link from Heathrow to Paddington, the **Heathrow Express**, costing £12 one-way and taking a mere 15 minutes.

All Heathrow terminals link up with the **London Underground** system, which runs from 5.30am to midnight. The Piccadilly Line service gets you into the centre in roughly an hour for about £4.50. If you have a lot of luggage and your destination is not on the Piccadilly Line, it may be worth getting off at ⊖ Earls Court or ⊖ South Kensington and proceeding by taxi.

There is also a **bus** service from Heathrow, which provides far more space for luggage but is also less frequent, slower (depending on traffic), quite a bit more expensive (about £7) and only runs until 7pm (℗ (020) 7222 1234 for more information). The A1 goes to Victoria Coach Station, with stops on the way at Earl's Court, Harrods, Hyde Park Corner and Victoria railway station. The A2 goes to King's Cross with stops at the Kensington Hilton in Holland Park Avenue, Notting Hill Gate, Queensway, Paddington, Marble Arch and Russell Square.

If all this sounds like too much hassle, you can take a **taxi**, but it will set you back £30 or more and, if you arrive during the rush hour, could take as long as 90 minutes.

Gatwick: The most practical way into town is by the **Gatwick Express** train; this non-stop service to Victoria station (cost: £9.50) leaves every 15 minutes from 5am until 12am, and every hour for the rest of the night. Look out for the signs in your terminal. There is a bus to Victoria Coach Station called **Flightlink** (℗ (020) 8668 7261), which is cheaper but takes nearly three times as long. Don't even think about a taxi.

Stansted: Just pop down one floor, and you are on the railway platform for London Liverpool Street. The journey takes 40–45 minutes and trains leave every half-hour. The fare is £10.40.

London City: Bus services (tickets £5) leave for Canary Wharf in Docklands and for Liverpool St every 20 minutes or so. A taxi ride into the City of London costs around £12. There is an executive helicopter service; if you need to ask the price, don't take it.

Luton: Almost as far away from London as Stansted, and in much the same direction, the airport has no direct rail link to the city. You have to take an airport bus to the station and then take an invariably crowded Thameslink commuter train in to King's Cross (about £10).

Arriving by Air in Amsterdam

Taxis will cost you at least ƒ60, and hardly seem worth it given the ease, frequency and price of public transport. **Trains** leave for Centraal Station every 15 minutes (until 1am, then hourly until 5am). The journey takes about 20 minutes and tickets cost ƒ5.75. Should you require them, there are trains from Schiphol to most of the suburban stations around Amsterdam.

Alternatively, you can swan into town on the plush **KLM Hotel Bus**. The service is available to anyone, even if you sneaked over on a bucket flight and intend sleeping in the Vondelpark. Buses leave at 15min intervals from 6.30am to 9.15pm and tickets cost ƒ17.50. Route A stops include the Pulitzer, Krasnapolsky, Jolly Carlton and Okura (i.e. mainly central Amsterdam). Route B focuses more on southern Amsterdam, stopping at such hotels as the Hilton, Beethoven and Apollo.

Waterloo station is just south of the Thames and is on the **Underground**'s Northern line and Bakerloo line, either of which will take you straight into the West End in a matter of 10 minutes. There is a direct link from the international terminal and it's about a five-minute walk inside the station; just follow the signs.

If you've got a lot of baggage it might be better to take a **taxi**, which will cost you from £5–10; there's a rank just as you exit the Eurostar gate. If you're taking a taxi to Waterloo from central London, make sure to specify the international terminal.

It's not a good idea to try to take a **bus** from or to Waterloo; the area just outside is a building site with the South Bank renovations and you would need to know where you were going.

Arriving by Train in Amsterdam

All major traffic comes into Amsterdam's **Centraal Station** and from here you can get to anywhere in the city by a variety of routes. Taxis line up outside to your right while two ranks of trams converge just outside. Dam Square is only a short walk away. Centraal Station has self-service lockers, staffed left-luggage (24-hr), a cashpoint machine accepting Eurocheque, Cirrus, Visa, Eurocard and Mastercard, as well as a number of shops and cafés.

Passports, Visas and Border Formalities

London: Britain has opted not to join the eight-strong group of European countries practising an open-border policy (the so-called Schengen Group), so EU citizens will still have to bring their passports or identity cards. That means a few delays and detours (particularly at the Channel Tunnel terminus at Waterloo), but basically they can expect to breeze through customs; there is even a separate queue for them to avoid hold-ups. Americans can expect a fair grilling, particularly at airports and particularly if you are not white.

There are very few **customs** restrictions if you are coming from another EU country. Otherwise, the usual limits on alcohol, cigarettes and perfume apply (roughly speaking, half a dozen bottles of wine or one bottle of spirits, plus 200 cigarettes). If you are a national of the United States, Canada, Australia, New Zealand, South Africa, Japan, Mexico or Switzerland, you won't need a **visa** to get into the country if you are just on holiday or on a business trip. Other nationalities should check with their local British consulate.

Amsterdam: EU nationals and citizens of Australia, Canada, New Zealand and the USA need only a valid passport to visit the Netherlands if their stay is for less than three months. If you intend to stay for longer than this you should get your passport stamped on entry, and will need a **residence permit**.

If you are coming from outside the EU and are over 17, you can enter the Netherlands with 200 cigarettes (or 50 cigars or 250g/8.82oz of tobacco), 1 litre of spirits (or 2 litres of fortified wine) and 2 litres of non-sparkling wine, 50g/1.76oz of perfume and *f*300 worth of gifts. If you've bought goods tax-paid within the EU then there are no restrictions, so long as you remain within reasonable limits.

The **exporting of flower bulbs** is permitted to the UK, but you need an inoculation certificate for the USA. It's best to have bulbs posted home to avoid border hassles. Most reputable dealers will do this, and the necessary paperwork, for you.

London Transport ✆ (020) 7222 1234, *www.londontransport.co.uk*

By Underground and DLR

London's **Underground** system (also known as the Tube) is 100 years old, and it shows. Creaky, unpunctual, smelly, unfriendly: it is everyone's favourite urban nightmare. The Tube is the most expensive city transport system in Europe, the most basic single adult ticket costing a staggering £1.50. For better or worse, though, it is still by far the quickest way to cross London and avoid the traffic, especially during office hours. Trains run from around 5.30am (7am on Sundays) until at least 11pm and as late as 1am on some lines (no service on Christmas Day).

The East End and Docklands, and now also Greenwich, are served by the **Docklands Light Railway,** or DLR, an overground monorail which links up with the Tube at Bank and Tower Hill (you can call the DLR 24-hour travel hotline for advice on journeys on ✆ (020) 7918 4000). DLR trains now run all week, until at least 11.30pm.

By Bus

London's buses are slightly cheaper than the Underground (£1 anywhere in central London (Zone 1) and 70p elsewhere), and at least you can see trees and sky, as well as the life of the city zipping by. Since the bus system was deregulated, many different private companies have been running services all over town, but all are integrated into the London Transport network. You can buy a Bus Pass, but your best bet is probably to buy a Travelcard which is valid for the Underground as well. If you plan to use the bus a lot, you should pick up a bus map, available from major Underground stations.

After midnight a large network of N-prefixed **night buses** takes over. You can get a map from Underground stations or just look on the bus stops for N numbers. The hub is Trafalgar Square. Note that One Day Travelcards are not valid on night buses and you will have to pay.

There is a vast range of **tourist buses,** with stops all over central London. One useful one to know about is the Hop-on Hop-off, which takes you round all the main tourist sights of the centre and allows you to get on and off as many times as you like. Call ✆ (01708) 631122 for details of the route so you know where to catch it.

By Train

Overground trains around London are integrated into the London Transport system and can be useful for crossing large chunks of town, or else for accessing certain parts which the Underground neglects. Three useful services are the **Thameslink**, which starts at Luton Airport and snakes through West Hampstead, Kentish Town, King's Cross and Blackfriars through to the south London suburbs including Greenwich; the north London **Silverlink**, which starts in Richmond and goes through Kew Gardens, Hampstead and Highbury on its way through to the East End; and the quick and efficient **Waterloo and City** line between Waterloo and Bank. The rail lines are all marked on the larger Underground maps (called Journey Planners), and you don't have to pay extra if you have a Travelcard.

Information: ✆ (0345) 484 950 or ✆ (020) 7222 1234.

Tickets and Passes

The Underground fare system is organized in concentric zones, Zone 1 being the centre, and Zone 6 being the outermost ring including, among other things, Heathrow Airport. Pick up a map from any station and you will see that the lines are colour-coded to make them easier to follow.

The most practical kind of ticket is a **One Day Travelcard**, which you can buy to cover all zones (prices start at £3.90 for Zones 1 & 2) and which is valid on buses and overground trains as well. Daily Travelcards are available after 9.30am; weekly and monthly passes are available any time, although you'll need a passport photo to get these; Zone 1 tickets are now sold in useful **carnets** which cost £10 for 10 tickets (saving you £5). You can also buy a **Weekend Travelcard** for £5.80, less than the price of two One Day Travelcards and valid for night buses on the first night.

Never ever travel beyond the zone or bus stop you have bought a ticket for. Even if you present yourself openly to the excess fares window, you will be liable for an instant £10 'penalty fare' (£5 on buses) and there's absolutely no sympathy to be gained from the steely staff.

By Taxi

Taxis are part of the mythology of London, perhaps because their drivers are the only people who can make sense of the great metropolitan labyrinth. Cabbies have to train for three years to take their qualifying exam, known as The Knowledge, in which they are expected to be able to locate every street, every major building and all the main tourist attractions as well as memorizing 468 basic routes. For years taxis conformed to a single sleek black design, but recently there have been some changes, notably the advent of advertising and different body colours. You can still recognize them, however, by the distinctive For Hire signs on the roof, which light up in orange when the cab is free.

During the day it is easy to hail a taxi off the street, unless it's raining when they all disappear. All licensed cabs are metered. They are more expensive than in most cities, but you can be confident of getting to your destination by the quickest route. For lost property ✆ (020) 7833 0996. If you want to order a taxi, contact **Dial-A-Black-Cab**, ✆ (020) 7253 5000.

Black cabs are harder to find at night, and you may need to call a **minicab**. These tend to be cheaper, less reliable and occasionally a little hazardous. Some good ones are:

Atlas Cars, ✆ (020) 7602 1234.

Greater London Hire, ✆ (020) 8340 2450.

Town and Country Cabs, ✆ (020) 7622 6222, ✉ (020) 7622 6000, *www.taxi. co.uk*. For South and Central London, male or female drivers, as requested.

Lady Cabs, ✆ (020) 7254 3501, a specialist service run by women for women.

By Car

Traffic in London moves at an average of 11 miles an hour during the day, so you will be much better off forgetting about a car. Parking is also a huge problem. Car parks and meters are very expensive and can prove ruinous if you outstay your welcome—at least £30 for a parking ticket (or £60 if you leave it for longer than two weeks). Restrictions on parking, both on meters and on single yellow lines, vary wildly from borough to borough and catch out even switched-on Londoners by changing with no notice. If you're very unlucky you will have a nasty yellow clamp placed around one of your wheels. There is one even worse horror that could befall you, and that is having your car towed away altogether. Call ✆ (020) 7747 4747 to find out where your vehicle is and bring at least £135 in cash to the vehicle pound.

A car can nevertheless be a blessing in London, particularly for trips out of town. Familiarize yourself with the British Highway Code (available from newsagents) and take particular note of the strict drink-drive laws. You don't need to carry your driving papers with you, but if you are stopped you can be asked to show them at a police station within five days.

If you are hiring a car, you need to be over 21 and have at least one year's driving experience. Here are some addresses:

Hertz, ✆ (0990) 996699/ **Avis,** ✆ (0990) 900500, open 24 hours.

Supercars, 11c Greens End, SE18 6HX, ✆ (020) 8317 1414. Much cheaper.

On Two Wheels

Despite the traffic and pollution, cycling is a good mode of transport in London. It is faster than going by car, at least during the day, and more pleasant than the Tube, especially if you make use of London's extensive parkland. For safety's sake, helmets are a must.

On Your Bike, 52–4 Tooley St (by London Bridge), ✆ (020) 7378 6669.

Dial-a-Bike, ✆ (020) 7828 4040, delivers to major hotels in London.

You could also telephone the **London Cycling Campaign,** ✆ (020) 7928 7220, for advice and maps of safe routes around the city.

By River

An excellent Riverbus service that used to ply the Thames all day suffered a sad demise in the summer of 1993; now you have to try your luck with a plethora of commercial companies that run services from Westminster Pier or Charing Cross Pier, both just south of Trafalgar Square. Services upriver to Greenwich and the Thames Barrier—the most attractive destinations—run every half-hour and take about 45–50 minutes (✆ (020) 7930 4097 for up-to-the-minute information). In the other direction, services downriver to Kew, Richmond and Hampton Court are more erratic and may not run more than four times a day (✆ (020) 7930 4721 for information).

Getting Around Amsterdam

By Tram

Trams run from 6am Mon–Fri, 6.30am on Sat and 7.30am Sun. Last trams are around midnight. They hurtle about, bells clanging, scattering cyclists and pedestrians and forcing passengers to hang on for dear life. On most trams you can get on or off through any one of the three doors (which open after you press the adjacent metal button). Some lines have conductors, who sit at the back. On these trams you can only alight through the rear door. If it looks as if you're the only person due to get off, you'll need to tell the driver to stop by pushing one of the bell buttons inside (on older trams these are unmarked and can be quite obscure). Tram stops have yellow boards showing the numbers of the trams they serve and listing further destinations along the route. Of special benefit to visitors is the Circle Tram, running from Centraal Station to all the major sights and back.

By Bus

Buses work on the same system as trams, though you board at the front door. You're much less likely to use them, unless you need a night bus. A black square with the bus number printed on it is shown on the board of night bus stops. By some inscrutable logic the night buses decrease in frequency at about the time the bars close (2am). After this time there is only one bus an hour on some routes, and none at all until 4am on others.

By Metro

The metro is used mainly by commuters from the suburbs. There are only two lines, both terminating at Centraal Station. Running times and ticketing are the same as for trams.

By Taxi

Theoretically, you can hail an Amsterdam cab in the street, but you're unlikely to have any luck at all. Best bet is to pick one up at a rank, or telephone the 24-hour central control, © 677 7777 or © (0900) 0724. The main ranks are at Centraal Station, Rembrandtplein and Leidseplein. Cafés, restaurants or nightclubs will usually phone a cab for you, and one will arrive within minutes. When you set off, the meter should be blank, except for the minimum charge. Even short journeys are expensive, with a flat rate of ƒ5.80 for starters, then ƒ2.85 a kilometre (ƒ4.50 a mile) and increasing after midnight.

By Bicycle

The city has an excellent network of cycle lanes and bicycles are cheap to hire, though it can often be more economical to pick up a second-hand one. This you can do from markets or cycle shops for around ƒ150.

Hire charges vary according to season, but start at around ƒ10 a day. You'll need to take your passport, and a deposit. This ranges from ƒ50 to ƒ200, but you can usually get around it by leaving an imprint of your credit card.

Try **Rent-A-Bike** (Pieter Jacobsdwarsstraat 11, © 625 5029) or **Macbike** (Mr Visserplein 2, © 620 0985) and **Take-A-Bike** (Stationsplein 6, near Centraal Station, © 624 8391), which are a little cheaper.

Tickets and Travel Information

GVB (**Amsterdam Municipal Transport Authority**), Stationsplein 15, opposite Centraal Station (*open Mon–Fri 7am–7pm, Sat and Sun 8am–7pm,* © *(0900) 9292*) for maps, information and tickets.

A **strip ticket** (*strippenkaart,* ƒ11.75) is valid on the metro and on all buses and trains. The *strippenkaart,* available from stations, newsagents and the GVB, is divided into 15 units. Each time you make a journey allow 1 unit for 'boarding', then one for each of the zones.

Day tickets (*dagkaart*) allow unlimited travel in Amsterdam and cost ƒ12 for 1 day, ƒ15 for 2 days, ƒ19 for 3 days, ƒ23 for 4 days, and ƒ27 for 5 days. You can buy dagkaarten from drivers or the GVB.

By Water

The **Canal Bus** takes you on a gentle dawdle along some fine stretches of canal between the Rijksmuseum and Centraal Station, stopping at Leidseplein, Leidsestraat/Keizersgracht and the Anne Frank Huis. Buses leave at 45-minute intervals between 10am and 6pm. A day ticket costs *f*22. The new **All Amsterdam Transport Pass** is a day pass that includes all public transport as well as unlimited use of the canal bus and costs a mere *f*29.50.

You can hail **Water Taxis** as they putter past and can also order them from the **Water Taxi Centrale** (Stationsplein 8, ✆ 530 1090; *open daily 9am–1am*; major credit cards accepted). Fares are metered—an 8-seater boat works out at around *f*125 for the first half an hour irrespective of the number of passengers, and *f*75 for every subsequent half hour.

If you're feeling energetic you can hire a **Canal Bike** (a pedalboat that seats two or four people; costs *f*25 per hour for two people and *f*40 for four; deposit *f*50; no credit cards, ✆ 626 5574). **Canal Motor Boats** (on Kloveniersburgwal, ✆ 422 7007) offer electric boats for hire at *f*65 for the first hour, and a declining rate for subsequent hours.

By Car

Covered **car parks** are indicated by a white P on blue background and can be found at De Bijenkorf (on Beursplein), Byzantium (Stadhouderskade, opposite Leidseplein), Europarking (Marnixstraat 250), RAI (on the Europa Boulevard) and under the Muziektheater (Waterlooplein). Charges are around *f*5 an hour. Parking beside the road works out at about *f*4 an hour. Street parking works by the 'pay-and-display' method. If you park illegally your car will be towed away. It will cost you at least *f*400 to get it back from the pound (Daniël Goedkoopstraat 7, ✆ 553 0333), and they won't take credit cards. If you'd like to **hire a car**, you'll find the international companies well represented:

> **Avis**, Nassaukade 380, ✆ 683 6061
>
> **Budget**, Overtoom 333, ✆ 612 6066
>
> **Hertz**, Overtoom 85, ✆ 612 2441

An EU or international driving licence is valid. You'll also need your passport and a credit card (to pay a deposit).

Guided Tours

The **Amsterdam Tourist Board** (opposite Centraal Station at Sationsplein 10) not only takes bookings for canal cruises, but constantly comes up with new ideas for touring the city—its staff can suggest all sorts of walking and cycling routes in and about Amsterdam. **Yellowbike** (NZ Kolk 29, ✆ 620 6940) also offers guided cycle tours around the city and surrounding waterlands. **Audiotourist** (Oude Spiegelstraat 9, ✆ 421 5580) will rent you a personal stereo plus guided tour on cassette for *f*15 (plus deposit). There are three different walks that last two to three hours each.

More rewarding than the commercially organized tours are the informal walkabouts with old Amsterdam residents offered by **Mee in Mokum** (*open Mon–Fri 1–4pm*, ✆ 625 1390). The guides give a homely, resident's touch that you're unlikely to find elsewhere. The tours are usually given in Dutch, but since the groups are small (about eight people), it's often possible to arrange an English alternative. **Archivisie** (✆ 625 8908) offers specialist architectural tours

London: Introduction

Oh thou, resort and mart of all the earth
Chequer'd with all complexions of mankind
And spotted with all crimes, in whom I see
Much that I love and more that I admire,
And all that I abhor...

William Cowper, *The Task*, Book III
(1785)

London, like all great cities, has a habit of going through drastic mood swings: grey, worthy and dull one minute, hip and ultra-modern the next. Down its long history it has been accused of everything from provincialism to irredeemable sinfulness; at times it has positively creaked under the weight of its own impossible size and complexity. At others, it has been hailed as everything a city could ever hope to be: a beacon of wealth, liberty, cosmopolitanism and artistic flair. And so, just when it was being written off as the crumbling capital of a dead empire, London has come roaring back to life. Freed from the shackles of empire and the bitter ideological divisions of the Thatcher years, it is enjoying a renaissance of extraordinary dimensions. London has recovered a belief in itself that would have seemed inconceivable even a decade ago, when gloom was perennially written on the hangdog faces of its citizens and the streets emptied as soon as the pubs closed. Now, in Soho or Notting Hill or Islington, you can barely move for people thronging to the latest designer shop, the newest art opening, or the hottest ethnic restaurant. The capital is being redefined by a new, highly creative generation of artists and designers iconoclastic enough to break down the fusty London of the past and rebuild it in their own image. Suddenly, everything seems possible and Londoners are embracing the changes with barely a whiff of scepticism or critical distance. The city invents and discards fads at an astonishing rate: rocket and shaved parmesan salad, the innovative food obsession of the mid-'90s, is already looking passé, along with Damien Hirst, Oasis and Vivienne Westwood. Old definitions no longer fit the new trends: sculpture and painting have given way to new mediums such as video art; the erstwhile household design guru Terence Conran, meanwhile, has moved beyond the restaurant business into gastrodomes, veritable palaces of food consumption in custom-made settings like an old tyre factory, say, or a sports car showroom. This new London has even contrived to pretend that the weather is better: pavement cafés and al fresco dining are the new watchwords, along with Italian coffee and Mediterranean clothing styles. No city in Europe is so desired, or so desirable.

Be warned, however. Amidst this creative frenzy, the old caveats about London still apply. It may be the most exciting city in Europe, but it is not the most beautiful, nor the easiest to get around. Indeed, there are times when it seems like one of those eccentric English aristocrats who deliberately dress in rags and forget to wash for weeks at a stretch. A city of its size is inevitably stricken with great swathes of dullness, not to mention air pollution, gridlocked traffic, creaky public transport, damp, ageing houses and all the other banal horrors of modern urban living. This is not a city that shouts its beauties from the rooftops, and many visitors who expect too much too quickly come away with a sense of bewildered disappointment.

There is an art to exploring London; you cannot only do the rounds of its celebrated sights and museums and say you have seen it all. You have to engage on a personal level, ferreting out neighbourhoods you feel at home in, finding little backstreets you can admire without necessarily looking for them in a guidebook, discovering the museums and theatres and pubs that give you a sense of personal satisfaction. Two visitors meeting after a week in London might discover that one had hung around wine bars in Kensington, taken a river trip to Hampton Court and shopped at Harrods, while the other had sought out Freud's house, done some sketching in the Tate Gallery and sat in pub theatres at lunchtime. They would not have visited the same city at all, but they would both have been to London.

Once you have got over the sheer vastness and inconvenience, once you have traced out your route around the labyrinth, the sense of diversity and discovery can be immensely liberating. Nobody can know all of London—not poets, not politicians, not even guidebook writers. You have to make up your own version of it. Out of the chaos you produce a personalized sense of order, your own map of the city. Pop out of an Underground station at random and you may well find yourself in the sort of anonymous urban wasteland the city's millions of commuters pass through every morning and night; it is just possible, however, that you will discover a charming unknown corner of the metropolis you can call your very own.

Orientation

The wit and raconteur Max Beerbohm once said that showing a visitor round London made him feel like Virgil accompanying Dante through the circles of hell. That may not sound like much of a compliment, but in one respect at least the observation is acute: the best way to orient yourself is to picture the city as a series of concentric circles. On the outside is limbo, that endless stretch of characterless suburbia that makes no sense to anyone except a mapmaker or a statistician; then comes the ring of inner suburbs, a zone of varied and often unexpected pleasures; finally, at the centre, is London's diabolical heart.

The centre is of course the part with most history, but that does not mean that it is necessarily the most interesting or most enjoyable to visit. What is central geographically may be only peripheral in terms of interest, and vice versa. As in Dante's *Inferno*, appearances can be deceptive. Certainly you should make sure you get to the National Gallery and St Paul's, but it would be a mistake to skip Hampstead, Greenwich or Kew just because they are not slap bang in the centre of town. In the same way, it would be foolish to spend too long in Mayfair or the City just because they happen to be where they are.

The Pick of London in a Weekend

There's nothing more dreary than spending a week in London going round museum after museum. Variety should be the watchword, whether this is your first time in the city or your 50th. Treat the following not as a list of must-sees to check off one by one, but rather a rich menu from which to pick the items that suit you best on the day:

First-time visitors

National Gallery, Westminster Abbey and Tate Gallery, Soho, British Museum, St Paul's, the South Bank, Victoria and Albert Museum, Portobello Market, Greenwich (including a boat ride down there).

Occasional visitors

Banqueting House and Houses of Parliament, the John Soane Museum, the Clink and Old St Thomas's Operating Theatre, the Wallace Collection, Holland Park, Hampstead, Kew Gardens, Hampton Court.

Residents

Spencer House and the Queen's Chapel, Westminster Hall and, if you can, the Foreign Office, Jeremy Bentham's corpse, St Etheldreda, Kensington Palace, Leighton House, Carlyle's House, Highgate Cemetery, Rotherhithe. Note: some of these are pretty tough to get into, but the effort will be well rewarded.

Not been back lately

To catch a whiff of the extraordinary changes in London, all you really have to do is stand in the middle of Soho in mid-evening and marvel at the variety, exuberance and sheer numbers of the people around you. Eat at Terence Conran's futuristic gastrodome, Mezzo, or grab some conveyor-belt sushi served by robots on Poland Street. Further afield, there is the irrepressible trendiness of Notting Hill. For sightseeing, the South Bank is a must, particularly the newly refurbished Oxo Tower, the rebuilt Globe Theatre and the developments at Butlers Wharf— this is the spirit of the new London. Look out, too, for looming Millennium projects and quirky new places like the Aquarium at County Hall.

Not been back in years

In addition to the above, you'll probably want to have a sniff round the Docklands, not just the monster tower at Canary Wharf, but also less obvious novelties like the riverfront at Rotherhithe. Go to the action-packed Science Museum which has changed beyond recognition. If you remember the strict old licensing laws, you'll get a buzz just sitting in a pub mid-afternoon and ordering a drink. As for eating, just about anywhere should come as a startlingly pleasant surprise; try a modern riverside location (the Blueprint Café, Butlers Wharf, or Canteen, Chelsea Harbour).

Can't stand all this new-fangled stuff

If what you want is good, old-fashioned London, St James's and Mayfair are the places to start. No doubt you'll stay in a favourite quiet hotel in South Kensington, or even one of the posher establishments in Mayfair, but that shouldn't stop you dropping in on Brown's or the Ritz for tea—ideal stopping-off points during shopping sprees on Jermyn Street (bespoke clothes, as well as marmalade and Earl Grey at Fortnum's). Once you've exhausted sights like Buckingham Palace and the Wallace Collection, you might want to stroll around Chelsea, meet the eccentric pensioners at the Royal Hospital, or even venture out to the fine Adam houses at Syon Park and Osterley. Back in town, there are cocktails at the Café Royal and enticing dinner options around Covent Garden at Simpson's, The Ivy and Rules.

Romantic London

Okay, this isn't Paris or Venice, but London is more romantic than you might think. Anthony Minghella's film *Truly, Madly, Deeply* highlighted the heart-wrenching pleasures of Kenwood (those great views of the metropolis over the Heath) and the pavement cafés on the South Bank (don't forget the foyer jazz and cosy book-browsing possibilities inside the National Theatre, either). For dreamy walks, Holland Park or the riverside at Richmond and Twickenham are perfect. Hampstead is London's dinkiest neighbourhood—visit Keats' house to relive the poet's romance with Fanny Brawne, and find yourselves a quiet nook in the atmospheric Holly Bush pub. Otherwise try kite-flying on Parliament Hill (more good views as well as bracing air), or the canal walks and Georgian rows of Canonbury (plus the romantic association of penniless Lord Compton and the rich local merchant's daughter). Hazlitt's is a charming, centrally located hotel, while Clarke's (on Kensington Church St) or Lemonia (in Camden) make fine settings for a romantic dinner.

London: Practical A–Z

Actual dates for nearly all the events listed below change every year. Numbers for checking are given where possible:

January

1 January	*New Year's day Parade* Display of 6,000 real-American majorettes starting from Parliament Square at 12pm and finishing in Berkeley Square at 3pm.
Early January	Harrods' after-Christmas sale starts.
Mid-January to early February	*Chinese New Year* celebrations around Gerrard St in Soho. Lots of food and colourful floats.
February	Shrove Tuesday *Soho and Great Spitalfields Pancake Day Races.* Sprints down Carnaby Street and Spitalfields, with participants tossing pancakes in a pan; ✆ (020) 7375 0441.

April

1 April	Check newspapers for April Fool's Day hoaxes.
Sat before Easter	*Oxford and Cambridge Boat Race.* Teams from the rival universities row their hearts out from Putney to Mortlake; ✆ (020) 7730 3488.
Easter Sunday	*Easter Day Parade* in Battersea Park, complete with funfair and sideshows.
Mid-April	*London Marathon* from Blackheath to The Mall; ✆ (020) 7620 4117 for details of route and how to enter.
Ascension Day	*Beating the Bounds.* Boys of St Dunstan's beat on the City's boundary markers with willow sticks in an ancient ritual. Starts at 3pm at All Hallows' by the Tower.

May

Early May	*Museums Week*—special events at 850 museums; *www.museumsweek.co.uk*
Late May	*Chelsea Flower Show* at the Royal Hospital Gardens. Funfairs on Hampstead Heath, Blackheath and Alexandra Park on Spring Bank Holiday Monday, enquiries ✆ (020) 7630 7422, tickets ✆ (0990) 344 444.

June

First Saturday	*Derby* horse race at Epsom racecourse, Surrey.
Early June	*Coin Street Festival,* Gabriel's Wharf, London SE1 (*see* p.83): buskers and free street performances. *Greenwich Festival*: concerts, theatre and children's events, plus fireworks on the opening night. Also, *Hampton Court Festival,* opera music and dance; ✆ (020) 7344 4444 (*see* pp.34–5). Also, *Beating the Retreat,* floodlit evening display by Queen's Household Division outside Buckingham Palace.
Second Saturday	*Trooping the Colour.* The Queen's Guards in a birthday parade for Ma'am. The date is chosen by the palace and is usually the second.

	Saturday, but it does vary. It's difficult to get a ticket but people line The Mall to watch; ✆ (020) 7414 2497.
June (*cont'd*)	*Spitalfields Festival.* Classical music in Christ Church, plus guided walks of the area; ✆ (020) 7375 0441.
Mid-June	*Royal Ascot.* Society horse races at Ascot in Berkshire.
Late June	*Henley Royal Regatta.* Rowers row on the Thames while very posh spectators get sozzled in their champagne tents.
Late June–early July	*Wimbledon* tennis championships. Box office ✆ (020) 8944 1066.
Late June to July	*City of London Festival*: classical concerts around the City; ✆ (020) 7377 0540.
June to August	*Summer Exhibition* at the Royal Academy (*see* p.72). More than 1,000 works by living artists.
June to September	*Kenwood Lakeside Concerts.* Open-air concerts at the top of Hampstead Heath every Saturday. Magical if the weather's good; ✆ (020) 7973 3427.

July

	Gay Pride Day, first week of July on Clapham Common. Also, *Hampton Court Flower Show;* ✆ (020) 7821 3042 (*see* p.34).
Mid-July	*Royal Military Tattoo* pageants in Earl's Court; ✆ (020) 7799 2323. Also, *Doggett's Coat and Badge Race*, a rowing contest from London Bridge to Cadogan Pier.
July to September	*The Proms* in the Albert Hall; ✆ (020) 7589 8212 (*see* p.28).

August

August to September	Buckingham Palace open to the public.
Last Sunday and Monday	*Notting Hill Carnival.* Steel bands, dancing and general Caribbean fun, occasionally broken up by police, around Portobello Rd and Ladbroke Grove (*see* p.90).

September

Mid-September	*Chelsea Antiques Fair*, ✆ (01444) 482514.
Third week	*Open House Weekend*, for info at 60p a minute: ✆ (0891) 600061. Houses and buildings which are normally closed to the public open up for free, also walking tours.
Late September	*Clog and Apron Race.* A sprint through Kew by gardening students in strange attire; ✆ (020) 8940 1171.

October

First Sunday	*Pearly Harvest Festival* at St Martin-in-the-Fields (*see* p.65). Lots of folklore cockneys in their button-splashed coats playing ukeleles.

November

5 November	*Bonfire Night.* Fireworks and bonfires, plus plenty of booze, in parks all over London (Highbury Fields and Battersea Park are good venues, but telephone the London Tourist Board ✆ (0839) 123456 or check

	Time Out for details) to commemorate Guy Fawkes's attempt to blow up parliament in 1605.
Early November	*State Opening of Parliament.* The Queen sets out from Buckingham Palace for Westminster where she reads out the government's programme for the forthcoming year. Crowds follow her around. Date varies a lot: check on ✆ (020) 7219 3107.
First Sunday	*London to Brighton Veteran Car Run.* Starts in Hyde Park; ✆ (01753) 681736 for details.
	London Film Festival, based at the NFT on the South Bank (*see* p.82) but with showings all over town; ✆ (020) 7815 1323.
Second Saturday	*Lord Mayor's Show.* The new Lord Mayor goes on a grand procession through the City in his 18th-century gilded coach. Most people stand around St Paul's to watch, but you can sit down if you ask the Pageant Master: ✆ (01992) 505 306.
Sunday nearest 11 November	*Remembrance Day Service* to commemorate war dead at the Cenotaph in Whitehall.
November to December	Christmas lights go on in Oxford Street, Regent Street, Bond Street and Trafalgar Square.
December	
31 December	New Year's celebrations beneath the Christmas tree in Trafalgar Square (*see* pp.45–6).

Consulates in London

You can always find the number of your consulate or embassy by calling directory enquiries (✆ 192). Here are a few:

US Embassy, 24 Grosvenor Square, ✆ (020) 7499 9000, open Mon–Fri 9–6. There is a 24-hour helpline for US citizens.

Australian High Commission, Australia House, The Strand, ✆ (020) 7379 4334, open Mon–Fri 9–5.15.

Canadian High Commission, 38 Grosvenor St, ✆ (020) 7258 6600, open Mon–Fri 8–11am, with 24-hour telephone helpline.

Crime and Police

The British downmarket newspapers are full of lurid crime stories, usually involving children being attacked or abducted, or policemen being shot by crazed drug-dealers. Something of a siege mentality has set in, which is curious because serious crime in London has been stable for several decades. You won't be at greater risk in London than in any other biggish city in Europe; the greatest hazard is petty theft and pickpocketing, for which the usual precautions apply. Although usage is unmistakably on the increase, drugs are yet to become the kind of overwhelming crime problem they are in the United States or parts of southern Europe; firearms are extremely uncommon and even police officers do not carry them. Don't hang around lonely neighbourhoods late at night—Hackney or Tottenham spring to mind—and don't leave valuables in your hotel room. Women have a far more hassle-free time in London than in Rome or Madrid, and it is accepted as normal for a woman to be out on her own. They should watch out on the Underground, however, particularly late at night.

You'll find the authorities sometimes jumpy about the risk of terrorist attack, particularly in the City: waste-bins have been removed from the Underground, automatic luggage lockers have been taken out of railway stations and many buildings bristle with security guards. Don't let reports of terrorist bombs put you off coming to London, though. You are more likely to die on the aircraft into London than in an attack once you get here; and you stand a far greater chance of being run over outside your house than ever dying on an aircraft.

The police are usually friendly enough, although you might encounter suspicion or idle prejudice if you are Irish or black. If you need to go to the police to report a theft or other crime, simply visit your nearest station and you should receive a civil hearing—though you probably won't get your stolen goods back. In case of emergency, dial either ✆ 999 or ✆ 112. If you yourself get picked up by the police, you must insist, if you feel it necessary, on calling your embassy or consulate, or a lawyer if you know one. Keep your cool and remain polite at all times. Be particularly careful how you drive around Christmas time, as the drink-drive police are out in force.

Finally, to retrieve **lost property**, try the London Transport Lost Property Office at 200 Baker St, open weekday mornings only, ✆ (020) 7486 2496; or the Black Cab Lost Property Office, 15 Penton St, Islington, ✆ (020) 7833 0996, open Mon–Fri 9–4.

Disabled Travellers

London is reasonably wheelchair-conscious, certainly by comparison with the rest of Europe, and most of the major sights have proper access and help on hand if necessary. There are still problems, however, with the transport system and many theatres and cinemas. The London Tourist Board has a special leaflet which you can find in tourist offices called *Information for Wheelchair Users Visiting London* which covers hotels, tourists sights and transport. A fuller guide is *Access in London*, a booklet available at Books Etc on Charing Cross Road or by post from the Access Project at 39 Bradley Gardens, London W13 8HE (a donation of £7.50 for printing costs is requested). London Transport publishes *Access to the Underground* with information on lift access to Tubes, available free from Tube stations or by post from the London Transport Unit for Disabled Passengers, 172 Buckingham Palace Road, London SW1W 9TN, ✆ (020) 7918 3312. Otherwise, bear the following addresses in mind:

Artsline, ✆ (020) 7388 2227. Free information on access to arts venues.

Holiday Care Service, ✆ (01293) 774535. Advice on hotels.

Shape, ✆ (020) 7700 8138. Offers cheap tickets for arts events.

Tripscope, ✆ (020) 8994 9294. Telephone helpline for people touring in London and the whole of Britain.

Finally **The Greater London Association for Disabled People** publishes a free *London Disability Guide*, available by post from 336 Brixton Road, London SW9 7AA.

Electricity

Britain uses three-prong square-pin plugs quite unlike anything else in Europe or North America. So far, the British government has resisted conforming to the rest of Europe on safety grounds—all British plugs have detachable fuses of three, five or 13 amps. So you will need an adaptor for any electrical device you bring in from abroad. The airport is as good a place as any to find one. Note also the electricity supply is 240 volts AC.

Health

Citizens of the European Union and some Commonwealth countries enjoy free medical care in Britain under the state National Health Service. The days when you could get free treatment on production of just a passport are probably over, so you'll need to fill out the appropriate paperwork before you leave home (in the EU the form is called an E111). Thus armed, the only things you will have to pay for are prescriptions and visits to the optician or dentist, although these should not cost more than a few pounds.

Anyone else, and that includes Americans, Africans, Indians and Canadians, should take out medical insurance.

If you need urgent medical treatment, you should head for one of the casualty departments (what in the United States are known as emergency rooms) of the major hospitals. These include St Thomas's on the South Bank, University College Hospital on Gower St in Bloomsbury, Guy's in Southwark, the Charing Cross Hospital on Fulham Palace Rd, Bart's in Smithfield and the Royal Free in Hampstead. You can call an ambulance by dialling ✆ 999 or ✆ 112.

Note also the following numbers:

Bliss Chemist, 5 Marble Arch. Stays open until midnight every day. Details of other late-opening chemists are available from police stations.

Dental Emergency Care Service, ✆ (020) 7935 4486. An advisory service open 24 hours which will direct you to the nearest clinic for emergency dental care.

London Rape Crisis Centre, ✆ (020) 7837 1600. Open 10am–10pm at weekends and 6pm–10pm Mon-Fri.

Samaritans, ✆ (020) 7734 2800. Helpline for any emotional problems, open 24 hours.

Family Planning Association, ✆ (020) 7837 4044. Will tell you where your nearest family planning clinic is and give you advice on morning-after pills, abortions and so on.

London for Free

You'll hear plenty of moans about the high cost of living in London, so here as an antidote is a list of things to do without spending a single penny:

Museums and galleries: Many of London's best museums have traditionally been free, but it is turning into a losing battle because of wavering government commitment to the necessary subsidies. Museums still hanging on by their fingernails include the National Gallery, National Portrait Gallery, the RIBA Heinz Gallery, Tate Britain (although it is considering charging for special exhibitions at the Tate Modern at Bankside), British Museum, Dulwich Picture Gallery, Bethnal Green Museum of Childhood, The Percival David Foundation for Chinese

Art, The Royal College of Art, William Morris Gallery, Keats' House and the National Army Museum. The Victoria and Albert Museum, Museum of London, Natural History Museum, Science Museum and Imperial War Museum all waive their charge from 4.30–5.50pm.

Other sights: Churches, with the exception of Westminster Abbey and St Paul's Cathedral, are all free. So, too, are the Guildhall, the Changing of the Guard outside Buckingham Palace, court cases at The Old Bailey or The Royal Courts of Justice on the Strand, the Sunday afternoon haranguing sessions at Speakers' Corner and the more regular haranguing sessions at the Houses of Parliament. London's wonderful riverside walks and parks—St James's, Battersea Park, the 19th-century dinosaurs in Crystal Palace Park, Hampstead Heath, Hyde Park and Regent's Park—are always free. So also are the beautiful cemeteries in Kensal Green, Highgate, Brompton and the Pet Cemetery in Hyde Park.

Shopping: Some of the fancier delicatessens in Soho and St James's (for example, the cheese sellers Paxton and Whitfield in Jermyn Street) will give away free nibbles, although you are under some pressure to purchase something in return. Food markets (try Berwick Street for starters) sometimes knock down the price of fruit and vegetables at the end of the day so far that they are as good as free.

Entertainment: There are free foyer concerts at the National Theatre and Barbican in the early evening. Covent Garden boasts plenty of street theatre and music, although you should offer something as the hat comes round. If you turn up to concert or theatre venues at the interval, you will often find people leaving and if you ask nicely they will give you their tickets. Another option in the summer is to go up to Kenwood on Hampstead Heath on a Saturday evening. You can sit on the rolling hills and listen to the outdoor concerts there without actually paying to get in.

Maps

London is one city where wandering around clutching a map will not automatically mark you out as a visitor; few Londoners venture out of familiar territory without a copy of the *London A–Z Street Atlas*, an inch-thick book of maps with an index of street names to help you find your destination. Bus and Tube maps are available from most main Underground stations; the large Journey Planner maps show both Tube and British Rail links. Cyclists will find the *Central London Cyclists' Map* a helpful guide to the quickest, safest and most pleasant routes through London's traffic mayhem. Published by the London Cycling Campaign, it can be bought from their office at 228 Great Guildford Business Square, 30 Great Guildford St, London SE1 0HS, ✆ (020) 7928 7220 and from some bookshops and cycle shops.

Many other maps can be found at London's largest specialist map shop, **Stanford's**, 12–14 Long Acre, Covent Garden.

Money and Banks

The currency in Britain is the pound sterling, divided into 100 pence. You'll come across notes worth £5, £10, £20 and £50, and coins worth 1, 2, 5, 10, 20, 50 pence, £1 and £2. London is also fully up to speed on credit card technology, and many shops, restaurants and hotels will accept Visa, Mastercard or American Express for all but the smallest purchases.

Minimum banking hours are Mon–Fri 9.30am–3.30pm, although many banks in Central London stay open later and, in some cases, on Saturday morning too. Most branches have automatic cash dispensers open 24 hours a day; check the stickers to see if your card and usual PIN number will be accepted, although if you don't have a British card you can expect your bank to charge a commission fee for any transaction.

You can change travellers' cheques at any bank or bureau de change, but remember to bring a passport or similar ID along with you. By and large, the big banks offer a better rate and lower commission fees, but shop around. If you need non-British currency, *bureaux de change* will be more likely to stock it. Try:

American Express, 6 Haymarket, © (020) 7930 4411.

Chequepoint, 548 Oxford St, and branches, © (020) 7723 1005.

Thomas Cook, Victoria Station, Marble Arch and many other branches, © (020) 7828 4442.

National Holidays

With the exception of Christmas and New Year's Day, Britain's national holidays, known as **bank holidays**, shift slightly every year to ensure they fall on a Monday. This avoids being 'cheated' out of holidays, as happens in continental Europe when they fall on the weekend, but it also leads to the absurdity of May Day being celebrated as late as 7 May. Banks and many businesses close down on bank holidays, but quite a few shops and most tourist attractions stay open. Public transport theoretically runs a Sunday service, but in practice tends to be very threadbare. The full list is: New Year's Day (plus the following Monday if it falls on a weekend), Good Friday, Easter Monday, May Day (first Monday in May), Spring Bank Holiday (last Monday in May), Summer Bank Holiday (last Monday in August), Christmas Day and the next day, known as Boxing Day (plus 27 December if one of them falls on a weekend).

Opening Hours

Traditionally, shops and offices stay open from around 9 to 5.30 or 6—significantly earlier than the rest of Europe. Pubs and bars still have fairly strict licensing rules and many of them will not serve alcohol after 11pm. Late opening for shops is becoming more and more common, however, particularly on Wednesdays and Thursdays, and Sunday trading is much more flexible than in the past: areas like Queensway and the Edgware Road, Hampstead, Greenwich, Tottenham Court Road and even most of the Oxford Street department stores are worth visiting.

Post Offices

Post offices are generally open Mon–Fri 9–5.30 and Sat 9–noon; avoid going at lunchtime as they can get very crowded. They are marked on most London maps (in the A–Z, for example, by a black star). You will be able to buy stamps at many newsagents. Two of the biggest post offices are at 24 King William IV St next to Trafalgar Square (*open Mon–Sat 8–8*) and at King Edward St near St Paul's Cathedral. Both have stamp shops and a *poste restante* service, as well as a very useful mail collection on Sunday evenings.

Postcodes: London postcodes are fairly confusing, and rely on an intimate knowledge of city geography to be intelligible. Postcodes begin with a direction (W for West, WC for West Central, N for North, NW for Northwest, and so on) and a number from 1 to 28. The full postcode then adds a letter immediately after the number, followed by a space, a number and two more letters. So a postcode might read EC1R 3ER—gobbledygook to anyone but a post office computer. This book uses postcodes sparingly, preferring to indicate the geographical district.

Pronunciation

Modern English spelling was standardized at the end of the 18th century by a small group of educationalists who evidently thought it would be hilarious to make pronunciation as difficult as possible for the uninitiated. Foreign tourists are forever inviting ridicule by asking for Glaw-sister Road or South-walk; it is hardly their fault if they are merely following the written word. Here is a survival guide to some of London's more common spelling anomalies:

Written	Spoken
Balham	Bal'm
Berkeley Square	Barkly Square
Berwick St	**Ber**rick Street
Cadogan (Square or Guides)	Cad**ugg**an
Charing Cross	Charring Cross
Cheyne Walk	Chainy Walk
Chiswick	Chizzick
Cholmondeley Walk	Chumly Walk
Clapham	Clap'm
Dulwich	Dull Itch
Gloucester Road	Gloster Road
Greenwich	Gren Itch
Grosvenor Place	Grove-ner Place
Holborn	Hoe Burn
Leicester Square	Lester Square
London	Lun Don
Southwark	Suth'k
Thames	Tems
Wapping	Wopping
Woolwich	Wool Itch

Religion

The state religion in Britain is Anglicanism, a peculiar hybrid of Protestant theology and Catholic ritual that developed after Henry VIII broke with the Roman Church to divorce his first wife, Catherine of Aragon. The biggest **Anglican** churches are St Paul's Cathedral, which has the finest organ in London, and Westminster Abbey. If you want to attend a service, a smaller church may be more to your liking. Leaf through some of the churches in the index for ideas. The biggest **Catholic churches** are Westminster Cathedral (off Victoria St) and the Brompton Oratory near the South Kensington museums. A more intimate place is St Ethel-dreda's in Ely Place off Holborn Circus.

London also has a sizeable **Jewish community**, concentrated around Golders Green and Stamford Hill in north London. For information about services and activities contact the

Liberal Jewish Synagogue, 28 St John's Wood Road, NW8, ✆ (020) 7286 5181; West London Synagogue (Reform), 33 Seymour Place, W1, ✆ (020) 7723 4404; or the United Synagogue (Orthodox), Adler House, 735 High Road, N12, ✆ (020) 8343 8989.

The Pakistani immigrants of the 1950s, supplemented by Bengalis, Indians and Arabs from many countries, form the backbone of the **Islamic community**. The London Central Mosque at 146 Park Road near Regent's Park, ✆ (020) 7724 3363, is a magnificent building which also contains a library and nursery school. Another popular place for Friday prayers is the East London Mosque at 84–98 Whitechapel Road, ✆ (020) 7247 1357.

For other denominations, note the following addresses:

London Baptist Association, 1 Merchant St, Bow, ✆ (020) 8980 6818.

The Buddhist Society, 58 Eccleston Square, Pimlico, ✆ (020) 7834 5858.

Evangelical Alliance, Whitefield House, 186 Kennington Park Rd, ✆ (020) 7723 4787.

Greek Orthodox Cathedral, Aghia Sophia, Moscow Rd, Bayswater, ✆ (020) 7229 7260.

Hindu Centre, 7 Cedars Rd, Stratford, ✆ (020) 8534 8879.

Central Church of World Methodism, Central Hall, Storeys Gate, Westminster, ✆ (020) 7222 8010.

Assemblies of God Pentecostal Church, 141 Harrow Rd, ✆ (020) 7286 9261.

Religious Society of Friends (Quakers), Friends House, 173–7 Euston Road, ✆ (020) 7387 3601.

Smoking

Britain has caught on to the anti-smoking craze in a big way, and you will find total bans in theatres, cinemas, museums, buses and Underground stations. Most restaurants have non-smoking areas, and some bars and pubs are introducing a similar partition. If you are invited to someone's home, ask in advance if smoking will be tolerated. It is considered quite normal to send guests wanting a puff into the garden or street.

Students and Pensioners

Students and pensioners are entitled to discounts on transport passes, air and rail travel and entry to many museums and shows. You should have some appropriate ID; in the case of students, an ISIC card is the most practical and is recognized worldwide. Students with queries should address themselves to the University of London Union (ULU) in Malet St behind the British Museum, ✆ (020) 7580 9551.

Telephones

In this era of privatization and information superhighways, telecommunications is becoming a highly competitive field, with more servers offering their services all the time. The two biggest companies remain British Telecom, the former national monopoly privatized in 1984, and Mercury, its most prominent competitor. Watch out whose phone you use if you buy a phonecard (they are company-specific but widely available, for example from newsagents). Cash, of course, works fine anywhere. For prices and information on cheap times to call, check with your local post office (the rates are constantly changing). Obviously, though, evenings and weekends are cheaper, particularly for international calls.

London phone numbers come with the prefix (020), which until April 2000 you must include even when dialling within the local area. Anyone calling from abroad must dial the country code 44, and then the prefix but without the first 0.

You can reach directory enquiries on ✆ 192. The general operator's number is 100, the international operator is on 155 and international directory enquiries are on 153. The international dialling code is 00, followed by the country code in question (1 for the United States and Canada, 353 for Ireland, 33 for France, 39 for Italy, 49 for Germany, 61 for Australia, 64 for New Zealand). You'll find a vast range of services in the phone book, from a speaking clock to an alarm call service. These are rather expensive, and you'll probably spend less buying a basic clock of your own. The emergency number for police, ambulance, or fire brigade is either ✆ 999 or ✆ 112.

Finally, Britain has peculiar telephone jacks that are wider than the US variety. If you need to plug in a telephone or computer, make sure you buy an adaptor, available at decent-sized general stores.

Time

Britain is one hour behind the rest of western Europe, just to be difficult. During the winter (roughly the end of October to the third week of March) it follows Greenwich Mean Time; in the summer it follows British Summer Time which is one hour ahead of GMT. After years of poor synchronization, Britain has at last agreed to change its clocks at the same time as the rest of Europe and North America. New York is 5 hours behind London time, San Francisco 8 hours behind, while Tokyo and Sydney are 10 hours ahead.

Tipping

Britain does not have the United States' established tipping code, but 10–15 per cent is considered polite in restaurants, taxis, hairdressers and the posher hotels.

Toilets

The old-fashioned underground public toilets are disappearing fast—and with good reason, given their dubious hygiene record and reputation for attracting gay men on the prowl for casual sex. In their stead you will find free-standing automatic 'Super-Loos' which are coin-operated (20p) and smell of cheap detergent (there is one, for example, in Leicester Square). Generally speaking, you'll have a more salubrious experience in pubs, bars and restaurants. If you don't want to buy anything, just pop in to the toilets discreetly, and nobody should give you a hard time.

Tourist Information

London is one of the tourist brochure capitals of the world; show one faint sign of interest and you will be inundated in glossy paper. The main tourist offices, which can also help you find accommodation, can be found at the Underground station for Heathrow Terminals 1, 2 and 3; at Liverpool St Underground station; on the forecourt of Victoria Station; and in the basement of Selfridge's department store on Oxford St. Many districts also have local tourist information offices, which can be excellent and provide guides to show you round for the appropriate fee. The centres at Greenwich (✆ (020) 8858 6376), Islington (✆ (020) 7278 8787) and Richmond (✆ (020) 8940 9125) also have accommodation services, but often don't even try to help you in high season. You'll have to visit their offices, as none of them takes phone bookings The London Tourist Board has a recorded telephone service with up-to-date information (✆ (0839) 123456); it is, however, rather expensive (up to 48p a minute, so look in the phone book or call (020) 7971 0026 first to find out exactly which recording you want to access). The Tourist Board also has a website on *www.LondonTown.com* with details on restaurants, shops, 3D maps and current attractions.

For more unusual tours of the city, contact the following: Supersky Trips, ✆ (0345) 023842: panoramic views from a 400ft-high balloon tethered in Vauxhall Spring Gardens (open 10–dusk, seven days a week: £12 or £7.50 for children, for 15 mins); Open Top Taxi Tours, ✆ (01525) 290800 (£15 for 2 hours if there are five of you, but £75 if you are alone): excellent tours of London in convertible taxis kitted out with sound systems, mini-fridges and instant cameras; Big City Scenic Flights, ✆ (01275) 810767: expensive aeroplane flights 1000ft over London with in-flight commentary. There are any number of other guided tours, including guided walks. They are listed at tourist offices and in the pages of *Time Out.*

London: Essential Sights

Albert Hall

Kensington Gore; ● *South Kensington, High Street Kensington; bus 9, 10, 52. Call ℂ (020) 7589 8212 for details of concert programmes and other events.*

As a concert venue the Albert Hall has one unforgivable flaw: an echo that has been the butt of jokes ever since the Bishop of London heard his prayers of blessing reverberate around the red-brick rotunda at the opening ceremony in 1871. The irascible conductor Sir Thomas Beecham remarked that the hall was fit for many things, but playing music was not one of them. But the Albert Hall is still well loved. Visually, it is one of the more successful Victorian buildings in London, and the high frieze around the outside depicts the Triumph of Arts and Sciences—a most Albertian theme. The hall is huge (capacity 7,000 or more) and remarkably versatile; through the year it hosts symphony orchestras, rock bands, conferences, boxing matches and tennis tournaments. Every summer it becomes the headquarters of the Proms, a series of cheap concerts widely broadcast on radio and television, the last night of which, in early September, is a national institution, *see* p.173.

Albert Memorial

Kensington Gore, opposite the Albert Hall.

The notion of honouring Queen Victoria's beloved husband Albert with a memorial was mooted even before the prince's untimely death in 1861. His over-eager homage-payers had to bide their time, though, if only because Albert himself was adamantly opposed to the idea. 'It would disturb my rides in Rotten Row to see my own face staring at me,' he said, 'and if (as is very likely) it became an artistic monstrosity...it would upset my equanimity to be permanently ridiculed and laughed at in effigy.' As it turned out, the prince's fears were only too well founded. The widowed Queen Victoria launched a competition for a memorial the year after her husband's death and picked George Gilbert Scott, nabob of neo-Gothic excess. The 175ft-high monument he built is a bloated, over-decorated stone canopy housing an indifferent likeness of Albert reading a catalogue from the Great Exhibition by John Foley: a ponderous pickle of allegorical statuary and religious imagery decked out in far too much marble, mosaic panelling, enamel and polished stone, and now, after recent restoration, clad in startling resplendent gold to boot. It was a big hit with the Victorians and remained popular well into the 20th century. Osbert Sitwell described it in 1928 as 'that wistful, unique monument of widowhood'. It took a writer as cynical as Norman Douglas to puncture the myth. 'Is this the reward of conjugal virtue?' he wrote in 1945. 'Ye husbands, be unfaithful!'

London Aquarium

County Hall, Westminster Bridge Rd; ● *Waterloo, Westminster; bus 12, 53, 109; ℂ (020) 7967 8000; www.londonaquarium.co.uk*

Open daily 10–6, last adm 5pm, holidays and summer till 6.30pm; adm.

To the left of Westminster Bridge, directly across the river from the Houses of Parliament, is **County Hall**, a grand grey stone public building in the pompous Edwardian 'Wrenaissance' style. Until 1986 it was the headquarters of the Greater London Council, the elected city government that proved such a threat to Margaret Thatcher that she abolished it.

County Hall has now been converted into a multi-purpose centre for residential housing, hotel accommodation and conferences. The basement already houses one of London's newer attractions, the **Aquarium**. Here, in spectacular three-storey fish tanks set among kitsch Roman ruins, you can say hello to sharks, stingray, octopus, sea bass, cuttlefish, umbrella-like jellyfish, piranha and wondrous shoals of sea bass, and even touch some of the gentler ones. The Aquarium is primarily entertainment and unfortunately fails to tell the visitor much about either the fish or the environment, but children will love it.

British Museum

Great Russell Street; ✪ *Tottenham Court Road; bus 7, 10, 24, 29, 134;* ✆ *(020) 7636 1555; www.british-museum.ac.uk*

Open Mon–Sat 10–5, Sun 12–6; free; guided tours (adm) are available.

Back in the 1770s, the grumpy novelist Tobias Smollett complained that the fledgling British Museum was too empty and lacked a decent book collection. The museum has certainly made up for both deficiencies since. Stuffed with treasures gathered from the farthest reaches of the British Empire, and boasting one of the finest and fullest libraries in the world, it became an irresistible magnet for visitors and scholars of every temperament and interest. It is by far the most popular tourist attraction in London: triumphant proof that real quality beats the tackiness of the Tower of London or Madame Tussaud's any day.

There is more in the museum than can possibly be described below; what follows is a guide to its most famous and appealing artefacts. Your best strategy is to pick up a floor plan and make up your own mind what to see.

Between 1997 and 2000, the Museum has been organizing its most exciting and complicated reshuffle ever, as the British Library moves to new premises in St Pancras. The move (especially the removal of the Library's ugly postwar bookstacks) has liberated a massive 40 per cent of the Bloomsbury site for redevelopment. For the new British Library, *see* p.54.

Ground Floor

The Round Reading Room

Between 1997 and 2000 the Round Reading Room and the area around it was completely redeveloped though it is still out of bounds to the general public.

This is one of the best loved rooms in the world, with a beautiful cavernous dome bigger in diameter than St Paul's or St Peter's in Rome. Although designed by Sydney Smirke, it was the brainchild of Sir Antonio Panizzi, an Italian exile who invented the systems for labelling and cataloguing that are used in libraries to this day. A steady stream of the world's political thinkers and revolutionaries came to this wonderfully spacious domed circular room, among them Marx (who wrote *Das Kapital* in Row G), Mazzini and Lenin. Other writers who have found inspiration, consolation and even, occasionally, love among its 18 million tomes include Macaulay, Thackeray, Hardy, Dickens and Yeats.

Western Asia

Western Asian treasures are spread throughout the British Museum, but the most accessible, the Assyrian relics of Nineveh, Balawat and Nimrud, are here on the ground floor. The Assyrians, occupying an exposed area in what is now northern Iraq, constructed a civilization essentially built on war with their neighbours, especially the Babylonians, between the 9th and 7th centuries BC. Their palaces are decorated with figures of wild animals, mythical creatures and magic symbols as well as depictions of conical-helmeted soldiers at arms with their chariots, battering rams and pontoons. The most extraordinary artwork depicts a **royal lion hunt**; the dying animals, shot through with arrows, are sculpted with great emotional force.

Egypt

There are more lions here in the Egyptian sculpture gallery, this time red and black ones carved in granite and limestone for the tombs of Pharaohs; Ruskin described them as 'the noblest and truest carved lions I have ever seen'. Among the huge Pharaohs' heads and ornate sarcophagi, look for the likeness of Amenophis III, an 18th Dynasty ruler, and the gilded coffin containing Henutmehit, the Chantress of Amen-Re, from around 1290 BC. Many of the riddles of the ancient Egyptian world were solved through the **Rosetta Stone**, a slab of black basalt discovered by Napoleon's army in the Nile Delta in 1799, which by extraordinary good fortune reproduces the same text in three languages: Greek, demotic and Egyptian.

Greece

Two monuments overshadow the Greek collections: the Nereid Monument and the Elgin Marbles. The **Nereid Monument** is a reconstruction of a vast tomb found at the Greek colony of Xanthos in Asia Minor. Built like a temple with a pediment supported by Ionic columns, it is a stunning tribute to the Lycian chieftains who are buried there; it also features remarkable frieze sculptures.

As for the **Elgin Marbles**, they have aroused so much controversy for being in Britain rather than Greece that their artistic merit is sometimes entirely overlooked. The Elgin Marbles are the frieze reliefs from the Parthenon, the temple to Athena on top of the Acropolis, and are considered some of the finest sculptures of antiquity. Depicting a Panathenaic festival to commemorate Athena's birthday, they reveal a remarkable mastery of detail and human feeling. Lord Elgin, the British Ambassador to the Ottoman Empire, discovered the stones when he visited Athens in 1800. The Parthenon, from which the marbles came, had been half wrecked in a skirmish between the Turks and a Venetian fleet besieging them in 1687, when a supply of gunpowder kept in the building exploded and brought many of the colonnades crashing to the ground. Elgin obtained a licence from the Turkish Sultan in 1802 and proceeded to transport the treasures back home.

The British Museum has them displayed in a vast room giving an idea of the scale of the Parthenon itself.

Oriental Collections (halfway between Ground and Upper Floors)

These rooms cover a huge amount of ground, from Chinese Tang dynasty glazed tomb figures to Turkish and Syrian ceramic work, by way of Thai banner painting and religious monuments from India and Nepal. Perhaps the most impressive section for the non-specialist is the room devoted to South and Southeast Asia.

Upper Floor

Egypt (continued)

The display of **Egyptian mummies and sarcophagi** is the most popular section of the British Museum, no doubt for its addictive gruesomeness. Here is the Egyptian way of death in all its bizarre splendour: rows and rows of spongy bodies wrapped in bandages and surrounded by the prized belongings and favourite food of the deceased.

Western Asia (continued)

The collection is more eclectic here than downstairs: Bronze Age tools from Syria, a mosaic column from Tell-al-Ubaid, reliefs from Kapara's palace in Tell Halaf (now in northeastern Syria) as well as further relics from Nimrud (ivory carvings) and Nineveh (tablets from the royal library). The two highlights are a collection of magnificently preserved funerary busts from Palmyra dating from the 1st and 2nd centuries AD, and the extraordinary sculpture *The Ram in the Thicket* from Ur, the birthplace of Abraham.

The Italy of the Greeks, Etruscans and Romans

Have a look down the western staircase, which is adorned with a Roman mosaic. On the walls are more mosaic fragments, this time from Greek palaces in Halicarnassus, Ephesus and Carthage. The collections themselves are a bit of a mixed bag: Greek red-figure vases found in Lucania and Apulia in southern Italy (1400–1200 BC), a carved stone Etruscan sarcophagus found at Bomarzo north of Rome (3rd century BC) and plenty of bronze heads of Roman emperors. The highlight of the Roman collection, though, is the **Portland Vase**, so called because the Barberini family sold it to the Dukes of Portland. The vase, made around the time of the birth of Christ, is of cobalt-blue glass and coated in an opaque white glaze depicting the reclining figures of Peleus and Thetis, with Cupid and his love arrows hovering overhead.

Romano-British Section

The oldest and most gruesome exhibit here is **Lindow Man**, the shrivelled remains of an ancient Briton preserved down the centuries in a peat bog. The body, which has been dated between 300 BC and AD 100, shows evidence of extreme violence. All you see here is his torso and crushed head, freeze-dried like instant coffee, with a hologram giving you a better idea of what he originally looked like.

Excavations in Britain have provided more pleasant surprises, notably the **Mildenhall Treasure**, 34 remarkably well-preserved pieces of 4th-century silver tableware dug up from a field in Suffolk in 1942. There are some beautiful mosaics, the largest of them a 4th-century floor from Hinton St Mary in Dorset which appears to be Christian in inspiration.

Medieval Antiquities

Here you will find more extraordinary finds from digs around the British Isles. You should not miss the **Lewis chessmen**, a collection of 78 pieces in walrus ivory discovered in the remote Outer Hebrides in 1831. The farmer who first came across them fled thinking they were elves and fairies, and it was only the fortitude of his wife that persuaded him to go back for another look. The figures do not make up complete chess sets and are thought to have been left by a travelling salesman, possibly from Scandinavia, some time in the 12th century.

Prints and Drawings

The museum's vast collection is displayed in rotation. On a good day you can find Michelangelo's sketches for the roof of the Sistine chapel, etchings and sketches by Rembrandt and a large selection of anatomical studies by Albrecht Dürer. Look out, too, for William Hogarth's satirical engravings, notably *Gin Lane* which castigates the corrupting influence of drink on 18th-century London, and his extraordinary series on cruelty.

Buckingham Palace Road; ⊖ Green Park, Victoria; bus (closest stop Royal Mews) 2, 8, 16, 36, 38, 52, 73, 82; info © (020) 7799 2331; © (020) 7321 2233 to book in advance; www.royal.gov.uk

Open Aug and Sept, at least in 2000, 9.30 daily for 1½-hour guided tours, last entry 4.15, ticket office closes at 4; adm exp. The ticket office, an elegant tent structure designed by architect Michael Hopkins, is at the western end of St James's Park just off the Mall, and the entrance is at Ambassadors' Court on the south side of the building.

On 7 August 1993, miracle of miracles, Buckingham Palace opened its doors to the public for the first time. For generations, royalists had invoked the need to preserve the mystery of the monarchy and refused, in the words of Walter Bagehot, to 'let daylight in upon its magic'. But by the early 1990s the British monarchy was in a crisis of quite astonishing proportions. Two royal marriages had broken up in quick succession, Princess Diana's struggles with bulimia and depression had been made glaringly public, Prince Charles had allegedly been taped telling his mistress on the telephone how he fantasized about being her tampon and, to top it all, half of Windsor Castle had burned down.

Little knowing the revelations and tragedies that were still to come, the Queen herself dubbed 1992, the year of most of these misfortunes, her '*annus horribilis*'. To rally public opinion back behind the monarchy she made two unprecedented concessions. The first was to agree to pay income tax for the first time. The second was to unveil some of the mysteries of Buckingham Palace for two months of the year, for an initial period of five years (it will stay open until in 2000). As a public relations coup, opening the doors of the queen's official residence proved less than spectacular. Quite a few newspaper critics, their knives already well sharpened by the preceding flurry of royal scandals, complained that the tour was impersonal, poorly put together and even boring. The public seemed more forgiving, fawning happily over every precious object listed in the official catalogue.

So what exactly is all the fuss about? What do you get to see? Certainly not a glimpse of the 'working palace' constantly alluded to by the Queen's public relations office. The tour takes in just 18 of Buckingham Palace's 661 rooms, and even these feel as though they have been stripped down to the bare minimum to ensure they are not sullied by the savage hordes. The original carpets are rolled away each summer and replaced with industrial-strength red Axminster rugs that clash awkwardly with the fake marble columns, greens, pinks and blues of the flock wallpapers and gold and cream ornamental ceilings.

The place feels hollow and spookily empty; in fact it is hard to imagine that anybody lives or works in such soulless surroundings. Perhaps it's just as well that there is no café or refreshment stall for the public, as the toilets are right at the end of the tour, in some tents in the Palace gardens. As for the personal touch, there is not so much as a photograph of the royal family on the whole tour, let alone a flesh-and-blood prince or princess to welcome the guests.

The tour route leads you to the inner courtyard and thence to the back part of the palace overlooking the gardens. The Grand Staircase, with its elegant wrought-iron banister, leads up to the first of the state rooms, the Green Drawing Room. The attractions are on the whole fairly obvious, and although there is no free groundplan to help you get your bearings the wardens are exceptionally helpful and friendly. All the rooms are filled with ostentatious chandeliers, somewhat chintzy furniture and ornate gilt and painted plaster ceilings. Whether you are in the Green, Blue or White Drawing Room you can't help feeling as though you are trapped in a Dairy Milk chocolate box. And the incidental decoration does not really improve as the tour goes on. The real highlight is the 155ft-long **Picture Gallery** (the third room on the tour), which is crammed from floor to ceiling with the cream of the royal collection of some 10,000 paintings. The walls are a bit crowded for comfort, but the gems stand out easily enough: Van Dyck's idealized portraits of Charles I, Rembrandt's *Lady with a Fan, Agatha Bas* and *The Shipbuilder and His Wife*, landscapes by Ruisdael, Poussin and Claude Lorrain, portraits by Frans Hals, Rubens' underwhelming *St George and the Dragon*, Albert Cuyp's *Landscape with a Negro Page*, and much more besides. Apart from Charles I, the only royal to receive anything like pictorial justice in Buckingham Palace is Victoria, whose family is cosily captured in Franz Winterhalter's 1846 portrait in the East Gallery (the room after the Picture Gallery).

The lower floor of the tour holds few new surprises, although you can have some fun in the 200ft **Marble Hall** with its yards of sculpture—look out for Canova's sensuous *Mars and Venus*, which George IV commissioned from Napoleon's pet artist after the British victory at Waterloo. A saunter through the **Bow Room** brings you out into the garden where Palace 'air hostesses' will deliver any bags and coats checked in at the beginning of the tour.

Here in the **garden** you may linger and enjoy some fine views, before moving on to the highlight of the tour which is the souvenir shop. In many ways this is the most telling part of the trip, with mugs and videos and other royal memorabilia displayed to the public in glass cabinets. At the top end of the scale, you can pick up a perfectly frightful crystal bowl or enamel box for roughly the same price as a dinner in a three-star restaurant. Better value (and more appetizing) are the Buckingham Palace Belgian chocolates moulded into the shape of the crown, or the attractive-looking Buckingham Palace gold tooth-mug, an ideal Christmas present for regally inclined mothers-in-law.

Globe Theatre

New Globe Walk; ❷ *Mansion House, Blackfriars, Borough; bus 149 to Southwark Bridge or to London Bridge, 35, 40, 43, 47, 48, 133, 149;* ℂ *(020) 7902 1400; box office* ℂ *(020) 7401 9919; www.shakespeares-globe.org*

May–Sept 2 performances daily, tickets from £5; exhibition open daily all year round 10–5; adm.

The original Globe was in fact a few hundred feet away from this building site, on the corner of present-day Park Street and Southwark Bridge Road. When London's first playhouse, The Theatre, was forced to move off its premises in Finsbury Fields, just north of the City, in 1598, its manager Richard Burbage had it dismantled and reassembled here on Bankside where the Rose Theatre had taken root 12 years earlier. Shakespeare helped finance Burbage's enterprise and had many of his plays, including *Romeo and Juliet, King Lear, Othello, Macbeth* and *The Taming of the Shrew* performed in its famous O-shaped auditorium for the first time. Bankside was the perfect location for theatrical entertainment; all manner of pursuits not deemed proper across the river in the stiff-collared City had moved here, and the area was already notorious, among other things, for its taverns and its whorehouses.

The Globe never properly recovered from a fire in 1613 and was finally demolished during the Civil War. This reconstruction was the brainchild of the late American actor Sam Wanamaker, who devoted most of his retirement to realizing the scheme, which remained unfinished when he died in December 1993 at the age of 72. The theatre finally opened for business four years later, following a remarkable fundraising effort in which actors, politicians and members of the general public volunteered to sponsor every last paving slab and brick.

The construction is remarkably faithful to the original, from the distinctive red of its brick-work, to its all-wooden interior and thatched roof (the first of its kind to appear in London since the Great Fire of 1666). If you are in London during the summer you should try to see a performance (box office ℰ (020) 7401 9919) to appreciate the peculiarities of Elizabethan theatre. The huge stage, with its vast oak pillars holding up a canopy roof, juts out into the open area holding up to 500 standing members of the audience (known as groundlings). The rest of the public is seated on wooden benches in the circular galleries, giving a peculiar sense of intimacy and audience involvement. Again, there are a few concessions to modern sensibil-ities: the seating is more spacious and comfortable than in Shakespeare's day, and performances take place in the evening as well as the traditional afternoon slot.

Whether or not you come for a play, you can visit the **Shakespeare Globe Exhibition** which charts the building of both the original and the reconstructed theatre and offers a guided tour around the auditorium itself. Wanamaker's Globe is more than just a venue for authentic performances of Shakespeare, however: there is also a study centre and library, open to scholars and theatre performers.

Hampton Court

East Molesey, Surrey. If you don't travel by river (by far the most pleasant but slowest means), go by train from Waterloo to ⇌ Hampton Court, or else catch a bus: the 267 comes from Hammersmith and the R68 from Richmond; ℰ (020) 8781 9500; www.hrp.org.uk

Open Mon 10.15–6, Tues–Sun 9.30–6, earlier closing mid-Oct–Mar; adm.

Hampton Court Palace is one of the finest Tudor buildings in England, a place that magnifi-cently evokes the haphazard pleasures and cruel intrigues of Henry VIII's court. We are lucky to have it. Oliver Cromwell meant to sell off its treasures and let it go to pieces, but then fell in love with it and decided to live there himself. A generation later, Christopher Wren had every intention of razing it to the ground to build a new palace; only money problems and the death of Queen Mary prevented him from wreaking more damage than he did.

Hampton Court started as the power base of Henry VIII's most influential minister. Cardinal Thomas Wolsey bought the property from the Knights of St John in 1514, one year before he became Lord Chancellor of England. As his influence grew, so did the palace: at its zenith it contained 280 rooms and kept a staff of 500 busy, constantly entertaining dignitaries from around Europe. Seeing the grandeur to which his chief minister was rapidly allowing himself to become accustomed, Henry VIII grew nervous and threatened to knock Wolsey off his high perch. Wolsey responded in panic by offering Hampton Court to the monarch; Henry was unimpressed and at first snubbed him by refusing to take up residence there. Wolsey was then given the impossible task of asking the Pope to grant Henry a divorce from his wife, Catherine of Aragon. When he failed, his possessions were seized by the crown, he was arrested for high treason and eventually died as he was being escorted from his archbishopric in York to London.

Henry first got interested in Hampton Court as a love nest for himself and his new flame, Anne Boleyn. The two of them moved here even before Henry had annulled his first marriage and set about effacing every possible trace of Wolsey. They removed his coat of arms, since restored, from the main entrance arch and renamed it **Anne Boleyn's Gateway**—a magnificent red brick structure with octagonal towers at either end. In 1540, Henry added a remarkable astronomical clock, and renamed the main courtyard within Clock Court.

The mid-1530s were Hampton Court's heyday. Henry built the **Great Hall**, with its 60ft-high hammerbeam roof and its stained-glass windows, amended right up to the end of his life to include the crests of each of his wives, even the ones he repudiated or executed. The king also established the gardens, planting trees and shrubs, notably in the Pond Garden, and built a **real tennis court** which still survives in the outhouses at the northeastern end of the palace. Hampton Court began to turn sour for him after Jane Seymour died in 1538 while giving birth to his much anticipated son and heir, Edward.

For a century after Henry's death, Hampton Court continued to thrive. The Great Hall became a popular theatrical venue, and the state rooms filled with fine paintings, gold-encrusted tapestries, musical instruments and ornaments. Charles I built the gardens' fountains and lakes as well as the long waterway, originally cut to provide the palace with water at the expense of neighbouring communities. Charles also accumulated a vast collection of art including the wonderfully restored *Triumph of Caesar* series by Mantegna, which hangs in its own gallery at the south end of the palace.

By the time William and Mary came to the throne, appreciation of Tudor architecture had waned considerably. The apartments at Hampton Court were considered old-fashioned and uncomfortable, and Christopher Wren was drafted in to build an entirely new palace to rival Louis XIV's extravaganza at Versailles—a project that, perhaps fortunately, never saw the light of day. The bulk of Wren's work is at the eastern end of the palace and centres around the cloisters of **Fountain Court**. The new apartments were decorated by the likes of Antonio Verrio, James Thornhill, Grinling Gibbons and Jean Tijou in sumptuous but stilted fashion; the **Chapel Royal** was also rebuilt, with only the Tudor vaulted ceiling surviving from the original. The best work carried out under William III was in the gardens, notably the lines of yew trees along the narrow strips of water, the herb garden (now beautifully restored) and the famous **maze**. Originally the maze was considered a religious penance to impress upon ordinary mortals the labyrinthine complications of a life in the service of Christ. Now it is a popular diversion, particularly for children too small to peer over the hedges to see what is coming next.

Houses of Parliament and Big Ben

❧ Westminster; buses 3, 11, 12, 24, 53, 77A, 88, 109 all go to Parliament Square.

*To visit the **Houses of Parliament**, you should head for St Stephen's entrance, which is roughly half way along the complex of buildings. Visiting arrangements for parliament are phenomenally complicated, and vary according to your nationality; you might well find that telephoning in advance (✆ (020) 7219 3000 , or ✆ 7219 4272 for information on what is being debated) will avoid wasting time. If you turn up on spec, you must queue outside St Stephen's entrance; don't expect to sit down before 5pm. Note that both houses have long recesses, particularly in the summer, and that debates of particular public interest are likely to be very crowded.*

To see the rest of the Palace of Westminster (notably Westminster Hall) you need to apply for a permit about two months in advance from your MP or embassy. It's a good idea whatever your arrangements to bring your passport and leave behind any large bags or cameras. You should also dress reasonably formally. The one bit of good news is that the Houses of Parliament, once you get in, come free of charge.

The best way to approach the Palace of Westminster is to imagine it as a multi-layered onion. Most of today's building is the dizzy virtuoso work of Charles Barry and Augustus Pugin, two Victorian architects working at the height of their powers to replace the old parliament destroyed by fire in 1834.

The story of the palace begins with **Westminster Hall**, which has survived the centuries more or less intact. The hall was originally a banqueting chamber built by King William Rufus, the son of William the Conqueror, in 1097. The Hall was the meeting place of the Grand Council, a committee of barons which discussed policy with the monarch in an early incarnation of parliament. Westminster Hall also became the nation's main law court. From about 1550, the lower house of parliament, known as the House of Commons, began meeting in St Stephen's Chapel in the main body of the palace. It may seem odd to convene parliament in a religious setting, but the juxtaposition is curiously appropriate: ever since the Reformation, parliament has been a symbol of the primacy of Protestantism in English politics. Pugin and Barry recognized this, and incorporated the chapel into their design. It was only when St Stephen's was destroyed in the Blitz that the House of Commons became an entirely secular chamber.

The inadequacies of the old Palace of Westminster were recognized as early as the 1820s. A new building might have been proposed there and then, but it took a calamity to spring them into action. On 16 October, 1834, the Clerk of Works, a Mr Richard Wibley, was asked to destroy several bundles of old talley-sticks in a cellar furnace. The fire raged out of control, and the whole palace was soon engulfed in flames. Augustus Pugin had been an eyewitness to the 1834 fire and revelled in every minute of it. He hated neoclassical architects and was only too happy to see their various improvements to the old parliament go up in smoke. Fearing that a neoclassical architect would be asked to design the new parliament, Pugin put his name forward and, although he was only 24 at the time, was named assistant to the older, more experienced Charles Barry. Theirs was a near perfect partnership. Barry sketched out the broad lines of the design, while Pugin attended to the details of ornamentation. Some of Pugin's work was lost in the bombing of the Second World War; you can nevertheless admire the sheer fervour of his imagination in the sculpted wood and stone, the stained glass, tiled floors, wallpaper and painted ceilings. Despite Pugin's rantings against the classicists, he was happy to go along with Barry's essentially classical design and Gothicize it to his heart's content. The Palace of Westminster's blend of architectural restraint (Barry) and decorative frenzy (Pugin) is one of its most appealing aspects.

Pugin went mad and died in 1852, and so never lived to work on the most famous feature of the new building, the clock tower at the eastern end known universally by the name of its giant bell, **Big Ben** (*visits to the clock must be arranged through an MP or serving member of the House of Lords, or, for horologists with a specific interest in the clock, directly through Chris Hillier on ✆ (020) 7219 4874*). Nowadays the clock is renowned for its accuracy and its resounding tolling of the hour, but the story of its construction is one of incredible incompetence and bungling. The 320ft-high clock tower was finished in 1854, but because of a bitter disagreement between the two clockmakers, Frederick Dent and Edmund Beckett Denison, there was nothing to put inside it for another three years. Finally a great bell made up according to Denison's instructions was dragged across Westminster Bridge by a cart and 16 horses. But, as it was being laid out ready for hoisting into position, a 4ft crack suddenly appeared. Similar embarrassments ensued over the next two years, until a functioning but still cracked bell was at last erected at the top of the tower. It remains defective to this day. As for the name, the most common explanation is that the bell was named after Sir Benjamin Hall, the unpopular Chief Commissioner of Works who had to explain all the muddles in his project to the House of Commons. Another theory has it that Big Ben was in fact Benjamin Caunt, a corpulent boxer who owned a pub a couple of hundred yards away in St Martin's Lane. The chimes, well known around the world, are a bastardized version of the aria 'I Know That My Redeemer Liveth' from Handel's *Messiah.*

From the moment that Barry and Pugin's building opened in 1852, it set an entirely new tone to proceedings in parliament. It was no longer just a legislative assembly, it was a *club.* Like so many British institutions, parliament is a place of deeply embedded rituals, established by a ruling order intent on protecting itself and its idiosyncratic ways; even if the institution has changed, the rituals have survived out of a quirky fondness for the past. Whatever its modern way of functioning, parliament still *feels* like the exclusive terrain of upper-class men who drink and smoke cigars together and decide the fate of the nation in an atmosphere of elegant sparring.

Kensington Palace

Kensington Palace Gardens; ✚ *Queensway, High Street Kensington, bus 12, 94 stopping to the north of the palace on Bayswater Road, and 9, 10, 52 stopping to the south on Kensington Road;* ✆ *(020) 7937 9561; www.royal.gov.uk*

Open April–Oct daily 10–5; Nov–Mar Wed–Sun 10–4; adm; includes small café.

Since the death of Princess Diana, Kensington Palace has become something of a shrine to her memory; this was where she, along with that other well-known royal divorcee, Princess Margaret, lived after the failure of her marriage to Prince Charles. You won't be able to visit her private apartments, but the Palace offers other delights in their place.

The tour is divided into two sections: the historic apartments, and an exhibition of royal clothes including the coronation robes worn by monarchs from George II onwards. The most interesting aspect of the apartments is the decoration work by William Kent: a beautifully patterned ceiling in the Presence Chamber, some fine *trompe l'œil* murals of court scenes on the King's Staircase and painted episodes from the *Odyssey* on the ceiling of the King's Gallery. The Cupola Room plays clever optical tricks to make you believe the ceiling is taller and more rounded than it is; from the King's Drawing Room there is a fine view over Kensington Gardens, the Serpentine and Hyde Park.

The fashions in coronation garb charted by the special exhibition give a good reading of the changing status of the monarchy itself. The over-confident Georges wore ermine galore, particularly the profligate George IV who sported a ludicrously flamboyant white feather hat and a train as thick as a shag-pile carpet. William IV and Victoria, whose coronations went almost unnoticed by a populace more interested in democratic reform than regal pomp, were sober almost to the point of blandness. Edward VII, who helped restore the monarchy's image, showed renewed confidence with his bright military uniform and ermine mantle braided with gold.

Millennium Dome

*⊖ North Greenwich. The nearest **rail** station is ⇌ Charlton, from where you have to get an M1 bus. By far the pleasantest way of getting there is via ferry or cruise **boat**: there's a **shuttle** service called the Maritime Greenwich–Dome Fast Ferry, costing £1.90 and taking 10mins. The M2 **bus** runs from ⇌ Greenwich and the Cutty Sark.*

The Millennium Experience is open daily in 2000, 10–6. Tickets available from travel operators, rail and bus stations and National Lottery outlets; Ticketline, © 0870 606 2000; or www.dome2000.co.uk. Adm very exp.

The Dome cost £758m to build, more than half of which has been paid for by the public via the National Lottery. The enormous semi-sebaceous cyst is made of Teflon and fibreglass and supported by 12 steel masts attached to 70 kilometres of wire cable. It is big enough to hold two Wembley Stadiums and as tall as Nelson's Column. Around the central arena are the fourteen 'Zones'—from work, rest and play, to body, faith and a 'celebration of all things British' sponsored by Marks & Spencer. The Dome opened on Millennium Eve to the general public and a sceptical British press and has subsequently suffered a lot of criticism in the media. Whether the Dome will ultimately prove to be a failure with the people, remains to be seen; certainly by February 2000 there was already a serious shortfall in ticket sales and the organizers admitted that improvements were necessary.

The Dome's future remains uncertain, though several consortia have put in bids to buy it for use as film and TV studios. A more permanent fixture on the site should be the Millennium Village, a 'model village' of 1,400 sustainable homes nearby.

National Gallery

Trafalgar Square; ⊖ Charing Cross, Leicester Square; bus: very nearly all of London's day and night bus services go around Trafalgar Square; © (020) 7747 2885.

Open daily 10–6, Wed 10–9; free.

The National Gallery is an astonishing collection of West European painting from the 13th to the early 20th centuries, including masterpieces from virtually every major school. Its great names include Leonardo da Vinci, Piero della Francesca, Van Eyck, Raphael, Titian, Veronese, Rubens, Poussin, Rembrandt, Velázquez, Caravaggio, Turner, Constable, Delacroix, Monet, Van Gogh, Cézanne and Picasso.

The National Gallery is very much a 19th-century phenomenon: a catalogue of paintings from the Grand Tradition reflecting the pride and power of the collector nation. Many of the gallery's masterpieces were bought in the Victorian era, particularly under its first director Charles Eastlake. The picture buying has continued ever since; and although money has grown tighter in recent years the annual budget remains well over £2 million.

The first work of art, which most visitors miss, is a mosaic of Greta Garbo's head by Boris Anrep (1933) on the floor of the main entrance hall. Pick up a floor plan from the information desk and you'll see that the gallery's four wings each concentrate on a different historical period, starting with early medieval Italian painting in the new Sainsbury Wing and moving gradually eastwards towards the 20th century.

Rooms devoted to individual painters are clearly marked. At the entrance to each wing, you are given the names of the major paintings to look out for. The gallery is magnificently lit, with intelligent explanations displayed alongside each picture. There is a computer database in the Micro Gallery in the Sainsbury Wing, where you can look up and print out detailed information on pictures or artists. There are also organized lectures on individual pictures, as well as a changing special exhibition in the Sunley Room to the left of the central hall, where paintings from the collection are grouped to illustrate a specific theme. And if that is not enough for you, there are hundreds of minor paintings stored on lower floors available for public view.

Natural History Museum

Cromwell Road; ● *South Kensington; bus C1 from Victoria, 74 from Baker St, 14 from Tottenham Court Road;* ℂ *(020) 7938 9123; www.nhm.ac.uk*

Open 10–5.50 Mon–Sat, 11–5.50 Sun; adm but free after 4.30 Mon–Fri, children age 5–16 free.

This place looks for all the world like a cathedral, but you are soon jolted out of any notion that this is a place of worship by the giant dinosaur in the central hall. This skeletal creature, a 150-million-year-old plant-eating beast called a diplodocus, that warded off predators with its giant tusks and whiplash tail, really sums up what is best and worst about the Natural History Museum. Our prehistoric friend *looks* very impressive; the trouble is, he's a fake, just a cast. Ever since *Jurassic Park*, the **dinosaurs** have been the museum's main attraction. The special section devoted to them is long on history but short on real skeletons, though one display gives an intriguing list of theories on why prehistoric monsters died out.

Much of this museum resembles a science classroom. There are games explaining human perception and memory, interactive displays on creepy-crawlies and a politically correct **Ecology Gallery** explaining the importance of the rainforests in the world's ecosystem. All of this is fine for children, but not so great for adults. For grown-ups, the museum only really gets going with the **Bird Gallery**, featuring a remarkable collection of stuffed birds and wild animals from the 18th century onwards, and a geological section known as the **Earth Galleries**, which are filled with beautiful stones and gems, and where there's a chance to step inside the 'Earthquake Experience'. Right next to the Exhibition Road side entrance you can really go for the broad view with an audiovisual experience called the **Story of the Universe**. Again, it is instructive, but not very inspiring. A newer part of the museum is the **Earth Lab Datasite**, an educational resource where you can investigate UK geology using an extensive on-line database.

Science Museum

Exhibition Road; ● *South Kensington; bus C1, 14, 74;* ℂ *(020) 7938 8080; www. nmsi.ac.uk*

Open daily 10–6; adm.

The Science Museum has done perhaps more than any other institution in London to make itself accessible and popular, undergoing constant updating and improvement. Children have always loved it; one of the latest gimmicks is to allow them to sleep at the museum overnight. Anyone between eight and eleven who brings a sleeping bag will be treated to an after-hours tour of the building, a choice of workshops and bedtime stories before lights out (children may also be accompanied by adults: phone the museum on ℂ (020) 7938 8008 for details).

For less privileged visitors, the best place to start is with the synopsis on the mezzanine above the **Ground Floor**, giving an overview of industrial and technological progress across the centuries. Here you can disabuse yourself of a few basic misconceptions: Jethro Tull was not just a bad 1970s heavy metal band but also an 18th-century agricultural pioneer who introduced rowcrop farming. Nearby, the Power section gives a brief history of engines including pioneering models by Boulton and Watt from the 1780s. Then comes a Space section, complete with Second World War V2 rocket and Apollo 10 command module. Beyond, the Land Transport section traces the history of automobiles from Stephenson's Rocket to the Morris mini, the latter bisected from top to bottom. One of the most recent additions is the Challenge of Materials, a new 'gallery of the future' whose centrepiece is a spectacular glass and steel bridge which spans the main hall of the museum, and whose exhibits celebrate British industry, manufacturing and design.

Moving up to the **First Floor** you come to one of the highlights for children, a gallery full of interactive games called the Launch Pad. Children are taken in groups at a time to be explained the rudiments of such diverse phenomena as bicycle gears and hangovers. For grown-ups the most fascinating section on this floor is Time Measurement, tracing the technology of clocks from the first Egyptian timepieces, based on water, to modern quartz and atomic clocks. Next to the tickers is Food for Thought, which explains everything you wanted to know about nutrition (and a few things you didn't—a group of see-through plastic vats, for example, demonstrating all too graphically how much urine, faeces and sweat a 10-year-old boy produces in a month).

The highlight of the **Second Floor** is the Chemistry section, exploring the history of the science through the discoveries of such pioneers as Priestley, Dalton, Davy and Faraday. Under Living Molecules you'll find Crick and Watson's metal-plate model of the structure of DNA. Further along the floor are displays on the development of computers and an overview of nuclear physics, as well as a beautiful collection of model ships. On the **Third Floor** most children head for the Flight Lab, featuring simulators, a wind tunnel and a mini hot-air balloon. The main Flight section is a display of more than 20 historic aircraft, plus a collection of models and an ingenious air traffic control display. Equally intriguing is Optics, a collection of spectacles, telescopes, microscopes and the like, leading up to such modern developments as lasers and holograms. The **Fourth and Fifth Floors** are devoted to medicine.

Children in need of tiring out can be taken directly to the **Science of Sport** gallery, on the ground floor, where they can see a genuine £2 million Formula 1 McLaren, or practise rock-climbing an indoor mountain, try out their snowboarding skills or experience the thrills and spills of a simulated penalty shootout.

St Paul's Cathedral

St Paul's Churchyard; ✆ *St Paul's; bus 8, 25, 242 from Oxford Street, 11, 15, 26 from the Strand,* ✆ *(020) 7236 4128, www.stpauls.london.anglican.org*

Open Mon–Sat 8.30–4.30, last admission 4; adm.

St Paul's is more than just a cathedral or famous landmark. It is an icon for a whole city. Get to know St Paul's and you understand many of the ambitions and failings of London itself.

For nearly 1400 years, succeeding buildings on this site have sought to express the material confidence of a powerful capital while at the same time delineating its spiritual aspirations. Back in the 7th century, St Paul's was England's first major Christian temple; in its medieval incarnation it was the largest single building in the land. In the hands of Christopher Wren, who rebuilt it from scratch after the Great Fire, it was hailed as an architectural masterpiece. Since then St Paul's has dutifully propped up all the myths of the nation: as the burial place for heroes during the glory days of empire, as a symbol of British endurance during the Second World War when it miraculously survived the Blitz, or as the fairy-tale setting for Prince Charles's marriage to Lady Diana Spencer in 1981.

And yet St Paul's has often shared more with the commercial world outside its doors than with the spiritual world celebrated within. Back in the Middle Ages the cathedral was itself a kind of market, with horses parading down the nave and stallholders selling beer and vegetables to all-comers. Even today, the first thing confronting the swarms of tourists who come here is a cash register, a sign of St Paul's' peculiar ease in reconciling religious faith with the handling of money. It is a cool, cerebral place. While we admire Wren's pure lines and lofty vision, we feel little warmth or sense of a living church community. St Paul's is a monument to wealth first, and God second.

By the time of the Great Fire of London, old St Paul's was so dilapidated that several architects wanted to pull it down and rebuild it from scratch. Christopher Wren, commissioned to consider the cathedral's future in 1663, called it 'defective both in beauty and firmness...a heap of deformities that no judicious architect will think corrigible by any expense that can be laid out upon it'. He did not have to lobby long for the merits of demolition. On 4 September 1666, the first flames of the Great Fire of London reached St Paul's and proceeded to engulf it entirely.

Nothing was easy about the rebuilding. Wren initially used gunpowder to clear the wreck of old St Paul's but had to resort to battering rams instead after terrified locals complained of rogue pieces of stonework flying through their living-room windows. As for the design, Wren set his heart on building a dome in the manner of the great Italian Baroque churches. That idea, too, met stiff resistance—it was considered excessively Popish in those religiously sensitive times. You can see his magnificent 20ft oak replica of the Great Model on display in the crypt. Eventually the dome problem was solved through a mixture of guile and compromise. Wren submitted a third plan dispensing with a dome in favour of a steeple, and had it approved in 1675; in return the royal warrant giving him the go-ahead granted him the liberty 'to make some variations rather ornamental than essential, as from time to time he should see proper'. By the time the cathedral opened 35 years later, the dome was back, as were many of the architect's other rejected ideas.

The sheer imposing scale of St Paul's is apparent as soon as you approach the entrance at the west front. The broad **staircase** leads up to a two-tiered portico upheld by vast stone columns and flanked by two clocktowers. Dominating the high pediment in the centre is a statue of St Paul, with St Peter to his left and St James to his right. It is surely no coincidence that these three figures look down on the sovereign of the day, Queen Anne, whose statue stands on the ground outside the entrance. The ensemble, the work of a single artist, Francis Bird, forges a clear mystical link between the City, the crown and the church.

The **nave** is vast but remarkably simple in its symmetries; concentrate on the harmony of the architecture and try to blank out the largely hideous statuary and incidental decoration added well after Wren's time. As you walk beneath the dome, look down at the marble floor and you'll see the famous epitaph to Wren, added by his son after his death in 1723, '*Lector, si monumentam requiris, circumspice*' (Reader, if you seek a memorial, look around you).

Look, in particular, up towards the magnificent **dome**. This is something of an optical illusion, nowhere near as big on the inside as it is on the outside. In fact, Wren built a smaller second dome inside the first to keep the interior on a manageable scale. The story goes that the first stone used to construct the dome was a relic from the old St Paul's which by coincidence bore the Latin word *resurgam* (rise up). Wren took it as a good portent and had the word inscribed in the pediment above the south door, adorning it with an image of a phoenix rising from the ashes. You can climb up into the dome, or domes, from a staircase on the south side of the cathedral, in exchange for another cash contribution.

The first stopping-off point is the **Whispering Gallery** 100ft up, so called because you can murmur with your face turned towards the wall and be heard with crystal clarity on the other side of the dome, 107ft away. You can also admire James Thornhill's series of frescoes on the life of St Paul which stretch all the way around the gallery. Vertigo permitting, you can continue on up to the Stone Gallery, the Inner Golden Gallery and the Outer Golden Gallery, offering panoramic views over London from just below the ball and cross at a height of 365ft.

And so down to the **crypt** (entrance near the south door), whose highlight is undoubtedly Wren's Great Model (*see* above) and the fine exhibition that accompanies it. Most of the space, though, is taken up with tombs commemorating Britain's military leaders. Among the rows and rows of nonentities you can find the Duke of Wellington in his pompous porphyry casket and, directly beneath the dome, the black marble sarcophagus honouring Horatio Nelson. The Florentine sarcophagus, by Pietro Torrigiano, was originally commissioned by Cardinal Wolsey back in the 16th century, but was deemed too good for him and spent three centuries unused and neglected in Windsor Castle until Nelson's mourners unearthed it for his funeral in 1805.

Tate Britain

Millbank; ❷ *Pimlico; bus 77A from Strand;* ✆ *(020) 7887 8000, www.tate.org.uk*
Open daily 10–5.50; free, with free guided tours Mon–Fri at 11.30, 2.30 and 3.30.

This gallery, founded at the end of the 19th century by the sugar baron Sir Henry Tate of Tate & Lyle, was once known simply as The Tate and housed the second great London art collection after the National Gallery. In spring 2000 the collection divided into two: 20th-century international art moved across the river to **Tate Modern** at Bankside (*see* p.84) while here at Millbank, **Tate Britain** reverted to the original purpose of its founder as the national gallery of home-grown art, with a full panorama of works from the Middle Ages until now. By 2001, there will be a new entrance, five new exhibition galleries, nine reno-vated galleries and more display space to allow works by Hogarth, Gainsborough, Stubbs, Blake, Constable, the Pre-Raphaelites, Spencer, Sickert, Bacon and Moore to be brought out of years of storage. Contemporary painters will also get a better airing with more works by Anthony Caro, Richard Hamilton, David Hockney, Eduardo Paolozzi, Lucian Freud, Howard Hodgkin (winner of the 1985 Turner prize), Richard Long and Frank Auerbach seeing the light of day.

Highlights of the Gallery

Room 2, which is almost entirely devoted to **Hogarth**'s finest satire, *O the Roast Beef of England*, a depiction of the greed and corruption of France.

Sir Joshua Reynolds, *Three Ladies Adoring a Term of Hymen*, which turns four upper-class English sisters into gossiping Greek nymphs with delicate complexions and dainty clothes.

Room 7, devoted to the terrifying Manichean world of **William Blake** (1757–1827), a man who turned his vivid Biblical and literary nightmares into extraordinarily enigmatic poetry, pen and ink watercolours and prints.

Victorian painting: starts with the Romantic John Constable and his lyrical depictions of Malvern Hall in Warwickshire and Salisbury Cathedral.

Pre-Raphaelites: among the works to look out for are Waterhouse's *Lady of Shalott*, Burne-Jones's *King Cophetua and the Beggar Maid* and Millais' *Ophelia*, floating lifelessly in a marshy brook. The best pieces here are by foreigners working in England, like the American James Whistler whose *Nocturne in Blue-Green* is a compelling cityscape of the Thames at Chelsea.

Turner Collection—the Clore Gallery. It is hard to pick out individual pictures, especially since the displays tend to change, but try to see some of the following: *Rome from the Vatican* (1820), an idealized portrait of the Eternal City reflecting many of Turner's artistic preoccupations; *Snow Storm: Steam-boat off a Harbour's Mouth*, a virtuoso whirl of chaos on the waves; *A City on a River at Sunset*, a gorgeous, warm study of sky and water, probably in Rouen; and *Peace—Burial at Sea*, a tribute to Turner's fellow painter David Wilkie in which light, mist and smoke mingle in Turner's typical sea setting.

Modern art: Highlights in the main modern galleries include Magritte's disturbing dreamscapes and the desolate cities of Giorgio de Chirico (*Uncertainty of the Poet*). Matisse dominates Room 24, particularly his early *Inattentive Reader* (1919) and his experiment with paper cut-outs, *The Snail* (which one of the guards insists is called *The Snail* because a tiny nick at the very top of the picture looks exactly like a snail making its way slowly across the picture). Abstract painting is well represented by Jackson Pollock and Mark Rothko; pop art by Roy Lichtenstein's comic-book *Whaam!* and Andy Warhol's *Marilyn Diptych* which parodies the movie superstar's transformation into a vulgar commodity.

10, Downing Street

Off Whitehall; ❂ *Westminster; bus 3, 11, 12, 24, 53, 77A, 88, 109*

Downing Street has been home to British Prime Ministers on and off since 1735. Unfortunately, you won't be able to sidle up to the famous Georgian front door at No.10 without a security pass; the best you can hope for is a glimpse through the heavy iron gates installed in 1990. Next door at No.11 is the Chancellor of the Exchequer, the British equivalent of treasury secretary or finance minister, and next door to him, at No.12, is the government whips' office, where the party in power keeps tabs on its members in parliament.

It is rather pleasing to think that this street, the scene of many a heated cabinet meeting and ministerial bollocking, was once an open venue for cock fighting. A theatre dedicated to the proposition that encouraging animals to tear each other apart with spurs is just as entertaining as watching politicians doing the same thing in the Palace of Westminster stayed in business on this site alongside the Axe brewhouse until about 1675. It was only then that a rather modest building development, later to become the powerhouse of the British establishment, was undertaken by one George Downing, a slippery fellow who managed to spy for both Oliver Cromwell and Charles II during the Civil War and come out of it not only alive but stinking rich into the bargain. It was more accident than design that led to Downing Street's lasting fame. When the prime minister, Robert Walpole, succeeded a certain Mr Chicken as tenant in 1735 he never meant to establish No.10 as an official residence, and indeed many of his successors preferred to conduct the business of government from their more lavish homes elsewhere in London. Only in the early 19th century was 10 Downing Street kitted out with proper facilities, such as John Soane's sumptuous dining room; only in 1902 did it become the prime minister's home as well as office. The shortcomings of the place have never gone away, though; when Tony Blair became prime minister in 1997, he installed his family in the more spacious No.11 next door, swapping places with his unmarried Chancellor, Gordon Brown.

Tower Bridge

⊖ *Tower Hill; bus 42, 78 from the City , or 15 to the Tower of London*

Tower Bridge Experience, ℂ (020) 7403 3761. Open daily April–Oct 10–6.30; Nov–Mar 9.30–6, last entry an hour and a quarter before closing; adm.

Tower Bridge is one of the great feats of late Victorian engineering, half suspension-bridge and half drawbridge, linked to two neo-Gothic towers. Designed by an engineer, John Wolfe-Barry, and an architect, Horace Jones, working in tandem, it has become one of London's most recognizable landmarks. Its fame was not exactly instant; indeed, at its opening in 1894, the critics found its evocation of medieval style crude. *The Builder* called it 'the most monstrous and preposterous architectural sham that we have ever known...an elaborate and costly make-believe.' There is still a reasonable case to be made that Tower Bridge is a kind of Victorian Disneyland, but time has mellowed its vulgarity and made it both awe-inspiring and loveable. Its two bascules, the arms that rise up to let tall ships through, weigh an astonishing 1000 tonnes each. Despite the decline of river freight traffic, the bridge still opens at least once a day on average; phone ahead (ℂ (020) 7403 3761) to find out the times. At the southern tower you can join the **Tower Bridge Experience,** a hi-tech retelling of the history of the bridge, plus a chance to enjoy the view from the overhead walkways and admire the giant Victorian hydraulic engines that once operated the bridge (it is now done with electric power).

Tower of London

Tower Hill; ⊖ Tower Hill; bus 15; ℂ (020) 7709 0765 or 7680 9004; www.hrp. org.uk

Open March–Oct, Mon–Sat 9–6 and Sun 10–6; Nov–Feb Mon–Sat 9–5 and Sun 10–5, last adm all year round an hour before closing; adm expensive.

The Tower is one London sight that everyone knows but nobody particularly likes. Ever since the monarchy moved out in the early 17th century, the Tower has existed principally as a stronghold of historical nostalgia, a place that owes its appeal more to romantic notions of the past than to real past events. Modern Americans might want to compare it to the fantasy castles of Disneyland, especially if they follow the **Tower Hill Pageant** (entrance near All Hallows' Church), a 15-minute underground ghost-train ride, complete with commentary, and nasty smells and sounds, past tableaux of famous episodes in London's history.

So what is the big attraction? First of all the site, which is one of the best preserved medieval castles in the world. The **White Tower**, the keep at the centre of the complex, dates back to William the Conqueror and includes the magnificent heavy round arches and groin vaults of the 13th-century **St John's Chapel**. More importantly, the Tower corresponds to every myth ever invented about England. Its history is packed with tales of royal pageantry, dastardly baronial plots, ghoulish tortures and gruesome executions. The Tower is still guarded by quaint liveried figures, the Beefeaters, who obligingly conduct their Ceremony of the Keys at 9.45 each evening. And, of course, the Tower contains the Crown Jewels.

Under Henry III the Tower expanded considerably and included for the first time a menagerie, complete with lions, leopards, a polar bear and an elephant. Prisoners were brought in from the river through **Traitor's Gate**, which you can still see today.

Inevitably, you also will be drawn towards the **Crown Jewels**. You'll probably have to share the spectacle with the entire adult population of Cleveland, Ohio, not to mention several thousand Euro-teenagers, but at least there is a decent attempt at crowd control, thanks to a relatively new conveyor-belt system. There are two main crowns: St Edward's Crown, a heavy, somewhat unwieldy piece used only during the coronation ceremony itself; and the golden Crown of State, encrusted with 3,000 gems, which was originally made for Queen Victoria and is still used for grand occasions such as the state opening of parliament. Next are the jewelled sword and spurs, also used to anoint the new monarch, followed by the orb, bracelets and two sceptres which symbolize the sovereign's secular and divine mission. The orb represents the spread of Christianity around the world, the sceptres forge the link between the monarch and his or her subjects, while the bracelets are an emblem of Britain's link to the Commonwealth. The Ring of Kingly Dignity is a sapphire mounted with rubies, while the Great Sword of State, the sovereign's symbolic personal weapon, is decorated with a lion and unicorn as well as the royal arms.

Trafalgar Square

Back in the 1810s and 1820s, when Britannia really did rule the waves and London was the capital of a burgeoning empire, a hitherto taboo concept suddenly came into fashion: urban planning. Previously it had been considered perfectly proper for London to develop organically according to the whims of private landowners. But then industrialization arrived, threatening to stifle the capital in factory smoke if the *laissez-faire* planning policy persisted. At the same time, Britain's victory in the Napoleonic Wars unleashed a broad desire for some decent monumental architecture. The Prince Regent, an ardent patron of grand building schemes, was only too happy to sponsor major projects, and soon architects were putting forward proposals for the wildest and most outlandish schemes.

It was in such an atmosphere that Trafalgar Square was first conceived. The Prince Regent (later crowned George IV) and his chosen architect, John Nash, wanted to create a vast open space glorifying the country's naval power which would also provide a focal point from which other urban projects could spread. It was a fine idea, but one that was destined to be cruelly truncated by the vagaries of history. George developed a reputation as a spendthrift and a philanderer, and as economic crisis gripped the nation in the mid-1820s all his dreams were brought to a halt by a hostile parliament. Nash was dismissed as soon as George died in 1830, and from then on Trafalgar Square was left at the mercy of successive parliamentary committees who argued for the best part of a generation over its final form.

Modern Trafalgar Square evolved partly out of a desire to raise the tone of the Charing Cross area. Nash pulled down the old King's Mews (incidentally, a fine Georgian building by William

Kent) to make room for his planned ensemble of grand classical buildings. But he never got to build them before his fall from grace. The whole Trafalgar Square project might have been abandoned had it not been for a lingering determination to bestow grand honours on Horatio Nelson, the country's legendary naval commander who had died at sea during the Battle of Trafalgar in 1805. In 1808, the essayist William Wood wrote a rousing eulogy of England 'proudly stemming the torrent of revolutionary frenzy', and proposed erecting a giant pyramid to his hero. Over the years 120 official proposals were submitted, including a myriad columns, pyramids and even a Coliseum. In the absence of a co-ordinating architect, however, the scheme made painfully slow progress. Where Nash had been extravagant, the special select committee of the House of Commons proved downright stingy. The new planners were not interested in producing monumental architecture unless it could be done on the cheap.

As for **Nelson's Column**, it did not see the light of day until 1843. The Corinthian column, topped by an unremarkable and scarcely visible likeness of Nelson in his admiral's three-cornered hat, by E. H. Baily, was erected on a sloping concrete basin prepared by the neoclassical architect Charles Barry. Railton based his design on a triumphalist precedent from ancient Rome, the Temple of Mars in the Forum of Augustus. The bronze bas-reliefs at the base of the column represent Nelson's four greatest victories, at Cape St Vincent, the Nile, Copenhagen and Trafalgar, while the surrounding statuary is of Nelson's generals. The two granite fountains at the base arrived in 1845, while the bronze lions, the most appealing feature of the ensemble, appeared a quarter of a century later.

Trafalgar Square is the point from which all measurements in London are drawn; there is a plaque indicating this on the corner of Charing Cross Road. On the eastern side of the square is South Africa House, where anti-apartheid protesters maintained a constant vigil through the latter part of Nelson Mandela's 26-year imprisonment. Next door is James Gibbs's church of St Martin-in-the-Fields. In the southeastern corner stands a lamppost known as the smallest police station in the world, which contains a telephone linked up to police headquarters at Scotland Yard. On the western side, in a building designed by Robert Smirke, builder of the British Museum, is Canada House, home to the Canadian High Commission.

Victoria and Albert Museum

Cromwell Road and 2nd entrance on Exhibition Road; ⊖ *South Kensington, bus C1, 74, 14;* ℗ *(020) 7938 8500; www.vam.ac.uk*

Open Mon–Sun 10–5.45, in summer also Wed late view 6.30–9.30; adm, free after 4.30.

This huge, sprawling museum is nominally dedicated to applied art and design, but in fact even such a broad definition does not sufficiently cover the sheer vastness of its collections. Over the years it has become the nation's treasure trove. You could liken it to a magical chest in some long-forgotten attic; but the V&A has also kept bang up to date, displaying everything from Donatello to Dalí, from medieval reliquaries to Reebok sneakers. Its former director, Sir Roy Strong, once defined it as an 'extremely capacious handbag'. Unlike most large museums, you would be ill-advised to pick and choose your way around the V&A on a first visit. To get a proper feel of it, you should aim to get hopelessly lost along its seven miles of corridors.

Pick up a free **museum guide** at the reception desk. It tells you where the most famous exhibits are, and provides detailed maps of the two main floors, plus the six storeys of the Henry

Cole wing. There are guided tours through the day, which are recommended for an hour's concentrated stimulation. Neither the museum guides nor this book would be foolhardy enough to undertake an exhaustive description of the whole place: what follows is a broad-brush and personalized account of what to expect.

Highlights of the Museum

Level A: Dress

An enthralling starting point is the room dedicated to European fashion across history. Watch how the flamboyant clothes of the 17th and 18th century gradually grow more restricted by corsets and bodices, then become blander and fussier in the 19th century, turn morose in the 1930s and 1940s before exploding in new-found freedom and colour in the 1960s and beyond. Up a spiral staircase from the dress section are **Musical Instruments**, a range of historical music boxes, virginals and a Dutch giraffe piano with six percussion pedals, as well as the usual strings, wind and brass.

Italy 1400–1500

The V&A calls this the greatest collection of Renaissance sculpture outside Italy. The pieces here are so disparate they could have come from some glorified car boot sale held by the great churches of Tuscany and northern Italy. There are rood sculptures and reliefs, and beautifully decorated cassones in gilt and gesso; a *Neptune and Triton* by Giovanni Bernini and *Samson Slaying a Philistine* by Giovanni Bologna. The greatest treasures are two delicate reliefs by Donatello, the *Ascension With Christ Giving The Keys To St Peter*, which may have been commissioned for the Brancacci chapel in Santa Maria della Carmine in Florence, and a *Dead Christ Tended by Angels*, which may have been intended for Prato cathedral.

Poynter, Gamble and Morris Rooms

On your way through the Italian section you pass the world's first museum café-restaurant. Each of the three rooms is a rich, highly decorated example of Victorian design. The Poynter Room, originally the grill room, is decked out in blue tiles depicting idyllic country harvest scenes in between allegories of the seasons and the months of the year. The Gamble Room, used for the cold buffet, is a throwback to the Renaissance with its gold and blue tiles, enamelled metal ceiling and apt quotation from Ecclesiasticus around the walls: 'There is nothing better for a man than to eat and drink.' The last room is the work of William Morris, famous for the vegetal inspiration of his wallpaper designs.

Plaster Casts

Two rooms, straddling the altogether disappointing collection of fakes and forgeries, are devoted to near-perfect copies of some of the most famous sculptures and monuments in the world. The effect is altogether surreal: how can you get your mind around seeing Michelangelo's *David* and *Moses*, Ghiberti's *Gates of Paradise*, Trajan's Column from Rome, the *Puerta de la Gloria* from Santiago de Compostela and chunks of Bordeaux, Aix-en-Provence, Amiens, York and Nuremberg cathedrals all in one place?

Oriental Art

The central section of Level A is devoted to art from the Islamic world, India, China, Japan and Korea. The most famous piece is **Tipu's Tiger** in the Nehru Gallery of Indian Art. This is an adjustable wooden sculpture dating from 1790 in which a tiger can be seen mauling the neck of an English soldier. There are Indian sculptures of deities dating back to the 1st century BC, and paintings and artefacts giving an overview of two millennia of Indian decoration.

The Toshiba Gallery of **Japanese Art** boasts some particularly fine lacquer work: tables, trays and some amazing playing-card boxes. There are also some interesting ceramics, including a huge porcelain disc originally shown in Europe at the 1878 Paris Exhibition.

The **Chinese Art** section focuses principally on fine objects used in everyday life, particularly ceramics and a collection of ornaments and figurines used in burial ceremonies. Grander pieces include a large Ming dynasty canopied bed and a Qing dynasty embroidered hanging for a Buddhist temple. The **Korean Art** gallery also focuses on everyday objects, including some ancient metalwork, and ceramics from the Koryo and Choson dynasties that go back to the 9th century. Finally the section on **Art in the Islamic World** contains a pot pourri of carpets and prayer mats from Egypt and Turkey and finely decorated bowls and earthenware from Persia.

The Rest of Level A

Sandwiched in the middle of the oriental art sections is the **Medieval Treasury**, a beautiful collection of mainly religious artefacts from the 5th to the 15th century. The other remaining highlight of Level A is the **Raphael Cartoons**, sketches for the great religious and philosophical frescoes he painted for the Papal apartments in the Vatican. Dotted around the corridors of Level A are European works of all kinds dating from 1100 to 1800.

Level B: 20th Century Gallery

This series of altogether enthralling rooms is a far more engaging history of 20th-century design than the Design Museum at Butler's Wharf. The focus is on household furniture, but within that remit is everything from Marcel Breuer's pioneering Bauhaus chair to Salvador Dalí's totally frivolous lipstick-pink sofa in the shape of one of Mae West's kisses.

Tapestries

Beyond the 20th Century Gallery you have to walk through yards and yards of unexciting silver pots, metalwork and armour before reaching the tapestry collection and, in particular, the medieval series known as the **Devonshire Hunt**. Famed for their beauty, wealth of detail and high standard of preservation, these tapestries were commissioned in the 15th century for Hardwick Hall, a country mansion in southwestern England.

Henry Cole Wing

This wing, named after the museum's founding director, comes closest to the chest-in-the-attic analogy: much of what is in here is junk, particularly the painting section on the fourth floor, but a bit of patient burrowing will be well rewarded.

On the second floor is the **Frank Lloyd Wright Gallery**, a series of rooms dedicated to the great 20th-century American architect and figurehead of the modern movement. Floor three is reserved for special exhibitions of prints. Floor four is crammed with mediocre painting, much of it British. Skip past the fifth floor, which is a print library not open to the general public, and you come up to a light, airy exhibition of some of the best of British painting, including a clutch of Turners and a broad selection of the work of John Constable.

The glittering **glass gallery** at Room 131 shouldn't be missed either, with its staircase made entirely of green glass blocks.

Parliament Square; ⊖ Westminster; bus 3, 11, 12, 24, 53, 77A, 88, 109;
ℂ (020) 7222 5152; www.westminster-abbey.org

Admission to the Abbey is free for services or prayers. For visitors the nave is open
Mon–Fri 9–4.45, last adm 3.45, and Sat 9–2.45, last adm 1.45; adm. Late night
Weds 6–7.45pm, when amateur photos are allowed. The Cloisters are open daily
8–6; free. The Royal Chapels, Statesman's Aisle and Poets' Corner are open Mon–Fri
9–4.45 and Sat 9–2.45; adm. The Chapter House, Pyx Chamber and Undercroft
Museum are open daily 10.30–4; adm. Guided tours conducted by the vergers are
also available, call ℂ (020) 7222 7110 to book.

It is impossible to overestimate the symbolic importance of Westminster Abbey in English culture. This is where monarchs are crowned and buried, where the Anglican Church derives its deepest inspiration, and where the nation as a whole lionizes its artistic and political heroes. No other country invests so much importance in a single building.

Architecturally the abbey derives its inspiration from the great cathedrals at Reims and Amiens and the Sainte-Chapelle in Paris. 'A great French thought expressed in excellent English,' one epithet has it. The abbey's origins go back to the mists of the Dark Ages; it found a mystical patron in Edward the Confessor, saint and monarch; it was rebuilt from scratch in the finest Gothic traditions from the 13th until the 16th century; and it was completed in 1745. Thus the abbey spans virtually the whole of modern English history. To be buried there, or at least to have a plaque erected, is still the highest state honour for an English citizen. The tombs of the medieval kings and other relics bestow much of the legitimacy to which the modern monarchy can still lay claim. If St Paul's is a monument to the secular wealth of London, Westminster Abbey enshrines the mystical power of the crown.

It was Westminster's association with the crown that saved the abbey during the dissolution of the monasteries in the late 1530s, when it escaped with just a few smashed windows and broken ornaments. The royal connection made it a target during the Civil War, when Cromwell's army used it as a dormitory and smashed the altar rails. Cromwell succumbed to its lure once he was Lord Protector, however, and had himself buried in the abbey after his death in 1658. His body was dug up at the Restoration and eventually reburied at the foot of the gallows at Tyburn. After the Civil War, the abbey was once again given over to burials and coronations. Aside from royals, the place is stuffed with memorials to politicians (in the Statesman's Aisle), poets (in Poets' Corner), actors, scientists and engineers.

The coronation ceremony has become familiar around the world thanks to television re-runs of the investiture of Elizabeth II in 1953, the first coronation to be televised. But ceremonies have not always gone as smoothly as the establishment might have liked. Richard I had a bat swooping around his head during his ceremony, a sign perhaps of bad luck to come. Richard II lost a shoe in the Abbey, while James II's crown wobbled and nearly fell off during his parade down Whitehall. George IV was so weighed down by his outrageously extravagant coronation garb that he nearly fainted and had to be revived with smelling salts.

Pick up a floor plan at the entrance. Everything west of the choir screen is free; beyond is the old east end, now St Edward's Chapel; and beyond that the late-Gothic extension including the Henry VII Chapel. The cloisters and Chapter House are off the end of the south transept.

The Nave

Measuring 103ft from floor to ceiling, the nave of Westminster Abbey is by far the tallest in England. But the nave is very long as well as high, giving an impression of general grandeur but not necessarily of loftiness. The columns, made of Purbeck marble, grow darker towards the ceiling, thus further deadening the effect of height. And the ceiling decorations push the eye not upwards, but along towards the altar. Overall, ornamentation is just as important as effects of perspective. As you come in, there is a 14th-century gilded painting of Richard II. The north aisle of the nave has become crowded with memorials and stones to politicians, earning the nickname **Statesman's Aisle**. Plenty of other walks of life are celebrated in this part of the abbey, notably scientists and engineers including Michael Faraday (a memorial tablet) and Sir Isaac Newton (a splendid monument against the choir screen by William Kent).

The Choir and St Edward's Chapel

The first attraction beyond the ticket counters, the choir screen, is a 19th-century reworking by Edward Blore of the gilded 13th-century original. Note the elegant black and white marble floor, and the heraldic shields commemorating the families who gave money to construct the abbey in the 13th century. Behind the High Altar is St Edward's Chapel, the epicentre of the abbey with its memorials to medieval kings around the Coronation Chair. Until November 1996, when it was finally removed to Edinburgh Castle, the simple gilded wooden chair contained the Stone of Scone, the most sacred symbol of the kings of Scotland, which was stolen by Edward I in 1279 and arrogantly kept for five and a bit centuries here in England.

Henry VII Chapel

The penny-pinching Henry VII managed one great feat of artistic patronage during his reign, this extraordinary fan-vaulted chapel, which is nominally dedicated to the Virgin Mary but is in fact a glorification of the Tudor line of monarchs. Henrys VII and VIII, Edward VI, Mary and Elizabeth I are all buried here in style, along with a healthy sprinkling of their contemporaries and successors. Elizabeth shares her huge tomb with her embittered half-sister Mary in a curious after-death gesture of reconciliation. The bodies believed to be the two princes murdered in the Tower of London in 1483 also have a resting place here. The highlight of the chapel, though, is the decoration. The wondrous ceiling looks like an intricate mesh of finely spun cobwebs, while the wooden choir stalls are carved with exotic creatures and adorned with brilliantly colourful heraldic flags.

Poets' Corner

The south transept and the adjoining St Faith's Chapel are part of the original 13th-century abbey structure, and boast a series of wall paintings and some superbly sculpted figures of angels. Geoffrey Chaucer was buried in the south transept in 1400, and ever since other poets and writers have vied to have a place next to him after their deaths. When Edmund Spenser, author of *The Faerie Queen*, was buried in 1599, several writers tossed their unpublished manuscripts into the grave with him. His contemporary, the playwright Ben Jonson, asked modestly for a grave 'two feet by two feet' and consequently was buried upright. Few of the writers commemorated in Poets' Corner are actually interred here; among the 'genuine' ones are Dryden, Samuel Johnson, Sheridan, Browning and Tennyson. To free up more space in the increasingly crowded corner, the abbey authorities have recently installed a stained-glass window with new memorials to parvenus such as Pope, Herrick and Wilde.

London: Central Neighbourhoods

⊖ *Holborn, Euston, Russell Square, Goodge Street, Warren Street*

Bloomsbury, according to William the Conqueror's survey *The Domesday Book*, started life as a breeding ground for pigs, but it has acquired a rather more **refined** pedigree since. Home to London University, the British Museum, the new British Library and countless bookshops and cafés, it is the **intellectual** heart of the capital. George Bernard Shaw, Giuseppe Mazzini, Marx and Lenin all found inspiration among the tomes of the Reading Room in the British Library. Bertrand Russell and Virginia Woolf helped form an intellectual movement here, the Bloomsbury Group, whose members invited each other for tea and gossip in the area's Georgian town houses. More recently, Bloomsbury has become a favoured location for the publishing trade and the new wave of independent television production companies. It is a **quiet**, slightly shabby but youthful quarter of London. Much of your energy will inevitably be devoted to the vast collections of the British Museum. But there's a good sprinkling of other curiosities as well, including some

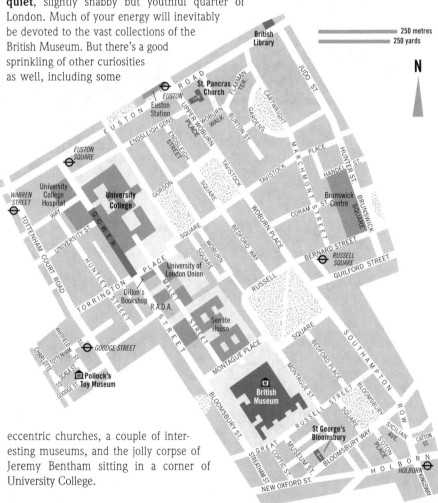

eccentric churches, a couple of interesting museums, and the jolly corpse of Jeremy Bentham sitting in a corner of University College.

Bloomsbury Square

This was the original London housing development based on the leasehold system, and the model for the city's phenomenally rapid growth throughout the 18th and 19th centuries. Nowadays it is one of the more elegant squares in central London, with a ring of stately Georgian homes surrounding a flourishing garden. The square also has a plaque commemorating the **Bloomsbury Group**, a movement most often associated with its brightest member, the novelist Virginia Woolf, but which also included Woolf's husband Leonard, the novelist E. M. Forster, the economist John Maynard Keynes, the philosopher Bertrand Russell and the essayist Lytton Strachey. The group had no manifesto or specific aim; it was a loose association of like-minded intellectuals (most of them politically on the soft left) who met to exchange ideas. Following the teachings of the philosopher G. E. Moore, they believed that the appreciation of beautiful objects and the art of fine conversation were the keys to social progress.

Russell Square and the University of London

On the western side of the square looms **Senate House**, one of the spookiest buildings in London, which stands at the heart of the schools and colleges of the **University of London**.

The School of Oriental and African Studies (SOAS) sits in the northwest corner of Russell Square. On the corner of Malet Street is the students' union (ULU). If you happen to be a student yourself, you can use its good cheap bar. Halfway down Malet Street is **Birkbeck College**, which in 1823 became the first college in England to run evening courses for the working classes. It joined London University in 1920. Continuing down Torrington Place, you come to **Gower Street**, the blackened brick terraces of which sum up everything the Victorians disapproved of in Georgian building. Ruskin called it 'the *ne plus ultra* of ugliness in street architecture'. You can see what he meant: the sameness of the houses, relieved only by the occasional splash of paint on the lower storey, and the arrow-like straightness of the street. Along on the right, **University College** is a fine, if rather heavy, example of the Greek Revival style by William Wilkins, the architect of the National Gallery. Many Victorians hated the place, combining their dislike of classical architecture with their disapproval for what they called 'the godless College in Gower Street'. Visitors should head straight for the South Cloister in the far right-hand corner. Near the door is the glass cabinet with the stuffed body of **Jeremy Bentham**, the utilitarian philosopher and political reformer who died in 1832.

Cafés and Pubs

Museum Street Café, 47 Museum St. Overhyped but excellent bistro-style café with exquisitely presented home-made food.

The Coffee Gallery, 23 Museum St. Grilled aubergines, fishcakes with rocket, and scrumptious Sicilian salads.

Town House Brasserie, 24 Coptic St. Eclectic modern French 'fusion' food in smartish restaurant offering set lunch for £9.95, or an early bird menu, 2 courses for £5.

Bush & Field's Café, 49 Museum St. Great salt beef.

Wagamama, 4 Streatham St. Cheap, popular, delicious Japanese noodle ('ramen') bar—you might have to queue. £5–10.

Mandeer, 21 Hanway Place. Elegant but cheap vegetarian Indian restaurant a stone's throw from Tottenham Court Rd Tube, serving a fantastic value canteen-style lunch for under £5. Wonderful value.

Malabar Junction, 107 Great Russell Street. Set lunch from £3.50 in sleek but laid-back restaurant close to the British Museum.

Fitzroy Tavern, 16 Charlotte St. Drinking hole of the 1940s literati.

The British Library

Midland Street, © (020) 7412 7332. Open Mon, Wed, Fri 9.30–6, Tues 9.30–8, Sat 9.30–5, Sun 11–5. Guided tours on certain days only; bookshops and a restaurant.

The history of this new building has been such a shambles that it came as a shock to most people when it finally opened, a decade late, in November 1997. Construction work on Colin St John Wilson's building began back in 1978 and took longer than the building of St Paul's cathedral. By the time it was completed, Wilson had overspent by £350 million, his practice had dissolved, and the building itself had been exposed to that peculiarly violent brand of venom that the British reserve for new architectural projects. Ironically, the building's most vicious critics have been stunned and delighted by the spectacular interior, with its vast scale, open tracts of white Travertine marble, and complex and fascinating spaces flooded with light. If the red brick exterior fills you with initial fear and loathing, remind yourself that the building is worth seeing for its three exhibition galleries and art treasures alone.

The big attraction is the library's vast number of **manuscripts**, from the sacred to the profane, from the delicate beauty of illuminated Bibles to the frenzied scrawl of Joyce's first draft of *Finnegan's Wake*; from musical scores to political documents, notebooks and private letters. Among the greatest treasures are the **Lindisfarne Gospels**, the work of a monk named Eadfrith who wrote and illuminated them on the island of Lindisfarne (also called Holy Island), off the northeastern coast of England, in honour of St Cuthbert. The other star exhibit is the **Magna Carta**. The British Library has two of the four surviving copies of this document, one of the founding texts of the modern democratic system signed by King John at Runnymede under pressure from his barons in 1215. Among the other manuscripts are Lenin's reapplication for a reader's ticket which he made under the pseudonym Jacob Richter. There is an extensive collection of literary manuscripts, including an illuminated version of Chaucer's *Canterbury Tales*, and—arguably the highlight—Lewis Carroll's beautifully neat handwriting and illustrations in the notebook version of *Alice in Wonderland*.

Stamp lovers should head for the **Philatelic Collections** which include first issues of nearly every stamp in the world from 1840 to 1890.

Also open here is the **British Library National Sound Archive** (*open Mon–Fri 10–5; free*). This wonderful collection includes early gramophones and record sleeves, and a series of priceless historical, literary and musical recordings: Florence Nightingale and Gladstone, Paul Robeson in a live performance of *Othello*, James Joyce reading from *Ulysses*, The Beatles interviewed by Jenny Everett, Charlie Parker's club performances (recorded on wire), and Stravinsky in rehearsal.

Pollock's Toy Museum

Corner of Scala St, © (020) 7636 3452. Open Mon–Sat 10–5; very cheap adm.

Benjamin Pollock was the leading Victorian manufacturer of toy theatres, and this small but very attractive museum is based on the collection that he left. It's an atmospheric place, the four narrow floors connected by creaky staircases. The theatres are on the top floor, and exhibits also include board games, tin toys, puppets, wax dolls, teddy bears and dolls' houses.

Also see: The **British Museum**, p.29.
Onwards to: **Covent Garden**, p.62; **Tottenham Court Road shopping**, p.123.

➔ *Bank, St Paul's, Tower Hill, Mansion House, Monument, Barbican*
➔ *City Thameslink, Barbican, Fenchurch Street*

The City is the heart of London, the place where the whole heaving metropolis began, and yet there is something so strange about it that it scarcely seems to be part of London at all. Tens of thousands of commuters stream in each morning, the bankers, brokers and clerks that oil the wheels of this great centre of world finance, spilling out of Liverpool Street or crossing over London Bridge towards their jumble of gleaming high-rise offices. During the lunch hour, you can see them scurrying from office building to sandwich bar to post office, a look of studied intensity stamped on their harried faces. By early evening they have all vanished again, back to their town houses and dormitory communities, leaving the streets and once-**monumental** buildings to slumber eerily in the silent gloom of the London night.

This is T. S. Eliot's 'Unreal City', a metropolis without inhabitants, a place of frenzied, seemingly mindless mechanical activity that the poet, back in the apocalyptic early 1920s, thought worthy of the lost souls of limbo. And yet it remains oddly fascinating, full of echoes of the time when it *was* London. Its streets still largely follow the medieval plan. Its fine churches and **ceremonial** buildings express all the contradictory emotions of a nation that built, and then lost, an entire empire. Its business is still trade, as it was in the 14th century, even if it is trade of a most abstract and arcane sort.

Wren's churches, and St Paul's Cathedral in particular, grace the skyline, but the area is also characterized by the bloody carcasses of Smithfield meat market and the grim legacy of Newgate prison, now converted into the Central Criminal Court.

At the other end of the Square Mile, the Tower of London is a striking relic of medieval London and a reminder of the constant **historical** struggle between wealth creation on the one hand and the jealous encroachment of political interests on the other. The City is a weekday place only, although you won't have any difficulty getting into the Tower or Guildhall on Saturday.

Temple Bar

In the Middle Ages this monument in Fleet Street was a barrier to control comings and goings into the City. So powerful were the City fathers that any unwelcome visitors were simply slung into the jail that stood on the site. The unlucky ones had their heads and pickled body parts displayed on spikes. Even the sovereign had to ask permission to pass this way, a tradition that has lasted in ritualistic form into the modern era. For 200 years an arched gateway designed by Wren marked this spot, but in 1878 it was removed because of traffic congestion and replaced with the present, rather modest monument by Horace Jones. The bronze **griffin** on top is one of the City's emblems, introduced by the Victorians who remembered that the griffins of mythology guarded over a hidden treasure of gold. They presumably forgot, however, that griffins also tore approaching humans to pieces as a punishment for their greed.

N

250 metres
250 yards

Middlesex
House of Detention

BOWLING GREEN LANE

CLERKENWELL CL

FARRINGDON LANE

CLERKENWELL GREEN

AYLESBURY ST

St James
Clerkenwell

St John
Clerkenwell

ST JOHN'S SQ

ST JOHN STREET

GOSWELL ROAD

F A R R I N G D O N   R O A D

CLERKENWELL   ROAD

Charterhouse

St John's
Gate

TURNMILL ST.

BIT ST.

ALBION PL.

ST JOHN'S LA.

BRITTON ST.

HATTON GARDEN

SAFFRON HILL

Farringdon

FARRINGDON

CONCROSS STREET

CHARTERHOUSE

SQUARE

BARBICAN

Barbican

BEECH STREET

Arts
Centre

LEATHER LANE

GREVILLE ST.

ELY PLACE

CHARTERHOUSE STREET

WEST SMITHFIELD ST.

LONG LANE

BARBICAN

St Bartholomew
the Great

CLOTH FAIR

ALDERSGATE ST.

Ironmongers'
Hall

St Giles
Cripplegate

St Ethelreda

Olde
Mitre
Tavern

Smithfield Market

SMITHFIELD

Museum of
London

St Bartholomew's
Hospital

LITTLE

Holborn
Circus

ST ANDREW STREET

HOLBORN VIADUCT

SNOW HILL

HOSIER LA.

GILTSPUR ST.

LONDON WALL

FETTER LANE

City
Temple

City
Thameslink

FARRINGDON ST.

St Sepulchre
without Newgate

Old
Bailey
(Central
Criminal
Court)

National
Post Office
Museum

Postman's
Park

BRITAIN

St Botolph

ST. MARTIN'S LE GRAND

GRESHAM STREET

Guildhall

NEWGATE STREET

KING EDWARD ST.

FOSTER LA.

ST BRIDE ST.

LUDGATE ST.

City
Thameslink

LUDGATE HILL

Paternoster
Square

Chapter Ho.

ST PAUL'S

ST PAUL'S CHURCHYD.

OLD BAILEY

WOOD STREET

MILK ST.

TRUMP ST.

STREET

St Lawrence
Jewry

CHEAPSIDE

Ludgate
Circus

St
Paul's
Cathedral

NEW CHANGE

Spire of
St Augustine's
St Mary-le-Bow

WATLING ST.

BOW LANE

KING STREET

ST PAUL'S CHURCHYARD

CARTER ST.

GODLMAN ST.

St
Nicholas

DISTAFF LANE

CANNON STREET

QUEEN VICTORIA STREET

VICTORIA

MANSION
HOUSE

QUEEN STREET

UPPER THAMES STREET

River Thames

SOUTHWARK BR.

Mansion House

Mansion House, the official residence of the Lord Mayor of London, was intended to be something of a trendsetter, the first project of the Georgian era to be designed in Palladian style. There is a story that a design by Palladio himself was proposed but rejected because the 16th-century Italian master was a foreigner and a Papist. In the end George Dance's building, erected on the site of the old Stocks Market, was completed in 1752, nearly 40 years after the project was first put forward. The end result is not a tremendous success; the awkward shape of the surrounding square does not allow the eye to be drawn towards its grandiose portico, which in any case is top-heavy and unwieldy with its six Corinthian columns.

Unfortunately Mansion House is now almost always shut and more or less the only way to get in is to apply in writing for a minimum of 14 people two months in advance.

Cafés and Pubs

Dirty Dick's, 202 Bishopsgate. Dirty Dick was a dandy called Nathaniel Bentley. His fiancée died on the eve of their wedding in 1787, and he never washed again. When he died in 1809, the house was in ruins. Rebuilt in 1870, it's now a jolly cellar bar; lunch is well-cooked bar food from £5–8.

Reynier Wine Library, 43 Trinity Square. Wine cellar deep in the city where customers choose a bottle of wine from the comprehensive 'library', and down it with cheese and pâté from the simple but tasty £10 buffet. Lunch only, from £13 upwards. *Open 10–6 Mon–Fri.*

Imperial City, basement of the Royal Exchange. A fine Chinese restaurant beneath vaulted brick ceilings. £16–35.

Obertelli's, 38 and 60 Lime St Passage. Sandwiches and café-style food. £3–6.

Poons in the City, 2 Minster Pavement. Stylish Chinese restaurant; lunch from £5 or £12 for the set meal.

The Place Below, St Mary-le-Bow, Cheapside. Award-winning, very popular, nutritious and vegetarian salads and soups in the basement undercroft of this historic City church. £3–7.

Simpson's of Cornhill, Cornhill. Traditional English food in a traditional eaterie off Cornhill: grills, bubble and squeak, steamed jam roll. £2–3 for starters, £5–7 for main courses.

The Greenery, 5 Cowcross St. Healthy veggie snacks, salads and sandwiches. Restaurant and take-away sections. £2–4.

Fox and Anchor, 115 Charterhouse St. Famous Smithfield pub serving full breakfast (£7) and steak for lunch from £6–10.

Guildhall

Open 10–5 daily except on special occasions, closed Sun Oct–April; free.

The Guildhall is the seat of the City's government, headed by the Lord Mayor and his Sheriffs and Aldermen and composed principally of the 12 Great Livery Companies, or guilds, that nominally represent the City's trading interests. Nowadays the governing body, known as the Corporation of London, is little more than a borough council for the City, but back in the Middle Ages it wielded near-absolute power over the whole of London. Even kings could not touch it, since the guilds generated much of the nation's wealth and made sure everyone knew it. Henry III tried to impose direct rule on London in the 13th century but eventually gave up, describing the City fathers as 'nauseously rich'.

First built in the 15th century, architecturally the Guildhall has also retained much from the medieval era, despite the calamities of the Great Fire and the Blitz. The building nevertheless bears the marks of countless renovations. The pinnacled façade looking on to Guildhall Yard is a bizarre 18th-century concoction of classical, Gothic and even Indian styles.

You'll need to make an advance booking for a group to see the **crypt**, the most extensive of its kind left in London.

Royal Exchange

The eight huge Corinthian pillars give this building a sense of importance to which it can no longer lay claim. The Royal Exchange was once the trading centre of the City *par excellence*, home to all of London's stock and commodity exchanges, but it lost this crucial role in 1939 when it was bought by the Guardian Royal Exchange insurance company. It now houses a number of company offices. This is the third Royal Exchange building to occupy the site. The present building, designed by Sir William Tite, dates from 1844, a rare example of neoclassical architecture from the Victorian era. Tite's Exchange comes complete with an equestrian **statue of the Duke of Wellington**, made in suitably triumphalist fashion from the melted-down metal of French guns. There is also a memorial to the war dead of London.

Bank of England Museum

Open Mon–Fri 10–5; free; follow the building round into Bartholomew Lane.

The playwright Richard Sheridan described the Bank of England as 'an elderly lady in the City of great credit and long standing'. Its record as prudent guardian of the nation's finances is well known; it rescued London from bankruptcy at the end of the 17th century, resisted the temptations of the South Sea Bubble and kept the country's economy buoyant throughout the trauma of the Revolutionary wars against France. As the bank of last resort it played a crucial role in the development of Britain's capitalist system during the 18th and 19th centuries.

But the Bank has had a tough time of it in recent years, particularly since the abandonment of worldwide currency controls in the 1970s. The rise of virtually unfettered currency speculation has severely limited its control over the value of sterling. At the same time, the changing nature of international capital has made it increasingly hard for the Bank to monitor the activities of the commercial houses. In compensation, it has won independence from the Treasury and is now free to set interest rates as it sees fit. But even this role is under threat from the single European currency and the establishment of a pan-European central bank in Frankfurt.

Architecturally, the Bank has a distinctly mixed record. At the end of the 18th century Sir John Soane, that most quirky and original of English architects, came up with a magnificently intricate neoclassical design, a veritable treasure trove of inter-connecting rooms each with its own peculiarities of light and decoration. In 1925 the Bank governors decided they needed more space, and instead of considering an extension or a new building they simply demolished Soane's work and replaced it with an unimaginative multistorey patchwork by Sir Herbert Baker. All that remains of Soane's original work is the secure curtain wall on the outer rim of the building and, thanks to a postwar reconstruction, the first room in the museum, the **Bank Stock Office**. Beneath Soane's vaulted roof, illuminated naturally through a series of skylights, the museum's displays recount the architectural fortunes of the Bank and show off some of the original mahogany counter-tops and oak ledger-rests. You are then led through a series of rooms, culminating in Herbert Baker's Rotunda, that give an account of the Bank's history.

The Old Bailey

The soaring gilt statue of Justice rising from the **roof** of the Old Bailey (*accessible via several flights of stairs only, open Mon–Fri, 10–1 and 2–when court rises, around 5, no cameras, large bags, drink, food, pagers, radios, mobile phones, etc., no children under 14, no cloakroom for bags; free*) has become such a potent symbol of temperance in the English legal system that it has eradicated virtually all memory of the barbarity once associated with this site. Until 1902 this place was Newgate Prison, one of the most gruesome of all jails, which Henry Fielding once described as a prototype for hell. Generations of prisoners were left here, quite literally, to rot; to this day judges wear posies of sweet-smelling flowers on special occasions as a grim reminder of the stench that used to emanate from the cold, filthy cells.

The mood now could not be more different. The nickname Old Bailey, referring to the alley running off Newgate Street, conveniently avoids all reference to the old prison. Ask about the place's history and you will be given a list, not of the horrors of incarceration, but of the famous names whose trials have taken place here: Oscar Wilde; the Edwardian wife-murderer Dr Crippen; and William Joyce, known as Lord Haw-Haw, who broadcast enemy propaganda from Nazi Germany during the Second World War.

You are welcome to attend a **court hearing** in one of the public galleries, although the tightly arranged wooden benches are not exactly designed for comfort. The rituals are similar to those of the civil courts, although the mood is inevitably more sombre.

St Mary-le-Bow

Wren almost certainly left the bulk of his church renovations to subordinates; it is hard to imagine that he had time to redesign all 52 himself. This church, however, bears all the signs of his own imprint. It is famous for two reasons. First for its massive, distinctive steeple, which soars 217ft into the sky, and secondly for its **Bow Bells** which have formed part of the mythology of London for centuries. It was their resounding peal that persuaded the fairy-tale Dick Whittington to turn again and return to London in search of fame and fortune. Ever since, the tradition has been that anyone born within earshot of the bells can call himself a true Londoner. There is a third, less well known, reason why you should visit St Mary-le-Bow: its magnificently preserved Norman **crypt**. Along with the Guildhall's, it is one of the few left in London.

Lloyd's Building

The City's most innovative and challenging building is Richard Rogers' design for **Lloyd's of London**, the world's biggest insurance market. On Leadenhall St itself, to the right, you can see a fine façade from the 1925 incarnation of Lloyd's. The entrance to the Richard Rogers building is on Lime St, the continuation of St Mary Axe, although since the IRA bombs of 1992 and 1993 the building has been closed to the public (*group visits can be organized via the Communications Department on ☏ (020) 7327 1000*).

Monument

Viewing platform, accessible by spiral staircase, open 10–5.40; adm; ☏ (020) 7626 2717.

The Monument commemorates the Great Fire of London. On its completion in 1677 it was the tallest free-standing column in the world; now it is so obscured by office buildings it is easy to miss. The view from the top is obscured by office buildings but still enjoyable.

St Etheldreda's

Ely Place.

Etheldreda was a 7th-century Anglo-Saxon princess who had the distressing habit of marrying and then refusing to sleep with her husbands. When husband number two, Prince Egfrith of Northumbria, finally lost patience with her and made unseemly advances, she withdrew into holy orders and founded a double monastery at Ely in Cambridgeshire. Seven years later, in 679, she was stricken with a tumour on her neck and died. None mourned Etheldreda more than her sister, the unfortunately named Sexburga, who campaigned ardently to have her sanctity recognized. In 695, Sexburga had Etheldreda's coffin opened and found that the tumour had quite vanished. Her skin was now quite unblemished. A miracle!

Etheldreda became Ely's special saint and was the obvious choice of patron for this double-storeyed church, built in the 13th century as part of the Bishop of Ely's palace. The Gothic **upper church** is a warm, lofty room with a fine wooden-beamed ceiling and huge stained-glass windows at each end. The east window, behind the altar, is particularly striking with its depiction of the Holy Trinity surrounded by the apostles and Anglo-Saxon and Celtic saints including Etheldreda herself. The west window is much starker, portraying the martyrdom of three Carthusian priors at Tyburn in 1535 with Christ hovering over them. Both windows date from after the Second World War; their predecessors were shattered by German bombs. Downstairs, the lower church or **crypt** is much simpler, no more than a room with a plain altar and little decoration.

Smithfield Market

Smithfield has come a long way since the 14th century, when cattle was slaughtered in front of the customers and witches boiled alive for the entertainment of the populace. This is still where Londoners come to buy their meat, but nowadays it is a civil, sanitized sort of place. The carcasses arrive ready-slaughtered and are stored in giant fridges so you'll barely see a speck of dirt or blood. The covered market halls have been refurbished and are surrounded by restaurants and pubs.

Leadenhall Market

Leadenhall Market is a pleasant surprise: a whiff of real life among the office blocks. It has considerable charm, plenty of bustle, often live music and excellent food, particularly meat, fish and cheese. The prices match the clientèle, many of them businessmen doing some inexpert and usually extravagant housekeeping on behalf of their wives stranded in suburbia; hence the popularity of game and exotic fish.

Barbican Centre

The Brave New World architecture of the Barbican comes straight out of the 1950s, all high-rise concrete and labyrinthine walkways. The City's only residential area worthy of the name, rebuilt after wartime bombing, would not be out of place in a 1960s television escape drama, though there are some advantages to living here: the leafy balconies, the forecourts and fountains.

The main reason for coming, apart from the dubious pleasure of gaping and shuddering, is a trip to the **Arts Centre**, home to the Royal Shakespeare Company, an art gallery (*open 10–6.45 except Tues to 5.45, Wed to 7.45, Sun 12–6.45; adm*), three cinemas, a concert hall and a semi-tropical conservatory (*on Level 3, irregular opening on Sun only, call © (020) 7638 4141 for more details*). On the way, you pass **St Giles Cripplegate** (*open Mon–Fri 9.30–5.30*), where John Milton was buried in 1674. The church itself, mostly built in the 16th century, escaped the 1666 fire but was destroyed by wartime bombs and faithfully rebuilt in the 1950s. A stretch of the Roman city wall can be seen just behind it.

Clerkenwell

By turns a centre for monks, clockmakers, gin manufacturers and Italian labourers, Clerkenwell has the feel of a cosy village with its squares, winding streets and pretty churches. Its proximity to the City made it an ideal headquarters for the knights of the Order of St John, who stayed here until the dissolution of the monasteries in the 1530s. Then in the early 17th century the digging of the New River put Clerkenwell on the main freshwater route into London and so attracted brewers and distillers. In the 19th century much of Clerkenwell was slumland, and the Victorians built forbidding prisons there to cope with the overflow from the city jails. After decades of neglect, it is now undergoing something of a revival, its grimy backstreets filling with offices, converted lofts and cheap, attractive cafés.

The sites of Clerkenwell are all within easy reach from the Green, which was often used in the 19th century as a starting point for protest marches. The **Marx Memorial Library** at Nos.37–8 (*open Mon 1–6, Tues–Thurs 1–8, Sat 10–1, closed Fri; non-members are welcome to look around for free but cannot use the library or its lending facility unless they pay a modest membership fee*) has the best private collection of radical literature in the city; Lenin wrote pamphlets here in 1902–3. Clerkenwell Close (off to the left) leads to the attractive yellow brick **St James's Church**, once part of a Benedictine nunnery but rebuilt many times. The steeple, the latest addition, dates from 1849. Further up the Close (follow the signposts) is the alarmingly Gothic **Middlesex House of Detention** (*open 10–6; adm*), the site of one of the area's notorious Victorian prisons, itself a conversion of an earlier prison.

Also see: **St Paul's Cathedral**, p.40; the **Museum of London**, p.135.
Onwards to: **Tower of London**, p.44; the **South Bank and Southwark**, p.80.

⊖ *Leicester Square, Covent Garden, Charing Cross, Tottenham Court Road*

Covent Garden, home to the Royal Opera House and the converted fruit and vegetable market, is **teeming** with restaurants, natty boutiques and street performers. Sundays are rather quiet as the theatres are dark, but the market and shops are open. The Theatre Museum is shut on Mondays.

There are those who find modern Covent Garden too **ritzy** and spoiled with its boutiques, upmarket jewellery stalls and **prettified** pubs; too much of an easy crowd-pleaser with its mime artists and

Cafés and Pubs

Belgo, 50 Earlham Street. Frites, mussels and Belgian beer, high-tech interior décor, and fashionable metropolitan crowd; lunch from £5–20.

Neal's Yard Dining Rooms, 14 Neal's Yard. Cheap, tasty and filling home-made vegetarian 'worldfood', from Mexican to Indian and African street food. £6–8 for a full meal.

Café in the Crypt, church of St Martin-in-the-Fields. Self service, hot and cold food in this atmospheric vaulted brick crypt. Main dishes around £5–7.

Food for Thought, Neal Street. One of London's first vegetarian cafés and still maintaining high standards. £5–£7.50.

Calabash, 38 King St. Come here for unusual and excellent dishes from all over Africa (grillled plantain, groundnut stew, etc.). Downstairs in the Africa Centre. Main dish £7–9.

Joe Allen, 13 Exeter Street. Great burgers (not on the menu; you have to know to ask!) and American-style food and monster puddings for grown-ups. Theatrically 'luvvie' in the evenings. Good Sunday brunch. £20–25.

handclapping bands belting out yet another rendition of 'I'm a Believer' or 'The Boxer'; too much—heaven forbid—of a *tourist attraction*. Looking into the past, however, one should perhaps be relieved it is even half as pleasant as it is. When the wholesale fruit and vegetable market moved out to the south London suburbs in the 1970s, the London authorities initially wanted to build office blocks and a major roadway through here. Wouldn't that have been fun? It was the local traders and residents who saved Covent Garden with protests and petitions; it is also the locals who, by and large, have the run of the place today. Dig a little, and behind the obvious tourist draws are plenty of quieter, more discreet spots. If Covent Garden seems a little derivative, it is because it deliberately and self-consciously echoes its own past—a dash of Inigo Jones's original piazza with its street life and sideshows, several measures of Charles Fowler's covered market, plus plenty of the eating, drinking and general revelry that have always characterized this neighbourhood.

Covent Garden Market

With the loss of the original fruit and vegetable market, Covent Garden has undoubtedly lost its rough edges. The main hall, once littered with crates and stray vegetables, is now spick and span, while the Flower Market houses museums devoted to transport and the theatre. Unlike the disastrous redevelopment of Les Halles in Paris, however, the place has not lost its soul. You can still buy roast chestnuts or a greasy baked potato from a street vendor as Dickens did, or watch clowns and jugglers performing in front of St Paul's where Punch and Judy shows first caught the public imagination in the 17th century.

In the lower level of the market is the wonderful **Cabaret Mechanical Theatre** (*open school holidays Mon–Sat 10–7, Sun 11–7; termtime Mon–Fri 10–6.30, Sat 10–7 and Sun 11–6.30; adm cheap, children under five free, award-winning website www.cabaret.co.uk*). This small and eccentric compendium of automata is guaranteed to amuse practically anyone from anywhere, instantly. On one side there's a quirky but jolly amusement arcade, with handmade machines costing 10–20p a go; on the other a fascinating exhibition of over 64 push-button automata. Tickets to the exhibition are stamped by a wooden mechanical man; once you're inside, everything is push-button-operated and free.

Neal Street

This pedestrian alley is a pleasant throwback to the hippy era, all beads, home-made earrings and wholefood. While Carnaby Street, the in-place in the 1960s, has faltered and died, Neal Street, a development from the late 1970s, has survived largely thanks to its jolly shops and cheap vegetarian cafés. Turn left down Shorts Gardens and you come to distinctly New Age **Neal's Yard**, a tranquil triangular oasis planted with trees, and an excellent place to sit, away from the traffic fumes and confusion. There are plentiful cheap vegetarian eats here, a world-food café, a beach café, an East-West herb shop, a groovy hairdresser's, a walk-in backrub parlour, an excellent bakery, a natural cosmetics shop, and the famous Neal's Yard Therapy Rooms, offering the gamut of 'alternative' therapies, from acupuncture to lymphatic drainage, from past-life counselling to 'rolfing'. As a last resort, there's a host of New Age shops stuffed with rainbow crystals, candles, incense, holograms and books on mystical healing. On your way in, don't miss the Heath Robinson clock above the Neal's Yard Wholefood Warehouse.

On the other side of Shorts Gardens is **Thomas Neal's Arcade**, filled with designer shops. With its wrought iron lamps and glass roof, this is another derivative piece of modern London architecture, this time a throwback to the arcaded emporia of the 19th century.

Royal Opera House

Two of the most famous London theatres are a mere stone's throw away: the **Theatre Royal Drury Lane**, which is not in Drury Lane but on the corner of Russell St and Catherine St (you can see it as you come out of the Theatre Museum to your right); and the **Royal Opera House**, better known simply as Covent Garden, which is off to the left down Bow St. Both buildings have been scourged by fire in their lives, and the Royal Opera House was razed to the ground in 1856, except for its portico.

When the building work was underway the drama focussed around the scaffolding, flying sparks, lunging cranes, exposed steel and concrete frames as intensive construction works continued on a massive redevelopment of the opera house and an imaginative extension of the site surrounding it. These works were long overdue: the 1858 building has had no real main-tenance since the 1960s, and the cramped and stifling back-stage facilities used by two separate companies (The Royal Ballet as well as The Royal Opera) and a leaking roof were in dire need of repair and technical updating. The redevelopment—by architects Jeremy Dixon and Edward Jones—integrates the Opera House with Covent Garden market for the first time, replacing the Georgian houses on the north side of Russell Street with elegant glass and wrought-iron shopping arcades (also containing cafés, restaurants and a box office) and a loggia walkway above, all based on Inigo Jones's original piazza. It opened in late 1999.

Bow Street Magistrates' Court

Opposite the entrance to the Opera House is the old **Bow Street Magistrates' Court** where the Fieldings, Henry and John, held court in the 18th century. Henry, who was a trained barrister as well as the author of *Tom Jones*, used his tenure here to set up the Bow Street Runners, an informal plainclothes police force that worked to crack down on underworld gangs and challenge the infamous official marshals, or 'thief-takers', who were usually in cahoots with the thieves themselves. The Runners proved remarkably effective and soon became famous throughout the land, particularly for their role in thwarting the Cato Street conspiracy in 1820. Until Robert Peel's uniformed 'bobbies' appeared in the 1830s, they were the closest thing to a police force that London had.

St Paul's Church

Inigo Place; church and gardens open Tues–Fri 9.30–4.30, services Sun 11am,
© (020) 7836 5221.

Don't be surprised if you feel you are sneaking up to this church from behind. That is exactly what you are doing. Properly speaking, St Paul's is part of the original Covent Garden piazza (*see* below) which Inigo Jones built in mock-Italian style in the 1630s. Jones made one crucial oversight, however. He and his low-church patron, the Earl of Bedford, thought they could get away with putting the altar of their church at the western end, so breaking with convention which insists it should be in the east. The Bishop of London, William Laud, ordered Jones to put the altar where it traditionally belongs, in this case flush against the planned main entrance. The interior is of disarming simplicity: a double square, 100ft by 50ft. St Paul's is one of the few pre-Great Fire buildings still left in London, and the only significant part of Inigo Jones's piazza still standing. St Paul's quickly won the affections of the theatre folk of Covent Garden, who preached here as well as attending services. They nicknamed it the Actors' Church, and several luminaries of the stage are buried here, including Ellen Terry, the *grande dame* of the late-Victorian theatre, whose ashes are marked by a plaque in the south wall.

St Martin-in-the-Fields

Open 8.30–6; free lunchtime concerts at 1.05 on Mon, Tues, Fri, evening concerts
at 7.30 on Thurs, Fri and Sat; © (020) 7930 1862.

The church of St Martin-in-the-Fields is the oldest building on Trafalgar Square, and the only one truly to benefit from the exposure the square affords; its curious combination of Greek temple façade and Baroque steeple catches the eye, even if the mix is a little awkward. Its churchyard, now a daytime junk market (*open daily 10–5.30*), contains the graves of Charles II's mistress Nell Gwynne and the 18th-century painters Reynolds and Hogarth. The church has become popular for its concerts and resident orchestra, the Academy of St Martin-in-the-Fields.

St Martin's Lane

Already you have stepped into London's theatreland, as the black strip at the bottom of the street signs says. The theatres along St Martin's Lane—the Albery and Duke of York's, as well as the Coliseum—all date from the turn of the century and so were among the last great playhouses to be built in London. But as early as the 18th century the street was attracting such artistic residents as Joshua Reynolds, first president of the Royal Academy, and Thomas Chippendale, the furniture maker.

One of the main sites in St Martin's Lane is the distinctive globe of the **Coliseum** theatre (tickets and information, © (020) 7632 8300), home to the excellent English National Opera. Built in 1904, this was the first theatre in England with a revolving stage. Now the whole place is under threat, with the government planning to move the ENO into Covent Garden along with the Royal Opera and Ballet. So catch it while you can.

Also see: **National Gallery**, p.38; **National Portrait Gallery**, p.132; **Trafalgar Square**, p.45; **London Transport Museum**, p.137; **Theatre Museum**, p.140.

Onwards to: **The City of London**, p.55; **Soho and Chinatown**, p.73; **Covent Garden shopping**, p.128.

☻ *Bond Street, Green Park, Piccadilly Circus*

The May Fair was once exactly that: an annual festival of eating, drinking, entertainments and (usually) debauchery that took place in the first two weeks of May. The custom began in 1686 when the area was in its infancy; by the middle of the 18th century, the neighbourhood had gone so far upmarket that the residents described the fair as 'that most pestilent nursery of impiety and vice' and made sure it was shut down for good. Mayfair has been pretty **staid** ever since, the preserve of London's *beau monde* who want nothing more than to be left alone. You will nevertheless notice, particularly around Curzon Street, some fine 18th-century houses and a few oddities. If you have ever played the London version of *Monopoly*, you will know that Oxford Street, Bond Street, Regent Street, Park Lane and Mayfair itself are the most expensive and desirable properties on the board. But Mayfair has not lived up to its early promise. It is cosmopolitan and **expensive**, but not really fashionable; **elegant** and well maintained, but not sophisticated; central and self-important, but at the same time strangely quiet. In short, the place does not buzz.

So why visit at all? The main reason is a certain quirky charm which most visitors to the big shops of Oxford Street and Regent Street fail entirely to find. The eccentrically built jewellery shops on Old Bond Street, the bustle of Shepherd Market: these are all little-known curiosities within a stone's throw of the hordes that mill through London's main thoroughfares every day. Here in the heart of London you can enjoy a gentle stroll among Georgian mansions and fine shops, while having the streets virtually to yourself.

Bond Street

Two kinds of shopkeeper dominate Bond Street: jewellers and art dealers, whose gaudy if not always particularly attractive shop fronts make for a diverting stroll. **Old Bond Street**, the lower part of the thoroughfare, concentrates mainly on jewellery and includes all the well-known international names including Tiffany's at No.25 (note the distinctive gold-trimmed clock hanging above the entrance). Evidently these establishments have kept going through the recession thanks to the patronage of the Russian mafia, which has made London its main foreign outpost. Old Bond Street brought a rare piece of good luck to the inveterate 18th-century rake and gambler, Charles James Fox, who once made a bet with the Prince of Wales on the number of cats appearing on each side of the street. No fewer than 13 cats appeared on Fox's side, and none on the Prince of Wales's. Maybe, though, Fox should have taken his inauspicious number of cats as an omen and steered clear of the gambling dens of St James's, since he later went bankrupt and had to be bailed out by his father.

The turning on the left just after Stafford Street is the **Royal Arcade**. Built in 1879, it is one of the kitschier examples of the genre with caryatids painted orange and white above the entrance. Walk through the arcade to emerge on Albermarle Street. Across the road on the right is one of the entrances to **Brown's Hotel**. This old-fashioned hotel remains one of the quintessential addresses of aristocratic London. Founded by a former manservant in 1837, it retains the kind of service one imagines to have been quite commonplace in the houses of gentlemen of quality. Franklin and Eleanor Roosevelt spent their honeymoon here, while in room 36 the Dutch government declared war on Japan during the Second World War. Nowadays, the time to come is for tea when, for a slightly cheaper rate than the Ritz, you can

Cafés and Pubs

Boudin Blanc, 5 Trebeck St. Cheap French bistro food. Popular, atmospheric and good value with a two-course set lunch from £6.95.

Al Hamra, 31–3 Shepherd Market. Upmarket Lebanese fare. Delicious but rather expensive. £20–30.

Sofra, 18 Shepherd Street. Attractive, more relaxed Middle Eastern alternative to the above, this time Turkish. £16–21.

Da Corradi, 47 Curzon St. All-day breakfast in this high-quality Italian greasy spoon. £10.

Ye Grapes, Shepherd Market (no number). Attractive and popular pub tucked into the corner of the main square of the market.

Ristorante Italiano, 54 Curzon St. Quaintly old-world, much-loved restaurant from the 1950s, serving London literary types with good traditional Italian pasta and main courses; lunch from £15 closed lunchtimes on Sat and all Sun.

Mirabelle, 56 Curzon St, ✆ (020) 7499 4636. Incredible-value set lunch from £14.50 in this glamorous Marco Pierre White restaurant, popular with the smart set. Reserve.

fill up on scones and cucumber sandwiches and enjoy the attentions of demure waiters in tails. Dress smart or they won't let you in (*see* p.158).

New Bond Street, the top half towards Oxford Street, is the province of high-class designer clothes and accessory shops, plus also the showrooms of art dealers like Bernard Jacobson and Le Fevre (or, on Cork Street, Waddington and Victoria Miro). Sotheby's, the famous auctioneers, are at Nos.34–5 New Bond Street; above the front door is the oldest outdoor sculpture in London, an ancient Egyptian figure made of igneous rock dating back to 1600 BC.

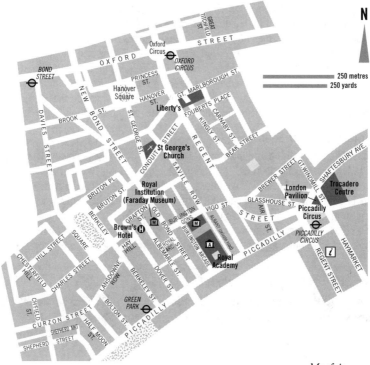

Royal Institution/Faraday Museum

21 Albermarle St. Open Mon–Fri, 10–6; adm.

This large, grand building, with its pompous façade based on the Temple of Antoninus in Rome, is to science what the Royal Academy is to the arts: the most prestigious association of professionals in the land. Founded in 1799, the Institution built up a formidable reputation thanks to early members such as Humphrey Davy (inventor of the Davy Lamp for detecting methane down mines) and his pupil, Michael Faraday. The small museum (the only part of the building regularly open to the public) is in fact Faraday's old laboratory where he carried out his pioneering experiments with electricity in the 1830s; his work is explained with the help of his original instruments and lab notes. The Royal Institution also organizes excellent lectures, including series specially designed for children.

Shepherd Market

There may not be any more May Fairs in Mayfair, but this enchanting warren of cafés, restaurants and small shops nevertheless comes as a nice surprise after all the stuffiness of its surroundings. Back in the 17th century, this was where the fire-eaters, jugglers, dwarves and boxers would entertain the crowds in early spring. The entrepreneur Edward Shepherd then turned the area into a market in 1735 (notice the attractive low Georgian buildings), and it has been a focus for rather more low-key entertainment ever since.

Berkeley Square

This is a key address for debutantes and aristocratic young bucks, who come for the annual Berkeley Square Charity Ball and vie to join the square's exclusive clubs and gaming houses. The chief interest to the visitor is the elegant row of Georgian houses on the west side. The highlight is No.44, described by Nikolaus Pevsner as 'the finest terraced house in London', which was built in 1742–4 for one of the royal household's maids of honour. Unfortunately the house is now a private casino called the Clermont Club, and its stunning interior, including a magnificent double staircase designed by William Kent, is out of bounds to the general public. They say the house is haunted by the ghost of its first major-domo, who can be heard coming down the stairs with his slight limp; one can only hope that one day he will spook the gamblers off the premises and allow everyone else a closer look.

St George's Hanover Square

A neoclassical church with a striking Corinthian portico, St George's was built in 1721–4 as part of the Fifty New Churches Act. It is the parish church of Mayfair and has proved enduringly popular as a venue for society weddings, including the match between Shelley and Mary Godwin. The interior, restored at the end of the Victorian era, has some fine 16th-century Flemish glass in the east window and a painting of the Last Supper above the altar attributed to William Kent. Notice also the cast-iron dogs in the porch; these once belonged to a shop in Conduit St and were brought here in 1940 after their original premises were bombed.

Also see: **Bond Street shopping**, p.122.

Onwards to: **Royal Academy**, p.72; **Piccadilly**, p.71; **Green Park**, p.111; **St James's and Royal London**, p.76; **Oxford Street shopping**, p.120.

⊖ *Leicester Square, Piccadilly Circus, Green Park*

The Piccadilly area has long been considered rather **vulgar**. The strange name derives from the fortunes of Robert Baker, a 17th-century tailor who made a fortune and built himself a mansion here on the proceeds in 1612. At the time, the land was totally undeveloped apart from a windmill (which inspired the name of the street leading off to the north of Piccadilly Circus, Great Windmill Street). Baker's peers thought his ostentation ridiculous and nicknamed his house Pickadilly Hall to remind him of his humble origins, a *pickadil* being a contemporary term for a shirt cuff or hem.

The development of St James's and Mayfair in the 18th century made Piccadilly one of the busiest thoroughfares in London. The area grew more **crowded** still in the late 19th century with the construction of Shaftesbury Avenue and a flurry of new theatres. Bus routes multiplied and an Underground station was constructed, followed by vast advertising hoardings on the side of the London Pavilion music hall. Virginia Woolf and others thought it was all marvellous; she described Piccadilly Circus as 'the heart of life...where everything desirable meets'. After the Second World War the ads went international—Coca Cola rather than Bovril—and **electric**, giving a touch of modernity to the 'swinging' city of Europe.

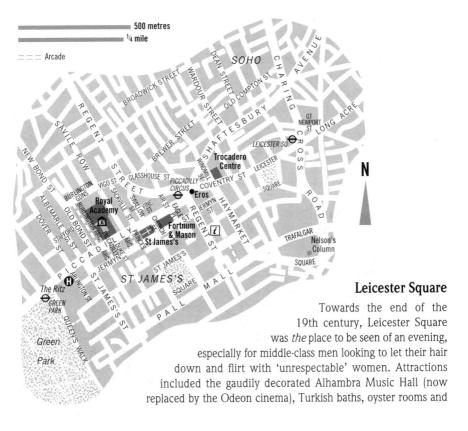

Leicester Square

Towards the end of the 19th century, Leicester Square was *the* place to be seen of an evening, especially for middle-class men looking to let their hair down and flirt with 'unrespectable' women. Attractions included the gaudily decorated Alhambra Music Hall (now replaced by the Odeon cinema), Turkish baths, oyster rooms and

Cafés and Tearooms

Photographers' Gallery Café, 5 Great Newport Street. This peaceful, friendly café in the tiny free gallery is filled with London's arty in-crowd eating bowls of healthy salad and home-made cakes and discussing creative endeavours over a cappuccino.

Café Rimini, Cranbourn Street. A gaggle of touristy cafés lines the south side of the street; this one stands out for excellent espresso and good falafel and sandwiches.

The Criterion, 224 Piccadilly (at Piccadilly Circus). Quality cuisine in a wondrous high decibel neo-Byzantine grotto; worth visiting for the interior alone. £14.95 for a two-course meal is one of London's better restaurant bargains.

Royal Academy Restaurant, Burlington House, Piccadilly. Self-service coffee, lunch and tea in an airy room. In summer there's a small café in the elegant courtyard. Open 10–5.30.

Fortnum & Mason, Jermyn Street and 181 Piccadilly. The luxury food shop has three traditional English restaurants, the posh Patio (£20 for a basic lunch menu; open till 6pm), the even posher Fountain on the ground floor (serving afternoon tea for £12.50; open till 8pm), and the St James's on the fourth (for a smart lunch from £16.95; open till 6pm). Something of a tourist trap and overpriced, but good nonetheless.

Ritz Hotel, 150 Piccadilly. Tea at the Ritz (a steep £24.50 a head) is a London institution, a challengingly priced indulgence that permits you to spend an hour or two immersed in an Edwardian paradise of gilded statues, ornate filigree roof decorations, interior waterfalls and exotic plants in the Palm Court. The food isn't bad either: cucumber or salmon sandwiches, plus scones with clotted cream and jam (a cheaper and less filling alternative to tea would be to have a cocktail at the bar).

---

dance halls. But all the fine buildings of the past, including the 17th-century Leicester House which gave its name to the square, are long gone. The Blitz was largely responsible for destroying the buildings and spirit of the place.

Leicester Square has nowadays recovered some of its happy-go-lucky spirit; the square has been pedestrianized and the central garden tidied up. Come here at more or less any time of the day or night and you will find a rough and ready crowd of cinema-goers, student tourists, buskers, street performers, portrait painters and pickpockets. For the dedicated sightseer, however, the only historical curiosity is a bronze statue of Charlie Chaplin with his bowler hat and walking stick.

Piccadilly Circus

The car horns and neon advertising hoardings of **Piccadilly Circus** have become synonymous with London, along with red double-decker buses and the Queen. Quite why is something of a mystery. For some inexplicable reason, hordes of European teenagers are prepared to spend whole afternoons trudging across Piccadilly Circus's crowded traffic islands, from Burger King to the Trocadero Centre to Tower Records, in search of the ultimate cheap thrill. The best thing about Piccadilly Circus is the view down Lower Regent Street towards St James's Park.

Two curiosities are nevertheless worth a moment's attention. The first is the **Criterion Restaurant** on the south side of the Circus, which has a long dining room sumptuously adorned in neo-Byzantine style, with a gilt ceiling, marble pillars and ornamental tiles. The second attraction of Piccadilly Circus is the **Eros statue** at its centre, a winged aluminium figure fashioned by Sir Alfred Gilbert in memory of the Victorian philanthropist Lord Shaftesbury and unveiled in 1893. The figure is not in fact supposed to be Eros, the cherubic god of love, at all; Gilbert intended it to be an Angel of Christian Charity, in memory of Lord Shaftesbury's work with destitute children.

Walking towards Leicester Square, on the north side of Coventry Street is the **London Pavilion**. This was once a music hall but has now been tarted up and revamped as the **Rock Circus** (*open 10–8, except Tues 11–8 and Fri and Sat 10–9; adm expensive*). This can be quite fun in a tacky sort of way—a sanitized history of rock'n'roll told with the help of wax figures from Madame Tussaud's and a vast array of lighting tricks, and a revolving theatre featuring an automaton of the Beatles. Right opposite the London Pavilion, with entrances on Great Windmill St, Coventry St and, round the back, on Shaftesbury Avenue, is the **Trocadero Centre**, a mélange of overpriced theme-u-rants, screaming kids and intimidating teenagers. Amidst the horrors, there are some thrilling and expensive virtual reality simulators, a dodgem ride (also thrilling and expensive) and a 3-D IMAX cinema.

Regent Street

Regent Street was once the finest street in London, although you might not think so to look at it now. In fact, all it boasts are a few fine shops (particularly men's clothes stores) and some rather stuffy, impersonal buildings livened up just once a year by the overhead display of electric Christmas decorations. The street could scarcely be further from the original plan, drawn up in 1813 by John Nash for the Prince Regent, which intended to bring revolutionary changes to the way London was organized. Nash's idea was to make Regent Street the main north–south artery linking the prince's residence at Carlton House on The Mall to the newly landscaped expanse of Regent's Park; as such it would have been the centrepiece of a carefully planned ensemble of squares, palaces and public thoroughfares.

One address that has not changed too much is the **Café Royal** at No.68 on the right-hand side of The Quadrant. A liveried doorman stands guard over one of the most fashionable addresses of the decadent years leading up to the First World War. Its extravagant mirrors, velvet seats and caryatid sculptures have remained more or less as they were when Oscar Wilde, Aubrey Beardsley and Edward, Prince of Wales, held court here in the naughty 1890s.

Piccadilly

From Piccadilly Circus to Green Park, this wide, straight, busy thoroughfare is the southern edge of Mayfair (*see* p.66) and it shows. Here you can find **Fortnum & Mason**, the ultimate old-fashioned luxury English food shop (*℗ (020) 7734 8040; open till 8 with a good value afternoon tea for £16.50 from 3–5.30*), and the **Ritz Hotel**, where afternoon tea is a London institution. Small high-class shops can be found in the streets to either side: Jermyn Street and Savile Row (*see* p.124), and small, elegant shopping arcades.

St James's Piccadilly

Open daily, with lunch-time recitals and evening concerts; call ahead on ℗ (020) 7381 0441 for details.

St James's (1684) seems curiously at odds with the rest of the neighbourhood, being totally unmarked by either pretension or exclusivity. Nowhere here do you see the trappings of wealth or snobbery; instead there is a flea market in the churchyard (*Wednesday–Saturday, with an antiques market on Tuesday*), a café (*open till 7; later if there's a concert*) in the annexe, a Centre for Healing, and a message of warm welcome on the notice-board in the porch. Nevertheless, from an architectural point of view, St James's is an object lesson in effortless grace and charm. It is the only church that Christopher Wren built from scratch in

London (the others were all renovations or rebuildings on medieval sites), and as such most clearly expresses his vision of the church as a place where the relationship between the priest and his congregation should be demystified. St James's is airy and spacious, with the altar and pulpit in full view and accessible to all. An elegant gilded wooden gallery with rounded corners runs around the western end, supported by Corinthian pillars in plaster adorned with intricate decorations. There are some beautiful carvings by Grinling Gibbons, notably on the limewood reredos behind the altar (fruit and nature motifs) and on the stone font.

Royal Academy

Burlington House, Piccadilly, © (020) 7300 8000. Open 10–6 daily; adm.

In 1714, the third Earl of Burlington took a trip to Italy and, rather like Inigo Jones exactly one century earlier, came back an ardent convert to Palladian architecture. But where Jones failed to start a general trend, Lord Burlington succeeded triumphantly; Palladian buildings were soon sprouting all over London. One of the first was the earl's private residence here in Piccadilly, completed in 1720 to the designs of James Gibbs, Colen Campbell and the earl himself. The gate leads into a grand courtyard graced with a colonnade. The house was based on Palladio's Palazzo Porta in Vicenza, a classic exercise in harmony and simple lines.

Burlington House was lived in for more than a century, until the government bought it in 1854 to house the Royal Academy of Arts. It has been one of London's most important exhibition venues ever since, staging major retrospectives as well as the famed Summer Exhibition, a traditional but fairly underwhelming showcase for over a thousand amateur British artists.

The RA also has a permanent collection with works from each of its prestigious members (Reynolds, Gainsborough, Constable and Turner for starters), as well as a marble relief sculpture by Michelangelo of the *Madonna and Child with the Infant St John*. You won't get much sense of the original Palladian mansion, however, because the building was radically altered by the Victorian architect Sydney Smirke in 1872. The bronze statue in the centre of the courtyard is of Sir Joshua Reynolds, the founder of the Royal Academy, shown with palette and paintbrush. It dates from 1931.

Burlington Arcade

London never really went in for shopping arcades the way that Paris did at the beginning of the 19th century; nowhere in this city will you find the graceful iron and glasswork of the Parisian *passages*, the precursors of the modern department store. Arcades nevertheless enjoyed a brief popularity in the final decade of George IV's life. The most famous is Burlington Arcade (1819), no doubt because of its top-hatted beadles who enforce the arcade's quaint rules: no whistling, no singing and no running. Originally it had a magnificent triple-arched entrance, but in 1931 the shopkeepers of the arcade demanded more girth to take deliveries, and the arches were destroyed. Nowadays it is elegant enough, its high-ceilinged halls decorated in green and white, and is home to up-market shops.

Also see: **Jermyn Street and Savile Row shopping**, p.124; **Green Park**, p.111; **Faraday Museum**, p.68.

Onwards to: **Mayfair**, p.66; **Covent Garden**, p.62.

❖ Leicester Square, Piccadilly Circus, Tottenham Court Road, Oxford Circus

Here, halfway between the clubbish pomp of Westminster and the venal frenzy of the City, is where Londoners come to enjoy themselves. Soho still thrives off its reputation as a seedy but **alluring** hang-out for **exotic** freaks and sozzled eccentrics who made the place famous after the Second World War. The establishment has always been suspicious of this area; the artistic community has never shown such squeamishness—indeed, this is the heart of London theatreland. Nowadays the sleaze is slowly disappearing, supplanted by the **flashy** cars and modish whims of the advertising and media darlings.

It was after the war that Soho really came into its own. In the 1950s it became the centre of the avant-garde in jazz, new writing, experimental theatre and cinema. In many ways Soho prefigured the social upheavals of the 1960s, creating a youth subculture based on rebellion, permissiveness, *joie de vivre*, booze and drugs. Above all, Soho developed its own community of intellectuals and eccentrics, people of all classes mingling, borrowing money off each other and getting pleasantly tippled in pubs or illicit 'near-beer' bars that stayed open outside the stringent licensing hours. Like all golden ages, 1950s Soho and its low life came to a some-what sorry end. The liberalizations of the 1960s and 1970s brought peepshows and strip joints galore that nearly caused the destruction of the neighbourhood. The planning authorities, outraged by prostitutes openly soliciting on every street, threatened to bulldoze the whole district to make way for office blocks. It wasn't until the mid-1980s that new laws regulated the pornography business and Soho regained some of its spirit. The number of peepshows is strictly controlled, and most of the prostitutes now solicit via cards left in telephone booths. So attractive has Soho become that the trendies have inevitably moved in to join the fun. Not a week goes by without a new bar, a new restaurant, a new fad. Today it might be sushi served by robots, or caramelized onions; next week these will be passé and the new obsession will be pine-scrubbed noodle bars, or cafés that look like middle-class living rooms.

Soho Square

This was where Scott built his mansion Monmouth House (long ago destroyed). A contempo-rary statue of Charles II by Caius Gabriel Cibber still stands in the square gardens, looking somewhat worse for wear behind a mock-Tudor toolshed which covers an underground air vent. On the north side of the square is the **French Protestant Church**, originally built for the Huguenots and then reworked by the Victorians in flamboyant neo-Gothic style. To the east is the red-brick tower of **St Patrick's Roman Catholic Church**, which holds weekly services for the local Spanish and Cantonese communities in their own languages.

Frith Street and Dean Street

The Frith Street Gallery at No.60 specializes in works on paper. In Frith Street you will also see **Ronnie Scott's** famous jazz club at No.47 (Scott, a jazz saxophonist, died in 1996, but his dingy basement club still gets high-profile bookings) and a plethora of restaurants including Jimmy's at No.23, a basement Greek café serving cheap moussaka and chips that has changed little since the Rolling Stones ate there in the 1960s.

Many phantoms also haunt Dean Street. No.49 is the **French House**, which became the official headquarters of the Free French forces under Charles de Gaulle during the Second

World War. Now it's a lively pub-cum-wine bar. Two clubs further down the street illustrate the changes in Soho since the 1950s. The Colony, at No.41, was once described as 'a place where the villains look like artists and the artists look like villains'. The Groucho—so called because of Groucho Marx's one-liner that he never wanted to join a club that would have him as a member —opened at No.44 in 1985 and has been a hit with the world of television, music, comedy, publishing and film ever since.

Quo Vadis, the restaurant at No.28, became instantly trendworthy in 1996 after it was bought from its original Italian owners by Marco Pierre White (famous London superchef) and Damien Hirst (Britpack conceptual artist-cum-restaurateur) and completed refurbished. Downstairs are works by Hirst and Marcus Harvey. Upstairs is where Karl Marx lived with his family from 1851–6 in a two-room attic flat in conditions of near abject penury (now a building site as it undergoes extensive refurbishments).

Cafés and Pubs

Mezzo, 100 Wardour Street. Ultra-sophisticated brasserie food in massive restaurant owned and operated by interior designer Terence Conran; with a 2-course £8.50 before 7pm special.

Soupworks, 9 D'Arblay St. Huge variety of soups, from traditional to spicy Thai, hot and cold. £2–5.

Wagamama, 10A Lexington St. Busy and popular Japanese noodle restaurant, where you sit at long communal tables.Be prepared to queue. £5–10.

Mildred's, 58 Greek St. Classy vegetarian fare, including tostadas, stir-fries and delicious desserts. Very popular. Under £10.

Italian Graffiti, 163 Wardour St. Great Italian-style pizza and pastas in a friendly setting. £6–10.

Maison Bertaux, 28 Greek St. Mouthwatering French pastries. Lovely stopping-off point for excellent-value tea, gateaux and pastries.

Pâtisserie Valerie, 44 Old Compton St. More delicious croissants, cakes and savoury vol-au-vents. Very crowded and a bit self-consciously arty.

Bar Italia, 22 Frith St. Open 23 out of 24 hours, a Soho institution for everyone from after-hours clubbers to tourists: arguably the best espresso and cappuccino in town. Some snacks.

The New Diamond, 23 Lisle St. One of the best establishments in Chinatown (though there's not much to pick between them), with an enormous menu and seating on two floors. £7–18.

Old Compton Street and Wardour Street

In many ways Old Compton Street is the archetypal Soho street, as well as the heart of gay London. Here you'll find cafés like the Pâtisserie Valerie at No.44, restaurants, delicatessens, gay clubs and bars, and modest-looking newsagents stocking every conceivable title on the planet. Wardour Street, once known for its furniture and antique stores, is now occupied by film companies who advertise their forthcoming productions in the high glass windows on the left-hand side of the street.

Berwick Street Market and Brewer Street

Berwick Street Market (*open Mon–Sat 9–4, early closing Wed*) always has beautifully fresh produce at incredibly low prices for central London. Ever since Jack Smith introduced the pineapple to London here in 1890, the market has also had a reputation for stocking unusual and exotic fruit and veg. The houses behind the stalls date, like the market itself, back to the 18th century. There are a couple of old pubs (The Blue Posts is the most salubrious), a scattering of noisy independent record stores and several excellent old-fashioned theatrical fabrics shops specializing in unusual silks, satins, velvets, Chinese printed silks and printed cottons, sold by the metre and the place to go if you're looking for something exotic for yourself or your sofa.

At the southern end of Berwick St is a poky passage called **Walker's Court**, dominated by peepshows and the London equivalent of the Moulin Rouge, Raymond's Revue Bar. Turn right into **Brewer Street**, the ultimate Soho mixture of sex-joints and eclectic shops. As you wander down it you will notice discreetly signposted peepshows, an excellent fishmonger's, a well-stocked poster shop and, at No.67, the shop Anything Left-Handed.

Chinatown

London's Chinese population came mostly from Hong Kong in the 1950s and 1960s, victims not so much of the political upheavals in the region as the cruel fluctuations of the Asian rice market. Back then Gerrard Street, like the rest of Soho, was cheap and run down and welcoming to foreigners. It took more than a generation for the new community to be fully accepted, however, and it was not until the 1970s that this street was pedestrianized and kitted out with decorative lamps and telephone boxes styled like pagodas—a spectacular backdrop to the Chinese New Year celebrations which take place here at the end of January or early February. Many of the older generation have only a rudimentary grip of English, and remain suspicious of their adoptive environment. The younger generation has integrated rather better; those born here are mockingly nicknamed BBCs (British-born children).

London's Chinatown is still very small—just Gerrard Street and Lisle Street really—and the trade is overwhelmingly in food and restaurants. There are a few craft shops, and there's always been a discreet illegal business in gambling—underground dens for mah jong, pai-kau and fan tan. The eastern end of Gerrard St and Newport Place are crowded with Chinese supermarkets and craft shops, which are well worth poking around for a bargain.

Onwards to: **Covent Garden**, p.62; **Bloomsbury**, p.52; **Charing Cross Road shopping**, p.123; **Oxford Street shopping**, p.120.

❸ *Green Park, Charing Cross, Victoria*

St James's is the fairyland of London, a **peculiarly British** kind of looking-glass world where everyone eats thickly cut marmalade sandwiches and drinks tea from Fortnum & Mason, where the inhabitants are for the most part kindly middle-aged gentlemen with bespoke tailored suits and ruddy complexions, where shopkeepers are called purveyors and underlings wear livery coats. What's more, this **fairy tale** comes with its very own queen, who lives in a palace surrounded by broad lush parks and guarded by toy soldiers in busby hats and red, blue and black uniforms. Everything is clean and beautiful in fairyland, even the roads, some of which have been coloured pink to add to the general feeling of well being. St James's is the preserve of the **establishment**, not the vulgar money-making classes of the City but an older, rarefied pedigree which whiles away the hours in the drawing rooms of fine houses and private clubs. It is a world that has been endlessly depicted and lampooned on film and on television; incredibly, it still exists.

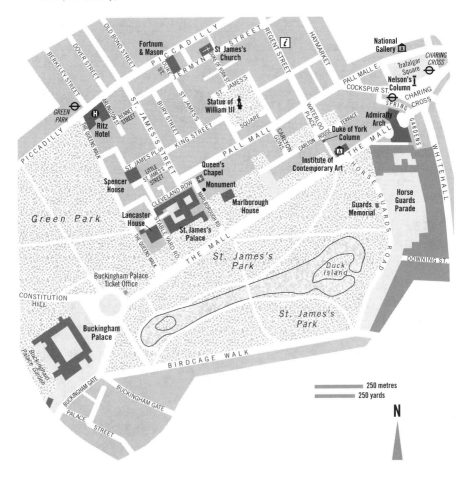

The Mall

A sense of place, and occasion, is immediately invoked by the grand concave triple entrance of **Admiralty Arch**, the gateway to St James's and start of the long straight drive along The Mall up to Buckingham Palace. Passing through the arch, you'll appreciate the full splendour of St James's Park (*see* p.117) ahead to your left; notice, too, the white stone frontings to your right. These are part of **Carlton House Terrace**, the remnants of one of London's more lavish—and ultimately futile—building projects. In the early 18th century this site was home to Henry Boyle, Baron Carlton. The Prince of Wales (later George IV) decided he rather liked the place and hired the architect Henry Holland to spruce up the house to the standards of a royal palace. For 30 years Holland and his associates toiled away, adding Corinthian porticoes here, brown Siena marble columns there. One contemporary critic said the end result stood comparison with Versailles; that did not stop the extravagant George from declaring himself bored with the new palace and having most of it demolished. It was left to John Nash to salvage what he could from the wreckage of Carlton House and construct these elegant terraces in their place. They have housed many a club and eminent society in their time; now the most interesting address is No.12, the **Institute of Contemporary Arts**. Perhaps surprisingly given the setting, the ICA is a mecca for the 'Britpack' school of art, the pre-post-avant-garde and the obscure. There is a modest day-membership fee to get into the main shows and the excellent café; otherwise you are restricted to the foyer and bookshop.

Horse Guards Parade (the Changing of the Guard)

The Horse Guards in question are the queen's very own knights in shining armour, properly known as the Household Division. Altogether, seven regiments are allocated the task of dressing up in chocolate-soldier costumes and parading in front of Buckingham Palace. Housed both here and at Wellington Barracks on the south side of the park are the Household Cavalry (look out for the horses), the Life Guards, the Blues and Royals, the Grenadiers, the Coldstream Guards and the Scots, Irish and Welsh guards. The best time to see them is on the first weekend in June, when they all take part in a grand parade in front of the Queen known as **Trooping the Colour**. Otherwise you can make do with the **Changing of the Guard** (*outside the Horse Guards at 11am daily or outside Buckingham Palace at 11.30am daily from May–Aug, and every other day the rest of the year*).

Cafés and Pubs

ICAfé, The Mall. Decent Italian bistro food inside the trendy arts centre, though you'll have to pay day membership (£1.50) to get in. £5–10. Spicy 'street food' served after 5.30 at £2.50 a dish.

Spreads Café, 15a Pall Mall. Breakfasts, pasta and sandwiches to eat in or out. The least pretentious spot in St James's, next door to a shop selling large yachts. £4–5.

Wiltons, 55 Jermyn St, best to reserve in advance on ℂ (020) 7629 9955. English, strong on fish, in a setting resembling a gentleman's club. £30–40.

The Avenue, 7/9 St James's St. Attempt at a Manhattanesque sophisticates' restaurant serving elegant 'modern' food (crab and prawn galette, calf's liver, rabbit confit with fig chutney, their own fish fingers, etc.). The set lunch is especially good value: from £17.50 for two courses (ℂ (020) 7321 2111 for reservations).

Quaglino's, 16 Bury St. Ferociously trendy Italian food in an ornate ballroom setting. £25 or so for lunch, reservations on ℂ (020) 7930 6767.

Pall Mall and Clubland

The street's curious name derives from an ancient Italian ball game called *palla a maglio*, literally ball and mallet. Charles II liked it so much that he built this pall mall alley close by St James's Palace.

If you enjoy birdwatching (*see* below), maybe you should pull your binoculars back out for some ornithological study of a different kind here in Pall Mall, the high street of London's **clubland**. The rare bird you are after is male, 50-ish and invariably well dressed; he tends to stagger somewhat, especially after lunch, and looks rather like one of those old salt-of-the-earth types that Jack Hawkins or Trevor Howard used to play. The author and former club *maître d'* Anthony O'Connor has defined the London club as a place 'where a well-born buck can get away from worries, women and anything that even faintly smacks of business in a genteel atmosphere of good cigars, mulled claret and obsequious servants'. The end of the empire and the emancipation of domestic servants brought about a sharp decline in clubland: before the Second World War there were 120 clubs in London; now there are less than 40.

The **Athenaeum** on Waterloo Place, designed by Decimus Burton, is one of the best Greek Revival buildings in London, its frieze inspired by the relief sculptures from the Parthenon housed in the British Museum. The club was known in the 19th century as the haunt of the intellectual élite, which explains the gilt statue of Athena, goddess of wisdom, above the entrance and the Greek letters of Athena's name in the mosaic above the porch.

As you walk past the Athenaeum down Pall Mall, look out for the brass plates announcing a host of other clubs, including the Travellers', the Reform, the Royal Automobile, the United Oxford and Cambridge and the Army and Navy Club. The **Reform Club**, at Nos.104–5, is where Jules Verne's fictional hero Phineas Fogg made his wager and set out to travel around the world in 80 days.

St James's Street

Along with Pall Mall, St James's Street is clubland *par excellence*, although in the past it has enjoyed a less than irreproachable reputation because of its gambling dens. **White's**, the oldest London club may well have instituted the national mania for bets and betting in the mid-18th century when it ran books on everything from births and marriages to politics and death. White's was soon eclipsed, however, by **Brooks** down the road. One particularly obsessional gambler, Charles James Fox, ran up debts of £140,000 and was seen cadging money off the waiters at Brooks before his father, Lord Holland, stepped in to bail him out in 1781.

St James's Street has changed quite a bit in the 20th century. The bottom end, at the junction with Pall Mall, is dominated by two turn-of-the-century office buildings by Norman Shaw. There is an astonishing office block that resembles a bronze spaceship, currently unoccupied. More striking still is the **Economist Building** at Nos.25–7, a series of three concrete hexagonal towers designed by Peter and Alison Smithson for the weekly news magazine *The Economist* and completed in 1964. Much praised at the time, the building is certainly one of the more successful of London's experiments in 1960s modernism.

St James's Square

This square was where St James's turned from a mere adjunct to the royal palaces into a fashionable residential district in its own right. Just before the Great Fire of 1666, Charles II had granted a lease to Henry Jermyn, Earl of St Albans, charging him to build 'palaces fit for the dwelling of noblemen and persons of quality'. The result was to set the tone for nearly all of London's squares, creating a haven of privacy and seclusion. The equestrian statue in the middle is of William III; his horse has one hoof atop the molehill which caused the king's fatal riding accident in 1702. Nowadays there are no more private residences in the square's spacious, mainly Georgian houses; they have been replaced by a succession of clubs, eminent institutions and company offices.

St James's Palace

St James's Street. Closed to the public.

For more than 300 years this was the official residence of England's kings and queens; indeed, foreign ambassadors are still formally accredited to the Court of St James even though they are received, like every other official on royal business, at Buckingham Palace.

Although endowed with fine buildings (of which only the octagonal towers of the gatehouse survive), St James's Palace became known as a raucous place of ill manners and debauchery, particularly under Queen Anne and the early Hanoverians who used it to hold drunken banquets. Anne was well known for her unseemly appetite for food and drink, particularly brandy, and for the bodily noises she frequently emitted at table. Not surprisingly, the place soon came to be described as 'crazy, smoky and dirty'. The Prince Regent celebrated his disastrous marriage with Caroline of Brunswick here in 1795, spending his wedding night fully dressed in a drunken slumber in the fireplace of the bridal chamber. Soon afterwards he moved into Carlton House, and the palace's somewhat tarnished glory days were over. A fire destroyed most of the original buildings in 1809; the rebuilt courtyards now house offices for members of the royal household.

Spencer House

27 Queen's Walk, open Sun 10.30–5.30, last adm 4.45, except Jan and Aug; adm £6/£5. Visit by guided tour only; tours begin at regular intervals and last an hour.

This gracious Palladian mansion was born in sorrow: its original backer, Henry Bromley, ran out of money and shot himself moments after reading his will over with his lawyer. The site was then taken over by the Spencer family (ancestors of Princess Diana) who hired a bevy of architects including John Vardy and Robert Adam to produce one of the finest private houses in London. Completed in 1766, Spencer House boasts magnificent parquet floors, ornate plaster ceilings and a welter of gilded statues and furniture. The highlight is Vardy's Palm Room, in which the pillars are decorated as gilt palm trees with fronds stretching over the tops of the arched window bays. James Stuart's Painted Room features classical murals, graceful chandeliers and a fine, highly polished wooden floor. The whole house was renovated by its current owners, RIT Capital Partners, in 1990 and looks magnificent. Unfortunately only eight rooms are open to the public; the rest are kept for the pleasure of the financial executives who occupy it during the week.

Also see: **Buckingham Palace**, p.32; **St James's Park**, p.117; **Jermyn Street and Savile Row shopping**, p.124; **Green Park**, p.111.

Onwards to: **Piccadilly**, p.71; **Mayfair**, p.66.

↔ *Waterloo, Embankment, London Bridge*

Southwark, the London borough stretching from Waterloo Bridge to the other side of Tower Bridge, has seen it all: butchers, leathermakers, whores, corrupt bishops, coach drivers, actors, bear-baiters, railwaymen and dockers. Shakespeare's Globe Theatre was here, and so was the notorious Marshalsea debtors' prison. It is one of the most **atmospheric** and **historic** parts of London, used over and over by the city's novelists, particularly Dickens.

In the 17th century, Bankside and the whole borough of Southwark were bywords for a raucous good time. The **boisterous** character of the area is easily explained by history. When the Romans first built London Bridge in AD 43, Southwark developed naturally as a small colony and market town opposite the City of London. As the City grew in wealth and importance, Southwark attracted some of the dirtier, more unpleasant trades that might have offended the rich merchants across the river. In 1556 Southwark came directly under the City's jurisdiction and cleaned up its act somewhat. The theatres made the available entertainment a little more thought-provoking, if only for a brief period. And then local industries sprang up: Bankside was bustling with wharves, breweries, foundries and glassworks.

Southwark remained a promising, if still raucous area until the mid-18th century, when the construction of Westminster Bridge and the first Blackfriars Bridge diminished its importance as the most accessible of London's southern satellites. The arrival of the railways in the Victorian era made it even more isolated, reducing it to no more than a row of warehouses stuck between the noisy train tracks. Further decline came after the Second World War, as the

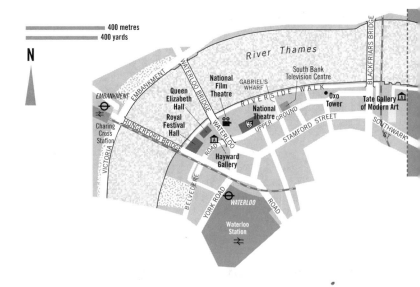

Cafés and Pubs

Gourmet Pizza Company, Gabriel's Wharf. Pizza with lovely views of the Thames from a riverside terrace. £4.75–8.50, with exotic toppings.

Doggett's Coat and Badge, 1 Blackfriars Bridge. Large, rambling renovated pub named after an annual boat race from London Bridge to Chelsea. Good beer, river views. Food so-so.

La Spezia, 33 Railway Approach. Typical Italian restaurant tucked away behind London Bridge station (it rattles!). £20–25.

Café Rouge, Hay's Galleria. Bustling café-brasserie in a converted wharf. £5–10 for a main course.

Blueprint Café, Design Museum, Butler's Wharf. Inventive and tasty Mediterranean cuisine attracting crowds from all over London. Worth booking (℗ 0171–378 7031). £20–25.

Fina Estampa, 150 Tooley Street. London's only Peruvian restaurant—tasty and delicious ceviche lunch from £15.

The Apprentice, 31 Shad Thames. A training school for Conran chefs and waiters—usually excellent gourmet food and extremely cheap, from £10.50.

The Fire Station, 150 Waterloo Rd. Renovated fire station opposite the Old Vic Theatre, serving fashionable modern British cuisine and Sunday roast lunches, from £10.95.

Le Pont de la Tour, Butler's Wharf. Sophisticated Conran-owned brasserie with spectacular views of the river and the City. Weekday set lunch from £28.50.

Oxo Tower: includes Bistrot 2—an informal café and bar serving cocktails and light snacks on the second floor, and the Oxo Tower Restaurant and Brasserie on the 8th floor, both managed by Harvey Nichols, with highly eclectic food. The Restaurant is more expensive and formal, with a good value but very filling set lunch for £26.50, the Brasserie and Bar cheaper and higher decibel. Both restaurants have wonderful views of the London skyline.

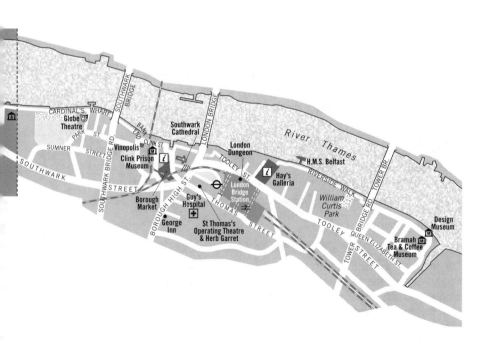

London docks became obsolete and the area's wharves and warehouses closed. Today, like so many neglected areas of London, it has only its past to turn to as a source of income, and is busy devoting itself to the heritage industry.

Nowadays, the atmosphere is very much intact, but in a wholly new form. The South Bank has become one of the most vibrant, fastest-changing parts of the city. Museums and arts venues have flourished where industrial life has curled up and died. Art galleries and restaurants have moved into the derelict wharves, and trendy new housing developments have livened up the old railway sidings. Even the Globe Theatre is back, not quite where it was in Shakespeare's day, but almost (*see* p.33). Best of all, these attractions are now linked by a wonderful river walkway stretching from Westminster Bridge to London Bridge and beyond—so you encounter little more than the distant rumble of traffic along the way.

The South Bank is where it was all happening in the run up to the Millennium. The area was then, and still is, in a frenzy of refurbishment, rebuilding and future planning. So be prepared to see a few new and surprising apparitions along the route of this walk. Biggest and weirdest is the **Millennium Wheel** just next to Westminster Bridge. The newly refurbished Oxo Tower will eventually be graced with a **Floating Lido** right on its doorstep, complete with Olympic-length swimming pool, aquarium-lined changing rooms and retractable roof that can be converted into a sports arena or dance floor. At Bankside, the satanic old power station has been converted into the **Tate Modern** (opened May 2000) with another pedestrian river crossing designed by Norman Foster, **Bankside Bridge**, that will connect the new gallery to St Paul's Cathedral (opened Summer 2000).

The South Bank Centre

From the outside, the buildings lying at the heart of the South Bank Centre look rather forbidding—lumps of dirty grey concrete streaked with rain, and proof if ever it was needed that concrete does not suit the English climate. Aesthetics apart, though, the South Bank works remarkably well as a cultural complex. The **Royal Festival Hall** is the South Bank's main concert venue; there's also the **National Film Theatre**, the **Hayward Gallery** (for major international exhibitions), **Queen Elizabeth Hall** and **Purcell Room** (also for concerts), and the three-stage Royal National Theatre. Everything is easily accessible, well signposted and free of traffic. The concerts and plays are subsidized and tickets relatively cheap. People enjoy coming not just for the scheduled events, but also to hang out in the spacious halls with their plentiful cafés, occasional musicians, elegant bookstalls, piers and river views. The merits of the various venues are dealt with in 'Entertainment and Nightlife'. The **National Theatre** foyers have excellent bookshops, particularly for drama, as well as free live concerts in the early evenings. The **Festival Hall** has a varied programme of free lunch-time concerts.

Sadly, the entertaining **Museum of the Moving Image** is closed for restoration until 2003.

Millennium Wheel

To book © (0870) 500 0600; adm £8.50, children £5.

This breathtaking construction is a peculiarly British take on the giant wheel in Vienna's Prater amusement park and a stunning addition to the London skyline. The oversized bicycle wheel is solar- and wave-powered; passengers board 32 pod-like capsules to be taken a dizzying 450ft into the city sky. The wheel is the fourth-highest structure in London; each revolution takes 30 minutes, and views stretch as far as Windsor to the west and Gravesend to the east.

IMAX Theatre

© (020) 7902 1234/1200. Open daily 11–8.45, Sat and Sun 11–10; adm £5–6.50.

Rising phoenix-like from a depressing roundabout outside Waterloo Station, this shiny £20m glass drum is the biggest, newest, most technically-advanced IMAX in Europe. Inside the 500-seat theatre 2- and 3-D films are shown on a 10-storey screen via a projector that is about the size of two small cars. For the time being the library consists of 125 films, ranging from the stupendous (documentaries such as *Into the Deep*, exploring the underwater coast of Southern California) to the wondrous and bizarre (Paul Cox's *Four Million Houseguests*—a fascinating journey via an illuminator super-microscope through a galaxy of giant-size carpets, rotting fruit and Velcro).

Gabriel's Wharf

This is an attractive square set back from the river. Formed by the backs of warehouses painted in *trompe l'œil* fashion to resemble house-fronts, it is occupied by sculpture, ceramics, fashion and jewellery workshops. There are some good cafés, bars and restaurants here if you want to stop for a drink.

Oxo Tower

Oxo, the stock cube people, neatly sidestepped the strict advertising regulations of the 1930s by working the letters 'OXO' into the design of the tower itself. In 1996 the Art Deco warehouse was magnificently restored by the Coin Street Community Builders, and it now contains over 30 retail units selling high quality textiles, furniture, clothing and jewellery at a fraction of West End prices (try Studio Fusion for the finest enamelled jewellery in the country). Above the workshops is a modestly priced café/bar (Bistrot 2) and several floors of co-op flats; at the very top is a free public viewing gallery with glitzy views of the London skyline, and the chi-chi Oxo Tower Restaurant and Brasserie.

Southwark Cathedral

You can enter through the modern annexe slightly to your left. Once inside, there is a café to the left and the cathedral entrance to the right.

Southwark Cathedral has a past almost as chequered as the neighbourhood, suffering fire, neglect and patchwork reconstruction over a history stretching back to the 7th century. It started life as the parish church of St Mary Overie (which despite the weird name merely means 'St Mary over the river'), built according to legend by the first boatman of Southwark to ferry gentlemen to and from the City. It burned down at least twice before being incorporated into a priory belonging to the Bishop of Winchester sometime around 1220. In the Civil War it was a bastion of Puritanism where preachers denounced the Bankside playhouses as offences to the Almighty. By the 19th century it had largely fallen to pieces, and the nave was rebuilt— twice as it turned out, since the first attempt was considered an appalling travesty. By the 20th century, with a little help from the restorers, Southwark was elevated to the rank of cathedral for the whole of south London. The architecture is still predominantly Gothic, particularly the choir, fine retrochoir and altar, making it something of a rarity in London. The tower is 15th century, although the battlements and pinnacles weren't completed until 1689. The nave is the only significant portion from a later era, although you will also notice Victorian statues atop the reredos behind the altar.

Tate Modern

Bankside, ℗ (020) 7887 8000. ⊖ *Southwark and Blackfriars. Open Sun–Thur 10–6; Fri & Sat 10–10; adm free. A free bus service runs between Tate Britain and Tate Modern in the summer.*

Looking like a set from Fritz Lang's *Metropolis*, this dour fortress was designed by Sir Giles Gilbert Scott in 1947. The power station has now been gutted and flooded with natural light via a glass canopy designed by the Swiss architects Herzog & de Meuron. More light shines down courtesy of illuminated balconies (windows of light) which cost a cool half a million yet still don't look as the architects originally envisaged. The glass roof spans the entire building, adding two floors to its height, and gives visitors spectacular views across the City. The main entrance, the former turbine hall, is cavernous – even a huge and grizzly spider-like creation by the French artist Louise Bourgeois seems somewhat lost. The 100,000 square feet of galleries inside house three temporary loan exhibitions a year plus the whole of the Tate's modern art collection (Picasso, Matisse, Brancusi, Dalí, Pollock, Giacometti, Warhol, Hockney, etc). The rooms are arranged thematically rather than chronologically (unusual for a museum) to draw out unexpected resonances. Thus, despite being born a century apart, you will find Claude Monet's *Water-Lilies* next to Richard Long's mud wall paintings to highlight both artists' sense of immersion in landscape. There are plenty of controversial art works on show, the kind which the general public loves to hate, including Carl André's *Equivalent Viii* (a pile of bricks) and Marcel Duchamp's hugely influential *Fountain* (a urinal). It's not all serious stuff (kids will probably love it here). In one room, devoted to the Fluxus Collective, you can play Fluxpingpong using absurd bats – one bat has a large hole while another has a tin can nailed to it. The game is impossible but quite a giggle.

Clink Prison Museum

Clink Street, ℗ (020) 7378 1558. Open daily approx 10–6; summer daily 10–10; adm.

The Clink was the Bishop of Winchester's private prison, where anyone who dared to challenge the extortion rackets he ran on Bankside would be locked up in gruesome conditions. The name Clink is familiar enough nowadays as a synonym for jail; it derives from a Latin expression meaning, roughly speaking, 'kick the bucket', which gives a good indication of the fate a prisoner could expect inside. The exhibition in this macabre museum highlights the cruelty of life in medieval Bankside, particularly the barbaric treatment of women both in prison and outside. Wives deemed too talkative would wear a scold's bridle, an iron gag shoved into their mouth, and be left there for days; sometimes the gag would be spiked. Crusaders off to the Holy Land would lock their womenfolk in chastity belts which prevented not only sexual contact but all possibility of genital hygiene.

George Inn

George Inn Yard, off Borough High Street.

The coaching inns were like the railway stations that eventually superseded them, each one providing a transport service to a specific group of destinations. Unlike railway stations, however, the inns had no fixed timetable but functioned according to demand. The George Inn goes back to the 16th century, although the present buildings date from shortly after the Great Fire. It is an elegant terrace of small interconnecting wooden bars with a quiet courtyard. During the summer you can see morris dancing and open-air productions of Shakespeare.

St Thomas's Operating Theatre Museum and Herb Garret

9a St Thomas's Street. Open Tues–Sun and most Mons 10–4; adm cheap.

The old church tower you enter used to be attached to the chapel of St Thomas's, one of the biggest hospitals in London, founded on this site back in the 12th century. The hospital moved to Lambeth in the 1860s to make way for London Bridge railway station, and all the old buildings except this one were destroyed. For a century the chapel was considered a mere curiosity, an unspectacular relic from a bygone age. Then, in 1956, a historian named Raymond Russell noticed a curious hole above the tower belfry. He squeezed through and discovered a garret containing a 19th-century operating theatre, the only one of its kind to have survived in the country. It was restored and in 1968 turned into a museum charting the tower's history, first as a medieval garret devoted to herbal remedies, then as an operating room attached to a women's ward in the next building. It is a fascinating, if grim place; nowhere else in London will you get such a graphic insight into the horrors of medicine before the modern age.

The museum also gives a lightning account of the history of apothecaries and of herbal and surgical medicine in London, accompanied by a display of gynaecological instruments that would not look out of place in a torture chamber.

The most famous woman in the hospital's history was Florence Nightingale, the legendary nurse of the Crimean War who set up London's first nursing school at St Thomas's in 1858.

London Bridge

'London Bridge is falling down' goes the cheery old nursery rhyme. Too right it is. In fact London Bridge has fallen down so often that there's nothing left to see. No, it's not the one on all the postcards that opens in the middle (that's Tower Bridge), although God knows there are enough tourists who haven't realized this yet (and one American who, back in the 1960s, actually bought the previous incarnation of London Bridge and had it reconstructed stone for stone back home in Lake Havasu, Arizona—how disappointed his friends must have been when they realized his mistake). London Bridge stopped being interesting some time around 1661, when the spikes used to display the severed heads of criminals were finally removed. It ceased to be London's one and only river crossing about a century later with the construction of Westminster and Blackfriars Bridges. Now London Bridge is nothing more than a cantilevered lump of concrete with four busy lanes of traffic on top, just one nondescript bridge among many. And it hasn't fallen down for centuries. The only striking feature of London Bridge now is the building at the Southwark end, **One London Bridge**, a 1980s office complex in shining chrome and glass that links up with the dinky shops and restaurants of Hay's Galleria (*see* below).

London Dungeon

Nos.28–34 Tooley Street. Open summer daily 10–last adm 5.30; winter daily 10.30–last adm 4.30; adm exp.

'Enter at your peril,' says the sign above the door. It is an appropriate warning for a museum that strives to make a spectator sport out of medieval torture but can only manage the ketchup-splattered inauthenticity of a 1950s Hammer horror movie. In the first place, this is not a dungeon at all, but in actual fact a converted warehouse underneath the arches of London Bridge station. And secondly, there is scarcely a genuine historical artefact to be found in the place.

Hay's Galleria

London's oldest wharf dates back to 1651, but the present structure is dominated by the tall yellow brick façades of the Victorian dock buildings, covered with a barrel-vaulted glass roof to form a pleasant arcade of shops, cafés and restaurants. The best feature is the central fountain sculpture, *The Navigators* by David Kemp, a fantasy in which a Viking galley is overtaken by naval commanders, astronomers and modern sailors with half-umbrellas for hats.

Butler's Wharf and the Design Museum

Museum open daily 11.30–6, last adm 5.30; adm; Ⓣ (020) 7378 6055 for details of temporary exhibitions. Includes a Conran restaurant (The Blueprint Café).

Created by Terence Conran and Stephen Bayley, the Design Museum is the only museum in the world devoted to industrial design and the cult of consumerism. A bower bird's shrine on the second floor showcases such mass production classics as the car (including designs by Le Corbusier from 1928), the vacuum (Dyson et al), early televisions and radios, telephones, tableware (by Enzo Mari) and chairs (by Charles and Ray Eames), while the ground floor is devoted to a diverse and diverting range of temporary exhibitions, from Porsche cars to Bosch washing machines. The museum is based in a disused warehouse which Conran and his partners rebuilt and—in a somewhat wistful homage to the International Style—painted white. Upstairs there are stunning views of Tower Bridge from the pricey Blueprint Café terrace.

The complex of buildings around the Design Museum is known as **Butler's Wharf**. As recently as the 1950s it was a hive of trade in commodities from tea and coffee to rubber, spices, wines and spirits. The rise of container shipping sounded the wharf's death knell; now only tourism and service industries can save it.

Vinopolis

1 Bank End, Clink Street, SE1; Ⓣ (020) 7940 8300; ⊖ Cannon St, Borough; bus 40, 133, 149. Open daily 10–5.30; adm.

A brand-new museum on all imaginable aspects of wine culture, history and vineyards; five tastings included in the admission price. The *Cantina Vinopolis* restaurant will be joined in due course by a brasserie, coffee shop and wine bar and you can purchase the tipple of your choice in the Wine Warehouse.

Also see: **London Aquarium**, p.28; **Globe Theatre**, p.33; **Bramah Tea and Coffee Museum**, p.139; **The *Golden Hinde***, p.136.

Onwards to: **Docklands**, p.94; **The City of London**, p.55.

London: Villages

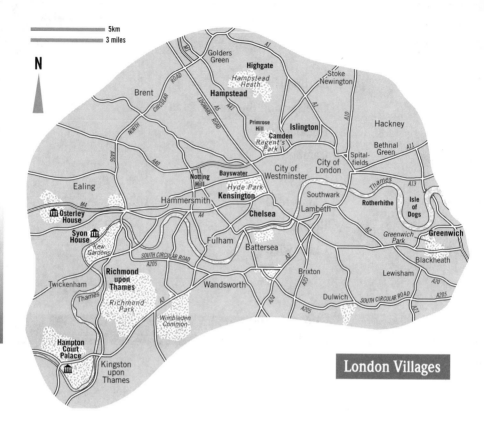

The London that stretches away beyond the centre is often described as a series of villages. Indeed, some of the geographical terms used to describe the various districts—Highgate Village, Camden Town, and so on—encourage this way of thinking, as though the outskirts of the city were a patchwork of truly autonomous communities separated by fields and trees.

To compare anything within the London urban area to village life is, of course, wishful thinking; there is little of a real village's close-knit sense of community, only hints of the unbroken greenery of the countryside, and none of the gossiping about the neighbours. It is important when visiting outer London, therefore, not to think that you are heading off into the sticks, as you might if you strayed 10 or 15 miles out of the centre of Paris or New York. Rather you should think of yourself as exploring another side of a multi-faceted city. Each outer satellite has a distinct identity of its own and a sense of integration with the whole.

Partly for this reason, the point at which central London ends and outer London begins is not easy to define. You might justifiably feel that Camden, Notting Hill and Chelsea are really part of the centre and do not belong in this section at all. The difference is that the wealth of history and culture is less focused. What you find instead is a sense of identity and atmosphere that can be described more usefully than an exhaustive list of tourist attractions.

The 'villages' below are arranged roughly in order of their distance from the city centre.

⊖ *Notting Hill, Ladbroke Grove, Westbourne Park*
Buses 23, 12, 94, 27, 31, 52

Notting Hill conjures up many images: of imposing pastel-stuccoed or gleaming white terraced houses, of antiques dealers on the southern end of Portobello Road pulling a fast one on unsuspecting tourists; of young Caribbeans dancing in the streets during the annual carnival; of arty types standing in line outside the Gate cinema; of young people riffling through second-hand records and cheap jewellery underneath the A40 flyover; of Moroccans and Portuguese chatting away in the ethnic cafés of Golborne Road; of affluent professional families relaxing in their large gardens in Stanley Crescent or Lansdowne Rise. To say Notting Hill is a melting pot is both a cliché and an understatement. It has been an emblem of **multicultural** London ever since the big immigrant waves from the Caribbean in the 1950s.

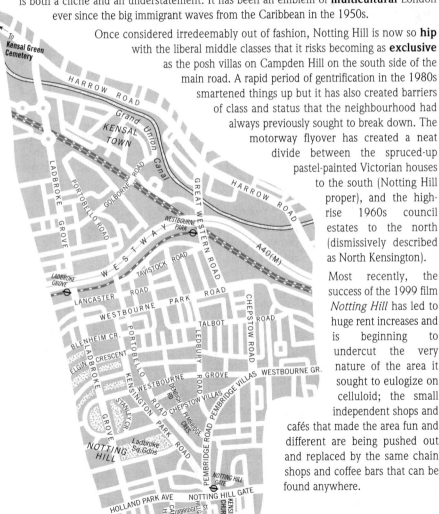

Once considered irredeemably out of fashion, Notting Hill is now so **hip** with the liberal middle classes that it risks becoming as **exclusive** as the posh villas on Campden Hill on the south side of the main road. A rapid period of gentrification in the 1980s smartened things up but it has also created barriers of class and status that the neighbourhood had always previously sought to break down. The motorway flyover has created a neat divide between the spruced-up pastel-painted Victorian houses to the south (Notting Hill proper), and the high-rise 1960s council estates to the north (dismissively described as North Kensington).

Most recently, the success of the 1999 film *Notting Hill* has led to huge rent increases and is beginning to undercut the very nature of the area it sought to eulogize on celluloid; the small independent shops and cafés that made the area fun and different are being pushed out and replaced by the same chain shops and coffee bars that can be found anywhere.

The Notting Hill Carnival

By the mid-1960s the Notting Hill Carnival, held on the last weekend in August, had become a permanent fixture. For two days each year, on the Sunday and Bank Holiday Monday, the streets throb with steel bands and soca music. The crowds sway giddily to the conga while balancing glasses of Jamaican draft stout and getting pleasantly high on some choice Caribbean weed. Everywhere is the tangy smell of saltfish, goat curry, fried plantain and patties. It is not always a peaceful affair. Relations between residents and police are tense at the best of times, and every few years that tension spills out at the carnival. Many of the middle-class residents of Notting Hill pack up the family Volvo and motor the hell out on Carnival weekend—not exactly eloquent testimony to their liberal credentials, but there you are. The impeccably liberal newspaper the *Guardian* once described the carnival as an 'all-singing, all-dancing Benetton advert viewed through a haze of marijuana', and included in its list of things to expect 'the contents of someone else's pitta bread dribbled down your back in the crush; vegetarian samosas embedded in the soles of your shoes; and a bassline that will reverberate through your ribcage for days'.

Notting Hill Gate and Around

Most visitors pile out of Notting Hill and head straight for Portobello Market. It's worth dallying for a while, though, to look at the pretty mews-style houses on **Uxbridge Street** and **Hillgate Street** behind the Gate cinema, and to head up **Campden Hill Road** to peek through the box hedges at the grandiose properties overlooking Holland Park. This is one of the most attractive residential areas in London, especially in the springtime when the small private gardens and trees are in bloom. It is also dotted with good restaurants and pubs like the Uxbridge Arms and Malabar on Uxbridge Street, and the Windsor Castle pub on Campden Hill Road.

Notting Hill Gate and **Pembridge Road** contain a mixture of excellent second-hand record, book and computer stores, cheap chain restaurants and, towards Holland Park, sofabed stores, beauty salons and the posey Damien Hirst restaurant Pharmacy.

Portobello Road

> *Antiques market Sat (7am–5pm); fruit and vegetable market Mon–Sat till 5 with early closing at 1 on Thurs.*

The antiques stalls start at the southern end of Portobello Road towards Notting Hill, and the rather shabbier furniture, food, jewellery, cheap records, books, postcards and funky bric-à-brac are at the north end, towards the A40 flyover. In between is a stretch of fruit and vegetable market popular with the whole community. The street is also lined with quirky, individual shops, some cheap, some expensive. Mingling among these counter-culture vultures are smarter, more self-conscious types on their way to the Travel Bookshop, Books for Cooks, Graham & Green, Ceramica Blue, Neal's Yard, the delicatessen Mr Christian or restaurants like 192 or Osteria Basilico on the side streets **Blenheim Crescent**, **Elgin Crescent** and **Kensington Park Road**.

Broadly speaking, the crowd gets more unorthodox and eclectic the further north you go. Under the flyover is a bric-a-brac and cheap clothes market, as well as vegetarian cafés and an indoor arcade called Portobello Green packed with young designers. Further north still, among

Cafés and Pubs

The Gallery, 5 Tavistock Rd. Unpretentious vegetarian, organic café.

Sausage and Mash Café, 268 Portobello Rd. Delicious, inventive speciality sausages and mash.

Market Bar, 240a Portobello Rd. Atmospheric wooden bar with a good Thai restaurant on the first floor.

Courtyard Café, 59a Portobello Rd. French-style sandwiches and salads and excellent coffee served in a hidden leafy courtyard. Profits go to charity.

Books for Cooks, 4 Blenheim Crescent. Test out their recipe books in the café. (You'll buy the book.)

Café Grove, 253a Portobello Rd. Popular terrace overlooking the market, serving good breakfasts and snacks.

Babushkas, 41 Tavistock Rd. Fashionable but laid-back bar with a garden for summer and cosy fires in winter.

The Pharmacy, 150 Notting Hill Gate. Restaurant/bar designed by Damien Hirst with clientele to match.

the ugly modern brick housing estates, you stumble across small art dealers, the excellent jazz shop Honest Jon's and the Spanish restaurant Galicia. Finally, off to the right is **Golborne Road**, a bustling short street divided between Portuguese and Moroccan communities.

Westbourne Grove and Ledbury Road

The Portobello Road end of **Westbourne Grove** is home to Agnès B, Tom's delicatessen, jewellery designer Dinny Hall and scores of antiques shops; in a traffic island you can't miss award-winning eau-de-Nil public toilet designed by Piers Gough, with one of London's best flower stalls attached. The Oxfam shop is one of London's best, with designer cast-offs. Further east towards Queensway are innovative home design shops like Aero, and Planet Organic, a wholefood emporium serving juices by the glass.

Ledbury Road is also packed with fashion and accessory designers, including Ghost (No.36), Molly K (63a), Lulu Guinness (66), Roger Doyle (38) and Nick Ashley (57).

Kensal Green Cemetery

Open Mon–Sat 9–5.30, Sun 10–5.30, closes an hour earlier in winter. Walk up Ladbroke Grove (several blocks) and turn left after the canal into Harrow Rd. The cemetery entrance, an imposing Doric arch, is opposite the William IV pub.

The large entrance arch frames an avenue leading to the Anglican Chapel, itself adorned with Doric pillars and colonnades. The chapel stands atop a layered cake of underground burial chambers, some of which used to be served by a hydraulic lift. Around the rest of the cemetery are extraordinary testimonies to 19th-century delusions of grandeur: vast ornate tombs worthy of the Pharaohs, decorated with statues, incidental pillars and arches. What made Kensal Green such a hit was a decision by the Duke of Sussex, youngest brother of George IV, to eschew royal protocol and have himself buried among the people, so to speak. Eminent fellow-occupants include Thackeray, Trollope, Wilkie Collins, Leigh Hunt and the father and son engineering duo Marc and Isambard Kingdom Brunel.

Onwards to: **Kensington Gardens**, p.114; **High Street Kensington**, p.125; **Holland Park**, p.113.

⊖ *Sloane Square, South Kensington*
Bus 137a, 19, 22, 239, 31, 49

Chelsea was an attractive riverside community long before it was ever integrated into greater London. The humanist and martyr Thomas More made the district fashionable by moving here in the 1520s, and soon every courtier worth his salt, even Henry VIII himself, was building a house near his. By the mid-19th century, Chelsea had turned into a **bustling** little village of intellectuals, artists, aesthetes and writers as well as war veterans—the so-called Chelsea pensioners who lived in the Royal Hospital built by Christopher Wren for Charles II.

Chelsea in the first half of the 20th century turned into little more than an annexe of South Kensington—a little more **classy** perhaps, a little more established, but just as snobbish and sterile. In the 1950s and 1960s, it became the refuge of the dying aristocracy, as films like Joseph Losey's *The Servant* (shot in Royal Avenue) showed to withering effect. In the 1980s, the sons and daughters of these last-ditch aristos mutated into a particularly underwhelming social animal known as the Sloane Ranger—a special kind of upper-class twit with deeply misguided delusions about being trendy. Male Sloanes wore corduroy trousers, striped shirts and tweed jackets, while the female of the species went in for frilly white shirts and pearls.

Chelsea's **artistic** streak never entirely disappeared, however, and in the 1960s and early 1970s it flourished with a vengeance along the King's Road. Like Carnaby Street in Soho, the King's Road let its hair down and filled with cafés and fashion shops selling miniskirts and cheap jewellery. The Royal Court Theatre, opposite Peter Jones, came into its own as a venue for avant-garde writers like John Osborne (the original Angry Young Man), Edward Bond and Arnold Wesker. Mods, later replaced by punks, set the fashion tone for whole generations of young people.

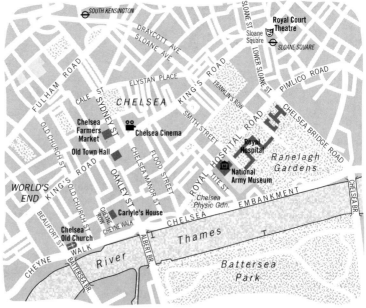

Cafés and Pubs

Habitat Café, King's Road. Airy, colourful room on the top of the shop, with big scrubbed wood tables and plants, and a daily Italian-inspired lunch menu, good coffee and scrumptious cakes.

King's Head and Eight Bells, 50 Cheyne Walk, Chelsea. Enjoy the antiques displays in this 16th-century building. There are views of the Battersea peace pagoda across the river.

Phene Arms, Phene St, off Oakley St. Small old pub with a courtyard garden in a quiet residential street, with surprisingly adventuous food.

Chelsea Kitchen, 98 King's Rd. Continental food and wine for less than £10.

Bluebird, 350 King's Rd. Part of the Conran empire, a converted 1930s garage containing a luxury food store, restaurant and café.

The King's Road

During the 1960s, old-fashioned shops were superseded by the likes of Terence Conran, who opened his first household store **Habitat** on the King's Road as a direct challenge to the fusty, old-fashioned goods then on sale at **Peter Jones** department store by Sloane Square. Meanwhile most of the boutiques have either gone upmarket or been replaced by generic highstreet chainstores. Some of the 1960s spirit lives on, however, in the delightfully sprawling **antiques markets** on the south side of the road. You might also want to take a look at the **Chelsea Farmer's Market**, Sydney Street, with its cafés and craft shops.

Chelsea Riverside

The heart of old Chelsea is down by the river. Either take the bus to Battersea Bridge, or walk down Old Church Street until you reach the water. Just to the left of the bridge is **Chelsea Old Church**, which preserves the memory of Sir Thomas More, author of the humanist tract *Utopia* and the first man to lose his head for standing up to Henry VIII over his break with the Pope. The church's history goes back to Norman times, but most of it was rebuilt in classical style in the 17th century. The churchyard has been converted into a small park.

Stretching to the east, just behind the Chelsea Embankment, are the delightful 18th-century brick houses of **Cheyne Walk**, one of London's most fashionable addresses for the past 200 years. Amongst the famous residents have been George Eliot, who died at No.4; Henry James, who spent the latter years of his life in Carlyle Mansions, a Victorian house standing just beyond the King's Head and Eight Bells pub; Whistler, who was living at No.101 when he produced some of his most extraordinary paintings of the Thames; and Turner, himself no mean painter of the Thames, who used No.119 as a retreat. The Queen's House at No.16 was shared during the 1860s by a trio of poets, Dante Gabriel Rossetti, Algernon Swinburne and George Meredith, who kept a whole bestiary of animals including some noisy peacocks.

The most interesting address, however, is 24 Cheyne Row just around the corner: **Carlyle's House** (*open April–Oct Wed–Sun 11–4.30; adm*). Few houses in London evoke such a strong sense of period or personality as this redbrick Queen Anne building, where the historian Thomas Carlyle, author of *The French Revolution* and *Frederick the Great*, lived with his wife from 1834 until his death in 1881. It has been kept almost exactly as the Carlyles left it. Even the old man's hat still hangs on the peg in the entranceway.

Also see: **Chelsea Physic Garden**, p.110; **King's Road shopping**, p.125.
Onwards to: **Knightsbridge shopping**, p.126; **Battersea Park**, p.110.

⊖ *Bank, Tower Hill, Wapping, Rotherhithe*

DLR *Tower Gateway, Shadwell, Canary Wharf, Mudchute, Island Gardens; ✆ (020) 7918 4000 for 24-hour travel information*

Buses: *100 from Liverpool Street for Wapping and Shadwell, P11 from Waterloo to London Bridge, D1 from London Bridge for the Isle of Dogs*

Boats *from Charing Cross or Westminster Pier every half-hour or so (less often in winter) 11am–5pm, stopping at London Bridge, St Katharine's Dock, Canary Wharf, Greenland Dock (in the Surrey Quays), Greenwich and the Thames Barrier. London Tourist Board recorded river service information line: ✆ 0839 123 432; Westminster Passenger Services: ✆ (020) 7930 4097; Thames Cruises (020) 7930 3373.*

*Travelcards are valid on the DLR. A **Sail and Rail** ticket entitles you to a day's unlimited travel on the DLR plus a riverboat trip from Westminster or Greenwich Piers, and*

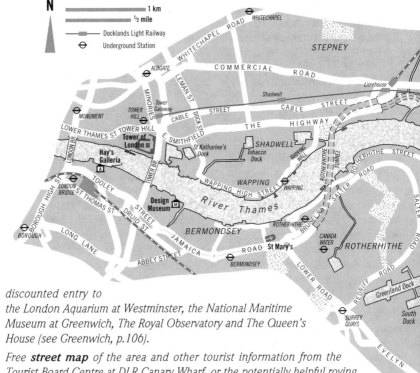

discounted entry to the London Aquarium at Westminster, the National Maritime Museum at Greenwich, The Royal Observatory and The Queen's House (see Greenwich, p.106).

*Free **street map** of the area and other tourist information from the Tourist Board Centre at DLR Canary Wharf, or the potentially helpful roving Tourist Assistants employed by DLR.*

To head downriver from the Tower is to enter a different world— more in tune with the Emerald City in *The Wizard of Oz*. The converted Docklands show the face of a city of the future: a vision of **shimmering** high-rise glass and steel reflected in the lapping tides of the

River Thames, a Phoenix risen from the ashes of the derelict wharves and warehouses of a bygone age. It's **disorientating**, endlessly surprising, pock marked by building sites, mud and cranes, and—in terms of sheer visual impact—extraordinarily **impressive**.

The Docklands were built in the 1980s without a shred of planning or civic sense and as a result were a spectacular financial flop. The development failed to respect its environment and the wishes of local people, many of whom were pushed out of their modest homes to make way for a higher-class breed of resident. Furthermore, nobody thought to provide proper services or adequate transport links, so the gleaming palaces were almost impossible to get to or live in. When recession struck at the end of the 1980s, hundreds of speculators went bust because they simply could not attract tenants. The place has become a bit of a ghost town: office blocks with bland reflective façades, impersonal shopping centres the same as you find in any New Town suburbia, luxury housing estates where the main luxury is a near-total absence of an identity.

The Docklands redevelopments continue out east all the way to London City Airport and beyond, featuring hi-tech office architecture by the likes of Richard Rogers and I. M. Pei,

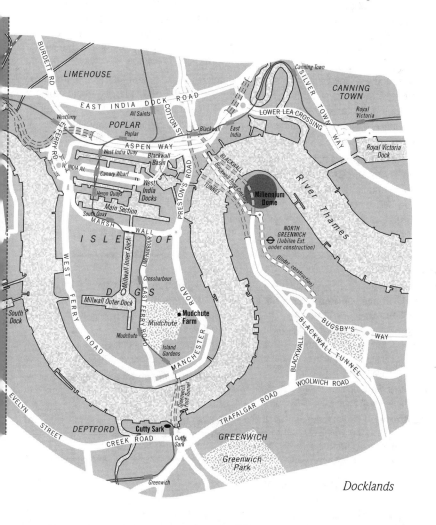

Docklands

which for the moment remain rather stranded as building works continue to develop an 'urban village' and a university campus on land where the Royal Docks used to be.

You can see a great deal of the Docklands by taking the overland **Docklands Light Railway** (DLR) from Bank or Tower Gateway to Island Gardens on the Isle of Dogs or Beckton. This elevated railway is like the futuristic monorail in Truffaut's *Fahrenheit 451*, the trains are computerized and quite eerily driverless. A ride on it—sitting next to the unmanned emergency driving position where you get panoramic views as you go, and getting on and off to explore—makes for an entertaining day out in itself. If you board at Tower Gateway on the hour between 10 and 4 you are treated to a commentary on your trip all the way to Crossharbour.

The Isle of Dogs and Canary Wharf

The **Isle of Dogs** is a peninsula defined by a tight loop in the river and crisscrossed by artificial waterways. There is no hard evidence that it ever had any association with dogs, although there are folk tales that the royal kennels were once kept here. Most likely, 'dogs' is a corruption of 'docks'; after all, that was what provided the area's livelihood from 1802 until the second half of the 20th century. The southern end of the Isle of Dogs is littered with failed upmarket residential estates as well as a sprinkling of older lower-class council houses. There's no mistaking the main attraction around here. The 812ft glass and steel tower block at the centre of **Canary Wharf** soars over the Docklands skyline, the flashing light atop its pyramidal apex winking 40 times a minute. Cesar Pelli's monster tower (*closed to visitors*), officially known by its address One Canada Square and completed in 1991 after just 18 months under construction, is the tallest building in London by far. This is Europe's largest single property development and clustered around the tower is a series of lower-lying buildings (mostly hi-tech reworkings by American architects of Edwardian styles), courtyards, shopping plazas, waterside footpaths, a car park, a fountain, incidental artworks and sculpted metal railings.

Continuity with the past is not its strong point, as traditionalists have been quick to point out. It bears no resemblance to the Canary Wharf of the 19th century, so-called because it took deliveries predominantly from the Canary Islands. The Pelli tower is the first skyscraper in the world to be clad in stainless steel. It is 50 storeys high, has 32 passenger lifts, 3960 windows and 4388 steps in its four fire stairways. Building materials included 27,500 tonnes of steel, 500,000 bolts and a staggering 90,000 sq ft of Italian, Spanish and Guatemalan marble in the

Cafés and Pubs

Canary Wharf restaurants, inside the complex, include **Café Rouge**, **Gourmet Pizza Co**, and the healthy **Soup Opera** and **Cranks**.

The Prospect of Whitby, 57 Wapping Wall, charming pub with loads of history—starting in 1543. With a hangman's noose to remind us of the executions once held there.

The Widow's Son, outside Devon's Road DLR station, an inn with an interesting story.

The Mayflower, 117 Rotherhithe St, and the **Angel**, 101 Bermondsey Wall East. Both have fine views over the river, the Angel is better for food.

Corney and Barrow, off Cabot Square, is shiny and you can sit outside.

Brera, Cabot Place West, deliciously sophisticated Italian sandwiches.

Chili's Grill & Bar, 2nd floor, Cabot Place East, serves a Texan lunch above Canary Wharf.

Babe Ruth's Legendary Eating Place, opposite Tobacco Dock, London's best themed restaurant.

Dickens Inn, St Katharine's Dock, where the food is pretty good if a little expensive.

lobby alone. Every feature is state of the art. There are so many fax machines and photocopiers in the building that heating is quite unnecessary, even in the dead of winter. The fountain in Cabot Square is computer-controlled, adjusting the jet intensity according to wind strength so that passers-by never get splashed.

The **Storm Water Pumping Station** on Stewart Street off Marsh Wall is well worth a visit—but to get there you will have to get out at South Quay and walk along Marsh Wall (about 10–20 minutes). Built by John Outram in 1988, the enormous pump station looks like an outsized Chinsese temple, and is one of the most successful buildings in the Docklands.

Further south, **Mudchute** is one of a number of city farms dotted around east London, a 32-acre patchwork of vegetable allotments and open fields. A little further down Eastferry Road is **Island Gardens**, a small riverside park with an outstanding view across the river to Greenwich. You can walk over to Greenwich through the **foot tunnel** built in 1902 beneath the river, its two onion-domed brick towers marking the entrances at either end. The Light Railway has also decided to tunnel south under the river, and there is an extension to Cutty Sark, Greenwich and Lewisham.

Wapping

Until the 16th century, when the land around it was drained, Wapping was little more than a sliver of land hemmed in by swamps to the north and the river on the south. It has almost always been poor: John Stow described Wapping High Street in his *Survey of London* (1598) as 'a filthy strait passage, with alleys of small tenements or cottages'. Sailors made up the bulk of its modest population, later replaced by dockers. The waterfront near **Wapping Wall** known as **Execution Dock** earned its name because pirates and smugglers used to be hanged there and then displayed in chains for as long as it took for three tides to wash over them.

This was where some of the first failed luxury flats of the 1980s were built. Some of the architecture is truly dire, and although the area is now more or less fully inhabited Wapping still has no soul. The ambitious and attractively converted **Tobacco Dock** on The Highway, for example, is supposed to be a thriving new shopping centre, but in fact it is rather forlorn.

St Katharine's Dock looks benign enough now, with its yachts and cafés, but it was once one of the most callous of riverside developments. To build the docks and commodity warehouses here in the 1820s, the authorities knocked down 1250 houses and made more than 11,000 people homeless. For all that, the dock was not a great financial success and lost money until its closure in 1968. Now prettified with boats and bright paint, its walkways are linked with a series of attractive iron bridges. It is an obvious lunch spot after a hard morning's sightseeing at the Tower of London, along a signposted walkway. There is a free hour-long guided walk of the docker's way of life leaving on Saturdays at 1pm and 3pm from the East Gate of the Tower of London. Call London Walks, © (020) 7624 3978, for details of others.

Opposite the Murdoch empire is Nicholas Hawksmoor's church **St George in the East** (1714–29) with its broad, tall tower with pepperpot turrets. The docks were heavily bombed during the Blitz, when the interior of St George was destroyed. It has now been redesigned as an intriguing hybrid—part church, part block of flats, part courtyard.

Limehouse

A more complete Hawksmoor church can be found a mile or so to the east, past Limehouse Basin off the Commercial Road. The chunky tower of **St Anne Limehouse** has been a guide to ships coming into London ever since it was completed in 1724. Named after the lime kilns which used to operate here, Limehouse bears the vestiges of the mini-Chinatown it was before the 1980s property bonanza and it has a little-publicized reputation for good cheap Chinese restaurants. In the 19th century the area was considered an iniquitous den of vice; this was where Oscar Wilde set the opium-smoking scene in his novel *The Picture of Dorian Gray*.

Rotherhithe

Rotherhithe was where the Pilgrim Fathers set out for America in their ship the *Mayflower* in 1620. You might think hordes of American tourists come to pay homage to their forefathers, but in fact Rotherhithe is a delightfully unspoiled, relatively unknown part of riverside London and one of the most successful of the Docklands redevelopments. The old warehouses have been repaired but not tarted up, the streets have been kept narrow, and the green in front of St Mary's Church lends an air of village-like cosiness.

Originally Rotherhithe was part of the estate of the great abbey of Bermondsey, which was destroyed at the Reformation. The monks used to drink in a tavern called The Salutation, since renamed **The Angel**. The present pub was built, probably in the 17th century, as a drinking haunt for sailors. The departure of the Pilgrim Fathers is commemorated in the **Mayflower** pub, which is partly built out of the broken up segments of the original ship and has a model of the vessel hanging outside its front door. Because of its tourist clientele, the pub is allowed to sell postage stamps, including American ones. This was probably the tavern where Captain Christopher Jones and his crew spent the night before their departure for the Americas. Within two years, the ship came back from its expedition, and Jones was eventually buried, along with the three co-owners of the *Mayflower*, in the churchyard of **St Mary's** opposite. The church itself, which was attractively rebuilt in the 18th century, contains a plaque to Jones as well as remains of the *Fighting Temeraire*, the battleship whose demise was so poignantly captured by Turner in his famous painting in the National Gallery.

Because of its isolation on a bend in the Thames, Rotherhithe became rather dilapidated after the Second World War. Its recent redevelopment, however, has attracted a modest number of artists and artisans, and by the river is an intriguing sculpture park called the **Knot Garden**.

Surrey Docks and Deptford

Southeast of Rotherhithe, if you can bear the noisy walk down Lower Road and off to the left down Redriff Road, are the old **Surrey Docks**, part of which have been converted into a yachting and pleasure-boat marina. Some of the hi-tech modern buildings are rather successful. **Greenland Dock** (used by the whaling trade in the 19th century) and **South Dock** are ideal for a stroll or a spot of rowing.

To the south is **Deptford**, famous as the place where Christopher Marlowe was stabbed to death in a tavern brawl in 1593 and where Peter the Great rode in a wheelbarrow in John Evelyn's garden during a state visit to the naval dockyard established there by Henry VIII.

Also see: **Millennium Dome**, p.38; **Tower of London**, p.44.

Onwards to: **Greenwich**, p.106; the **South Bank and Southwark**, p.80; the **City of London**, p.55.

✪ *Camden Town, Chalk Farm; bus 24, 29, 31*
Visit at the weekend to see the area at its liveliest.

Cafés and Pubs

Silks and Spice, 28 Chalk Farm Rd. Thai and Malaysian café-restaurant. Lunch from £4.95.

Crown and Goose, 100 Arlington Rd. Award-winning pub and wine bar with real ale, good food and friendly service.

Café Delancey, 3 Delancey St. Laid-back brasserie.

Dublin Castle, 94 Parkway. Rowdy but friendly Irish pub with live music.

Marine Ices, 8 Haverstock Hill, near ✪ Chalk Farm. Traditional old Italian ice cream restaurant, one of the best in all London.

Camden is above all its buzzing **open-air** market, or rather series of markets, that have sprung up around the canal and the surrounding streets. There is something for everyone: cheap clothes, pianos, herbal cures, tarot card readings, off-beat bookshops, furniture stores, pubs and lots and lots of restaurants. At the weekends, traffic comes to a standstill. The atmosphere is very **relaxed, young** but not overly self-conscious or trendy. You can easily spend hours sorting through the leatherwear and second-hand records, stopping for a drink or snack from a street stall; later, you can head off for a meal or a spot of dancing; or you can easily escape the crowds by strolling away along Regent's Canal. Camden's modern identity as a haven for artists and small shopkeepers was established in the 1970s, when the market started and the old Victorian warehouses were slowly converted into artists' studios, music venues and restaurants.

Markets and Shops

The nerve centre of the market is at **Camden Lock**, just next to the canal off Chalk Farm Road (the extension of Camden High Street). Some but not all of the stalls and shops stay open all week. In the middle of the market is a covered three-storey building with narrow staircases and passages selling jewellery and crafts; in the immediate vicinity are stalls selling clothes, antiques, books and records. The stalls then continue for about 500 yards up the Chalk Farm Road, in an area known as **The Stables**. **Chalk Farm Road** itself has interiors shops with an ethnic slant. Some of the most interesting shops are on **Camden High Street**, which is really a market unto itself; the Electric Ballroom nightclub doubles on Sundays as a bazaar for cheap designer fashions and jewellery. Finally, there is a fruit and veg market on **Inverness Street**, between the High Street and Gloucester Crescent, which is open Mon–Sat.

Jewish Museum

129–32 Albert St, (020) 7284 1997. Open Sun–Thurs 10–4; adm.

This celebration of Jewish life in England from the Middle Ages, formerly in Woburn House on Tavistock Square, is notable mostly for its collection of old ritual objects from London synagogues. The centrepiece is an elaborately carved 16th-century Venetian Synagogue Ark. There are also attractive illuminated marriage contracts and some Torah bells fashioned by the 18th-century silversmith Abraham Lopes de Oliveira.

Onwards to: **Regent's Park and London Zoo**, p.116.

⊖ Angel, ⊖/⇌ Highbury and Islington
Bus 19, 73

In the 1950s you wouldn't have found much in Islington apart from a clapped-out old music hall, a few eel and pie shops and an extended series of slummy terraced houses. How times have changed. Now it is one of the liveliest and trendiest districts in the capital, a Mecca for liberal-minded **arty** professionals, particularly writers and broadcasters, who live in attractively refurbished Georgian townhouses and eat out in expensive ethnic restaurants. The place is packed with pubs, cafés, designer bars and shops, and **alternative** theatres.

During the 1980s Islington was associated with a certain kind of earnest, occasionally radical left-wing politics that jarred completely with the prevailing Thatcherite ideology of free markets and individual responsibility. The borough council spent money on crèches and facilities for the disabled and was dismissed as a cabal of the 'loony left' for its pains. More recently, Islington has been taken to task in the right-wing press for spawning a more **comfortable** breed of liberal lefty who likes to discuss the meaning of socialism over a fancy plate of rocket and shaved parmesan. The occasion of this new wave of Islington-bashing has been the rise of Prime Minister Tony Blair, an Islingtonian of long standing.

In fact, the pleasures of Islington have been well known for centuries and were only seriously interrupted by the industrial revolution. In the 16th century it was popular as a royal hunting ground and noted for its pure spring water and good dairy farms. The open fields were dotted with well-appointed mansions, gardens and orchards. Elizabeth I used to meet her favourites here, and people from all walks of life came to enjoy the bowling greens, dance floors and taverns. The extension of Regent's Canal (here called the Grand Union Canal) and the advent of the railways in the 19th century did similar damage in Islington as it had in Camden; the attractive Georgian terraces which had sprung up in the district became dilapidated and dirty, as the local population, mostly made up of labourers, swelled uncontrollably. Soon Islington became a byword for everything that was *un*fashionable in London. In 1928, the novelist Evelyn Waugh ran away from Canonbury Square after just a few months in a rented house because he was fed up having to explain to his friends why he lived in such a backwater.

Just 20 years later, though, there was nothing marginal about Islington at all. The Camden Passage antiques market arrived in 1964, and pub theatres led by the King's Head on Upper Street began to flourish soon after. The old Collins Music Hall burned down and was replaced with the Screen on the Green cinema. Nowadays the changes in Islington come so fast it is hard to keep track of them: a Lebanese restaurant closes there, a Cuban bar opens here. The area retains a certain self-conscious shabbiness, but that is part of its charm. Islington doesn't have any tourist attractions in the traditional sense of the word, just bags of atmosphere. The best way to visit is to start at the Angel and work your way slowly northwards.

Camden Passage

Open Wed 7.30–5, Sat 9–5.30, some stalls open 10–5 other days, closed Mon

This is a cobbled row of elegant antiques shops and stalls, most of which open their doors on Wednesday mornings and Saturdays only. The market is ideal for browsing, since everything looks perfect and the prices of the furniture, prints, silverware and jewellery are probably too high to consider seriously for purchase.

Cafés and Pubs

Santa Fe, 75 Upper St. 'New Mexican' food (pot roast with garlic mash, quesadillas, lots of lime and chilli, great desserts) in a large, bright, trendy bar/restaurant. Lunch £4–9.

King's Head, 115 Upper St. Great theatre pub with plush seats and bags of atmosphere.

Granita, 127 Upper St. *The* Islington restaurant and New Labour meeting place. Minimalist décor matched by trendy menu. Lunch served Wed–Sun 12.30–2.30. £15–20.

Pasha, 301 Upper St. Spicy Turkish food, with lots of choice including many vegetarian dishes. Set lunch menus from £5.

Upper Street Fish Shop, 324 Upper St. Perhaps the best fish'n'chips in London. From £2–3 take-away; £12 for a 3-course sit-down menu.

Almeida Theatre Café, 7a Almeida St. Baguettes, soup, etc. from £2–3.

Angel of the North, 353 Upper St. Pleasant café serving breakfasts, salads, burgers. £5–8.

Upper Street

All the streets around here, from Upper Street across to St Peter's Street and down to City Road, are a delight for strollers—small, relatively traffic-free and packed with elegant houses, cafés and restaurants. The area to the east, along the Grand Union Canal, is particularly charming and dotted with pretty Georgian houses. In the 1950s and 1960s this was the distinctly unfashionable home of the playwright Joe Orton and his lover Kenneth Halliwell.

Just to the north, back on Upper Street, is the lumbering hulk of the **Business Design Centre**. This rather clumsy building is a redevelopment of the old Royal Agricultural Hall, a fine Victorian hangar made of iron and glass used for agricultural shows and industrial exhibitions. The Design Centre now hosts conferences, the Islington Art Fair and other odd art shows. On either side of the Design Centre, Upper St is packed with the restaurants and offbeat shops that characterize Islington, including several shops selling a fascinating variety of old furniture (try Castle Gibson, No.106a) and others even more miscellaneous, like After Noah (No.121), with its array of old and new lamps, clocks, soaps and old comics. Behind, on Liverpool Road, is **Chapel Market**, a lively fruit, veg and clothes market, open every day but Monday.

Triangular **Islington Green**, where Upper Street meets Essex Road, is more of a meeting place than a spot of any great beauty. Heading north on Upper St, you come to the **King's Head** theatre pub, which as a gimmick still counts money in the pre-decimal currency of pounds, shillings and pence (12 pence to a shilling, 20 shillings to a pound). The streets to the left of here, forming the beginning of the area known as Barnsbury, contain some fine Georgian townhouses. Theberton Street, not far from the pub, leads to the pale brick splendour of Gibson Square. One block further up is Almeida Street, home to the highly successful fringe theatre of the same name. The crowds and the trendiness factor gradually ebb away the further north you walk up Upper St. It is worth continuing for five minutes, past the town hall, to turn right on Canonbury Lane and explore one of the most unspoiled areas of Georgian housing in north London. The name **Canonbury** recalls Islington's roots as the burgh, or district, of the canons of the priory of St Bartholomew at Smithfield. Then, as now, the most imposing building in the neighbourhood was **Canonbury Tower** on Canonbury Place, a building of mythical reputation whose history goes back to pre-Roman times; no fewer than 24 ley lines meet at the point where the central pillar of its main staircase stands.

Onwards to: **Camden**, p.91; the **City of London**, p.55.

⊖ *Hampstead, Belsize Park,* **⇌** *Hampstead Heath (Silverlink)*
Bus 24, 46, 210, 268

Hampstead is a pretty **hilltop** village of Georgian rows and Victorian mansions, surrounded by the vast expanse of the Heath. Throughout its history, it has provided a refuge when life in the city has become too much. John Constable came here and painted some distant cityscapes that were barely distinguishable in tone from his great rural idylls. No wonder: the air is so **pure** and the Heath so big and wild you can feel you are lost in the deep heart of the English countryside. Nowadays Hampstead has an unmistakable air of *established* comfort. More cosmopolitan than Camden and Islington, it is full of lively restaurants, bars and theatres frequented by its well-off, generally New Labour residents. But in contrast to its north London neighbours, Hampstead, for all its liberal credentials, is a staid and remarkably **conservative** place, everything carefully planned and lovingly looked after, from the window boxes in the Georgian houses on Holly Hill to the fish stall next to the community market.

Hampstead Village

The real pleasure of Hampstead village is in getting lost in the winding backstreets. Up near Whitestone Pond, Lower Terrace takes you past the entrance to **Judges Walk**, the legendary 'substitute' law court of the Great Plague which is now just a driveway to a couple of tumbledown houses. A little further down to the left is **Admiral's Walk**, which contains a splendid Georgian house with multi-levelled rooms and balconies, where at various times the novelist John Galsworthy and the architect George Gilbert Scott have taken up residence. At the other end of Admiral's Walk, Hampstead Grove takes you down to **Fenton House**, a splendid brick mansion dating from 1693 (**©** *(020) 7435 3471; open Sat and Sun 11–5, Wed–Fri 2–5; adm*). Aside from the elegant rooms and fine garden, the house has collections of early keyboard instruments and fine porcelain. At the bottom of Hampstead Grove, the narrow road up to the left is **Hollybush Hill**, a cul-de-sac lined with beautiful small houses including the 17th-century Hollybush pub. Just after the pub is a steep staircase plunging down towards Heath Street. Better, however, to retrace your steps and head down **Holly Walk**, another delightful cobbled path flanked by fine houses and a small flower-filled cemetery. At the bottom of the hill is **St John's**, an attractive 18th-century church with a tall tower and, inside, a balustraded gallery and a bust of Keats beside the lectern. Constable is buried in the churchyard. The road from the church back to Heath Street, called **Church Row**, is one of the most elegant lines of Georgian housing in London.

Heath Street is one of two Hampstead thoroughfares lined with fine shops, delicatessens, cafés and restaurants. The other, the **High Street**, can be reached through **Oriel Place**, which has an old plane tree growing in a minuscule patch of ground halfway along. Cross the High Street and you come into **Flask Walk** with its second-hand bookshops, galleries, children's boutiques, and posh tea and coffee merchant. Along with its continuation **Well Walk**, this is where fashionable folk came to take the Hampstead spa waters in the 18th century.

The Spaniards Inn

The 16th-century **Spaniards Inn** at the junction of Hampstead Lane and Spaniards Road, named after two Spanish proprietors who killed each other in a duel, owes its fame to the 18th-century highwayman Dick Turpin who used to stop for drinks here in between coach

Cafés and Pubs

Ye Olde White Bear, New End Square. Friendly pub in the maze of streets behind Hampstead tube. Food served outside and all day.

Toast, 51–3 Hampstead High St. Smart new restaurant/bar above Hampstead tube. Lunch from £15.

The Flask, Flask Walk. Rambling traditional pub behind flower-bedecked façade, just off the High Street.

Maison Blanc, 62a Hampstead High St. Chic pâtisserie serving excellent pastries and coffee.

Coffee Cup, 74 Hampstead High St. Much-loved but rather shabby café with seats outside.

The Crêperie, corner of Hampstead High St and Perrin's Lane. Tiny stall selling freshly made sweet and savoury crêpes.

Giraffe, 46 Rosslyn Hill. Funky café serving international menu accompanied by world music.

---

hold-ups. During the Gordon Riots of 1780, a group of mobsters dropped by on their way to Kenwood House, which they intended to destroy. The publican offered the rioters pint after pint of free beer and soon the men weren't in a fit state to walk to Kenwood, let alone burn it down. You can see their muskets hanging on the wall in the saloon bar.

Keats' House

> *Wentworth Place, Keats Grove (walk down Hampstead High St and its continuation Rosslyn Hill, then turn left on to Downshire Hill and take the first right); © (020) 7435 2062. Open April–Oct Mon–Fri 10–1 and 2–6, Sat 10–1 and 2–5, Sun 2–5; Nov–Mar Mon–Fri 1–5, Sat 10–1 and 2–5, Sun 2–5; free.*

The main attraction is the plum tree in the garden, under which Keats wrote 'Ode to a Nightingale' in 1819 (if you think the tree looks a bit young, you're right; it is a replacement). In all, Keats spent only two years here as a lodger of Charles Armitage Brown, a literary critic specializing in Shakespeare's sonnets. It was nevertheless an eventful time. He produced some of his best and most famous work, fell in love with Fanny Brawne who lived in the other half of the house, and contracted the consumption that was to kill him two years later at the age of 25. Keats used one living room downstairs and one bedroom upstairs. Memorabilia are strewn in every room; these include a lock of Keats' hair and some of his manuscripts and books.

Kenwood House

> *Hampstead Lane; entrance opposite Bishops Avenue; © (020) 8348 1286. Open April–Sept daily 10–6, closes 4 in winter; free. For Hampstead Heath, see p.112.*

The unpretentious atmosphere at Kenwood is a breath of fresh air after the stuffily earnest stately homes dotted around the rest of London. The expanse of the Heath rolls away to the south and its breathtaking views over Highgate and central London. Kenwood is famous for its summer concerts held by the lake at the bottom of the garden; the orchestra sits under a white awning and the audience watches from across the water. The house itself dates back to 1616 but was given a facelift by Robert Adam in the 1760s. He stuck on the white neoclassical façade, and reworked most of the interiors. The pictures, bequeathed by Lord Iveagh, include works by Rembrandt (a remarkable self-portrait), Vermeer (*The Guitar Player*), Van Dyck, Gainsborough, Guardi, Reynolds, Landseer and Turner.

Also see: **Hampstead Heath**, p.112; the **Freud Museum**, p.138.
Onwards to: **Highgate Cemetery**, p.112.

⊖/⇌ *Richmond*
Bus 65, 391

Richmond is a **tranquil**, affluent **riverside** community of attractive Georgian and neo-Georgian houses, flanked on all sides by wide expanses of greenery. On a sunny day it is an ideal place to walk along the river; the compact town centre beside Richmond Green has a pleasant **villagey** feel and there are plenty of cafés and riverside pubs. Richmond's sense of community is such that it boasts not one but two theatres: the Richmond Theatre on the Green, and the Orange Tree near the station.

Richmond Palace and the Green

In medieval times, the focal point of the district was Shene Palace, a relatively modest manor house used as a lodge for the excellent hunting in the surrounding hills. The village green (today's Richmond Green) became a popular venue for pageants and jousting tournaments. Henry VII was so attached to the place that he changed its name from Shene to Richmond, after his earldom in Yorkshire, and entirely rebuilt the palace after a fire in 1497.

The new Richmond Palace must have been quite something, a riot of spires and turrets which you can see reconstructed as a model in the Richmond Town Hall's small **museum** (*entrance on Red Lion Street, © (020) 8332 1141; open May–Oct only, Tues–Sat 11–5, Sun 1–4; adm*). Sadly, almost nothing survives of medieval Richmond in real life. A charterhouse which stood a few hundred yards to the north was destroyed during the Reformation, and the palace followed suit immediately after Charles I's execution in 1649. All that remains is a stone gateway off Richmond Green, bearing Henry VII's coat of arms, and the palace wardrobe, or household office, to the left just inside Old Palace Yard.

Political upheaval could not disguise the basic attraction of Richmond, and by the early 18th century building had begun again in earnest. In Old Palace Yard is **Trumpeters' House**, an elegant mansion built by a pupil of Christopher Wren and subsequently used as a refuge for Prince Metternich after the upheavals in Vienna of 1848. Further fine Georgian houses are to be found in neighbouring streets, such as Old Palace Terrace and Maids of Honour Row.

The Riverside

Today, as ever, the biggest attraction of Richmond is the riverside, which boasts, amongst other things, the elegant five-arched **Richmond Bridge** dating from the 1770s. The houses on the north side have been extensively redeveloped as a neo-Georgian terrace of shops, restaurants and offices called **The Riverside**, opened in 1988. The architect responsible was Quinlan Terry, a chum of Prince Charles much in sympathy with the Prince's traditionalist leanings. Most critics were appalled by this piece of unadventurous pastiche, while Prince Charles called it 'an expression of harmony and proportion'. The development nevertheless does its job well enough, and on summer days its layered terraces descending towards the water are crowded with strollers, sunbathers and the spillover customers of the surrounding pubs. At the top of the bridge, Richmond Hill leads to wild Richmond Park (*see* p.117), famous for its deer.

Cafés and Pubs

Bellini, 12 The Quadrant. Fish, pasta, *gnocchi* and singing waiters in flamboyant Italian eaterie (from £15).

Café Parisien, 7 Lower George St. Superior filled baguettes and toasted sandwiches; outdoor seating; exceptionally friendly service (from £5).

Pierre's Brasserie du Liban, 11–13 Petersham Rd. One of the best Lebanese restaurants in London (from £30); take-away sandwiches (from £3).

White Swan, 26 Old Palace Lane. Traditional riverside pub hidden in a tiny street of cottages.

Beeton's, 58 Hill Rise. Unusual modern British cuisine.

Caffè Mamma, 24 Hill Street. Superior pasta café decorated like an Italian courtyard.

White Cross Hotel, Richmond Waterside Ordinary pub fare, but a delightful spot. Crowded in summer.

Ham House

Ham Street, off Sandy Lane and Petersham Road; ☎ (020) 8940 1950; bus 371 from Richmond. Grounds open Sat–Wed 10.30–6; adm; house open Sat–Wed 1–5; adm.

Ham House is one of the grandest surviving Jacobean mansions in London, a magnificent three-storey redbrick house that has been restored to something approaching its original splendour. Built in 1610 and nicknamed the 'sleeping beauty' for its tranquil position, it became the home of William Murray, a friend of Charles I, who as a child had acted as the future King's whipping boy. In gratitude, Charles offered the adult Murray a peerage (he became the Earl of Dysart) and all the property around Ham and Petersham including this house.

The highlight is the **Great Hall**, a wonderfully airy room decorated in blue, with a gallery overlooking the black and white checked floor. The rest of the house, some of which is still under reconstruction, boasts a profusion of tapestries, velvet drapes and plaster ornamentation on the staircases and ceilings. The gardens have retained their original 17th-century formal layout; the hedges and rows of trees intriguingly conceal the house from the river, lending an air of mystery and anticipated pleasure as you approach from the ferry stop.

Marble Hill House

Richmond Road, Twickenham; ☎ (020) 8892 5115; ⇌ St Margaret's; bus 490, 33, R70 from Richmond. Open April–Oct daily 10–6; Nov–Mar Wed–Sun 10–4; adm.

From the Twickenham side of Richmond Bridge you can enjoy a delightful mile-long walk along a stretch of the Thames that seems almost entirely rural. Marble Hill House is a simple white Palladian villa built in 1729 for Henrietta Howard, the 'exceedingly respectable and respected' mistress of George II. Henrietta could not stand the pressure of life at court, where she had to negotiate a tricky path between her lover and her influential husband, and so with a little help from the royal purse she set up home here, some 10 miles out of central London. The house is rather empty, having been neglected for 200 years and depleted of most of its furniture. But the park is open and very green, affording the broadest possible view of the river. A series of annual open-air concerts is staged here every summer; it is a delightful venue when the weather holds.

Also see: **Richmond Park**, p.117.
Onwards to: **Kew Gardens**, p.114; **Syon Park**, p.118.

➔ *Jubilee line (North Greenwich)*

⇌ *Greenwich (a bit off to the west) or Maze Hill (a bit off to the east) from Charing Cross, Cannon St and London Bridge.* **DLR** *to North Greenwich*
Bus *53 and 188 from Trafalagar Square and Waterloo*
By **boat** *from Charing Cross, Tower and Westminster Piers daily*

Greenwich has been a place of pleasure since the 15th century, when Henry V's brother, Duke Humphrey of Gloucester, built the first royal palace. While neighbouring districts like Deptford and Woolwich have always had to live by their wits and the hard graft of building and unloading ships, Greenwich has concentrated on **idle pleasures** like hunting and jousting, or rarefied pursuits like astronomy. Thanks to the contributions of Jones, Wren, Hawksmoor and Vanbrugh, it also boasts a remarkable **architectural** heritage, evident from the moment you look up from the ferry pier. It is an ensemble of great grace and proportion, which in recent years has spawned an **affluent** community of middle-class Londoners in fine Georgian houses up Crooms Hill or on the grassy verges of Greenwich Park and Blackheath.

Henry VIII was born at Greenwich and, after a boyhood spent jousting, hunting and attending balls, never lost affection for the place. Henry married his first wife, Catherine of Aragon, in the palace's private chapel and watched in frustration and rage as six of their seven children—four of them the boys he so desired—died here within a few weeks of their birth. The latter half of Henry's reign, when Hampton Court took over as the 'in' palace, saw a decline at Greenwich. Edward VI was sent here to convalesce in 1553. Queen Elizabeth I came here occasionally, and it was here that Sir Walter Ralegh magnanimously threw his cloak on a 'plashy place' (i.e. a puddle) so Her Majesty would not get her feet muddy. But it was the Stuarts who breathed new life into Greenwich with the fine buildings we see today.

The village is mobbed at weekends by bargain-hunters coming for the markets: crafts in the covered market off Nelson Road, and antiques, bric-a-brac, and vintage clothing around Stockwell Street.

Royal Naval College

King William Walk, on the site of the old Palace of Placentia. Open daily 10–4; free. The Pepys Building inside the college was home to the Millennium Visitors' Centre until Oct 1999 when the tourist information office moved there (open Mon–Fri 11–7, Sat–Sun 10–6).

Charles II's first thought when he restored the monarchy was to rebuild Placentia, but he didn't have the money and gave up soon after the foundation stone was laid. Queen Mary had another idea after she witnessed the terrible wounds inflicted on British sailors at the battle of La Hogue in 1692: she commissioned Christopher Wren to clear the ruins of the old palace and build a naval hospital in its place. Mary and Wren did not enjoy an altogether happy collaboration, since Mary insisted that the Queen's House should be visible from the river (something that was never the case when Placentia was still standing), and that the path of the Deptford to Woolwich road, which at the time ran through the middle of the building site, should be undisturbed. As a result, Wren and his successors, Hawksmoor and Vanbrugh, were obliged rather against their will to come up with a design based on four separate buildings, with its majestic neoclassical façades overlooking the river and pepper-pot towers at the back.

Cafés and Pubs

Bar du Musée, 17 Nelson Rd. French-style bar with a garden, good wines and a mellow ambience.

Spread Eagle, 2 Stockwell St. Small, plush, friendly restaurant serving delicious traditional English food, with a French twist. Good value menu.

Time Bar and Restaurant, 7a College Approach. This new sleek and spacious loft-style bar also functions as a gallery. The restaurant serves excellent modern British cuisine.

North Pole, 131 Greenwich High St. Fashionable bar and restaurant dishing up good modern European food to a cheerful crowd.

Peter's Café, 21 Greenwich Church St. Easygoing café serving cream teas, cakes and lunches. Tiny terrace.

Saigon, 16 Nelson Rd. Long-standing Vietnamese.

Goddard's Ye Old Pie House, 45 Greenwich Church St. Goddard's is a local haunt serving great pie and mash.

The hospital was eventually closed, and the Royal Naval College moved here in 1873. Now it houses the University of Greenwich. Only the chapel and Painted Hall are open to the public. The former is based on a design by Wren, but was entirely refurbished by James Stuart after a fire in 1779. It has an intricate plaster-moulded ceiling, and a fine painting of *St Paul at Melita* by Benjamin West above the altar. The **Painted Hall** is a magnificent ensemble of three rooms painted in opulent style by James Thornhill, the man who also decorated the cupola of St Paul's.

Queen's House and National Maritime Museum

Romney Road. Open daily 10–5; adm. Combined ticket for attractions available.

The **Queen's House** (undergoing repairs until late 1999) was Inigo Jones's first experiment in Palladian architecture after his return from Italy in 1615. James I's wife Anne of Denmark was the queen in question, who wanted her own private villa as an extension to the Palace of Placentia. For years after Anne's death in 1619 the house languished unfinished, but the project was taken up again by Queen Henrietta Maria in 1629. So happy was she with the final result, completed in 1640, that she nicknamed it her 'house of delights' and returned to live in it as the Queen Mother after the Restoration. The building is a textbook exercise in Palladian classicism—simple and sober on the outside, and full of 'licentious imaginacy', as Jones put it, on the inside. Much of the decay which the Queen's House suffered in the 18th and 19th centuries has been reversed, thanks to a recent restoration bringing the building back to something close to its 1660s state. The centrepiece is the **Great Hall**, a perfect 40ft cube immediately inside the main entrance with an elegant gallery at first floor level. Note the **Tulip Staircase** at the eastern end of the hall, a wrought-iron helix staircase which twists its way up to the Queen's Bedroom. This was the first open-well staircase to be built in England. The floral decorations on its banister are not tulips at all, but fleurs-de-lys.

The **National Maritime Museum** has recently reopened after a £40 million overhaul and is now the most up-to-date museum in the UK. A whole floor is devoted to interactive learning, ostensibly for kids, but everyone seems to enjoy shooting water pistols or blowing hair dryers at model ships. The courtyard has been glassed over to airily accommodate the larger exhibits: an enormous propellor, a container, even a yacht. Historical memorabilia, particularly that of Napolean's era, still features but the focus has shifted from past history to an engagingly energetic portrayal of the high-tech world of modern shipping.

Old Royal Observatory

Greenwich Park. Open daily 10–5; adm. Combined tickets for major attractions available. For the park itself, see p.111.

Greenwich is, of course, a time as well as a place; Greenwich Mean Time, as measured at this observatory, has synchronized the world's watches and guided the world's ships since 1884. The first two things you see on approaching the museum entrance are the metal plaque marking 0° longitude and, next to it, a large red ball on a stick that lowers every day at 1pm precisely as a symbol of the accuracy and universality of GMT.

Why Greenwich? First, because this was where England's first Astronomer Royal, John Flamsteed, decided to build his home and observatory in 1675. And secondly, because Flamsteed and his successors did more than anyone to solve the oldest navigational problem in the book: how to measure longitude. Measuring latitude was relatively easy, as it could be ascertained from the angle of the Pole Star to the horizon. But longitude was something else. Scientists knew what they needed: a dependable and portable watch or clock with which to work it out. But for anything other than the shortest journeys no such timepiece existed. In 1754, parliament issued a Longitude Act, offering a reward of £20,000 to the person who could crack the problem. The first proposals ranged from the sublime to the ridiculous. It was a Yorkshire clockmaker called John Harrison who eventually broke the impasse. He constructed his first marine clock in 1730 and continued perfecting it all his life; by the time he came up with the prize-winning model in 1772 he was 79 years old. Captain Cook took Harrison's clock to Australia and called it his 'trusty friend'. The museum takes the history of navigation and time up to the present, including the 1884 Washington conference that selected Greenwich as the Prime Meridian, and the invention of atomic clocks based on the nine billion vibrations per second of a caesium atom. The observatory itself is also worthy of note, particularly Flamsteed's original observatory, the **Octagon Room**, designed by Christopher Wren.

The *Cutty Sark* and the *Gipsy Moth IV*

On the quay by the ferry pier; open daily 10–5; adm. Combined tickets for major attractions available.

Much is made of the *Cutty Sark* as the last of the great tea clippers that plied the route from England to the Far East. Built in 1869, it was certainly one of the fastest sailboats of its time, winning the annual clippers' race in 1871. Its commercial usefulness was rather limited, however, since steam ships soon took over the bulk of maritime trade, and the opening of the Suez Canal took a lot of the time pressure off merchant vessels. The greatest pleasure afforded by the *Cutty Sark* now is its magnificent gilded teak fittings, the rigging on its three masts and its fine collection of figureheads and other maritime memorabilia. The name, by the way, comes from Robert Burns's poem 'Tam O'Shanter', in which a witch called Nellie is described as wearing only a *cutty sark*, a corruption of the French *courte chemise*, or short shirt. You'll notice the female figurehead on the prow is dressed in this manner. Next to the Cutty Sark, the *Gipsy Moth IV* was the ketch in which the British mariner Sir Francis Chichester made his solo round-the-world voyage in 1966–7, completing the trip in nine months and one day.

Also see: **Greenwich Park**, p.111; **Fan Museum**, p.140; **Dome**, p.38.
Onwards to: **Docklands**, p.94.

London: Green Spaces

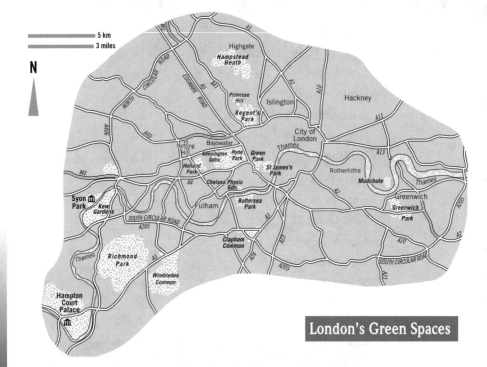

London's Green Spaces

Battersea Park

≥ *Battersea Park (from Victoria), Queenstown Road (from Waterloo)*
⊖ *Vauxhall and then bus 344 or 44;* ⊖ *Sloane Square and then bus 19 or 49*

Battersea Park is an all-action activity centre with a café, children's zoo, tennis courts, a bowling green and a running track. Although opened by Queen Victoria in 1853, the park really came into its own in 1951 when it was one of the centrepieces of the Festival of Britain. Near the boating lake at the southern end is a Henry Moore statue entitled ***Three Standing Figures***. Near the river, about two-thirds of the way over towards Albert Bridge, is the **Battersea Peace Pagoda**, built by a group of Japanese Buddhist monks in 1985 and now one of London's most distinctive riverside landmarks.

Chelsea Physic Garden

✆ *(020) 7352 5646; Cheyne Walk; enter from the back on Swan Walk. Open April–Oct Wed 2–5 and Sun 2–6; adm.*
⊖ *Sloane Square then a walk: Lower Sloane St, and left down to the end of Royal Hospital Road.*

This wonderfully unusual garden of rare trees, plants, herbs and seeds has a history stretching back to 1676 when it was founded by the Apothecaries' Company. Some of England's first cedar trees were cultivated here in the 1680s and the hardiest of them lasted until 1903. In the 1730s the Physic Garden sent out the seeds that allowed James Oglethorpe, the colonist of

Georgia, to sow the southern United States' first cotton fields. Among the wonders still visible today are the world's first rock garden, built in 1772 with old bits of stone from the Tower of London, a Chinese willow pattern tree, and a 30ft-high olive tree that once produced seven pounds of olives in a season (something of a miracle in rainy old England). The statue in the garden is of Sir Hans Sloane, the physician and philanthropist who saved the gardens from bankruptcy in 1722. Sir Hans owned large tracts of Chelsea (hence the number of streets named after him) and built up a huge collection of art and antiquities that were bequeathed to the nation after his death and provided the foundation of the **British Museum** (*see* p.29).

Also see: **Chelsea and the King's Road**, p.92.

Green Park

☻ *Green Park, Hyde Park Corner*
Bus 8, 9, 14, 19, 22, 38

This pleasantly undulating expanse, which is green all year round, has much the same history as St James's Park (*see* p.117). It was originally a burial ground for Queen Matilda's lepers (and, in deference to the dead beneath it, has never been planted with flowers). Henry VIII made it a royal park, and Charles II laid out its walkways. Green Park, like its neighbour, was a haunt of troublemakers and duellists in the 18th century. On one occasion, Count Alfieri returned to the nearby Haymarket Theatre for the last act of a play after sustaining a duelling wound to his arm from Lord Ligonier, his mistress's husband. Deckchairs can be hired and you can pop next door to tea at the Ritz (*see* p.158).

Also see: **Buckingham Palace**, p.32.

Greenwich Park

≈ *Greenwich*
☻ *North Greenwich*
DLR to Island Gardens and then foot tunnel to Greenwich.

The park, along with Blackheath beyond, was the hunting ground that attracted Duke Humphrey to Greenwich back in the 15th century. It has been tamed considerably since then, particularly under Charles II who hired the great French landscape gardener André Le Nôtre, of Versailles fame, to help lay it out anew in the 1660s. There is no evidence Le Nôtre ever visited the site for himself; indeed to judge from the way the park falls away abruptly at the bottom it looks as though he didn't even realize it was on a hill. It is nevertheless an elegant place, unusually continental in its formality. Sadly, the deer that used to roam freely are confined to The Wilderness on the southeastern edge; they were isolated after a 19th-century stroller was gored and killed during the rutting season. On Chesterfield Walk, just beyond Croomshill Gate is **Ranger's House** (*open daily 9–1 and 2–6, earlier closing in winter*), an elegant mansion dating from 1699 which is no longer the residence of the park ranger but instead holds a collection of musical instruments and 17th-century portraits. On the opposite side of the park, at 121 Maze Hill, is the eccentric **Vanbrugh Castle**, where the eponymous architect lived for six years until his death in 1725. It is not open to the public.

Right in the centre of the park is a **statue of General Wolfe**, who died fighting the French in Quebec in 1759 and is buried at St Alfege's. Note the shrapnel scars, and then look out across the Thames: you quickly appreciate what a perfect bombing route towards the Docklands this was for German aircraft during the Blitz. The **Old Royal Observatory** (see p.108) is next to the statue.

Also see: **Greenwich**, p.106.

Hampstead Heath

➤ *Hampstead Heath, Gospel Oak*
⊖ *Hampstead, Belsize Park*
Bus 24 from Trafalgar Square, 268, C11

Hampstead Heath is so big and wild you can easily feel you are lost in the deep heart of the English countryside, yet there are amazing views over London. At the top (north) end is the superbly located, unpretentious white neoclassical **Kenwood House** (*see* p.103), famous for its idyllic summer concerts held by the lake at the bottom of the garden; the orchestra sits under a white awning and the audience watches from across the water. The hill down from Kenwood leads to **Highgate Ponds**, a series of open-air pools segregated by sex to encourage nude bathing. The ladies' pool, discreetly hidden behind some thick bushes, is nearest the top just off Millfield Lane; the men's pools are alongside the path nearer Highgate Road. Right down at the bottom of the Heath, should you stray that far, is **Parliament Hill**, site of an ancient barrow where the rebel queen Boudicca (Boadicea) is rumoured to have been buried. The view from the hill, no more than a bump compared to the heights of Kenwood, is rather disappointing, but the wind the site attracts is ideal for kite flying.

Also see: **Hampstead**, p.102.

Highgate Cemetery

⊖ *Archway, Highgate*
Bus 271, 210

To reach the entrance to the cemetery, start in Highgate High Street and turn right down the steep narrow hill called Swains Lane. At the bottom there are patches of gravel on either side of the road. To the right is the grand arched entrance to the western cemetery (open for guided tours only, usually every two hours during the afternoon, ✆ (020) 8340 1834; adm), and to the left is the more mundane iron grille leading to the eastern cemetery (open daily 10–5, closes at 4 in the winter; free).

Highgate Cemetery has been a tourist attraction ever since it opened in 1839, both for its magnificent funereal Victorian architecture and for its views. 'In such a place the aspect of death is softened,' wrote the *Lady's Newspaper* in 1850. The **western side** is the older and more splendid of the two halves, a maze of winding paths leading to an avenue of mock-Egyptian columns and obelisks, and a hemicycle of tombs around a cedar of Lebanon. Winding roads and footpaths lead up to the so-called Egyptian Avenue, which you enter through an arch flanked with obelisks and mock-Egyptian columns. The avenue leads beneath a bridge to the Circle of Lebanon, a complex of tombs constructed on each side of a circular path with a magnificent cedar tree in the middle. The spire of St Michael's parish church looms above at the top of Swain's Lane. The guide will point out the eminent dead occupying these hallowed tombs; they include the chemist Michael Faraday and the poet Christina Rossetti.

The **eastern cemetery**, which opened in 1857 to cope with the overload of coffins from across the road, is altogether wilder and spookier (it features in Bram Stoker's *Dracula*) where the cracked tombstones are covered in creepers and ivy. Here you can roam around at will. Most people head straight for the large black bust of Karl Marx marking the place where the much-maligned philosopher was buried in 1883. The eastern cemetery contains a sprinkling of other left-wing revolutionaries, mainly from the Third World, plus the remains of novelist Mary Ann Evans (a.k.a. George Eliot) and the radical conservative thinker Herbert Spencer who died in 1903.

Holland Park

⊖ *Holland Park, High Street Kensington*
Bus 94 (north side) from Oxford Street and Piccadilly, 9, 10, 49, 27 (south side)
Open daily 7.30am until half an hour before sunset. The best way to enter is through the wooded northern end. Take Holland Walk, a path opposite Holland Park Underground station, and look out for the first turning into the park, which is on the right after about 300 yards.

Holland Park turns reality on its head: it seems much bigger, much wilder, much more remote than it really is. Covering only about 40 acres (a fraction of the size of Kensington Gardens, for example), it feels like something out of a magical children's story, a maze of winding paths, wooded hideaways, rolling fields and formal gardens, wild flowers and birds. The park is what remains of the estate of **Holland House**, a grand Jacobean mansion devastated during the Second World War, which survives only in truncated form, about two-thirds of the way down towards Kensington High Street. You can see some of the ground-floor stonework of the original building, but little else. The east wing has been entirely rebuilt as a **youth hostel** (a wonderful place to stay if you are a student, *see* p.168), while part of the ruined main house has been converted into an open-air theatre with an summer season of opera (*see* p.173).

Around the house to the north is a series of formal gardens, all different in style, including the peaceful **Kyoto Garden** with its still lake, lawns lined with gentle blooms, and a square Elizabethan-style herb garden. On the south side is a calm terrace **café** overlooking a cricket pitch and tennis courts. Wild woodland areas surround the park on its outer edges. Wherever you walk, you will be startled by wild rabbits and peacocks and begged at by almost tame squirrels used to tourists and their sandwiches. Take nuts if you don't want to feel guilty.

Also see: **Leighton House**, p.134.

Hyde Park

⊖ *Hyde Park Corner, Marble Arch, Lancaster Gate, Knightsbridge*
Bus 12, 94 (north side), 9, 10, 52 (south side), 10, 2, 16, 36, 73, 74, 82 (east side)

Hyde Park is a remarkably large expanse of greenery for the centre of a big city. This end is rather hilly and open, giving views of the posh hotels along Park Lane up to Marble Arch. There are more trees towards Kensington Gardens, as the stretch beyond the Serpentine lake is known. **Rotten Row** is the sandy horse path running along the southern edge. Its name is a corruption of the French *route du roi* (royal road).

Hyde Park started out as part of the Westminster Abbey estate, a breeding ground for deer, boar and wild bulls. When Henry VIII dissolved the monasteries, he decided to keep it as a private hunting ground; it was not opened to the public until the beginning of the 17th century. William III hung lamps along Rotten Row to deter highwaymen while he made his way from Kensington Palace to St James's, instituting the idea of street-lighting in London. The park was a favourite hang-out for crooks of all kinds, and even George II was once robbed of his purse, watch and buckles while out walking. In the course of the 18th century it also became London's most popular duelling ground.

In 1730 Queen Caroline created the **Serpentine** by having the underground Westbourne river dammed. The L-shaped lake is still the park's most prominent feature, famous for its New Year's Day swims which are open to anyone foolhardy enough to jump into the cold (sometimes freezing) winter water (some years the swimmers have to break the ice before they start). The Serpentine has provided the focus for many other events, from funfairs to political demonstrations. The northeastern end of Hyde Park remains the only place in Britain where demonstrators can assemble without police permission, a concession made in 1872 in a truce between the Metropolitan Police and a succession of angry demonstrators. The spot is known as **Speaker's Corner**, and every Sunday afternoon you can hear impassioned crackpots droning on for hours about the moral turpitude of the world. Despite the fame of Speaker's Corner, it is hardly an impressive symbol of free speech. Microphones are banned, and most of the words are drowned out by the traffic on Park Lane. Nobody takes the place seriously, particularly in this media-saturated era. You can talk all you like, Speakers' Corner says; just make sure nobody can hear you.

Kensington Gardens

⊖ Queensway, Bayswater, Lancaster Gate, High Street Kensington
Bus 12, 94 (north side) 9, 10, 52 (south side)

The Serpentine divides Hyde Park from the westerly Kensington Gardens, originally the grounds of Kensington Palace (*see* p.37) with its **Round Pond** where you can play with model boats. George Frampton's famous statue of **Peter Pan** is by the lakeside towards the Bayswater Road. On the south side of the park, just behind the Albert Memorial (*see* p.28), is an attractive area of bushes and flowering plants known as the **Flower Walk**, and near the Serpentine is the **Serpentine Gallery**, famous for its shows of modern art. On summer weekends the park throngs with locals on rollerblades and playing ballgames.

Kew Gardens

⊖ Kew Gardens
⇌ Kew Bridge (from Waterloo)
Bus 391 from West Kensington, 190 from West Brompton

℡ (020) 8940 1171; www.kew.org. Gardens open 9.30–dusk; adm. The glasshouses and other buildings open at 9.30 as well but close at 5.30. Guided tours in the summer at 11am. There are several entrances to Kew Gardens, the most useful being the Victoria Gate on Kew Road, where guidebooks and free leaflets are available at the visitor centre and shop. Take sturdy shoes as there are around 300 acres of gardens to explore. Pick up a free map at Queen Victoria Gate, which will locate all the major sites for you. It is also colour coded for easier use.

For the visitor, Kew is a place of many wonders: 38,000 different plant species, some of them entirely extinct in the wild; vast glasshouses, historic houses and buildings and, above all, acres and acres of beautifully tended parkland, some of it wonderfully wild and remote, with views up and down the Thames. All year round, Kew provides a glorious array of colours: flowering cherries and crocuses in spring; roses and tulip trees in summer; belladonna lilies, heather and darkening leaves in autumn; strawberry trees and witch hazels in winter.

The Royal Botanical Gardens at Kew have always been more than a collection of trees, flowers and plants; they are more like a giant vegetable laboratory, sucking up new information about the botanical world and, through the power of their research, influencing the course of human history in all sorts of unexpected ways. In the 19th century, Kew's laboratories first isolated quinine and, realizing it was an efficient natural antidote to malaria, recommended putting it in the tonic water with which the colonial administrators of India and Malaya diluted their gin. Kew was also involved in the development of commercial rubber and helped produce artificial fibres like rayon and acetate. It is now actively researching plant substances for the treatment of AIDS. In these days of receding rainforests and dwindling numbers of species of all kinds, Kew also does vital work in cataloguing and preserving plant types and developing new, genetically engineered hybrids that stand a better chance of survival in the wild.

In the 18th century, Kew was part of the royal estates that stretched down as far as Richmond. Princess Augusta, the mother of George III, first had the idea of laying a botanical garden in the grounds of **Kew Palace** where she lived. This elegantly gabled two-storey Jacobean mansion (*open April–Sept daily 11–5.30 only; separate adm*) so endeared itself to George II and his wife Queen Caroline a generation before Augusta that they leased it for 99 years, for 'the rent of £100 and a fat doe'. The botanical garden was at first of only incidental importance to Kew; George III spent his energies commissioning a series of follies and outhouses from the architect William Chambers. These included three pseudo-classical temples, a ruined Roman arch, the handsome Wren-like Orangery, and—most striking of all—the **Pagoda**. Chambers took his inspiration for this 10-storey octagonal tower from a visit to China in his youth. When finished in 1762, it was the most accurate rendering of Chinese architecture in Europe—although to be truly accurate it should have had an odd number of storeys.

The botanical garden began to grow thanks to the enthusiasm of its keeper, Sir Joseph Banks, who organized Kew's first foreign plant-hunting expeditions and set about cultivating rare species. Banks's was nevertheless a small-scale enterprise, and Kew did not really take off until 1840 when it was handed over from the royal family to the state, opened to the public and expanded to more than 200 acres. The first director of the new public gardens, Sir William Hooker, put Kew on a firm scientific and research footing. Hooker's most lasting architectural influence was to commission two great glasshouses from Decimus Burton. The **Palm House** (1844–8) is a wondrous structure of curvilinear iron and glass, with a two-storey dome as its centrepiece. The **Temperate House**, built in the early 1860s and modified right up to 1898, is far bigger but more conventional in structure, using straight panes and iron rods to achieve its great height and width.

William Hooker's son Joseph took over as director in 1865 and established the **Jodrell Laboratory** to enhance Kew's research credentials. He also encouraged a young artist called Marianne North to set up a special gallery to display her collection of 832 botanical paintings based on her travels around the globe between 1871 and 1885 (left of Victoria Gate).

In this century, a number of new glasshouses have been added to the park, including the **Princess of Wales Conservatory**, containing Kew's collection of tropical herbaceous plants not least of which the incredible Titan Arum, which at two metres high is one of the largest flowers in the world. The newly refurbished **Museum No.1** contains Kew's fascinating 'Plants + People' exhibition of wood and plant materials which have been made into useful materials for man—a 200-year-old shirt made out of pineapple fibres, from the Caribbean, and an incredible collection of Japanese lacquer boxes.

Regent's Park and London Zoo

> ✆ *Baker St (for the boating lake and theatre), Regent's Park (for the theatre), Great Portland St (for the theatre), Mornington Crescent, Camden Town (for the zoo). Bus C2 from Oxford Circus (for east side), 13, 82, 113 and 274 (for west side).*

Regent's Park is the most ornate of London's open spaces, a delightful mixture of icing-sugar terraces, wildlife, lakes and broad expanses of greenery. It is the most rigorously planned of London's parks, the brainchild of George IV's favourite architect, John Nash, who conceived it as a landscaped estate on which to build several dozen pleasure palaces for the aristocracy. It was meant to be the culmination of a vast city rebuilding project, of which the centrepiece was Regent Street. Nash's dreams of a new London, endowing the city with a full sense of aristocratic majesty, were tempered by a succession of objections and financial problems; Regent's Park, however, perhaps comes closest to embodying the spirit of his plans. His stuccoed terraces around the perimeter of the park are at once imposing and playful; the handful of grand mansions inside the park exude the same air of nonchalant, summery elegance as the hunting villas and parks on the outskirts of central Rome; the park itself is beautifully manicured, giving it a curious air of exclusivity even though it is open to all; most delightfully, for the visitor, it is remarkably empty.

Within the Inner Circle of the park is **Queen Mary's Rose Garden**, a magnificent array of flowers and plants of all kinds. At the north end is the **Open Air Theatre** *(open May–Sept, ✆ (020) 7486 2431)*, a magical sylvan setting for summer productions of *A Midsummer Night's Dream* and *As You Like It*. On the west side of the Inner Circle (find the path next to the open air theatre) is the **Boating Lake**, a wonderfully romantic stretch of water where you can rent boats of all kinds for a balmy summer afternoon's idle dreaming.

London Zoo

> *London Zoo ✆ (020) 7722 3333; open April–Oct 10–5.30, Nov–Mar 10–4; adm exp.*

The Zoological Gardens in Regent's Park were where the term 'zoo' originated. The abbreviation, which first surfaced in the late 1860s, was immortalized in a music-hall song of the time beginning: 'Walking in the zoo is the OK thing to do'. In these post-colonial, animally correct times, zoos are not quite as OK as they used to be. But London Zoo has responded to debate about its role with some energy. The **Bear Mountain**, once horribly overcrowded and a place of abject misery, has been redeveloped, and houses just two bears. The delightful new **Children's Zoo** is built entirely out of sustainable materials, with a Camel House whose roof is planted with wild flowers and grass seed, a wonderful touch paddock, barn, and pet care centre. A new Lottery-funded **Conservation Centre**, with exhibitions explaining eco systems and animal diversity, opened in mid-1998.

One of the attractions of visiting the zoo now is the fine array of well-designed animal houses—the penguin pool by Lubetkin and Tecton (1936), Lord Snowdon's spectacular polygonal aviary (1964), Hugh Casson's elephant and rhino pavilion (1965) or the recently built Macaw Aviary. On your way round you will be invited to 'adopt' any animal that takes your particular fancy. Pay £20 for an exotic breed of cockroach, £6,000 for an elephant, or £30 for a part share in *any* animal, and you are assured the beast will be fed and nurtured for a year. Your name will also go on a plaque beside the animal's enclosure—you'll see plenty of these already in place.

Richmond Park

↔ *Richmond*
Bus 65 and 391, 337

At 2470 acres, Richmond is the largest urban park in Britain and one of the least spoiled in London. A few medieval oaks survive, as do many of the varieties of wildlife that medieval royal parties would have hunted. The deer are what make Richmond Park famous—around 350 fallow deer and 250 red deer, which do so well in the heart of London that there is an annual cull—but there are also hares, rabbits and weasels. In addition Richmond Park has two ponds for anglers, five cricket pitches, two golf courses, no fewer than 24 football grounds and numerous cycle paths.

At the top of Richmond Hill near the park entrance is the **Star and Garter Home**, once a humble tavern which rose to be one of the most fashionable addresses in outer London. Its Assembly Room was the setting for many a 19th-century wedding reception, and its modest bedrooms housed everyone from common wayfarers to continental royalty. In the 1860s the tavern was revamped as an imitation French Renaissance chateau, a project as unpopular as it was extravagant, and one that led to the establishment's demise at the turn of the 20th century. Used as a hostel for disabled soldiers after the First World War, it is now an old people's home. Few can enjoy its enviable views over Richmond and the river; it, however, is all too visible for a mile or more in each direction along the Thames towpath.

Also see: **Richmond**, p.104.

St James's Park

↔ *St James's Park*
bus (to Whitehall): 3, 11, 12, 24, 53, 77A, 88, 109

The dreamy expanse of St James's Park explains much about the spirit of the neighbourhood. Certainly it seems perfectly spruce nowadays, even rather romantic in a restrained sort of way, with its tree-lined pond and proliferation of city wildlife; but its elegance is a cunning artifice created to overcome centuries of turbulence and squalor.

Back in the early 12th century, Queen Matilda founded a women's leper colony on the site of what is now St James's Palace. By the mid-15th century leprosy had subsided and the hospital was turned into a special kind of nunnery; special because its young occupants were better known for administering to the flesh rather than to the spirit of the eminent men who called on them.

These so-called *bordels du roi* were closed by Henry VIII, who built St James's Palace in their place and drained the marsh to create a nursery for his deer. The first formal gardens were laid out under James I, who installed, among other things, an aviary (hence the name of the street on the south side, Birdcage Walk) and a menagerie of wild beasts including two crocodiles. The setting was romantic enough for Charles II to use it as a rendezvous with his mistress, Nell Gwynne; unfortunately it also attracted upper-class hooligans in search of both trouble and rumpy-pumpy with the local whores.

In 1672 Lord Rochester described the park as a place of 'buggeries, rapes and incest', a state of affairs not improved even after a decree issued by Queen Anne banning dogs, hogs, menials, beggars and 'rude boys' from the premises. James Boswell lost his virginity to a whore in St James's Park on 20 March 1763, an experience which brought him 'but a dull satisfaction'. It was only under George IV that the park developed its present dignity. George landscaped the lake as we see it today and added gas lighting to deter the ladies of the night. The sex-crazed aristocrat gave way to an altogether gentler breed, the birdwatcher, as St James's filled with more than 30 ornithological species. Look out for the pelicans, ducks, geese and gulls which have made the lake their home.

Also see: **St James's and Royal London**, p.76.

Syon Park

London Road, Isleworth, with another entrance off Park Road near the riverfront.

Open April–Sept Wed–Sun 11–4.15; Oct–Dec Sun 11–4.15; gardens open 10– dusk daily; adm.

Across the river from Kew Gardens, officially in Isleworth, is Syon Park, not so much a stately home as a kind of theme park *à l'anglaise*. Here in the large if rather empty park stretching down to the river are a butterfly house, a vintage car museum and a gardening centre housed beneath an impressive Victorian domed conservatory made of gunmetal and Portland stone.

The house itself, built in crenellated stone around a quadrangle, was once part of a monastery, but was seized by Henry VIII for his own private use after his break with the Roman church. He locked up his fifth wife, Catherine Howard, in Syon House before her execution on adultery charges; a few years later the gods got their revenge when a band of dogs discovered the half-open coffin containing Henry's remains and chewed on them all night long. Since 1594 Syon Park has belonged to the Percy family, holders of the Duchy of Northumberland. At first they let it slowly decline, but then in 1762 Robert Adam was commissioned to rework the interior, and the landscape architect Capability Brown was set to work on the grounds.

The house is particularly successful, using only the bare bones of the original structure to create a sumptuous classical atmosphere. The highlights are the Great Hall, which makes up for the unevenness of the floor with a series of small steps embellished with Doric columns, and the anteroom, which has a lavishly gilded plasterwork ceiling and a multicoloured marble floor. Osbert Sitwell once said this room was 'as superb as any Roman interior in the palaces of the Caesars'.

London: Shopping

LIBERTY

London...a kind of emporium for the whole earth.

Joseph Addison

London has been a cosmopolitan place to shop since the Romans traded their pottery and olive oil for cloth, furs and gold back in the 1st century AD. Until comparatively recently the best shopping was for the rich, channelled through prestigious department stores such as Harrods, or smaller establishments in St James's and South Kensington offering exceptional service and attention to detail. The Carnaby Street spirit of the 1960s changed that, and now you can find cheap clothes and jewellery, unusual music and exotic food all over town in flea markets and gaily coloured shops. Carnaby Street itself, regrettably, has long since sold its soul to the cause of tourist kitsch, but you will find its successors in Covent Garden, down the King's Road, around Notting Hill and at Camden Lock market.

A note on VAT: if you leave Britain for a non-EU country within six months of arriving, you are entitled to a refund on the Value Added Tax, or VAT, that you have paid on any goods you have bought from shops displaying a 'tax free for tourists' sign. You must pick up a form in the shop where you make your purchase, and then hand it in at the airport when you leave the country. Since the rate of VAT is 17.5 per cent, this is well worth the hassle, especially with larger items.

Opening hours: Traditionally, shops stay open from around 9 to 5.30 or 6—significantly earlier than the rest of Europe. Late opening for shops is becoming more and more common, however, particularly on Wednesdays and Thursdays, and Sunday trading is much more flexible than in the past: areas like Queensway and the Edgware Road, Hampstead, Greenwich, Tottenham Court Road and most of the Oxford Street department stores are worth visiting.

Oxford Street

Oxford Street is forever packed with shoppers and tourists, for whom its wide pavements and large department stores symbolize the very essence of the big city. This rather puzzling mystique is not really borne out by the reality, which is impersonal, uniform and unremittingly grey. In 1825 John Wilson Croker called Oxford Street 'thou lengthy street of ceaseless din', and the description still applies; even if cars have been banned during the daytime, there is still plenty of noise from the zillions of buses and taxis.

The most prestigious address, a few blocks off to the right beyond Duke Street, is **Selfridge's**, which for sheer size and range of goods is the closest rival in London to Harrods. The other department stores such as Debenhams, D. H. Evans and **John Lewis**, and outsize outlets of high street regulars like **Marks & Spencer**, River Island and The Gap, are not as much fun (or as cheap) as the specialist shops dotted around more intimate parts of London, but they do offer a one-stop shopping day. Most are open Sunday, except John Lewis.

Off and behind Oxford Street are a few side streets with interesting small stores: at the Selfridge's/Bond Street end try walking down **South Molton Street, Davies Street, St Christopher's Place, James Street, Duke Street** and **Wigmore Street,** and past Oxford Circus there's **Great Portland Street** and **Argyll Street,** and pedestrianized **Carnaby Street,** which bears no traces of its 1960s heyday but still has some odd little one-offs and its own array of even tinier side alleys.

Selfridge's, 400 Oxford St. Classic department store. There are also perfume and make-up demonstrations and a travel agents in the basement.

Marks & Spencer, 458 Oxford St and branches all over London. Suppliers of cheap, comfortable clothes and underwear to the nation—and the world. Don't overlook the food section, either, with excellent pre-prepared dishes and stunningly good ice cream that beats Haägen Dazs for both quality and price.

John Lewis, Oxford Street. With its slogan 'Never knowingly undersold', this cheerful and efficient department store promises to refund the difference if you find anything cheaper elsewhere. Well-stocked departments of household goods and accessories, and for decades one of London's largest retailers of dressmaking and furnishing fabrics and haberdashery. *Not open Sundays.*

Borders, 197 Oxford St. Huge branch of the US book and music shop, with readings, performances and a coffee shop. *Open till 11pm and on Sundays.*

H. R. Higgins, 79 Duke St. Purveyor of fine coffee to Her Majesty the Queen. Evokes the atmosphere of the old Jacobean coffee houses.

South Molton Drug Store, 64 South Molton St. Cheap end-of-line cosmetics.

Electrum Gallery, 21 South Molton St. Classic jewellery from around the world—at a price.

Browns, 23–7 South Molton St. Centre of a burgeoning empire of fashion shops along this bijou pedestrian street off Oxford Street. Lots of famous labels, not all of them unaffordable.

Vivienne Westwood, 6 Davies St. The punk queen of British fashion offers real clothes as well as eccentric pieces of tailoring art.

Gray's Antique Markets, 58 Davies St. An enclosed antiques market with over 200 dealers in a large Victorian building. Mainly silverware, glassware, jewellery, toys, ancient artefacts and china. Some odder stalls, such as Wheels of Steel model train sets stall or Pete McAskie's Dinky toys. The Thimble Society of London is a stall dedicated to antique and modern thimbles.

James Smith and Sons, 53 New Oxford St. Fend off the British weather with a trip to this Victorian shop dedicated to umbrellas. Also stocks walking sticks, often with carved handles.

Sonico, 47 Oxford St. Jeans galore at competitive prices.

NikeTown, Oxford Circus. Supermodel sports shop full of loud music, encouraging slogans ('Life is a Verb') and weird sculptures.

TopShop, Oxford Circus. Haven of cheap trendy gear for style-obsessed but cash-poor teenage girls.

A. K. Mowbrays, 28 Margaret St (basement of Waterstone's). Excellent religious bookshop.

Forbidden Planet, 71 New Oxford St. The best sci-fi bookshop around.

Muji, 26 Carnaby St and 187 Oxford St. Minimalist Japanese paper, fabric, fashion and edible goods.

Lush, 40 Carnaby St. You can smell this shop from yards away! Handmade soaps and toiletries using only natural ingredients.

Storm, 21 Carnaby St and 6 Gees Court. Unusual modern watches as well as fashion, sunglasses, lava lamps and so on.

Cerex, 11 Carnaby Street St. Inexpensive young-style shoes.

Octopus, 28 Carnaby Street St. All kinds of gifts and gimmicks: lamps made of brightly coloured rubber, bags with holograms on, glasses mounted on toy cars. Great fun.

Regent Street

Regent Street was once the finest street in London, although you might not think so to look at it now. In fact, all it boasts are a few fine shops (particularly men's clothes stores), the new *Cheers* theme-u-rant (at 72 Regent Street, overpriced and depressingly anonymous) and some rather stuffy, impersonal buildings livened up just once a year by the overhead display of electric Christmas decorations.

One address that has not changed too much is the **Café Royal** at No.68. If you're feeling tired, this is a good stopping off point for a cocktail or afternoon tea from 3–5pm.

Liberty, Regent St. A labyrinth of a store with warm wooden interiors. Famous for print scarves, also good for fashion, china, rugs and glass.

Dickins and Jones, Regent St. Department store for counties matrons. Very strong on cosmetics.

Aquascutum, 100 Regent St. Raincoats, cashmere scarves and endless sober suits. Clothes to last, not look hip in.

Boosey and Hawkes, 295 Regent St. Classical music.

Crabtree and Evelyn, 239 Regent St. Herbs and fruit scents, all beautifully packaged. Ideal for gift-hunting.

L'Occitane, 237 Regent St. Provençal herbs and fruit scents, also all beautifully packaged. Also ideal for gift-hunting.

Teddy Bear Shop, 153 Regent St, W1. Sells handmade (English) teddy bears. Traditional ones as well as more modern varieties.

Hamley's, 188 Regent St. London's biggest toy emporium.

Zara, Regent St. Stylish Spanish fashion store chain.

Grant & Cutler, 55–7 Great Marlborough St, off Regent Street. Uneven, but nevertheless the best bookshop in London for obscure and not so obscure foreign-language books.

The European Bookshop, 5 Warwick St, off Regent St. Makes up for Grant and Cutler's deficiencies, especially in French literature in which it excels.

Bond Street

Two kinds of shopkeeper dominate Bond Street: jewellers and art dealers, whose gaudy if not always particularly attractive shop fronts make for a diverting stroll. **Old Bond Street**, the lower part of the thoroughfare, concentrates mainly on jewellery and includes all the well-known international names including **Tiffany's** at No.25 and **Chatila** at No.22.

At the top of Albermarle St is the ultimate shop for country gents, **Asprey's**, whose windows are packed with rifles, shooting sticks and waders. If you walk through the shop to the Bond Street side you can also enjoy its extraordinary collection of military jewellery, including tanks and fighter jets made of gold and silver.

New Bond Street is famous for the showrooms of art dealers like Bernard Jacobson and Le Fevre (or, round the corner on Cork Street, Waddington and Victoria Miro). **Sotheby's,** the famous auctioneers, are at Nos. 34–5 New Bond Street.

Fenwick's, New Bond St. One of the more old-fashioned, very English, traditional department stores, strong on accessories and women's clothes.

Church's, 163 New Bond St. Solid, sober shoes to last half a lifetime.

Miu Miu, 123 New Bond St. The funkier offspring of Prada.

Calvin Klein, 55 New Bond St. (opposite Miu Miu). Famous for jeans, underwear and scents.

Donna Karan, 20 New Bond St. and **DKNY**, 27 Old Bond St. Trendy streetwear for women. DKNY includes a café.

Mulberry, 41 New Bond St. Traditional high-quality bags and leather goods, stamped with the recognizable mulberry tree symbol.

Yves Saint Laurent, 137 New Bond St.

Hermès, 155 New Bond St. Source of the famous scarves and accessories.

Louis Vuitton, 17 New Bond St. The famous monogrammed bags are back in trend.

Smithson, Stylish stationery for the swish set; uninspired designs but good quality paper, and fountain pens that will last a lifetime.

Bulgari, 172 New Bond St. Top Italian jewellery.

Chanel, 173 New Bond St for jewellery and 26 Old Bond Street for everything else.

The Spy Shop, 26 Conduit St. Everything you need for surveillance!

Tottenham Court Road

As late as the 1870s, cows grazed along this road which is now all too crowded with traffic. Its main attractions are its furniture stores—**Heals** (very classy and upmarket), **Habitat** (cheaper but duller) and shop after anonymous shop specializing in sofa beds and futons—and its **discount computer and hi-fi** shops. Visit plenty of shops, ask to see write-ups in the trade magazines to back up the recommendations and haggle the price down as far as you can. North Americans will find prices rather high, but Europeans will be astounded at how cheap everything is. Most shops open Sundays. Only a couple of specific addresses to recommend:

Habitat, 196 Tottenham Court Rd. Everything for the house, from glasses and corkscrews to fitted cabinets. Cheap and practical.

Heal's, 196 Tottenham Court Rd. Up-market sister to Habitat, with innovative designs.

Hi-fi Care, 245 Tottenham Court Rd. Accessories shop. Very useful for extension cords, speaker cable and all those other things you can't usually find.

Charing Cross Road

Charing Cross Road is the traditional centre of the London **book** trade, although the pressure of high rents is pushing many original establishments out into other areas. The once-gentlemanly publishing and book trade has become something of a cut-throat environment. Stores no longer stock the eclectic range of titles that they once did, preferring to focus on titles they know will sell in large numbers. On the plus side, many assistants still give expert advice on titles and subjects. Browsing is not only tolerated, it is welcomed.

The most famous bookshop on the street is **Foyle's**, at No.119. Don't be deluded by its reputation, however, which dates from the inter-war years: inside it is a chaotic, antiquated mess. Foyle's fame largely rests on the boast that you can find any book at all on its well-thumbed shelves. Sure you can, as long as you have about 36 hours to spare and the patience of a saint.

The modern chains just down the road, **Books Etc** and **Waterstone's**, are far more efficient general stores. Charing Cross Road's charm, however, lies in higgledy-piggledy secondhand bookshops such as **Quinto** (think *84 Charing Cross Road*) or its specialist shops. Collet's, the celebrated left-wing bookshop at No.66 where radicals lectured on revolution in the 1930s, went bankrupt in 1993. However, the expensive art bookshop **Zwemmer's**, at Nos.76–80, is still going and so are places like the **Silver Moon Women's Bookshop** at No.64–8 and small specialist bookshops come and go.

Waterstones, 121–5 Charing Cross Rd and many branches. Probably the best chain overall, with an outstanding selection at every branch.

Books Etc, 120 Charing Cross Rd and many branches. The most commercial of the quality chains, but strong on crime fiction and film screenplays. Charing Cross Rd has a permanent bargain basement.

Travellers' Bookshop, 25 Cecil Court, off Charing Cross Rd. Atmospheric shop in a Georgian building, with a broad range of travel titles.

Silver Moon, 64–8 Charing Cross Rd. Specialist women's bookshop.

Zwemmer, 80 Charing Cross Rd. London's leading art bookshop.

Murder One, 71–3 Charing Cross Rd. New and secondhand genre fiction, mainly science fiction and crime.

Henry Pordes, 58–60 Charing Cross Rd. One of many secondhand and antiquarian booksellers on the Charing Cross Rd and its offshoot, Cecil Court.

Jermyn Street and Savile Row

Jermyn Street boasts some of the fanciest shopping in town. Royal and aristocratic patronage has showered down over the years on the old-fashioned emporia lining it. The names of the establishments hark back to another era: Turnbull and Asser the shirtmakers, George Trumper, barber and perfumer, or Bates the hatter (the full spectrum, from flat caps to bowlers). The shop assistants more closely resemble manservants from the great aristocratic houses of the past than paid employees of ongoing business concerns. Deference and attention to detail are the watchwords, sometimes pushed to rather absurd extremes. At Trumpers clients are still asked, at the end of a haircut, if Sir would like 'anything for the weekend' (a wonderfully euphemistic way of avoiding any mention of the dread word 'condom'). Anyone buying a shirt is in for a treat of careful measuring, discreet compliments and nonchalant chitchat about the fluctuating quality of modern cloth (try Harvie and Hudson at No.97, with its attractive mid-Victorian fronting).

Jermyn Street also has several galleries selling old prints, silverware and antiques. Another fine establishment is **Paxton and Whitfield** the cheese-seller at No.93, where the freshest cuts of the day are advertised on a blackboard behind the counter and samples of unusual cheese types are offered for tasting with water biscuits.

Along Jermyn St you pass two arcades lined with more purveyors of quality goods: first Princes Arcade, with its brown and white décor and then, after Duke St, the lower-ceilinged, green and white Piccadilly Arcade. Halfway between them is the back entrance to **Fortnum & Mason**, the ultimate old-fashioned English food shop (*open till 8pm with a good value afternoon tea for £16.50 from 3–5.15pm*).

North of Piccadilly is the quintessential address for men's bespoke tailoring, **Savile Row**. Classic menswear like **Hardy Amies** can still be found here, although the styles on offer are beginning to look impossibly old-fashioned; suffice to say that one of the biggest contemporary fans is the puddingy French politician Edouard Balladur. The street has hit hard times recently, although you'll still find some atmospherically traditional establishments, and you can see tailors working away in the basements as you pass.

Also north of Piccadilly is **Burlington Arcade**, which contains a host of little shops selling Irish linens, old pens, leather, pashmina shawls, antique and modern costume jewellery, perfumes and accessories.

Gieves and Hawkes, 1 Savile Row. One of the last gentlemen's outfitters in Savile Row. Unwavering attention to detail, atmospherically traditional.

Turnbull and Asser, 69–72 Jermyn St. One of many old-fashioned clothing boutiques on Jermyn Street, with lots of shirts and silk ties.

Paxton and Whitfield, 93 Jermyn St. Impeccable, old-fashioned cheese shop with specials of the day and nibbles at the counter.

Floris, 89 Jermyn St. Old-fashioned, long established perfume shop.

Taylor of Old Bond Street, 74 Jermyn St. Old-fashioned barber paraphernalia: shaving brushes and so on.

Davidoff, 65 Jermyn St. Fine cigars.

Bates, 21a Jermyn St. Men's hatter, with straw Panamas and other traditional styles.

Immaculate House, Burlington Arcade. All manner of strange and wonderful objects for the home.

Au Bon Pain, Burlington Arcade. Bakery café.

High Street Kensington

This is a fun place to shop, and not that expensive either; in reality it's really a mini Oxford Street, more compact and less busy. It's got its very own department store, **Barker's**, recently completely redesigned and especially good for cosmetics and furniture and Christmas goods.

There are big branches of **Marks & Spencer, BHS** and **Boots**. At the western end of the High Street are all the women's fashion chains (**H&M, Kookai, Jigsaw, Warehouse, Hobbs, Monsoon, French Connection**) and a selection of shoe shops, but also a large branch of the booksellers **Waterstone's**. Turn right from the Underground station to find trendier clothes shops, notably the discount designer emporium Hype DF and, almost directly opposite, the bazaar-like **Kensington Market**. For antiques, look around the lower end of **Kensington Church Street** and the cobbled passage, **Church Walk**, that snakes behind the Victorian-era St Mary Abbots church. Late night shopping day is Thursday.

Muji, 157 Kensington High Street and branches. Minimalist Japanese store selling kitchen equipment and stationery.

Crabtree and Evelyn, 6 Kensington Church St and branches. Herbs and fruit scents, all beautifully packaged. Ideal for gift-hunting.

Amazon, many branches at the bottom of Kensington Church St. Well loved by locals for its discounted and end-of-line men's and women's clothes.

Cologne & Cotton, 39 Kensington Church St. Luxury linen for the stylish bedroom, mostly in tasteful white, cream and blues.

What Katy Did, 49 Kensington Church St. Cute kiddie clothes.

Hype DF, 26–40 Kensington High St. Indoor market-style showcase for young designer talent, a place to snatch the trendy stuff before it becomes really trendy (and expensive)

Howard Jones, 43 Kensington Church St. Silver and enamel gifts.

Inventory, 26 Kensington High St. Huge selection of cheap and cheerful household goods over three floors: from bathroom goods to candles.

Urban Outfitters, 36 Kensington High St. Kitsch, young and fun, but you have to be fit to climb the stairs to the cool café.

Claire's Accessories, 171 Kensington High St. Pink ribbons, plastic earrings and hairslides: a little girl's paradise.

Past Times, 179 Kensington High St. Gift shop trading on nostalgia for the British past in all its incarnations. Not as tacky as it sounds.

Snow and Rock, 188 Kensington High St. Everything necessary for skiing and mountaineering.

Ehrmann's, Lancer Square, off Kensington Church St. A vast range of tapestry kits and equipment: make your own medieval cushion.

King's Road

Like Carnaby Street in Soho, the King's Road let its hair down and filled with cafés and fashion shops selling miniskirts and cheap jewellery. Old-fashioned shops, including the delightfully named toilet maker Thomas Crapper, were superseded by the likes of Terence Conran, who opened his first household store Habitat on the King's Road as a direct challenge to the fusty, old-fashioned goods then on sale at **Peter Jones** on Sloane Square.

Nowadays, most of the boutiques have either gone upmarket or been replaced by generic high-street chainstores. Some of the1960s spirit lives on, however, in the delightfully sprawling antiques markets on the south side of the road: **Antiquarius** at No.137, the **Chenil Galleries** at No.181–3 and the **Chelsea Antiques Market** at No.253. You might also want to take a look at the **Chelsea Farmer's Market**, with its cafés and craft shops just off the King's Road on Sydney Street. Behind the King's Road to the north, Cale Street and Elystan Place have nice little shops and a certain charm. For a map of the area, *see* p.92.

Chelsea Antiques Market, 245–53 King's Rd. All sorts of antiques.

Designer Sale Studio, 241 King's Rd. Last season's collections at up to 70% off.

Monsoon, 33d King's Rd and branches. Strong-coloured cotton clothes with an oriental influence. Mostly for women. Unusual homewares department in this branch.

Rococo, 321 King's Rd. Zany chocolate shop; an Aladdin's cave of edible delights.

Habitat. Everything for the house, from glasses and corkscrews to fitted cabinets. Cheap and practical. Good café for people-watching.

Heal's, 196 Tottenham Court Rd and 234 King's Rd. Upmarket sister to Habitat, with innovative designs for furniture, beds, lighting, etc.

Daisy and Tom, 181–3 King's Rd. Children's emporium, complete with hairdressing salon, carousel, toys, clothes and shoes.

Designer's Guild, 269 King's Rd. Bright and colourful textiles, linens, pottery and furniture. At the cutting edge of the lime-green revolution.

Steinberg & Tolkien, 193 King's Rd. Vintage clothing and accessories beloved by the 'in-crowd'.

Brora, 344 King's Rd. Scottish cashmere, tweed and wool with a modern twist.

The Holding Company, 241 King's Rd. A wealth of storage solutions for every room in the home or office.

Bluebird, 350 King's Rd. Part of the Conran empire, a converted 1930s garage containing a luxury food store, cookware shop, flower stall, restaurant and café.

Peter Jones, Sloane Square. A West London institution; a branch of John Lewis renowned for wedding lists and Chelsea 'ladies who lunch'.

Chelsea Town Hall, corner of Manor Street and King's Rd. Venue for antique sales and craft fairs.

The Chelsea Courtyard, Sydney Street. Pleasant haven from the main drag, with Bikepark, a bike shop where you can buy, hire and park bikes and get them repaired; an antiques centre; and the only authentic Vietnamese street barrow in London.

John Sandoe Books, 10–11 Blacklands Terrace, just off the King's Rd. An old-fashioned, higgledy-piggledy bookshop with knowledgeable staff.

Boy London/Ad Hoc, 153 King's Rd. OTT selection of fun, kitsch clothing and clubbing accessories.

American Classics, 400 King's Rd. All you need for that authentic 'street' look.

R. Soles, 109a King's Rd. Cowboy boot heaven.

L'Artisan Parfumeur, 17 Cale St. Beautifully gift-wrapped, elegant scents and colognes.

V. V. Rouleaux, 54 Sloane Square, just behind Peter Jones. An irresistible shop filled to the ceiling with rolls of ribbon and brocade.

Knightsbridge and Brompton Cross

It was the Great Exhibition that turned Knightsbridge into the birthplace of the late Victorian department store. **Harvey Nichols**, the most stylish (and the absolute favourite of Patsy and Edina in *Absolutely Fabulous*), is on the corner of Sloane Street and Knightsbridge. Harvey Nicks is justly famous for its weird and wonderful window displays, and fifth floor food halls, where swishly packaged exotica of every description are sold under an equally exotic steel panelled corrugated canopy with views of the Knightsbridge skyline. (If you need a break, coffee or even a drink, it's well worth making a short detour from here to the food hall's glamorous café and bar).

The most famous department store of all, **Harrods**, is on the Brompton Road. Nowadays it is often mentioned in the same breath as the name of its owner, Mohammed Fayed—Egyptian tycoon, failed candidate for British citizenship and father of the ill-fated Dodi, last companion of Princess Diana. But its pedigree stretches back much further to the glory days of the 19th century. The vast, terracotta-fronted palace that Harrods now occupies was built in the first five years of the 20th century, at much the same time as the first modern luxury hotels like the Savoy and the Ritz. Indeed Harrods is itself in some ways more like a five-star hotel than a mere shop; service and indulgence towards the customer are paramount, and no request is ever too much trouble. The place is kitted out to provide a fitting welcome to the noblest of princes; particularly striking are the Food Halls with their beautiful food displays and Edwardian Art Nouveau tiles in the Meat Hall depicting hunting scenes. As you wander around, you are serenaded alternately by a harpist and a piano player. You'll find just about anything on its six floors, just as long as money is no object.

Both **Brompton Road** and **Sloane Street** parade classy designer shops, some of them too scary to enter. Nicole Farhi, Dior, Christian Lacroix, Chanel, Gucci, Kenzo and a clutch of others stretch down Sloane Street, while beyond Harrods in the Brompton Road you will find Emporio Armani and Issey Miyake. The streets behind Harrods have hidden treasures, and halfway down Brompton Road to the left is **Beauchamp Place**, lined with tiny exclusive shops selling anything from underwear to jewellery to designer cast-offs. Yet around the many exits of Knightsbridge tube are branches of Monsoon and Miss Selfridge, Jigsaw and Laura Ashley as well.

Harrods, Brompton Rd. A shopping institution of such proportions that it demands to be seen. Whether you want to buy anything is another matter. Exotic foods, kitchenware, silverware and toys are all excellent, clothes rather less so. Look out for bargains on mundane things like CDs during the sales.

Harvey Nichols, 109–25 Knightsbridge. High-class fashionwear, plus an excellent food hall and café on the fifth floor.

Scotch House, 2 Brompton Rd. Classic woollens, from socks to knitted ties, plus Scottish kilts and all the paraphernalia.

Descamps, 197 Sloane St. Fine French linen.

Gant USA, 17 Brompton Rd. American sportswear.

Graff, 55 Brompton Rd. Very expensive jewellery.

Space NK Apothecary, 305 Brompton Rd. Make-up and beauty products not available elsewhere: Nars, Kiehl's, Stila.

The Outlet, Brompton Rd. Discounted designer wear.

Emporio Armani, 191 Brompton Rd. Elegant cuts from the king of classic Italian tailoring.

Rigby and Peller, 2 Hans Road. Sublime underwear.

La Bottega del San Lorenzo, 23 Beauchamp Place. Divine Italian deli.

Isabell Kristensen, 33 Beauchamp Place. Ballgowns.

Mulberry, 185 Brompton Road. Classic English leather bags and luggage with the distinctive logo.

Brompton Cross

Further along the Brompton Road is a small enclave of shops and restaurants at the start of the Fulham Road known as Brompton Cross. The most striking building at its centre is Terence Conran's remarkable Art Nouveau **Michelin Building** (at No.61), which he renovated in the 1980s complete with glass cupolas and car-themed mosaics to create offices, a Conran Shop and the Bibendum restaurant and Oyster Bar.

Behind and parallel to the Brompton Road, first left off Draycott Avenue, **Walton Street**, like Beauchamp Place, is a quiet enclave of unmissable classy little shops.

Conran Shop, Michelin House, 81 Fulham Road. Baskets, chairs, lighting, even notebooks are all beautifully designed and presented in this tremendous Art Deco building.

Voyage, 115 and 175 Fulham Road. Bouncers decide whether you're elegant or trendy enough to be allowed in this designer clothes store.

Formes, 313 Fulham Road. Fashion for pregnant women.

The Ringmaker, 191–3 Fulham Road. Huge jeweller's with stylish designs.

Divertimenti, 139 Fulham Road. Pots and pans of the highest quality and inventiveness.

Agnès B, Fulham Road. One branch of the women's design shop: clothes and make-up.

Czech and Speake, 125 Fulham Road. Incense burning by the door lures you into this haven of scents for the body and home.

Jerry's Home Store, 163–7 Fulham Road. American household goods and food, including shiny chrome 50s blenders and ice-cream machines and authentic brownie mixes.

Dinny Hall, 54 Fulham Road. Resin and silver earrings from this trend-setting jewellery designer.

Bentley's, 190 Walton Street. Leather goods and luggage.

Maman Deux, 79 Walton Street. For the street-smart baby.

Jo Malone, 154 Walton St. Her own range of toiletries from the queen of the facial. Delectable and now legendary products for the face and body.

Nôm, 150 Walton St. Calm Japanese style for the home.

Sam de Teran, 151 Fulham Rd. Sailing, skiing and sports gear.

The Room, 158 Walton Street. Beautiful homewares that are almost works of art.

Cox and Power, 95 Walton St. Flamboyant modern jewellery.

Farmacia di Santa Maria Novella, 117 Walton St. Italian hand-milled soaps and fragrances.

Covent Garden

Apart from the market, there are many shops that make this a rewarding area to take your credit card. Neal Street, Seven Dials and the streets radiating from it, Thomas Neal's Arcade, Long Acre, New Row and the streets around the market are the places to head for.

The Astrology Shop, 78 Neal St. Have your personal horoscope read; also books, CDs and astrological objects.

Red or Dead, 43 Neal St. Trendy British shoe shop that now also sells clothes.

Janet Fitch, 37 Neal Street and 1 The Market. Jewellery shop with work by different designers.

Sam Walker, 33 Neal Street. Vintage clothing.

The Tea House, 15a Neal St. All kinds of teas from around the world: herbal, green, organic and fruit.

Neal Street East, 5 Neal St. An oriental emporium of books, clothes and home decorating ideas.

Michiko Koshino, 70 Neal St. Glad rags suitable for the high-class club circuit. Cool and dazzling.

Ray's Jazz Shop, 180 Shaftesbury Ave. Old classic LPs and new CDs on jazz and blues.

Neal's Yard Wholefood Warehouse, off Shorts Gardens. Organic everything.

Neal's Yard Remedies, 15 Neal's Yard. Lots of oils and homoeopathic remedies, all very natural.

Neal's Yard Dairy, 17 Shorts Gardens. More than 70 varieties of cheese, matured and served with love.

Duffer of St George, 29 Shorts Gardens. Very trendy menswear store, selling street and clubwear.

Dress Circle, 57 Monmouth St. 'The greatest showbiz shop in the world,' they claim, with sheet music, scores, books, posters and CDs.

Natural Leather, 33 Monmouth St. Leather jackets, jeans and bags.

Muji, 39 Shelton St, and branches. Minimalist Japanese store selling kitchen equipment and stationery.

Stanfords, 12–14 Long Acre. Map specialist, indispensable if you are travelling to the Third World where maps are virtually non-existent. Also travel guides, travel literature and walking guides.

Dillons Art Bookshop, 8 Long Acre. Books on art; also cards and postcards.

Nicole Farhi, 12 Long Acre and Unit 4, East Piazza. Stylish, elegant clothes for women.

Jones, 13 Floral St. At the cutting edge of fashion; here Gaultier and Galliano are old hat.

Paul Smith, 40–4 Floral St, Covent Garden. High-class gloss on the bovver-boy look. Mostly for men, but there is now a women's collection too.

The Tintin Shop, 34 Floral St. Books, videos and T-shirts.

Oasis, 13 James St and branches. Stylish, fashionable womenswear at reasonable prices.

Culpeper Herbalists, 8 The Market. Herbs, spices, bath salts and potpourri, mostly taken from homegrown sources.

Segar & Snuff Parlour, The Market. A tiny shop selling pipes, lighters, and hand-rolled cigars from Cuba.

Ordning & Reda, 21 New Row. Stylish, colourful, Swedish-designed stationery and office accessories.

Vertigo Galleries, 29 Bedfordbury. Vintage movie posters.

The Africa Centre, 38 King St. African crafts; also a restaurant/café.

Dr Martens Department Store, 1–4 King St. Four floors of DMs for men, women and children; also sells clothing.

Crime in Store, 4 Bedford St. Specialist crime and mystery bookshop, including many US titles unavailable elsewhere in Britain.

Penhaligon's, 41 Wellington St. Own-brand eau de toilette and other fragrances. Also delicious air freshener sprays.

Markets

Street markets are one of the best things about London. They are where the city comes alive, showing off the vitality and variety of the neighbourhoods lucky enough to have them. Some, such as Covent Garden and Portoballo, are described in the main sections of this book; what follows is a list of what to expect and details of opening hours.

Berwick Street, Soho. Outstanding fruit and veg (*open every day except Sun, with lunchtime closing on Wed*). *See* p.75.

Brick Lane, Whitechapel (*open Sun morning*). Very popular market where East End barrows try to offload their junk, especially furniture and old books. Keep a hard nose and you can haggle a real bargain.

Brixton, Electric Avenue (*open daily except Sun, with lunchtime closing on Wed*). London's biggest Caribbean market, with music, exotic vegetables, goats' meat and wafting spices.

Camden Lock, between Camden High St and Chalk Farm Rd (*open Sat and Sun*). A weekend institution, with an array of books, clothes, records and assorted antiques by the canal. Huge crowds guarantee a festive atmosphere, and there are lots of excellent refreshments on hand.

Camden Passage, Islington (*open Wed and Sat only*). High-class antiques market in a quiet street next to the bustle of Upper St.

Chapel Market, Islington (*closed Mon and at lunchtime on Thurs and Sun*). An exuberant north London food market, with excellent fish and, as a sideline, lots of household goods and cheap clothes.

Columbia Road (*off the Hackney Road about three-quarters of a mile north of Liverpool St Station, open 8am–1pm Sun morning*): Columbia market was set up in 1869 as a covered food market set in a vast neo-Gothic palace. The traders preferred to do their business on the street, however, and the venture failed. The shortlived market building was knocked down in 1958 to make room for the lively, modern, highly successful flower market. As well as a wide range of cut flowers and pot plants, you can buy homemade bread and farmhouse cheeses and enjoy the small cafés that line the street.

Earlham St, Earlham St, Covent Gdn, between Shaftesbury Ave and Seven Dials (*Mon–Sat 10–4*). Extraordinary flowers, and secondhand clothes.

Greenwich, College Approach, Greenwich (*Sat and Sun only*). Lots of crafts, books, furniture and coins and medals. Worth a detour.

Petticoat Lane, Middlesex St, Whitechapel (*open Sun morning*). Leather, cheap fashion and household goods at London's most famous Sunday market. Look out for the jellied eel and whelk sellers on the fringes.

Portobello Road, Notting Hill (*open Mon–Sat, with lunchtime closing Thurs; antiques Sat only*). Perhaps the most atmospheric market in London. The southern end is stuffed with antique dealers, while the northern end is a mixed bag of design shops, cafés, food stalls, jewellery stands, record stores and more. Has a real neighbourhood feel, culminating in the wonderful half-Portuguese, half-Moroccan Golborne Road. *See* p.90.

St James's, St James's Churchyard, Piccadilly (*Tues antiques, Wed–Sun 10–6*). Lots of books, old prints, coins and medals on a Tuesday, and ethnic crafts the rest of the time.

South Bank, Riverside Walk, in front of the NFT (*Sat and Sun*). Secondhand books and prints along the riverside, open rain or shine.

London: Museums and Galleries

Summer Exhibition

Courtauld Institute, Somerset House, The Strand, WC2, ✆ (020) 7845 4600; ⊖ *Covent Gdn, Temple. Open Mon–Sat 10–6, Sun 2–6; adm; full disabled access, café, entrance is to the right on the way in to Somerset House.*

Somerset House was the first Renaissance palace in England, built for the Duke of Somerset who in 1547 was named Lord Protector for nine-year-old Edward VI, and set about building a home grand enough to match his overweening ambitions. He knocked down two bishops' palaces, an inn of chancery and a church to make room for his super-palace, and pillaged two more churches to provide the stone. After his death the palace was a royal residence and a venue for peace conferences. It fell out of fashion in the 17th and 18th centuries and, despite boasting a chapel by Inigo Jones and the first example of parquet flooring in Europe, was demolished in the 1770s. The replacement, used to house Royal Societies, public records and the Inland Revenue service, is a fine Georgian building by William Chambers. Its great courtyard has recently been cleared of cars and redesigned by Sir Jeremy Dixon and Edward Jones as a setting for public performances, with a café and fountains.

Somerset House's chief attraction is the Courtauld Institute, with its exquisite collection of paintings, particularly of Impressionists and post-impressionists. Most of the paintings were a bequest by the philanthropist Samuel Courtauld, who also set up a school of fine art affiliated to London University. An elegant staircase leads to 11 smallish rooms spread over two floors. There is a magnificent *Adam and Eve* by Lucas Cranach the Elder, some fine Rubens including his early masterpiece *The Descent from the Cross*, and a roomful of unusual 18th-century Italian art including a series of Tiepolos. The Impressionists include a copy by the artist of Manet's *Le Déjeuner sur l'Herbe*, some wonderful Degas studies of dancers and moody Cézanne landscapes. Highlights from the 20th century include Kokoschka, Modigliani and some excellent contemporary British works donated in the early 1980s.

The Courtauld Institue has recently been joined in Somerset House by the **Gilbert Collection** of decorative arts.

Estorick Collection of Italian Art, Northampton Lodge, 39a Canonbury Square, N1, ✆ (020) 7704 9522; ⊖ *Highbury & Islington. Open Wed–Sat 11–6, Sun 12–5; cheap adm.* Fascinating private collection of Italian art, mainly futurist painters including Balla, Boccioni and Carra. With a library, café and shop.

Kenwood House, Hampstead Lane, NW3, ✆ (020) 8348 1286; ⊖ *Hampstead, Highgate. Open daily 10–6; Oct–Mar daily 10–4. See p.103.*

National Gallery, St Martin's Lane, WC2, ✆ (020) 7747 2885; ⊖ *Charing Cross, Leicester Sq. Open daily 10–6, Wed 10–9; free. See p.38*

National Portrait Gallery, St Martin's Lane, WC2, ✆ (020) 7306 0055; ⊖ *Charing Cross, Leicester Square. Open daily 10–6; Thurs and Fri 10–9; free.* This gallery is unique, and a true oddity. Unique, because no other Western country has ever assembled a similar collection of portraits of the glorious names populating its history. Odd, because the kings, generals, ministers, pioneers, inventors and artists on display here have not been chosen according to the quality of the painting—in fact some of it is downright lousy. They are here because the Victorian aristocrats who originally founded the gallery believed that it would serve as a stern kind of history lesson. Don't be too surprised, then, to find that in here you will see no revolutionaries, few union leaders, few true dissidents.

The gallery has over 9,000 portraits spread over five narrow floors (there's a new café/restaurant on the roof). Chronologically, the collection starts at the top with the Tudor age and works its way down towards the present day, with a magnificent new 20th-century wing designed by Piers Gough. The best paintings, technically speaking, are probably Holbein's vividly life-like versions of Henrys VII and VIII and Sir Thomas More. There are also magnificent renditions of the 19th-century prime ministers Disraeli and Gladstone by Millais, self-portraits by Hogarth and Reynolds, a distinctly ambivalent Churchill by Walter Sickert (all yellows and greens) and a Cubist T. S. Eliot by Jacob Epstein. Some of the portraits are so reverent as to be absurd. Lawrence of Arabia appears in stone effigy like some medieval king imbued with divine powers, and Jacques-Emile Blanche's James Joyce looks ludicrously respectable in a smart suit in front of an orderly writing desk.

Percival David Foundation of Chinese Art, 53 Gordon Square, WC1, ℗ (020) 7387 3909; ⊖ *Euston Sq. Open Mon–Fri 10.30–5; free*. This fine collection of imperial porcelain is named after the philanthropic collector who acquired its treasures. With its extensive library and superb ceramics, this is a vital stopping-off point for China scholars. The vases, which are beautifully documented and dated, range from the Sung dynasty of the 10th century up to the Qing dynasty of the 18th.

Royal Academy, Burlington House, Piccadilly, W1, ℗ (020) 7300 8000; ⊖ *Green Park, Piccadilly. Open daily 10–6; adm. See* p.72.

Tate Britain, Millbank, SW1, ℗ (020) 7887 8000; ⊖ *Pimlico. Open daily 10–5.50; free. See* p.42.

Tate Modern, Bankside, SE1, ℗ (020) 7887 8000; ⊖ *Southwark, Blackfriars. Open Sun–Thur 10–6, Fri & Sat 10–10; free. See* p.84.

The Wallace Collection, *Hertford House, Manchester Square, behind Oxford St, W1*, ℗ (020) 7935 0687; ⊖ *Marble Arch, Bond Street. Open Mon–Sat 10–5, Sun 2–5; free, donations welcome*. One could not hope for a more perfect monument to 18th-century aristocratic life than the Wallace Collection, a sumptuous array of painting, porcelain and furniture housed in a period mansion called Hertford House. The collection is the result of several generations of accumulation by the Hertford family, whose link with the art world had already begun in the mid-18th century, when the first Marquess of Hertford patronized Joshua Reynolds. Richard Wallace, who gave his name to the collection (as well as designing the Paris drinking fountains that still bear his name), was the bastard son of the fourth Marquess and acted as agent for his father in all his transactions. He later bequeathed the whole lot to the state, on condition that it remain on public view in central London.

Highlights include works by Frans Hals (*The Laughing Cavalier*), Rembrandt (*Titus*), Rubens (*Christ's Charge to Peter* and *The Holy Family*), Poussin (*Dance to the Music of Time*) and Titian (an extraordinary rendition of *Perseus and Andromeda* in which the Greek hero tumbles towards the open jaws of the sea monster with only his sword and shield to save him). Take your time around the rest of the collection to take in the finely carved wardrobes inlaid with tortoiseshell and gilt bronze, the delicate porcelain and any number of eccentric *objets d'art*.

Whitechapel Art Gallery, Whitechapel High St, ℗ (020) 7522 7888; ⊖ *Aldgate East. Open Tues–Sun 11–5; free*. A lively gallery focusing on contemporary and avant-garde work, housed in an interesting Art Nouveau building designed by Charles Harrison Townsend at the turn of the 20th century. It was the brainchild of Samuel Barnett, a local vicar who believed education could help eradicate the appalling poverty in the East End. Jackson Pollock and David Hockney both held exhibitions here early in their careers.

Design and the Decorative Arts

Clockmakers' Museum, Guildhall Library, Aldermanbury, EC2, ℗ (020) 7606 3030; ⊖ *Bank, Mansion House. Open Mon–Fri 9.30–4.45*. Here you'll find more than 700 timepieces of all shapes and sizes belonging to the Worshipful Company of Clockmakers. Look out for the silver skull watch said to have belonged to Mary, Queen of Scots, and the wrist watch worn by Edmund Hillary during the first recorded ascent of Mount Everest in 1953.

Commonwealth Institute, Kensington High Street, W8, ℗ (020) 7371 3530; ⊖ *High Street Kensington; bus 49, 9, 10, 27. Open daily 10–5; adm*. The shimmering green hyperboloid roof, made of Zambian copper, is only the first of many surprises at this highly imaginative cultural centre celebrating the diversity and imagination of Britain's former colonies, now grouped together as the Commonwealth. There are three floors of galleries, each dealing with a different country, where you can pluck a sitar, sit on a snowmobile or watch a model demonstrating the digestive system of a New Zealand cow. Children love it. The Institute also has a lively programme of lectures, concerts and art exhibitions; a shop jam-packed with craft work; and a restaurant offering indigenous dishes from around the Commonwealth. A new 'interactive' attraction called The Commonwealth Experience is a vertiginous and quite scary simulated helicopter ride over a rather more visible Malaysia than in real life.

Crafts Council Gallery, 44a Pentonville Rd, E3, ☎ (020) 7278 7700; ⊖ *Angel; bus 19, 38, 73. Open Tues–Sat 11–6, Sun 2–6; free.* Excellent exhibition of modern British crafts.

Design Museum, Butler's Wharf, SE1, ☎ (020) 7403 6933; ⊖ *Tower Hill. Open Mon–Fri 11.30–6, Sat and Sun 12–6. See* p.86.

Geffrye Museum, Kingsland Rd, E2, ☎ (020) 7739 9893; ⊖ *Old Street then bus 243. Open Tues–Sat 10–5, Sun 2–5; free.* A thoroughly absorbing series of reconstructions of British living rooms from Tudor times to the present, housed in a row of former almshouses, with a new extension focusing on design.

Leighton House, 12 Holland Park Rd, W14, ☎ (020) 7602 3316; ⊖ *Holland Park, High Street Kensington; bus 9, 10, 27, 49. Open Mon–Sat 11–5.30; free.* This apparently straightforward red-brick house opens into a grand extravaganza of escapist late Victorian interior design. Lord Leighton, one of the Pre-Raphaelite painters, used his imagination, his not inconsiderable funds and the inspiration of a number of friends to create an astonishing Oriental palace here in his London home. The highlight is undoubtedly the Arab Hall, which has a stained-glass cupola, a fountain spurting out of the richly decorated mosaic floor and glorious painted floral tiles which Leighton and his friends picked up in Rhodes, Cairo and Damascus. Dotted around the downstairs reception rooms, among the paintings of Leighton and his contemporaries Millais and Burne-Jones, are highly ornate details including Cairene lattice-work alcoves and marble columns decorated in burnished gold. *See also* p.113.

Sir John Soane's Museum, 12–14 Lincoln's Inn Fields, WC2; ☎ (020) 7430 0175, ⊖ *Holborn. Open Tues–Sat 10–5, with a £3 guided tour—which is free to students—on Saturdays at 2.30 and with visits by candlelight on the first Tuesday of each month from 6–9; free, but any donations are gratefully accepted.* John Soane (1753–1837) was a great English eccentric and also one of the great architects of his age. He was a fanatical

student of antiquity, and one of the towering figures of the neoclassical movement in Britain. One contemporary described him as 'personal to the point of perversity'. Soane did not seem unduly bothered by the relative paucity of high-profile commissions; he stayed busy throughout his professional life and won a formidable reputation as a lecturer. In later life he bought up and converted three adjacent houses here in Lincoln's Inn Fields, adapting each room to his quirky style and filling them with objects from his remarkable art collection. In 1833 (four years before his death in 1837), Soane saw through a private Act of Parliament in which he bequeathed the whole collection to the public, with the stipulation that the museum should be maintained forever as it was on the day of Soane's death.

One of the highlights is the Picture Room on the ground floor, containing two great satirical series of paintings by Hogarth: *The Rake's Progress*, which follows the rise and fall of a degenerate young man from the moment he comes into his inheritance to his untimely end in the madhouse, and *The Election*, four scenes satirizing the greed and corruption surrounding political ambition. The Picture Room also includes studies by Piranesi and architectural drawings by Soane himself. Soane's other prized exhibit is the sarcophagus of the Egyptian Pharaoh Seti I (1303–1290 BC) in the Sepulchral Chamber in the basement. This is the finest example of a sarcophagus you can see outside Egypt, beautifully preserved and covered in hieroglyphics honouring Osiris and Ra and adorned with a painted figure of the goddess Nut, to whom Seti had pledged allegiance, on the inside.

It would be a mistake, however, to visit this museum merely for its artistic highlights. Every room yields surprises, whether it is the enormous collection of plaster casts Soane made from classical models, or the classical colonnade running along the upstairs corridor, or simply the amazing ambiguities of light, which Soane manipulated so intriguingly in every area of the house with the aid of concave and then convex mirrors.

Victoria and Albert Museum, Cromwell Rd, SW7, ☎ (020) 7938 8500; ⊖ *South Kensington. Open Mon–Sun 10–5.45, summer Wed late view 6.30–9.30; adm, free after 4.30. See* p.46.

William Morris Gallery, Lloyd Park, Forest Rd, E17, ✆ (020) 7527 3782; ⊖ *Walthamstow Central. Open Tues–Sat 10–1 and 2–5, plus first Sun in the month 10–noon and 2–5; free.* A long way to go to see William Morris's childhood home and its fascinating exhibition on his life and work. Lots of Arts and Crafts wallpaper, stained glass, tiles and carpets. There is also an interesting collection of pre-Raphaelite paintings and drawings by Burne-Jones and Rossetti, plus a few Rodin sculptures.

Historical, Political and Military

Bank of England Museum, Bartholomew Lane, Threadneedle St, EC2, ✆ (020) 7601 5545; ⊖ *Bank. Open Mon–Fri 10–5; April–Sept Sun 11–5; free. See* p.58.

Cabinet War Rooms, Clive Steps, King Charles St, SW1 (entrance Horse Guards Rd), ✆ 0171 930 6961; ⊖ *Westminster. Open daily 9.30–5.50, last adm 5.15; adm.* Winston Churchill had the basement of a number of government buildings converted in preparation for war in 1938, and he, his cabinet and 500 civil servants worked here throughout the conflict, protected from the bombing by several layers of thick concrete. The floor below the present exhibition contained a canteen, hospital, shooting range and sleeping quarters. Churchill, whose office was a converted broom cupboard, kept a direct line open to President Roosevelt in Washington; all other telephone connections were operated from an unwieldy old-fashioned switchboard and scrambled, for perverse reasons of security, via Selfridge's department store. The War Rooms, with their Spartan period furniture and maps marking the British Empire in red, are a magnificent evocation of the wartime atmosphere. A pity, then, that the curators do not allow the place simply to speak for itself.

Clink Prison Museum, 1 Clink St, SE1, ✆ (020) 7403 6515; ⊖ *Borough; bus 40, 133, 149. Open daily 10–6; June–Sept 10–10; adm. See* p.84.

Imperial War Museum, Lambeth Rd, SE1, ✆ (020) 7416 5329; ⊖ *Lambeth North. Open daily 10–6; adm; free after 4.30pm.* Until the First World War this was the site of the notorious Bethlehem Royal Hospital for the insane, better known as Bedlam, where inmates were kept like zoo animals in cages and cells. The building is now used to illustrate Britain's wartime experiences from 1914 to the present day. Despite the intimidating pair of artillery cannon at the entrance, this museum does everything it can to illustrate the human side of war, not just the military hardware. Certainly, there are plenty of Zeppelins, Lancaster bombers, Cruise missile launchers—there is even a distasteful flight simulator for which visitors cough up extra money to 'experience' a World War Two bombing mission. Fortunately there are also exhibits on rationing and air raids, sound and light shows illustrating the terrors and privations of life in a First World War trench, and artworks including Henry Moore's drawings of London during the Blitz. Try as it might, however, the museum ultimately fails to convey the sheer barbaric awfulness of war and can't help wrapping the experiences it depicts in a coat of patriotic nostalgia.

Kensington Palace, Kensington Gardens, W8, ✆ (020) 7937 9561; ⊖ *High Street Kensington, Queensway. Open Mar–Oct daily 10–6; Nov–Feb Wed–Sun 10–3; adm. See* p.37.

Museum of London, 150 London Wall, EC2, ✆ (020) 7600 3699; ⊖ *St Paul's. Open Tues–Sat 10–5.50, Sun 12–5.50; adm, free after 4.30pm.* This ambitious and fast-changing museum sets out to tell the story of London from prehistoric times to the present, drawing on a vast collection of documents and historical relics. It is an ideal place to come if you want to familiarize yourself with the basic facts about the city. It is also a tremendous resource for students and researchers. The museum is very strong on early history, particularly the Roman era, and gives a rich impression of life in the 19th century. It also has an imaginative section on contemporary London. In other areas, perhaps inevitably, the museum is a bit patchy, since the quality of the displays varies according to the illustrative material available. The main problem, in the end, is that the museum's archive of documents is far richer than its collection of artefacts. That said, the museum is never boring. It is beautifully laid out over three descending levels. There are lucid explanations of the historical evidence yielded by lumps of Roman paving stone and recovered coinage. One angled window cleverly gives you a view down on to a piece of Roman wall (AD 200) on the ground outside. Many of the best displays in the rest of the museum are reconstructions of contemporary buildings: a 16th-century grocer's shop, a cell at Newgate Prison, a Victorian pub, a Second World War bedroom kitted out with a protective cage called a Morrison shelter. The museum also has a magnificent range of clothing, giving an insight into changing fashions since the 17th century. The undisputed centrepiece, though, is the **Lord Mayor's Coach**. Built in 1757 in blazing red and burnished gold, the coach is still used every November for the investiture of the new Lord Mayor. It looks the sort of thing Prince Charming might have used to drive Cinderella home; it is covered in allegorical paintings depicting both the virtues of modesty and the glories of wealth.

National Maritime Museum, Romney Rd, Greenwich, SE10, ✆ (020) 8312 6565; ⇌ *Maze Hill (from Charing Cross). Open daily 10–5; adm. See* p.107.

Royal Naval College, King William Walk, SE10, ✆ (020) 8858 2154; ⇌ *Greenwich; DLR Island Gdns; by river to Greenwich Pier; bus 188. Open*

Fri–Wed 10–5, Thurs 2.30–5, Sat and Sun 12–5; free. See p.106.

Winston Churchill's Britain at War Museum, 64–6 Tooley Street, SE1, ✆ (020) 7403 3171; ➌ *London Bridge; bus 47, P11. Open daily 10–4.30; adm exp.* This is the kind of museum you could cook up out of a recipe book. Take a popular subject (the Second World War), add plenty of period memorabilia (books, clothes, newspaper cuttings, radio broadcasts, etc.), mix in a couple of set-piece reconstructions (an Underground station during an air raid and a bombed-out house) and top with lashings of patriotism (Vera Lynn singing 'There'll Always Be An England'). There is not a drop of originality about the place. You'll see all of it, and more, at the Cabinet War Rooms in Whitehall.

The *Golden Hinde*, St Mary Overie's Dock, Clink Street, ✆ (0541) 505 041; ➌ *Borough; bus 40, 133, 149. Open daily 9–sunset; adm cheap; tea and coffee available.* A perfect replica of the galleon used by Sir Francis Drake to circumnavigate the world in 1580. The original rotted away in a berth in Deptford, and the reconstruction you see here is a working galleon which has sailed many more miles across the world than its progenitor. A crew of 15 lives aboard the ship.

Science, Medicine and Technology

National Postal Museum, King Edward St, EC1, in the post office in King Edward Building on the left-hand side of the road, ✆ (020) 7239 5420; ➌ *St Paul's. Open Mon–Fri 9.30–4.30; free.* This is a stamp collector's wet dream: three floors of postal memorabilia, from rare stamps to uniforms, Bantams (the motorbikes used for delivering telegrams) and red and green post boxes dating back to the 1850s.

Brunel Engine House, St Marychurch St, SE16; ➌ *Rotherhithe; bus 47, P11, 188. Open by appointment on* ✆ *(020) 7252 0059 or* ✆ *(020) 8748 3534; adm.* Rotherhithe acquired a new cause for celebrity in the early 19th century, when Marc Isambard Brunel made it the starting point for the first tunnel to run beneath the Thames. Brunel was born in France and fled the Revolution with a forged passport. Although a talented engineer—he invented a system of pulley blocks still remembered today—he had no financial sense and spent far too

much of his own money on his work. The Duke of Wellington had to haul him out of debtors' prison to start the tunnel from Rotherhithe to Wapping. The job took 18 years, from 1825 to 1843, and nearly ended in disaster on five separate occasions when the roof caved in. You can see the bright red pump that Brunel used to suck out the water, as well as a number of other memorabilia at the Brunel Engine House. The Thames Tunnel is now used by the East London Underground line; it is not to be confused with the adjacent Rotherhithe Tunnel, built for road traffic in 1908.

Faraday Museum, Albemarle St, W1, ✆ (020) 7409 2992; ➌ *Green Park. Open Mon–Fri 9–5; adm.* The Royal Institution building, with its pompous façade based on the Temple of Antoninus in Rome, is to science what the Royal Academy is to the arts: the most prestigious association of professionals in the land. Founded in 1799, the Institution built up a formidable reputation thanks to early members such as Humphrey Davy (inventor of the Davy Lamp for detecting methane down mines) and his pupil, Michael Faraday. The small museum (the only part of the building regularly open to the public) is in fact Faraday's old laboratory where he carried out his pioneering experiments with electricity in the 1830s; his work is explained with the help of his original instruments and lab notes. The Royal Institution also organizes excellent lectures, including series specially designed for children.

Florence Nightingale Museum, 2 Lambeth Palace Rd, SE1, ☎ (020) 7620 0374; ⊖ *Lambeth North, Waterloo; bus 507. Open Tues–Sun 10–5, last adm 4; adm*. You won't learn much more about the founder of modern nursing here than at the Old St Thomas's Operating Theatre (*see* p.85), but the museum nevertheless builds up a vivid image of her life and times. Here are the letters, childhood books and personal trophies that the 'Lady with the Lamp' brought back from the Crimean War. You can also see a reconstructed ward from the Crimea, contemporary nurses' uniforms and some of the equipment they used. 'Nursing is a progressive art, in which to stand still is to go back,' Florence Nightingale said towards the end of her long life (she died, aged 90, in 1910). Her influence is still being felt today.

London Planetarium, Marylebone Rd, NW1, ☎ (020) 7935 6861; ⊖ *Baker Street. Open June–Aug daily 9.30–5, Sept–May daily 12.20–5; adm. A joint ticket is available with Madame Tussaud's*. If you have children, you might enjoy the Planetarium, with its exciting and informative laser, sound and light show projected over a vast dome-shaped auditorium via a high-tech Digistar Mark 2 projector. The show explains how the solar system works, what the galaxy and the Milky Way are (apart from the chocolate bars you chomped in the queue), how earthquakes and volcanoes happen, and more.

London Transport Museum, 39 Wellington St, WC2, ☎ (020) 7379 6344; ⊖ *Covent Garden. Open Sun–Thurs and Sat 10–6, Fri 11–6; adm, full disabled access*. Londoners like to grumble about London Transport, but in their heart of hearts they are really rather fascinated by it. This cheerful museum celebrates everything that is excellent about the system, from the red London Routemaster bus to the London Underground map, designed in 1931 by Harry Beck, and never surpassed. In the main gallery, a glass walkway takes you past a series of historic buses, trams and steam locomotives, including the oldest surviving double-decker horse tram. In adjoining galleries you can see an original watercolour of Beck's Underground map, and a superb collection of Art Deco period posters. There's a simulated Tube train driving seat, actors dressed in period costume, educational 'Action Zones' and a museum shop. The museum also organizes a programme of talks and events (including a regular tour and lecture on London's disused Tube stations)

Natural History Museum, Cromwell Rd, SW7, ☎ (020) 7938 9123; ⊖ *South Kensington. Open Mon–Sat 10–5.50, Sun 11–5.50; adm. See p.39.*

Old Royal Observatory, Greenwich Park, SE10, ☎ (020) 8858 4422; ⇌ *Maze Hill (from Charing Cross); bus 188. Open daily 10–5; adm. See p.108.*

Science Museum, Exhibition Rd, SW7, ☎ (020) 7938 8080; ⊖ *South Kensington. Open daily 10–6; adm. See p.39.*

St Thomas's Operating Theatre Museum, 9a St Thomas St, SE1, ☎ (020) 7955 4791; ⊖ *London Br. Open Tues–Sun 10.30–4.45; adm. See p.85.*

Thames Barrier Visitor Centre, Unity Way, SE18, ☎ (020) 8854 1373; ⇌ *Charlton; by river from Westminster Pier; bus 188 then bus 472. Open Mon–Fri 10–5, Sat and Sun 10.30–5.30; adm*. A brief history of flooding in London, and an explanation on how the barrier works.

Famous Homes

Apsley House, Hyde Park Corner, W1, ☎ (020) 7499 5676; ⊖ *Hyde Park Corner. Open Tues–Sun 11–5; adm*. Wellington was given this house as a reward for his victories against the French, and he modestly dubbed it No.1 London (its real address being the more prosaic 149 Piccadilly). Robert Adam had built it half a century earlier for Henry Bathurst, a man generally reckoned to be the most incompetent Lord Chancellor of the 18th century. The Iron Duke succeeded in defacing Adam's original work, covering the brick walls with Bath stone, adding the awkward Corinthian portico at the front and ripping out much of the interior with the help of the architects Benjamin and Philip Wyatt. You feel the coldness of a man who terrified most who met him and who, according to legend, once defused a mounting riot in Hyde Park with a single crack of his whip. Sadly the museum does not own a pair of Wellington boots, the man's greatest legacy to the 20th century. The highlight is indubitably Canova's double-life-size sculpture of Napoleon, which Wellington stole from the Louvre after its megalomaniac subject rejected it.

Carlyle's House, 24 Cheyne Row, SW3, ✆ (020) 7352 7087; ⊖ *Sloane Square then bus 19, 22. Open April–Oct Wed–Sun 11–5; adm. See* p.93.

Dickens' House, 49 Doughty St, WC1, ✆ (020) 7405 2127; ⊖ *Russell Sq, Chancery Lane. Open Mon–Sat 10–5; adm*. The only one of Dickens's many London homes to survive. The furnishings have been drafted in from other Dickens homes; really just a collection of hallowed objects.

Dr Johnson's House, 17 Gough Square, EC4, ✆ (020) 7353 3745; ⊖ *Blackfriars, Temple. Open Mon–Sat 11–5.30 and 11–5 Oct–April; cheap adm*. This is the elegant 17th-century house where the Doctor lived from 1748 to 1759. For many of those years he was busy compiling his famous dictionary, the first of its kind in the English language. He worked in the attic, sitting in a rickety three-legged chair and ordering about his six clerks, who must have had a tough time coping with his boundless energies and inexhaustible wit. Boswell said the attic looked like a counting house. The chief legacy of the dictionary to modern lexicographers is its scrupulous references to literary texts.

But it is also full of jokey definitions that poke fun at anyone and everyone, including Johnson himself; a lexicographer is defined as 'a writer of dictionaries, a harmless drudge'. The dictionary, published in 1755, made Johnson's reputation as both a serious academic and a great wit. The house is of interest more for its atmosphere than its contents.

Freud's House, 20 Maresfield Gardens, NW3, ✆ (020) 7435 2002; ⊖ *Finchley Road; bus 46. Open Wed–Sun 12–5; adm*. This is the house where Freud set up his last home after fleeing the Nazis in Vienna in 1938. Six rooms have been left untouched since the founder of psychoanalysis died of throat cancer on the eve of the Second World War. Of greatest interest is the couch where his patients lay during sessions—if, that is, it is not on loan to another museum. You can also see Freud's collections of furniture and artefacts, including some extraordinary phalluses, and watch the home movies he made of his family and dog at home in Vienna in the increasingly dark days of the 1930s.

Hogarth's House, Hogarth Lane, Chiswick, W4, ✆ (020) 8994 6757; ⊖ *Turnham Green. Open Tues–Fri 1–5, Sat 1–6; winter closed 1hr earlier; closed Jan; adm*. This was where the great 18th-century painter and satirist, in the last 15 years of his life, came to get away from it all—hard to believe, given the current traffic level. It is no more than a curiosity, since the house itself is unspectacular and contains only prints of his most famous works, not the originals which are elsewhere.

Keats's House, Wentworth House, Keats Grove, NW3, ✆ (020) 7435 2062; ⊖ *Hampstead. Open April–Oct Mon–Fri 10–1 and 2–6, Sat 10–1 and 2–5; Sun 2–5; Nov–Mar Mon–Fri 1–5, Sat 10–1; 2–5; Sun 2–5; free. See* p.103.

Religion

Freemason's Hall, Great Queen St, WC2, ✆ (020) 7831 9811; ⊖ *Covent Garden. Open Mon–Fri 10–5 and Sat 1pm, guided tour only; free*. An intriguing PR exercise stressing Freemasonry's principles of truth and brotherly love. Lots of regalia but no elucidation of those handshakes. 'It is not a secret society,' explains a leaflet. Right, and the Pope's not Catholic.

Wesley's House, Wesley Chapel, 49 City Rd, EC1, ✆ (020) 7253 2262; ⊖ *Moorgate. Open*

Mon–Sat 10–4, Sun 12–2; adm. John Wesley's house, and the nonconformist chapel he built next door in 1778, with columns made from the masts of ships donated by George III. Lots of missionary paraphernalia, and the world's first electric chair (invented by Wesley).

Jewish Museum, 129–32 Albert Street, NW1, ✆ (020) 7284 1997; ⊖ *Camden Town. Open Sun–Thurs 10–4; adm. See* p.99.

BBC Experience, Broadcasting House, Portland Place, W1, ℂ (0870) 603 0304; ⊖ *Oxford Circus. Open daily 10–4.30, Mon 11–4.30; tour takes 2hrs; adm on the pricey side.* This rather grim 1930s building is the nerve centre of the British Broadcasting Corporation, better known by its initials, BBC. The Beeb (or Auntie as it is sometimes referred to) used to run its main radio operations here. There never used to be much for the visitor to see around here, but now the broadcasting grandees have thought fit to provide something called 'The BBC Experience'. This includes a guided tour of the building, a look at a collection of Marconi's earliest radio equipment, a shop and café, and various inevitable interactive displays in which visitors have the opportunity to direct a soap opera, read the weather forecast or 'be' a sports commentator.

Bethnal Green Museum of Childhood, Cambridge Heath Road, E2, ℂ (020) 8980 2415; ⊖ *Bethnal Green. Open Mon–Thurs, Sat 10–5.50, Sun 2.30–5.50; free.* This extension of the Victoria and Albert Museum is housed in the building once known as the Brompton Boilers where the decorative arts collections were kept during the 1850s (you'll notice the very Victorian mosaic frieze on the outside depicting Agriculture, Art and Science). Inside are some extraordinarily intricate children's toys, notably doll's houses, train sets, puppet theatres and board games; a shame, however, that they are displayed in such gloomy cabinets. (Cambridge Heath Road, incidentally, leads up to the East End extension of the Grand Union Canal and the western end of Victoria Park, the biggest piece of greenery in east London.)

Bramah Tea and Coffee Museum, Maguire St, Butler's Wharf, SE1, ℂ (020) 7378 0222; ⊖ *Tower Hill, London Bridge; bus 47, 188, P11. Open daily 10–6; adm cheap.* Coffee arrived in London in the 1640s and quickly became popular among the traders and brokers of the City. 'It is a very good help to digestion, quickens the spirit and is good against sore eyes,' remarked one contemporary quaffer. Coffee was very much a man's drink; indeed for a long time women were not admitted to coffee houses at all. They were expected to drink tea, which arrived in Europe at roughly the same time. This full fresh-flavoured museum was set up by a commodity broker, Edward Bramah, with his amazing collection of over 1000 tea and coffee pots which tell the intricate history of the commodities, from the 17th and 18th century coffee houses which spawned the Stock Exchange and Lloyds Insurance, to that most elegiac of 20th-century inventions, the mass-produced tea bag. A more authentic brew is made in the two cafés, and the shop sells a choice selection of leaf teas.

Dennis Severs' House at **18 Folgate Street**, E1, ℂ (020) 7247 4013 for times and booking; ⊖ Liverpool Street. *Open first Sun in the month 2–5pm; adm; and also for evening performances three times a week with a special Silent Night on the first Monday of each month when the house is lit by candles and no one speaks, so that a 'silent poetry' is created; adm exp.* This is not so much a house as a theatre, a place which offers a glimpse back into the past not by showing off well-preserved artefacts and objects in the way that National Trust homes do, but by forcing you to feel your way into the atmosphere of bygone eras, from neoclassical to romantic. Inside, each room is a living tableau, a lovingly constructed still-life time machine, where sheets are rumpled, candle wax is congealed on the floor and last week's vegetables sit half-eaten on the tables. The master of ceremonies is Dennis Severs himself, a mildly eccentric ex-pat American lawyer who dropped out of the southern Californian rat race in the late 1970s and bought this house as a way of getting back in touch with himself and with the past. In his startlingly original evening performances (for which you should book several weeks in advance since only eight people can attend at a time), Mr Severs evokes the lives of five generations of occupants of the house, the fictional Jervis family, through a mixture of sound effects, light, still-life décor and sheer acting bravado. Emma Thompson came here to prepare for *Sense and Sensibility*. The effect is almost that of a seance. Mr Severs calls this 'perceiving the space between the eye and what you see'. Or, to quote his motto, *aut visum aut non*—you either see it or you don't.

Fan Museum, 12 Croom's Hill, SE10, ✆ (020) 8858 8789; ⇌ *Greenwich. DLR Island Gdns by river to Greenwich Pier; bus 188. Open Tues–Sat 11–4.30, Sun 12–4.30; adm.* Delightful collection of fans from the 17th century to the present.

London Aquarium, County Hall, Waterloo, SE1, ✆ (020) 7967 8000; ⊖ *Waterloo, Westminster. Open daily 10–5. See* p.28.

Madame Tussaud's, Marylebone Rd, NW1, ✆ (020) 7935 6861; ⊖ *Baker Street. Open May–Sept daily 9–5.30, with slightly later opening the rest of the year; adm exp.* There is no escaping the horrendous queues, which are little shorter in the winter. Nearly three million people put themselves through the crush each year, although it is hard to see why—the only thing you can say in the end about a waxwork is whether it is lifelike or not—and most of the film stars, politicians and famous villains here fare pretty indifferently. Back in the 19th century, of course, waxworks made more sense as they provided the only opportunity for ordinary people to catch a glimpse of the rich and famous, albeit in effigy. Marie Tussaud was a Swiss modelmaker who trained with her uncle by making death masks of the victims of the revolutionary Terror in France. Her hallmarks were her attention to detail, particularly in the costumes, and her efforts to keep the exhibition bang up to date with the latest celebrities and figures in the news. One of Madame Tussaud's most inspired ideas, the **Chamber of Horrors**, survives to this day. The final section of Madame Tussaud's is called the **Spirit of London**, a funfair-type ride in a modified black cab featuring illustrations of London's history from the Great Fire to the swinging 1960s.

Museum of Garden History, St Mary's, Lambeth Palace Rd, SE1, ✆ (020) 7261 1891; ⊖ *Westminster; bus 77, 159, 170, 507. Open Mon–Fri 10.30–4; free (donations welcome).* The plants on display were first gathered by Charles I's gardener John Tradescant, who is buried in the churchwith his son. You can also see gardening tools dating back to the ancient world. The church, largely rebuilt in 1852 but still based on its 14th-century precedent, is curious for other reasons too. It contains the only full-immersion font in London. It is the last resting place of Captain Bligh, of *Mutiny on the Bounty* fame. And in the south chapel is a stained-glass window commemorating a medieval pedlar who grew rich when his dog unearthed great treasure while scratching around one day on a piece of waste land in the area. The pedlar left an acre of land to the parish when he died, but asked for the window for him and his dog in return.

Sherlock Holmes Museum, 221b Baker St, NW1, ✆ (020) 7935 8866; ⊖ *Baker Street. Open daily 9.30–6; adm.* The museum *says* its address is 221b Baker St, and certainly looks convincing enough to be the supersleuth's consulting rooms. Unfortunately, though, it is really No.239; the building encompassing No.221b (which never actually existed as a self-contained address) is the glass-and-concrete headquarters of the Abbey National Building Society. The museum is a lot of fun, if you enter into its spirit of artifice. You are greeted at the door by either a housekeeper or a policeman. Most entertaining of all is the folder containing Sherlock Holmes's fan mail.

Theatre Museum, Tavistock St, Covent Garden, WC2, ✆ (020) 7836 2330/7836 7891; ⊖ *Covent Garden. Open Tues–Sun 11–7; phone to check time of tours; adm.* This museum is confusingly laid out; by far the best way to see it is to join one of the very informative guided tours led by actors three times a day and free with the price of admission. A vast number of exhibits cover the history of the English stage from the Elizabethan public playhouses to the rise of the National Theatre, illustrated by period costumes and plenty of model theatres. Unfortunately all this wonderful stuff—from Edmund Kean's death mask to the psychedelic hand-printed costumes used by the Diaghilev Ballets Russes to premiere 'The Rite of Spring' in Paris in 1913—is displayed behind the smudged glass of dully lit fish tanks. Rather more engaging fun is to be had by submitting yourself to the free make-up displays; you may have noticed some eccentric-looking people with werewolf faces or Mr Hyde expressions on your way in.

Vinopolis, 1 Bank End, Clink Street, SE1, ✆ (020) 7940 8300; ⊖ *Cannon St, Borough; bus 40, 133, 149. Open daily 10–5.30; adm. See* p.86.

London: Children and Sport

Children's Activities

Children have traditionally come somewhere beneath dogs and horses on the scale of human affection in England. The prevailing view is that children should be neither seen nor heard in public. If some pubs, bars and restaurants now admit children, and even provide high chairs and nappy-changing facilities, it is more out of a sense of obligation than any real enthusiasm. Nevertheless, there is plenty to keep children occupied and amused in London. Aside from the ideas listed below, you can find out more through **Kidsline** on ✆ (020) 7222 8070 (*open during school summer holidays 8am–4pm*), or the London Tourist Board's **what's on for children line** on ✆ 0839 123 404 (*recorded information*).

Among the most popular and absorbing sights for children are: the **Science Museum** (where they can even spend the night), the Natural History Museum, the Commonwealth Institute and the three museums devoted to the younger generation: Pollock's Toy Museum in Fitzrovia, the Bethnal Green Museum of Childhood, the Cabaret Mechanical Theatre in Covent Garden, and the London Toy and Model Museum in Bayswater. For gore and ghoulishness, if you want to avoid the queues at such crowd-pullers as the London Dungeon and Madame Tussaud's, try instead the Clink Exhibition in Southwark or the **Tower of London**.

To keep the kids entertained there are many **funfairs** in the parks during the summer (*see Time Out*); Punch and Judy shows at Covent Garden; children's films at the National Film Theatre, the Barbican and the ICA. At Christmas time there are **pantomimes** galore all over London. During the rest of the year there are children's shows at the following theatres:

Little Angel Theatre, 14 Dagmar Passage, Islington, N1, ✆ (020) 7226 1787; ⊖ *Highbury & Islington/Angel*. A delightful puppet theatre. *Closed Aug.*

Polka Theatre for Children, 240 The Broadway, Wimbledon, SW19, ✆ (020) 8543 0363; ⊖ *Wimbledon*. A complex for the under-13s including the main theatre, a playground, two shops with cheap toys and an adventure room for under-5s. *Closed Sept.*

Unicorn Theatre for Children, 6 Great Newport St, Covent Garden, WC2, ✆ (020) 7836 3334; ⊖ *Leicester Square*. London's oldest children's theatre.

Rainforest Café, 20 Shaftesbury Avenue, W1, ✆ (020) 7434 3111; ⊖ *Piccadilly Circus*. Exciting rainforest eating place which will delight children, and an inspired alternative to the ubiquitous McDonald's. (Not only for children.) Top floor is a retail area.

No lack of outlets to shop *for* kids: for most emergency toy or clothing needs you should be satisfied by the many branches of the Early Learning Centre, Mothercare, Toys R Us, Next, Baby Gap or Gap for Kids. As for shopping *with* kids, here are a few key destinations:

Borders, 203 Oxford St, W1, ✆ (020) 7292 1600; ⊖ *Oxford Circus*. American bookstore on five floors; excellent children's section with places to sit and read, and storytelling sessions (call for details); nice café on the same floor.

Davenports Magic Shop, Charing Cross Underground Shopping Arcade, WC2, ✆ 0171 836 0408. ⊖ *Charing Cross*. Masks, practical jokes and hardware for magicians.

Disney Store, 140–4 Regent St, W1, ✆ (020) 7287 6558; ⊖ *Piccadilly Circus*. Anything Disney you or your kids could possibly desire, and more.

Hamleys, 188 Regent St, W1, ✆ (020) 7494 2000; ✆ *Oxford Circus*. One of the world's great toyshops with loads of puzzles, computer games, teddy bears and gadgets. The escalators alone can keep kids happy for hours. Expensive, though.

London Doll's House Co., 29 The Market, Covent Garden, WC1, ✆ (020) 7240 2288; ✆ *Covent Garden*. Everything for your child's doll at this delightful basement boutique.

Child-minding Services

Childminders, 6 Nottingham St, W1, ✆ (020) 7935 3000. An agency with a network of babysitters, nurses and infant teachers.

Universal Aunts, ✆ (020) 7738 8937. Provides babysitters, entertainers, people to meet children off trains, and guides to take children round London.

Pippa Pop-Ins, 430 Fulham Rd, SW6, ✆ (020) 7385 2458. This award-winning hotel for 2–12 year olds provides a crèche, nursery school and babysitting services.

Sports

London is rich in sports facilities and venues thanks to its extensive parkland and plentiful supply of ponds, reservoirs and lakes. It boasts several first-rate venues, including Wembley for soccer, Twickenham for rugby, Crystal Palace for athletics, Lord's and the Oval for cricket, and the mythical lawns of Wimbledon for tennis. For any sporting query, whether for spectating or taking part, call **Sportsline**, ✆ (020) 7222 8000.

Taking Part

For health fanatics in need of a workout, the **public sports centres** run by all London boroughs usually have good facilities—ask Sportsline for the most convenient one.

There are some superb outdoor venues for **swimming**, notably the Highgate and Hampstead Ponds on Hampstead Heath. The Hampstead Pond, which is mixed-sex, is best reached from East Heath Road. The single-sex Highgate Ponds are accessible from Millfield Lane. Other council-run lidos worth trying are Tooting, Brixton and Parliament Hill (lidos are large unheated open-air pools, usually built in the 1930s).

There are **tennis** courts in virtually every London park—check with Sportsline for details and booking procedure. Battersea Park has some of the cheapest courts, while Holland Park has the trendiest. Most charge a membership fee, but this may entitle you to play at other London venues. Often you have to book in person.

Queens Ice Skating Club, 17 Queensway, W2, ✆ (020) 7229 0172; ✆ *Queensway*. Lessons, ice discos and more at London's most famous club. Also ten pin bowling.

Regent's Park Boating Lake, ✆ (020) 7486 4759; ✆ *Baker Street*. Rent a boat during the summer and idle away a few hours on either the large adult or the tiny children's lake between the Inner and the Outer Circle of Regent's Park. Cheap and wonderful.

Ross Nye Stables, 8 Bathurst Mews, Bayswater, W2, ✆ (020) 7262 3791; ✆ *Lancaster Gate*. For riding in Hyde Park. *Horses on holiday mid-July–early Sept.*

Rowans Ten Pin Bowling, 10 Stroud Green Road, Finsbury Park, N4, ☎ (020) 8800 1950; ⊖ *Finsbury Park*. For a little late-night exercise.

Wimbledon Village Stables, 24a/b High Street, Wimbledon Village, SW19, ☎ (020) 8946 8579; ⊖ *Wimbledon*. Good for beginners, with the whole of Wimbledon Common and Richmond Park in which to roam free.

Spectator Sports

A game surely invented to be incomprehensible to the uninitiated, **cricket** incites great passions in its most ardent fans and sheer tedium in nearly everyone else. It would be foolhardy to attempt an explanation of the rules, which defy description, at least on paper. Atmosphere's the thing, and a visit to Lord's or the Oval usually provides plenty of good drink and conversation as well as an introduction to the world of silly mid-offs, follow-ons, googlies, chinamen, long legs and short legs.

Rougher and more complex than soccer, **rugby** football involves hand as well as foot contact and is played with an ovoid ball. Still an essential part of the summer season, the Wimbledon lawn **tennis** championships take place in the last week of June and the first week of July. The men warm up a couple of weeks' earlier in competition at the smaller Queens Club.

All England Lawn Tennis Club, Church Road, Wimbledon, SW19, ☎ (020) 8944 1066; ⊖ *Southfields*. You'll need to apply nine months in advance for a seat on Centre or Number One Court during the championships—they're allocated by ballot. However, if you turn up early in the competition you'll see plenty of action on the outside courts, and can still enjoy strawberries and cream under the pale English sun.

Crystal Palace Sports Arena, Ledrington Road, SE19, ☎ (020) 8778 0131; ⇌ *Crystal Palace*. Venue for national and international athletics events.

Highbury Stadium, Avenell Road, N5, ☎ (020) 7704 4000; ⊖ *Arsenal*. Home to Arsenal (the Gunners), Tottenham's arch-rival.

Lord's Cricket Ground, St John's Wood Road, NW8, ☎ (020) 7289 1611; ⊖ *St John's Wood*. The most famous cricket venue in the world, and home to the original governing body of the sport, the Marylebone Cricket Club (MCC), as well as the local county side, Middlesex.

The Oval, Kennington, SE11, ☎ (020) 7582 7764; ⊖ *Oval*. Home to Surrey, this vast pitch usually hosts the last test match of the summer.

Queens Club, 14 Palliser Road, W14, ☎ (020) 7385 3421; ⊖ *Baron's Court*. One-week men's competition just before Wimbledon gives a good idea of who's on form to win the big one. Some tickets available on the day.

Twickenham Stadium, Rugby Road, Twickenham, in southwest London, ☎ (020) 8892 2000; ⇌ *Twickenham*. International rugby fixtures and cup finals.

Wembley Stadium, Stadium Way, northwest London, ☎ (020) 8902 0902; ⇌ *Wembley Stadium*/⊖ *Wembley Park*. Major international soccer fixtures and cup finals. Also venue for pop concerts.

White Hart Lane, 748 High Road, N17, ☎ (020) 8365 5050; ⇌ *White Hart Lane*. Home to Tottenham Hotspur (Spurs), Arsenal's arch rival.

London: Food and Drink

Food, Glorious Food

Nice manners, shame about the food: nothing about the English has traditionally left foreigners so aghast as their dining habits. The horror stories are legion: of wobbly, green-tinged custard, of vegetables boiled until they are blue, of white bread so vile you can roll it into little balls and use it as schoolroom ammunition, of rice pudding so sickly and overcooked it makes you gag. No wonder visitors from abroad have often contemplated packing a few home goodies to keep the wolf from the door.

In fact, you can put away your prejudices; London is now one of the great gastronomic centres on the planet. Never in its history has the city been so cosmopolitan, and never has there been such a wide variety of cuisines to sample. Its cutting-edge chefs are treated like superstars as they vie to reproduce, and improve on, the best that world cooking can offer. London boasts the best Indian food outside of India, and the best Chinese food in Europe. There are excellent Caribbean restaurants, Lebanese restaurants, Italian, Greek and Spanish restaurants, Polish, Hungarian and Russian restaurants. Even the British restaurants aren't bad, and some of them are outstanding.

Restaurants

London restaurants tend to take lunch orders between 12.30 and 2pm, and dinner orders between 7 and 10pm, although you'll find cafés and brasseries that stay open all afternoon and accept orders until 11pm or even later. Listed restaurants are open every day for lunch and dinner unless indicated otherwise. Soho and Covent Garden are undoubtedly the most fertile areas, although there are excellent selections in Notting Hill, Fulham, Camden Town, Islington and Hampstead.

The one drawback is money—eating out in London is an expensive pleasure. There are some incredible bargains to be had, but overall you are lucky to get away with much less than £25–35 per head for a decent evening meal, roughly half as much again as you would in Paris, Rome or a number of North American cities. One reason for this is the wine, which can be cripplingly expensive without being especially reliable: watch out. Meal prices should be inclusive of tax (VAT), but an extra cover charge (no more than £2) may be added in swankier places. Look carefully to see if service is included. If not, leave an extra 10–15 per cent of the total, preferably in cash. As for prices, the lists below divide restaurants into the following categories, according to the price of a full meal with wine and service:

ᚑᚑᚑᚑᚑ	*luxury*	**more than £50**
ᚑᚑᚑᚑ	*expensive*	**£35–50**
ᚑᚑᚑ	*moderate*	**£25–35**
ᚑᚑ	*inexpensive*	**£15–25**
ᚑ	*cheap*	**under £15**

All but the cheapest establishments will take cheques or credit cards. If you are paying with plastic, the total box will inevitably be left for you to fill, in anticipation of a fat tip. Don't feel under any pressure, especially if service is already included.

Soho

Alastair Little, 49 Frith St, W1, ✆ (020) 7734 5183 (*closed Sun and Sat lunchtime*). One of the first and also the best of nouvelle British cuisine restaurants. The simplicity of the ingredients is echoed by the positively bare-essentialist décor. The menu changes according to what's fresh in the market.

The Gay Hussar, 2 Greek St, W1, ✆ (020) 7437 0973 (*closed Sun*). Velvet-upholstered Hungarian restaurant, famous for its wild cherry soup, goulash and dumplings, served on thick red-and-white china. The stylish, intimate setting is much beloved by the old left of British politics. The unchanging menu is calorific and filling.

L'Escargot, 48 Greek St, W1, ✆ (020) 7437 2679 (*closed Sat lunch, all day Sun*). This one-time bulwark of the Soho scene has reopened under new management, serving high quality, classic French food under the gaze of high modern art (Picassos, Mirós, Chagalls). The first-floor dining room is more formal than the magnolia room below, but both serve exquisite dishes in daring sauces. A speciality is *feuilleté* of snails served with bacon.

Vasco and Piero's Pavilion, 15 Poland St, W1, ✆ (020) 7437 8774. Sophisticated, friendly Italian restaurant serving immaculately presented dishes, e.g. grilled breast of guinea fowl with juniper berries. Cheaper two- or three-course set menus. Truffles from Umbria available in season.

Sri Siam, 16 Old Compton St, W1, ✆ (020) 7434 3544. Modern, minimalist and hip, a combination unusual in a Thai restaurant. The sleek, cream walls, adorned here and there by banana and palm leaf themes, host throngs of diners in the evening, although it can be empty at lunch.

Café Fish, 36–40 Rupert St, SW1, ✆ (020) 7287 8989 (*closed Sat lunch, all day Sun*). Although there is an underlying old French character to this bustling bistro, the accent is fish, obviously. And you can order fish and shellfish in most cooked forms, be it char-grilled, steamed, *meunière* or fried, or sometimes even marinated.

The Criterion, 224 Piccadilly, W1, ✆ (020) 7930 0488. (*Closed Sun lunch.*) A magnificent, Art Deco, gold mosaic interior, opened in 1870 and recently re-launched with Marco Pierre White as chef. The place has seen much drama—suffragettes met here in the 1910s when women were not allowed into pubs. While the service is sometimes impatient and the room crowded, the food is exquisite without being exotic.

Fung Shing, 15 Lisle St, WC2, ✆ (020) 7437 1539. Beautiful, delicate, mainly Cantonese Chinese food, served with style in a bright lemon, blond-wood-panelled dining room; there is also an airy veranda at the back. The menu includes some more traditional Chinese dishes. One of the classic dishes is braised suckling pig.

Mezzo, 100 Wardour St, W1, ✆ (020) 7314 4000. Reputedly one of the biggest, trendiest restaurants in Europe, which opened in 1995 to loud acclaim by the media, partly because of the prestige of the designer and owner, Sir Terence Conran. The basement restaurant is overpriced, and the service is erratic, but the place definitely has style. Prepare for noise. A high standard of cooking: fillet of beef, pesto and *pommes frites*; salmon, pickled eggplant and yoghurt. *Closed upstairs on Sundays.*

The Sugar Club, 21 Warwick St, Soho, W1R, ✆ (020) 7437 7776. One of the hippest places in London. Globally inspired dishes with particularly good contrasting textures and tastes, e.g. grilled scallops with sweet chilli sauce and crème fraîche.

Little Italy, 21 Frith St, W1, ✆ (020) 7734 4737. An offshoot of the famous Bar Italia, which was for many years the only place selling real espresso in London. The restaurant has a comparable authenticity that some of the more fashionable places may lack. Photographs of boxers adorn the walls.

Dell'Ugo, 56 Frith St, W1, ✆ (020) 7734 8300. A big statue sticks out of one of the windows. A three-storey building, each level being a separate, different restaurant. The ground floor hosts a fashion-conscious under-30s crowd. The upper floors are calmer and serve more serious dishes.

Quo Vadis, 26–9 Dean St, W1, ✆ (020) 7437 9585. Lime green airy interiors with meticulous table decoration. Positively serene compared with the new, trendy bustling bistros. Features spoof 'Brit Art' by chef-turned-artist Marco Pierre White, inspired in the wake of his recent and highly publicized fall-out by ex-partner Damien Hirst. French food with Mediterranean influences.

Frith Street Restaurant, 64 Frith St, W1, ✆ (020) 7734 4545 (*closed Sat and Sun lunch*). Modern Provençal food served in a cool interior of aquamarine walls, wood floors and comfortable leather chairs.

The Lexington, 45 Lexington St, W1, ✆ (020) 7434 3401 (*closed Sat lunch, Sun*). Modern European food: 2-course set menu for £10 which includes broad-shouldered dishes like roast pheasant and chorizo or suckling pig with butter bean and morel stew. Warm, purple and faintly psychedelic with modern art. Jazz pianist at night.

Andrew Edmunds, 46 Lexington St, W1, ✆ (020) 7437 5708. Simple, beautifully prepared dishes at low prices. Queues at the door, which makes the service understandably frenzied. Old-fashioned frontage, hard benches and restless sawdust effect belie the modern ethos and originality of the cooking. Menus change weekly.

Randall & Aubin, 16 Brewer St, W1, ✆ (020) 7287 4447. An old Victorian butcher's shop converted into an oyster and champagne bar, with a rôtisserie; the original tiled interior has been preserved. Specializes in seafood and spit-roasts, also langoustines, crabs, whelks—the ingredients can be made into sandwiches to order.

The Red Fort, 77 Dean St, W1, ✆ (020) 7437 2115. Northern Indian restaurant. Excellent Tandoori and Mogul specialities such as quail and a Rajasthani smoked kebab of fresh salmon. Recently refurbished decor has upped the prices. Indian food festivals occasion special menus.

French House Dining Rooms, 49 Dean St, W1, ✆ (020) 7437 2477 (*closed Sun*). Dark, worn wooden rooms above a pub of the same name. Atmospheric, 1920s ambience, much frequented by literati. Excellent British food, e.g. smoked eel salad, ox tongue, guinea fowl, confit of duck.

Kulu Kulu, 76 Brewer St, W1, ✆ (020) 7734 7316. Sushi is handmade at this busy Japanese eating spot. A long, narrow conveyor belt runs along the counter and the food is served on colour-coded plates.

Tokyo Diner, 2 Newport Place, W1, ✆ (020) 7287 8777 (*open from 12 every day—all year*). Japanese fast food—sushi and Japanese curries. One of the cheapest Japanese eateries in London. Noodles (about £6), donburi—rice and various toppings (£4–6). Ingredients are fresh and crisply cooked. Good service, authentic décor, no tips.

Soho Spice, 124–6 Wardour St, W1, ✆ (020) 7434 0808. One of the few Indian restaurants in Soho. Radiant blue, orange and magenta colour scheme makes for a modern Indian look. Genial service; also a bar.

Poon's, 27 Lisle St, W1, ✆ (020) 7437 4549. Recently expanded, this has lost some of its chaotic caffness. Famous for high-quality 'wind-dried' meats—especially the duck.

Jimmy's, 23 Frith St, W1, ✆ (020) 7437 9521. Moussaka and chips, as eaten by the Rolling Stones, among others, in the 1960s, is a mainstay of this basement Soho institution. Unchanging décor, green lino and cheap prices for standard Greek Cypriot dishes, like *taramá*, *afelia* and the like. Cosy in winter, hot in summer.

Mildred's, 58 Greek St, W1, ✆ (020) 7494 1634 (*open till 11*). Eclectic wholesome vegetarian fare from Brazilian casserole to Chinese black bean vegetables and vegetarian sausages. Vegan daily specials. Also seasonal organic produce and even organic wines. Good Sunday brunch.

Cranks, 8 Marshall St, W1, ✆ (020) 7437 9431. Popular, pioneering vegetarian restaurant with several branches around London. Warm, apricotty interiors. Good vegetarian food—roasted vegetables and couscous—and tasty salads, quiches, pies. Self-service.

Wagamama, 10A Lexington St, W1, ✆ (020) 7292 0990. Wagamama, now an institution in Bloomsbury, has opened a new branch in Soho. The philosophy of this Japanese noodle bar is 'positive eating, positive living'. Hi-tech, efficient, fast service on long communal tables. Long queues do not diminish the experience.

Café España, 63 Old Compton St, W1, ✆ (020) 7494 1271. Plain, authentic little Spanish restaurant—a far cry from self-conscious, un-Spanish tapas bars that have cropped up all over London. Good generous portions of Galician and Castilian dishes, emphasizing fish.

Covent Garden

The Ivy, 1 West St, WC2, ✆ (020) 7836 4751. The moody oak panels and stained glass dating from the 1920s are offset by vibrant modern paintings. The menu caters for elaborate as well as tamer tastes. Salmon fishcakes on a bed of leaf spinach is a signature dish. Takes orders from 12–3 and 5–12, which ensures a diverse clientèle, but particularly popular amongst the theatre comers and goers as well as the players.

Simpsons, 100 Strand, WC2, ✆ (020) 7836 9112. The ultimate, old-fashioned English restaurant, ideal if you like your roast beef and Yorkshire pudding served by deferential, tail-coated waiters in an aristocratic environment. Once a gentlemen's club and also a chess club, the ethos of which is preserved and refined. Also serves 'The Great British Breakfast' which includes the 'ten deadly sins' of liver, black pudding, sausages and the like.

Christophers, 18 Wellington St, WC2, ✆ (020) 7240 4222. The opulent curved stone staircase in the foyer recalls a 19th-century pleasure dome—reinforced when one realizes that this was once London's first licensed casino (and later a high-class brothel). Up the stairs, in the dining hall, a more restrained elegance pervades. As an American restaurant, the menu emphasizes steaks and grills, but there are also seafood inspirations.

Rules, 35 Maiden Lane, WC2, ✆ (020) 7836 5314 (*open all day*). The oldest restaurant in London (established 1798), with a long history of serving aristocrats as well as actors. Formal and determinedly old-fashioned, panelled in dark wood and decorated with hunting regalia. Specializes in game of the season: even rarities such as snipe, ptarmigan and woodcock. Dress smart.

Mon Plaisir, 21 Monmouth St, WC2, ✆ (020) 7836 7243. Jumbled, old bohemian charm, reminiscent of a convivial Rive Gauche brasserie, and a cluttered yet capacious dining area, thronged with rushing, Gallic waiters. Appetizing French provincial dishes, especially seafood.

Bertorelli's, 44a Floral St, WC2, ✆ (020) 7836 3969 (*closed Sun*). Conveniently located for opera-goers, 'Bert's' serves a broad range of proven Italian favourites, but also a more radical catalogue of Italian dishes, like *maltagliati* served with pumpkin, cream, chorizo, or antipasti of deep-fried mozzarella.

Orso, 27 Wellington St, WC2, ✆ (020) 7240 5269 (*open all day*). High-quality Italian fare, served in a graceful, terracotta, Venetian dining room. Mainly Tuscan food, interestingly and daringly interpreted, like pizza with goat's cheese and roasted garlic and oregano, or *puntarelle* with anchovy dressing.

Joe Allen, 13 Exeter St, WC2, ✆ (020) 7836 0651. Started out as an American restaurant, serving hamburgers and steaks, but now embraces modern British and European too. The result is a long menu, lacking character—but there are some delights, particularly if you're into monster puddings. Joe Allen's is traditionally a venue to be seen in and also for star-gazers. Rollicking atmosphere with last orders at 12.45am.

Café des Amis du Vin, 11–14 Hanover Place, WC2, ✆ (020) 7379 3444 (*closed Sun*). A cheap, quiet French brasserie, favoured by theatre goers. Caters for all tastes, from omelettes to stuffed trout. More formal upstairs dining room. A little pedestrian, but solid. Service can be slow.

Calabash, Africa Centre, 38 King St, WC2, ☎ (020) 7836 1976 (*closed Sat lunch, all day Sun*). Dishes from all over Africa are served at this basement restaurant under the Africa Centre. A surprisingly institutional feel pervades the dining room, partly because of the collegey canteen. *Egusi* (stew of beef, melon, shrimps cooked in palm oil) from Nigeria, couscous from the Maghreb, *dioumbre* (okra stew) from Ivory Coast, with lots of fried plantain.

Bloomsbury/Fitzrovia

Nico Central, 35 Gt Portland St, W1, ☎ (020) 7436 8846 (*closed Sat lunch, Sun*). Although this restaurant is no longer run by Nico Ladenis, the standards, as well as the good deals in the set menus, remain. Mostly Provençal-inspired creations. Sometimes smallish portions, but beautifully cooked, with interesting ideas such as boudin blanc with caramelized apple galette, and red snapper with couscous. Dream puddings.

Museum Street Café, 47 Museum St, WC1, ☎ (020) 7405 3211 (*closed Sat, Sun*). Sleek and spartan, emphasizing the '90s predilection for scarce décor. Excellent, unusual items, though standards are reputedly variable. Sample dishes include salad with *confit* of guinea fowl with roasted beets and walnut vinaigrette, and penne with roasted red peppers and basil cream.

Gonbei, 151 King's Cross Rd, WC1, ☎ (020) 7278 0619 (*closed Sun*). One of London's cheaper, but still excellent, Japanese restaurants. Only open in the evening (*6–11*). Delicious set dinners; also à la carte choices. Sushi is particularly recommended, as is noodle soup with tempura.

Elena's L'Etoile, 30 Charlotte St, W1, ☎ (020) 7636 1496 (*closed Sat lunch, all day Sun*). This historic Fitzrovian locale has appropriated Elena Salvoni's name to its title in tribute to her personal contribution to the Etoile. Faded grandeur and old photographs of fêted regulars serve as the backdrop. But the menu is no longer only traditional French fare: some modern touches especially in the Eastern influence of some recipes.

Alfred, 245 Shaftsbury Ave, WC2, ☎ (020) 7240 2566 (*closed Sat lunch, all day Sun*). A modern angle on old British favourites. Stark, no-nonsense décor with duck egg blue and nut brown walls and formica tabletops. This serves to underline the delicacy of the cooking. Straightforward dishes like roast pork combine with imaginative accompaniments.

Mandeer, 8 Bloomsbury Way, W1, ☎ (020) 7242 6202 (*closed Sun*). Appetizing vegetarian food from Gujarat and Punjab, including puffed lotus seeds and tofu curry. The place has been serving vegetarian dishes of this ilk since 1961. There are about five *thalis*—complete meals.

Townhouse Brasserie, 24 Coptic St, WC1, ☎ (020) 7636 2731. A fusion of modern French and international cooking, e.g. seafood tempura in French batter. Somewhat cramped quarters even though there is plenty of space. Fizzing and boozy atmosphere, and huge portions.

Chutneys, 133–5 Drummond St, NW1, ☎ (020) 7388 0604 (*unlicensed*). One of several extraordinarily cheap, vegetarian Indian restaurants along this narrow street just behind Euston Station. Watch out for unexpectedly high service charges.

Wagamama, 4 Streatham St, ☎ (020) 7323 9223. *See* under Soho, p.149.

October Gallery Café, 24 Old Gloucester St, WC1, ☎ (020) 7242 7367. Eclectic inspiration from around the world; busy, cosy and friendly. Two- or three-course meals for highly reasonable prices. A limited choice—but usually a vegetarian option. A courtyard to skulk in in summertime.

Marylebone

Stephen Bull, 5–7 Blandford St, W1, ☎ (020) 7486 9696 (*closed Sat lunch, all day Sun*). An excellent, original voice amongst the multi-faceted strains of modern European cooking. Bull believes strongly in simplicity in cooking, and emphasizes fresh ingredients and unfussy, non-gimmicky presentation. The result is highly sophisticated.

∞ **Singapore Garden**, 154–6 Gloucester Place, NW1, ✆ (020) 7723 8233. A spacious, light basement venue under Regent's Park Hotel, serving Singaporean food. Sometimes very hot, but successful seafood dishes. The service is very friendly, the environment a touch staid. Try the fried seaweed and squid and the mild fish curry.

∞ **Sea Shell**, 49–51 Lisson Grove, NW1, ✆ (020) 7723 8703. Arguably the best fish and chips in town. Fresh and crisp. Fine home-made fish cakes and, more's the rarity, home-made tartare sauce. Clean and attractive. Café-style eating as well as takeaway.

Mayfair/St James's

∞∞∞∞∞ **Connaught Hotel Grill Room**, Carlos Place, W1, ✆ (020) 7499 7070 (closed Sat afternoon). Steaks, grills, as well as unusual French delicacies are a treat in this most exclusive of surroundings. High quality but not wildly adventurous. A fine, apple-green room, chandeliers, banquettes. Serious but friendly waiters with impeccable sensitivity.

∞∞∞∞∞ **Le Gavroche**, 43 Upper Brook St, W1, ✆ (020) 7408 0881 (closed Sat, Sun). Albert Roux is one of the most revered cooks in Britain, the first this side of the Channel to win three Michelin stars. He has now delegated the cuisine to his son, Michel, but standards are still de luxe. Extraordinary creativity, from the sautéed scallops to the coffee cup desert. It doesn't come cheap.

∞∞∞∞∞ **Suntory**, 72–3 St. James's St, SW1, ✆ (020) 7409 0201 (closed Sun lunch). One of the best, most expensive Japanese restaurants in town, with a Michelin star and also prices to remind you of the fact. You can eat in the old-fashioned, paper screened dining room— or in a private room. Very delicate sushi.

∞∞∞∞ **Al Hamra**, 31–3 Shepherd Market, W1, ✆ (020) 7493 1954. Sophisticated if rather overpriced Middle Eastern restaurant in the heart of the cosmopolitan chic of Shepherd Market, where you can sit 'out' in the summer months. Select a meze of different dishes from the 48 delicacies.

∞∞∞∞ **The Greenhouse**, 27a Hay's Mews, W1, ✆ (020) 7499 3331 (closed Sat lunch). The principal idea behind this restaurant was to resurrect stale old English recipes into new categories. Liver and bacon or sponge pudding may sound dull, but they come to life here. Signature dishes include fillet of smoked haddock with Welsh rarebit.

∞∞∞∞ **The Square**, 6–10 Bruton St, W1, ✆ (020) 7839 8787 (closed Sat, Sun lunch). The Square has moved to a new Mayfair address, equally sleek and modern. Constantly changing menu, with strong emphasis on fish. Try the delicious seared tuna with niçoise dressing.

∞∞∞∞ **Le Caprice**, Arlington House, Arlington St, SW1, ✆ (020) 7629 2239. Fashion victims crowd this modish but imaginative restaurant. Essentially 'modern British' food, but eclectic choice, with lovely starters such as squash risotto.

∞∞∞ **Quaglino's**, 16 Bury St, SW1, ✆ (020) 7930 6767. Modern, designer restaurant in a converted, sunken ballroom, mainly Italian menu. Polished and gleaming, it is another facet of the growing Conran empire. The menu is equally design conscious, although there is a large choice. Good shellfish.

∞∞∞ **Sofra**, 18 Shepherd Market, W1, ✆ (020) 7493 3320. Excellent Turkish restaurant with all the usual meze dishes, a crushed wheat salad and delicious sticky filled pastries. An emphasis on fresh ingredients ensures high quality at reasonable prices.

∞∞∞ **Mulligans'**, 13–14 Cork St, W1, ✆ (020) 7409 1370 (closed Sat lunch, all day Sun). Hearty Irish cooking, but a new management has incorporated lighter dishes (such as smoked fish, or blue cashel cheese and artichoke and spinach salad), especially at lunch time. But you can still find beef cooked in Guinness. Wicked puddings.

∞∞ **Down Mexico Way**, 25 Swallow St, W1, ✆ (020) 7437 9895 (open from 12 noon everyday). London does not excel in Mexican food but this is one of the better addresses in town. Fish with chilli and almond, and lime-cooked chicken provide welcome variations on the usual enchiladas.

Condotti's, 4 Mill St, W1, ☎ (020) 7499 1308. A smart pizza parlour with white linen tablecloths and chic waitresses. Otherwise the pizzas are regular and juicy as opposed to thin and crusty. At lunchtime it is full of business clients, but in the evening it jollies up.

Kensington

Clarke's, 124 Kensington Church St, W8, ☎ (020) 7221 9225 (*closed Sat, Sun*). A Californian restaurant to the extent that there is an emphasis on fresh produce. The set menu changes nightly, including salad of roasted pigeon with watercress, blood orange and black truffle dressing, and chargrilled turbot with chilli and roasted garlic mayonnaise. Small, intimate, nearly prissy room, but cooking is precise and professional.

Phoenicia, 11–13 Abingdon Rd, W8, ☎ (020) 7937 0120. Swish, carpeted Lebanese restaurant attracting smartly dressed customers. Delicious meze selections—excellent *basturma* (smoked, cured Lebanese beef) and falafel—but portions can be modest. Makes much of pudding too: a variety of fresh cream and pastry dishes are given a dousing in aromatic syrups.

Wódka, 12 St Alban's Grove, W8, ☎ (020) 7937 6513 (*closed Sat, Sun lunch*). This site has been a Polish restaurant since the 1950s—but the current proprietor of this newish venture is intent on modernizing the image of Eastern European food in London. Plain interior with jazz backdrop. A list of 30 different vodkas and *eaux de vie*; also a daily changing set lunch at low prices. The result is both classy and professional.

Cambio de Tercio, 163 Old Brompton Rd, SW5, ☎ (020) 7244 8970. Exuberant contemporary Spanish cooking: delicate paella, skate wings, salt cod, octopus. Intensely popular; best to book ahead. Strong references to the bullring in the decorative theme. Some real tapas too to start with— *jamón serrano* with *fino* or *manzanilla*.

The Gate, 51 Queen Caroline St, Hammersmith, W6, ☎ (020) 8748 6932 (*closed Sat lunch, all day Sun*). First-rate vegetarian restaurant with mouth-watering fennel mousse, wild mushroom cannelloni and teriyaki aubergine. Sunflower walls and a leafy courtyard make an attractive ambiance.

Polish Air Force Association Club and Restaurant, 14 Collingham Gardens, SW5, ☎ (020) 7741 4052. Set three-course meal from £5.20. Atmospheric basement club founded after the War, filled with flying memorabilia, catering to local Poles but welcoming visitors. Hearty Polish cooking: *pierogis*, sauerkraut, meatballs: also *golonka* (pig's knuckle), and jam pancakes.

Chelsea and Fulham

La Tante Claire, Wilton Place, Knightsbridge, SW3, ☎ (020) 7823 2003 (*closed Sat, Sun*). Classic French cuisine, with three Michelin stars to its name. Lots of goose, foie gras and duck, as well as other Gascon-inspired compositions.

Bibendum, Michelin House, 81 Fulham Rd, SW3, ☎ (020) 7581 5817. Excelling in ultra-rich French regional food, set in the sumptuously restored Art Deco Michelin building (ex-headquarters of the tyre manufacturers, designed by an untrained architect in 1905, and restored by Conran in 1987). The oyster bar downstairs, with a shorter fish-oriented menu, is cheaper though less grand.

River Café, Thames Wharf Studios, Rainville Rd, W6, ☎ (020) 7381 8824 (*closed Sun dinner*). Simple, very tasty Italian food in a splendid riverside setting designed by Richard Rogers—and then redesigned by him. Rogers' wife, Ruthie, and her friend Rose Gray, are the chief chefs—and they have written a series of influential cookbooks.

Bombay Brasserie, Courtfield Close, Courtfield Rd, SW7, ☎ (020) 7370 4040. Near Gloucester Rd. Unlike most Indian restaurants in London, this is posh, in sumptuous colonial décor, and gastronomically flawless. Largely north Indian menu, including some unusual tandoori dishes. Beautiful veranda.

Canteen, Unit 4G, Harbour Yard, Chelsea Harbour, SW10, ✆ (020) 7351 7330. Part owned by the actor, Michael Caine, a resident of the harbour. Post-modern setting with playing-card upholstery. Dishes include *velouté* of artichokes, spinach and chestnut ravioli, and peppered duck breast, roast baby vegetables and pineapple *jus.*

Ken Lo's Memories of China, 67–9 Ebury St, SW1, ✆ (020) 7730 7734 (*closed Sun lunch*). Minimalist décor, but maximalist cooking. Ken Lo, one of Britain's best-known Chinese restaurateurs, who died a few years ago, founded this esteemed establishment which offers a stunning gastronomic tour of China to delight your eyes and satisfy every stomach. His daughter, Jenny Lo, has opened a similiarly impressive Chinese eatery, building on her father's inspiration, at Jenny Lo's Tea House, 14 Eccleston St, SW1, ✆ (020) 7259 0399.

Del Buongustaio, 283 Putney Bridge Rd, SW15, ✆ (020) 8780 9361 (*closed Sat lunch*). Tasty Italian regional specialities at very reasonable prices. Emphasis on seasonality: monthly changing menus, knowledgeably researched, e.g. baked goat with prosciutto and roasted vegetables.

La Delizia, 63–5 Chelsea Manor St, Sydney St, SW3, ✆ (020) 7376 5411. Good pizzeria with attractive outdoor seating and elegant indoor rooms. Often very crowded.

Montana, 125 Dawes Rd, SW6, ✆ (020) 7385 9500. Cooking from the American southwest: subtle chilli flavours, and lots of cumin, squash, tortilla and pumpkin. Some highly original combinations such as Navajo rabbit and fig *quesadilla.* Sophisticated blue and purple colour scheme.

Chelsea Kitchen, 98 King's Rd, SW3, ✆ (020) 7589 1330. Continental food and wine for less than £10. Known since the 1960s as a jostling, studenty joint for knock-down prices.

Stockpot, 6 Basil St, SW3, ✆ (020) 7589 8627. Three-course meals for not much more than a fiver. Strains of school dinner. Hardly makes pretensions at culinary art, but the quality isn't actually bad.

Notting Hill

Leiths, 92 Kensington Park Road, W11, ✆ (020) 7229 4481 (*closed all day Sun, lunch Sat–Mon*). An ultra-neutral environment, verging on the bland. This is doubtless to emphasize that the culinary delights on offer are not to be competed with. Presentation is as expert as the combination of ingredients. Roasted scallops and spiced lemon couscous amount to high art.

192, 192 Kensington Park Rd, W11, ✆ (020) 7229 0482. Once the early stamping ground of embryonic chefs such as Alastair Little. Now a very trendy French brasserie where food plays second fiddle to the posing: models and actors and the like come in their droves. Dishes include sea bass on samphire with *beurre blanc* and chives; duck confit with mash and apple sauce.

Alastair Little, 136A Lancaster Rd, W11, ✆ (020) 7243 2220 (*closed Sun*). New branch of famous Soho establishment (*see above*). Even more minimalist, but food just as marvellous.

Pharmacy Bar and Restaurant, 150 Notting Hill Gate, W11, ✆ (020) 7221 2442. The ultimate in tasteful conceptual art: a restaurant and café/cocktail lounge designed by formaldehyde artist Damien Hirst, with the help of a few consignments of pillboxes and specimen jars from St Mary's Hospital, Paddington. Waiters are dressed in hospital gowns designed by Prada. A small menu, and a trendy, arty crowd.

Dakota, 127 Ledbury Rd, ✆ (020) 7792 9191 (*closed Sun*). Increasingly popular amongst the great and the good of Notting Hill, this is one of the best in the area. Modern, elegant US cuisine boasting an impressive (delicious corn bread) menu. Impeccable service.

The Cow Dining Room, 89 Westbourne Park Road, W2, ✆ (020) 7221 0021. The relaxed, almost countrified atmosphere at the upstairs rooms above the trendy pub (of the same name) belies the precision cooking. Global inspiration but strong French strain, particularly in the sauces.

Orsino, 119 Portland Rd, W11, ✆ (020) 7221 3299. Sibling restaurant to Orso's and thus shares many of the latter's characteristics. Terracotta walls, Venetian blinds and simple but innovative cooking with Tuscan roots, like veal escalopes with sun dried tomatoes, sage and white wine.

Veronica's, 3 Hereford Rd, W2, ✆ (020) 7229 5079 (*closed Sat lunch, all day Sun*). A restaurant that has unearthed historical and regional British dishes—spring lamb with crabmeat or calf's liver and beetroot—and even relaunched recipes that date from the 14th century, sometimes adapting them to more modern tastes. Elizabethan puddings.

First Floor, 186 Portobello Rd, W11, ✆ (020) 7243 0072. Fantastical—some might say pretentious—upmarket brasserie above a loud drinking place with interesting concoctions, and verging on the weird with coffee-smoked ostrich fillet with mango sushi. The room itself is a haven of calm.

Kensington Place, 201 Kensington Church St, W8, ✆ (020) 7727 3184. Sleek, airy, noisy, modern dining room with bold garden frescoes and 'eclectic European' cuisine. The highest quality ingredients; venison, sirloin steak, wild sea trout, sorrel omelette. Full of publishers lunching out with their favoured writers and journalists.

Malabar, 27 Uxbridge St, W8, ✆ (020) 7727 8800. Quiet northern Indian restaurant with sumptuous, but unchanging choices. Very popular with Notting Hill regulars. Modern and wooden inside with white-washed alcoves. Dishes are served on large, shiny stainless-steel plates. Sleek, deferential waiters all dressed in black.

Galicia, 323 Portobello Rd, W10, ✆ (020) 8969 3539. Galicia jostles with a rum mixture of authentic 'Gallego' locals and a trendy crowd of 'Gatey Mates' (Notting Hill Gate fashion fiends). But the produce, the waiters and the 'feel' are uncannily real.

Mega Kalamaras, 66 Inverness Mews, W2, ✆ (020) 7727 9122. A high-quality, very friendly Greek restaurant. Good seafood and a wide variety of vegetarian dishes as well as the hearty meat standards. Its smaller, cheaper twin Micro Kalamaras is in a basement next door.

Anonimato, 12 All Saints Road, W11, ✆ (020) 7243 2808. Imaginative, inventive menu drawing on the unusual and the familiar (ostrich, seafood, ravioli). Blends trendy Italian and Pacific elements in airy, unfrenetic surroundings.

Mas Café, 6–8 All Saints Rd, W11, ✆ (020) 7243 0969 (*closed lunch Mon–Fri*). Swinging, bustling, loud, ultra-trendy restaurant. Starts buzzing late. Mediterranean food like baby squid; definite high-quality spicy cooking to boot.

Khans, 13–15 Westbourne Grove, W2, ✆ (020) 7727 5420. Hectic, helter skelter Indian restaurant; frantic waiters collide with waiting queues. Noise drowns intimacy, and yet the main dining room preserves its charm—painted clouds waft all about you and palm trees act as columns. Delicious food.

Osteria Basilico, 29 Kensington Park Rd, W11, ✆ (020) 7727 9372. Intensely popular, hence intensely noisy restaurant with warm ochre walls. New wave Italian dishes that are now becoming the norm, like spaghetti with fresh lobster and tomato, and linguini with spiced salami, parmesan, tomato and basil. Wooden kitchen tables and chairs, and echoey floors. Brazen staff.

Palio, 175 Westbourne Grove, W11, ✆ (020) 7221 6624. Cool yellow and black décor with big round staircase winding through to the first floor; jazz wafts through the rooms; dark and intimate and yet noisy. Italian food in bold combinations.

Geales, 2 Farmer St, W8, ✆ (020) 7727 7528 (*closed Mon*). Superior fish and chips (deep-fried in beef dripping for a touch of class). Very busy.

Standard Indian Restaurant, 23–4 Westbourne Grove, W11, ✆ (020) 7229 0600. First-rate tandoori restaurant with excellent pickles and friendly service. Unassuming name and room belie the high quality of the food.

∞ **Brasserie du Marché aux Puces**, 349 Portobello Rd, W10, ✆ (020) 8968 5828 (*open all day*). Inventive, café-style restaurant (the name means flea-market brasserie, as it's near Portobello market). Serves eclectic menu including an extraordinary haggis in filo pastry with quince purée. Old-fashioned but popular.

∞ **Casa Santana**, 44 Golborne Rd, W10, ✆ (020) 8968 8764. Neighbourhood Portuguese restaurant (Madeiran to be precise)—meat stews and smoked cod—with bags of character and good food. Triumphant desserts and Madeira beers.

◊ **Mandola**, 139–41 Westbourne Grove, W11, ✆ (020) 7229 4734 (*unlicensed*). Delightful Sudanese restaurant which has had to expand to cope with demand. Simple wooden décor with a few African exotica. Strong Arabic overtones to the dishes: *filfilia* (mixed vegetable stew), *addas* (lentil stew dressed with caramelised garlic).

◊ **Satay House**, 13 Sale Place, W2, ✆ (020) 7723 6763 (*closed Mon*). Small, intimate shop front serving delicious Malaysian food—most of the customers appear to be Malaysian which suggests authenticity. Strong flavours and a broad range of delicious recipes, chargrilled, baked and marinated. Karaoke on a Saturday night in the basement is popular amongst Malaysians too. Photographs of Malay pop stars adorn the walls downstairs.

◊ **Rôtisserie Jules**, 133a Notting Hill Gate, W11, ✆ (020) 7221 3331 (*closed Sat lunch, all day Sun*). A very welcome new venture in cheap but good restaurants. Good free-range chicken and other meats, with huge portions. Three courses for a very modest bill. Two other branches in Bute St, SW7, and 338 King's Rd, SW3.

∞ **Calzone**, 2A Kensington Park Rd, W11, ✆ (020) 7243 2003 (*open all day from 10am*). Wide thin-crust pizzas. The antidote to Pizza Express (whose pizzas are juicier)—particularly if you dislike chain restaurants. Calzone is situated in an interesting, curved glass-fronted room overlooking the juncture of four roads.

∞ **Manzara**, 24 Pembridge Rd, W11, ✆ (020) 7727 3062 (*open all day*). Good, cheap Turkish restaurant with a wide selection of meze dishes. Sometimes sloppily cooked—as in oily or overdone—but good value and some definitely tasty, fresh choices.

Camden

∞∞∞ **Café Delancey**, 3 Delancey St, NW1, ✆ (020) 7387 1985 (*open all day*). Charming, discreet French restaurant with robust, attractively presented dishes. Caters for all types. Brasserie food: venison but also snacks and soups.

∞∞∞ **Lemonia**, 89 Regent's Park Rd, Primrose Hill, NW1, ✆ (020) 7586 7454 (*closed Sat lunch and Sun eve*). Popular Greek Cypriot restaurant with a delightful conservatory for simulated *alfresco* dining in the summer. Very high standard Greek food, especially fish, although a particularly good *spanako pita* with fresh mint.

∞ **Vegetarian Cottage**, 91 Haverstock Hill, NW3, ✆ (020) 7586 1257 (*evenings only, closed Tues*). Excellent vegetarian Chinese restaurant, with inventive dishes including 'duckling' made entirely of soya, and water chestnut pudding. Essentially seeks to provide Buddhist vegetarian dishes—sometimes variable, but wonderful when good.

∞ **Camacheira**, 43 Pratt St, Camden, NW1, ✆ (020) 7485 7266. Portuguese cuisine, with a strong emphasis on meaty dishes, especially lamb, chicken and veal. Main courses start at £6.45.

∞ **Cheng Du**, 9 Parkway, Camden, NW1, ✆ (020) 7485 8058. Spicy Chinese Szechuan cooking in the heart of Camden. Often mixes Szechuan with more modern Chinese cooking. Attentive service.

Hampstead

∞∞∞ **Café des Arts**, 82 Hampstead High St, NW3, ✆ (020) 7435 3608. Classy French cooking and a beautiful 17th-century building make this one of the most appealing restaurants in north London. An open fire and wooden panelling impart warmth.

Byron, 3A Downshire Hill, NW1, ✆ (020) 7435 3544. Elegant English restaurant with good fishcakes and trimmings and excellent traditional Sunday lunches. Romantic Georgian townhouse setting, and long swirling taffeta curtains give a stagey feel. Cheap lunches in the week.

Islington

Granita, 127 Upper St, N1, ✆ (020) 7226 3222 (*closed Mon and Tues lunch time*). Eclectic Islington restaurant, with imaginative polenta, fish and meat dishes. Tony Blair is reputed to have dined here with Gordon Brown when they decided who should go for the leadership of the Labour Party in 1994.

Anna's Place, 90 Mildmay Park, N1, ✆ (020) 7249 9379 (*closed Sat eve, all day Sun*). A real oddity: a Swedish restaurant, and one that has made a mark on the local community. Lots of marinated fish and meat, plus home-made bread. Book in advance, especially for the terrace tables which are especially delectable in summer and heated in winter. Cottagey interior.

Upper St Fish Shop, 324 Upper St, N1, ✆ (020) 7359 1401 (*closed Sun*). Superior chippie with the option of grilled or poached fish as well as the traditional deep-fried. Plain wood panelled walls decorated with pictures of the mop-like former house dog, Hugo. House special is halibut.

Smithfield/East End

Quality Chop House, 94 Farringdon Rd, EC1, ✆ (020) 7837 5093 (*closed Sat lunch*). Superior English specialities like fishcakes, game pie and roast lamb, though a modern Mediterranean influence has crept on to the menu. All served in the highly atmospheric rooms of a former 19th-century working-class men's club.

Stephen Bull, Smithfields, 71 St John St, EC1, ✆ (020) 7490 1750 (*closed Sat lunch*). Innovative Mediterranean cooking, especially good fish and seafood. Strong Spanish influence, as well as Latin American *ceviches*.

St John, 26 St. John St, EC1, ✆ (020) 7251 0848 (*closed Sat lunch, all day Sun*). A converted smokehouse, still with an industrial feel to it. Hearty, meaty, ingenious British cooking with a difference: every conceivable part of the animal (trotters, oxheart, bone barrow) is presented in interesting dishes. No fussiness, crisp vegetables.

Alba, 107 Whitecross St, EC1, ✆ (020) 7588 1798 (*closed Sat, Sun*). Quietly excellent Italian restaurant, specializing in polenta, risotto and other northern or Piedmontese dishes. Pink and minimalist inside.

The Peasant, 240 St John St, EC1, ✆ (020) 7336 7726. A gaudy pub converted into an interesting restaurant—the aim being to make country food sophisticated, with delicious results. Upstairs you move from purple and blue Victoriana (the pub décor) to a white, pristine, wooden room. The food has Italian leanings.

F. Cooke, 9 Broadway Market, E8, ✆ (020) 7254 6458 (*open all day, closed Sun*). An authentic East End pie and mash shop that goes back nearly 100 years. The present owner, Bob Cooke, is grandson of the first.

Nazrul, 130 Brick Lane, E1, ✆ (020) 7247 2505 (*open late*). One of a number of incredibly cheap, unlicensed Bengali Indian restaurants on and around Brick Lane. Getting a little too well known for its own good, but still outstanding value.

South of the River

Le Pont de la Tour, Butlers Wharf, 36d Shad Thames, SE1, ✆ (020) 7403 8403 (*closed Sat lunch*). The flagship of Terence Conran's little restaurant empire at Butlers Wharf, with high-class French food and views of the river, Tower Bridge and the City. Everything, even the bread, is home-made. Chic but relaxed.

RSJ, 13a Coin St, SE1, ✆ (020) 7928 4554 (*closed Sat lunch, all day Sun*). Flamboyant, innovative French cooking, with a certain amount of global influence from Thailand and elsewhere. Extremely popular. Delightful upper rooms.

∞∞ **Blueprint Café**, Design Museum, Butlers Wharf, Shad Thames, SE1, ℰ (020) 7378 7031 (*closed Sun eve*). French and Italian food at the Pont de la Tour's less expensive sister establishment. Recently refurbished to include a new conservatory to emphasize the terrific views over the river and Tower Bridge, as well as Canary Wharf.

∞∞ **Buchan's**, 62–4 Battersea Bridge Rd, SW11, ℰ (020) 7228 0888. Just over Battersea Bridge, a popular wine bar and restaurant with a Scottish slant. The seasonal menu ranges from steaks, pheasant and wild boar to seafood, soufflés and salads.

∞∞ **Ransome's Dock**, 35 Parkgate Rd, Battersea, SW11, ℰ (020) 7223 1611. With its canal-side view, this periwinkle-blue converted warehouse provides an inventive modern-English menu with seasonal dishes. Good-value lunch and monthly changing menu. Reliable good cooking. Relaxed.

∞∞ **Riva**, 169 Church Rd, Barnes, SW13, ℰ (020) 8748 0434. It is worth making the journey to this foodie shrine, where the variations on Italian recipes are of a high standard: San Daniele ham and pears, bresaola with goat's cheese.

∞∞ **The Fire Station**, 150 Waterloo Rd, SE1, ℰ (020) 7620 2226. This former fire station has had its basic features preserved and been converted into an extremely fashionable restaurant, just opposite the Old Vic theatre. Serves excellent warm salads and Mediterranean dishes. Service a bit slow, especially in the afternoon.

Cafés, Teahouses and Snack Food

Ever since the rise of the City coffee house in the 17th century, London has been addicted to the relaxed charm of café culture. These days it seems to be labouring under one of its periodic illusions that Britain enjoys a Mediterranean climate: pavement cafés, along with al fresco dining, are all the rage. You will soon discover the new vogue for coffee, whether at one of the city's many Italian-style espresso bars or at the even newer chains offering much the same thing Pacific Northwest style: skinny wet caps and the rest, sweetened with a flavoured syrup if you so desire. Back indoors, you will still find a cosy kind of establishment geared towards the English ritual of afternoon tea and cakes. Tea, being the quintessential English drink, tends to be delicious; you'll be given a bewildering choice of varieties.

Soho and Covent Garden

Bar Italia, 22 Frith St, W1 (*open Mon–Thurs 7–5; 24 hrs Fri–Sun*). The café with the best coffee in town and it knows it. The mirrored bar, complete with TV showing Italian soccer games, could have come straight from Milan or Bologna. The seating is a bit cramped, but at least there are tables on the pavement. Better to stand.

Pâtisserie Valerie, 44 Old Compton St, W1 (*open Mon–Fri 8–8; Sat 8–7, Sun 10–6*). Excellent French cakes and coffee.

Bunjie's Coffee House, 27 Litchfield St, WC2 (*open 12–11pm, exc Sun*). Eccentric beatnik café, named after the founder's cousin's hamster. Vegetarian food and good coffee.

Maison Bertaux, 28 Greek St, W1 (*open Mon–Sat 9–8; Sun 9–1, 3–8*). Mouthwatering pastries in a slightly cramped upstairs tearoom which is always crowded.

Java Java, 26 Rupert St, W1 (*open Mon–Thurs 9.30am–10, Fri–Sat 10.30am–11pm; Sun 1–9pm*). Old French haunt frequented by international youth reading free magazines. Good coffee and unusual cakes.

Freuds, 198 Shaftesbury Ave, W1. Trendy basement bar with young, studenty atmosphere and intriguing menu design.

Beatroot, 92 Berwick St, W1 (*open 9–7*). Cheerful, down-to-earth vegetarian eat-in/takeaway café where you choose your size of food box and have it filled with any selection of hot dishes and salads from the food bar. Great puddings too.

Mayfair, Kensington, Chelsea

The Ritz, Piccadilly, W1, ✆ (020) 7493 8181. Tea sittings at 3 and 4.30 daily. The fanciest, most indulgent tea in town, served in the sumptuous Edwardian Palm Court. Worth splashing out, but you'll definitely need to book.

Brown's Hotel, Dover St or Albermarle St, W1. Tea served 3–6 daily. Very traditional English hotel serving tea to all-comers, as long as you dress to fit the part. A snip cheaper than the Ritz.

Harry's, 19 Kingly St, W1 (*open all night*). London's only all-night diner, with hearty fry-ups and reasonable coffee, featuring an eccentric cast of weirdos and insomniacs. During the day and early evening it serves Thai food. There's often a queue.

Pâtisserie Valerie, 215 Brompton Rd, SW3. Branch of the Soho French pâtisserie.

Muffin Man, 12 Wright's Lane, W8. Quaint all-day café just off Kensington High St. A variety of set teas include, as you would expect, home-made muffins galore.

Stravinsky's Russian Tea House, 6 Fulham High St, SW6. Enormous selection of teas, plus eastern European pastries, at very reasonable prices.

Notting Hill and Around

Julie's, 137 Portland Road, W11. Multi-levelled and multi-purpose establishment with eccentric décor that is part café, part wine bar and part restaurant. The place is at its best for afternoon tea when it is neither too expensive nor pretentious.

Grove Café, corner of Portobello Rd and Westbourne Park Rd, W11. First floor café with a terrace overlooking the market. Good coffee and newspapers to browse in the morning or afternoon.

The City and East End

Brick Lane Beigel Bake, 159 Brick Lane, E1. Round-the-clock bagels. Always crowded, even at three in the morning.

Whitechapel Café, 80 Whitechapel High St, E1. Wholefood café inside the Whitechapel Art Gallery.

Café Rongwrong, 8 Hoxton Square, N1. Beatnik café in one of London's trendiest east London squares. An old warehouse, full of graphic designers and video artists. Atmospheric.

North London

Louis Pâtisserie, 32 Heath St, Hampstead, NW3. Famous Hungarian tearoom which has been a haunt of middle-European emigrés for decades. Wonderful cheesecake and cream cakes brought on a tray for you to choose from.

Everyman Café, Holly Bush Vale, Hampstead, NW3. Atmospheric basement café beneath north London's best established rep cinema.

The Coffee Cup, 74 Hampstead High St, NW3. Dazzling menu including delicious raisin toast. Good for watching the beautiful people walk by.

Carmelli's, 128 Golders Green Rd, NW11. The best bagels in London, in the heart of Jewish Golders Green, though you can't eat them on the premises.

South of the River

Annabel's Pâtisserie, 33 High St, Wimbledon, SW19. Old-fashioned tearoom-cum-brasserie in the genteel atmosphere of Wimbledon.

Kew Greenhouse, 1 Station Parade, Kew. Cakes and pastries near Kew Gardens.

Pubs

The London pub—gaudily decorated with gleaming brass, ornate mirrors and stained glass—is still an essentially Victorian establishment, at least to look at. Even recently built pubs eschew modern décor in favour of mock-Tudor beams, leaded windows and reproduction hunting prints. Licensing hours, although now much extended, are still rigorously enforced; the landlord usually rings a bell when it is time to drink up, like a fussy schoolmaster. Gone, however, are the days when the pubs closed just when you were feeling thirsty; you can now drink without interruption between 11am and 11pm every day except Sunday, when there is still a break from 3–7pm. Many pubs in outer London still close every afternoon, however.

Beer remains the drink of choice. British beer is admittedly an acquired taste—stronger, darker and flatter than lager and served luke-warm rather than stone cold—but easy to get hooked on in time. Unfortunately, London pubs are being swamped, like everywhere else, with generic multinational lagers—Carlsberg, Heineken, Budweiser and the rest. This is far from good news for traditional local breweries, who are fighting an energetic rearguard campaign with the help of CAMRA, the Campaign for Real Ale. CAMRA's influence has been greater in country pubs and the cities of northern England than it has in London, where wine and American-style cocktails are more popular than in the rest of the country; in the capital you will nevertheless find decent bitters like Fullers London Pride and Youngs, and creamy, full-bodied ales like Theakston's, Abbot and Ruddles.

The following list is necessarily short, since few London pubs really shine above the rest. Most of them make the list because of their location—overlooking the river, maybe, or in a quiet row of Georgian houses—or because of a particular historical association. You'll notice their eccentric names, which date from a time when most drinkers were illiterate and recognized pubs only by their signs. Hence the preponderance of coats of arms (King's Arms, Queen's Arms, Freemasons' Arms etc) and highly pictorial appellations (Wheatsheaf, Dog and Duck, Nag's Head, Slug and Lettuce, etc). One thing to look out for is the name of the brewer that owns the pub. If the sign says 'Free House', that means the pub is independent and generally has a better range of beers. Quite a few London pubs are venues for theatre or concerts; where the entertainment is the main attraction, you will find them in the 'Entertainment' chapter rather than here.

Soho, Covent Garden, Fitzrovia

Lamb and Flag, 33 Rose St, WC2. One of few wooden-framed buildings left in central London, dating back to the 17th century, with low ceilings and a lively atmosphere. The pub was for a long time nicknamed the Bucket of Blood because it staged bare-knuckled fights. Now you just have to knuckle your way past the crowds at the bar.

Dog and Duck, 8 Bateman St, W1. Soho's smallest pub. Customers spill out on to the pavement in the summer, and huddle round the log fire in the winter.

The French House, 49 Dean St, W1. Meeting-place for De Gaulle's Free French during the Second World War; now adorned with pictures of famous Frenchmen.

The Sun, 63 Lamb's Conduit St, W1. A beer-lover's paradise: 15 real ales and the chance to tour the cellar with the landlord.

Fitzroy Tavern, 16 Charlotte St, W1. Dylan Thomas's main drinking haunt; see the literary mementoes on the walls downstairs.

Holborn and Fleet Street

Cittie of York, 22 High Holborn, WC1. The longest bar in London. Cosy, separate booths, ideal for winter lunch times.

Ye Olde Cheshire Cheese, Wine Office Court, 15 Fleet St, EC4. Dr Johnson's old haunt, with atmospheric beams but disappointing food.

The Eagle, 159 Farringdon Rd, EC1. New wave pub with less emphasis on drinking and more on food, good atmosphere and general hanging out.

East End

Ten Bells, 84 Commercial St, E1. The original Jack the Ripper pub, with oodles of memorabilia. Marred by the tourist coaches who drop in during the evening but friendly enough at lunch time.

The Ship and Blue Ball, 13 Boundary St, E2. First-rate organic beer from the independent Pitfield brewery. Try the brand called Dark Star.

Town of Ramsgate, 62 Wapping High St, E1. The pub where the merciless 17th-century Judge Jeffreys finally got his come-uppance. Friendly East

End atmosphere, with a riverside garden and view of the post where smugglers and pirates used to be condemned to hang in chains for the duration of three high tides.

Southwark, Rotherhithe, Greenwich

Anchor Inn, 1 Bankside, SE1. Superior food and excellent river views in this ancient Bankside institution where fugitives from the Clink prison next door used to hide in cubby holes.

Old Thameside Inn, Clink St, SE1. Shantymen perform sea shanties at lunch time on the last Sunday of the month at this pub with attractive riverside views from a concrete terrace.

The Angel, 101 Bermondsey Wall East, Rotherhithe, SE16. The pub where Captain Cook had his last drink before sailing to Australia. Notable for its ship's wheel, smugglers' trapdoor and balcony overlooking Tower Bridge and Execution Dock.

The Mayflower, 117 Rotherhithe St, SE16. Inn from which the Pilgrim Fathers set out for America, and the only place in Britain where you can buy US postage stamps. There's a long jetty from which to admire the river. Avoid the indifferent food.

Trafalgar Tavern, Park Row, Greenwich, SE10. Famous for its Whitebait Dinners, at which cabinet ministers and senior public figures would hold informal chats over seafood from the Thames. River pollution ended the tradition in 1914, though you can still eat rather indifferent whitebait from the pub menu. Nice views.

Islington, Highgate, Hampstead

King's Head, 115 Upper St, Islington, N1. Popular Islington pub, where the money is still counted according to the old pre-decimal system of pounds, shillings and pence. The pub theatre is excellent and the atmosphere is very genial.

Canonbury Tavern, 21 Canonbury Place, Islington, N1. Delightful garden pub with an unusual court for playing *pétanque*.

The Flask, 77 Highgate West Hill, N6. Friendly pub dating back to the 17th century at the top of Highgate Hill, with a garden and good food.

The Bull, 13 North Hill, Highgate, N6. A large tree-lined garden and patio are the most attractive features of this former drinking haunt for painters such as Hogarth and Millais.

Spaniards Inn, Spaniards Road, Hampstead Heath, NW3. Reputed as a highwayman's pub patronized by Dick Turpin and a host of scurrilous scribblers including Byron and Shelley. Wonderful garden and, of course, the expanse of Hampstead Heath just across the road.

The Holly Bush, 22 Holly Mount, Hampstead, NW3. Idyllic pub with five low rooms grouped around an old wooden bar.

Freemasons Arms, 32 Downshire Hill, Hampstead, NW3. Huge garden and terrace, fountain and pitch to play the ancient game of pell-mell. Gets crowded.

West London

Ladbroke Arms, 54 Ladbroke Rd, Notting Hill, W11. Very popular pub with flower-lined patio. Don't bring the car as there's a police station next door and they'll nick you for drink-driving.

Queen's Head, Brook Green (West Kensington), W6. Old coaching inn overlooking a green, with a beer garden at the back.

Anglesea Arms, 15 Selwood Terrace, SW7. Good beer in this local Chelsea haunt.

Havelock Tavern, 57 Masbro Road, W14. Popular pub serving high-quality pub food.

King's Head and Eight Bells, 50 Cheyne Walk, Chelsea. Enjoy the antiques displays in this 16th-century building. There are views of the Battersea peace pagoda across the river.

Dukes Head, 8 Lower Richmond Rd, Putney. Fine views along the river, though you have to put up with plastic cups if you sit outside.

The Ship, Ship Lane, Mortlake. The place to watch the end of the Oxford and Cambridge boat race in April. Fine river views and a tranquil setting the rest of the year.

The White Cross, Cholmondeley Walk, Richmond. A pub that turns into an island at high tide. Enjoy the real fires and fine food.

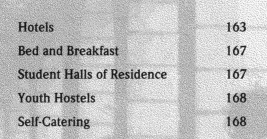

London: Where to Stay

There is only one word to describe London's hotels and that word is *nightmare*. Accommodation, although improving slowly, is on the whole shamelessly expensive and shamelessly shoddy. You can pay up to £80 for an ordinary double room with no guarantee of quality or even basic hygiene; and you can pay up to twice that without even approaching the luxury category. There is no universal rating system, and the variously sponsored star or crown systems are so unreliable as to be virtually useless. So your best bet is to dust down your address book and see if there isn't anybody in London who might be able to put you up. If that fails, don't lose heart: there are some cheap deals available, and some surprisingly enjoyable establishments. You must, however, be very wary of the pitfalls.

If at all possible, try to arrange accommodation from your home country. Flight and accommodation packages cover a wide price range and can work out to your advantage. Otherwise, try the numbers below. You can usually confirm your booking by giving a credit card number or sending a fax. The London Tourist Board also operates a telephone credit card booking service on ✆ (020) 7824 8844 which is open Mon–Fri 9.30–5.30. If you turn up in London without a room in your name and you get nowhere ringing the numbers listed below, you can line up outside a tourist office and try your luck there. Try Victoria station forecourt, Liverpool St station, the underground concourse at Heathrow Terminals 1–3, or one of the following local tourist offices: Greenwich (✆ (020) 8858 6376), Islington (✆ (020) 7278 8787) or Richmond (✆ (020) 8940 9125). Commission for all booking services is around £5. If you are travelling out of high season (i.e. not the summer), try haggling a bit and you might negotiate your own discount. Weekend rates are common, and if you stay for a week you might get one night free. You can further save your pennies by declining breakfast (a possible £10 saver, *see* Food and Drink for other places to go) or by asking for a room without a bath. In the cheaper establishments, the corridor bathrooms are usually better than the *en suite* kind, so this is not much of a sacrifice. The following Internet address may also be useful: hotels *www.demon.co. uk/hotel-uk/excindex.html.*

Most hotels are in the West End and around, Kensington, Chelsea, Earl's Court and west London. Try to avoid streets like Sussex Gardens in Bayswater, which is something of a hotel ghetto and rather miserable for it. Finding somewhere quiet can be a problem, especially in the busy summer months, but as a broad rule of thumb you will be disturbed less the further you are out of the centre. The best places to stay are in districts like Notting Hill and Holland Park, or else by the river—don't forget the newer hotels in the Docklands. Bloomsbury offers some excellent bargains as well as the proximity of the British Museum.

Prices given below are for a normal double room for one night, but—again—find out about discounts before dismissing a place as too dear. Remember that space is tight, so book as far in advance as possible, whatever the category of accommodation. Hotels are graded by price, as follows:

⬭⬭⬭⬭⬭	**luxury (£200 and over)**
⬭⬭⬭⬭	**very expensive (£150–200)**
⬭⬭⬭	**expensive (£100–150)**
⬭⬭	**moderate (£60–100)**
⬭	**cheap for London (under £60)**

Hotels

Mayfair

∞∞∞∞ **Brown's**, 19–24 Dover St W1, ℗ (020) 7493 6020. Old fashioned English establishment, with the air of a country house and impeccable, stiff-collar service. Attractive if smallish rooms. £250–750 + VAT.

∞∞∞∞ **Claridges**, Brook St W1, ℗ (020) 7629 8860. Art Deco bedrooms, black and white marbled foyer and a touch of royal class at London's most celebrated smaller luxury hotel. £280–3,500 + VAT (the latter for a 2-floor penthouse).

∞∞∞∞ **Connaught**, 16 Carlos Place W1, ℗ (020) 7499 7070. Attentive service commands a troupe of loyal devotees. An air of calm exclusivity presides. Outstanding restaurants; personalized formality. Book in writing well in advance. £215–360 + VAT.

∞∞∞∞ **Dorchester**, 53 Park Lane W1, ℗ (020) 7629 8888. Triple-glazed rooms (to foil the Park Lane traffic) and views over Hyde Park, plus a dazzling choice of fine restaurants and acres of gold and marble. £295 + VAT.

∞∞∞∞ **Ritz**, Piccadilly W1, ℗ (020) 7493 8181. Marble galore, gorgeous rococo carpets, plus glorious views over Green Park if you pick your room right. *Ancien régime* luxury. £260–300 + VAT.

West End

∞∞∞∞ **Savoy**, Strand WC2, ℗ (020) 7836 4343. A sleeker, more business-like luxury here. *Fin de siècle* dining room: a favourite venue for afternoon tea. Many restaurants and bars and discreet good service. £325 + VAT.

∞∞ **Bryanston Court**, 56–60 Great Cumberland Place W1, ℗ (020) 7262 3141. Business-like hotel with few frills but a pleasant atmosphere and an open fire in winter. £110.

∞∞∞ **Durrants**, George St W1, ℗ (020) 7935 8131. A former 18th-century coaching inn preserving many old-fashioned touches including silver plate covers in the restaurant.

Rooms are simple, a few on the small side. £135.

∞∞ **Hazlitt's**, 6 Frith St W1, ℗ (020) 7434 1771. Small Georgian rooms with some four posters and claw-footed iron baths in the former home of essayist William Hazlitt. Palm trees and classical busts adorn the premises. £170 + VAT.

∞∞ **Blandford**, 80 Chiltern St W1, ℗ (020) 7486 3103. Simple bed-and-breakfast-style hotel, offering decent rooms and a copious morning meal, in a quiet side street near Baker St station. £85.

∞∞ **Concorde**, 50 Great Cumberland Place W1, ℗ (020) 7402 6169. Plain and inexpensive but light and efficient, under the same management as the Bryanston Court. With self-catering options. £85 + breakfast + VAT.

∞∞ **Edward Lear**, 28–30 Seymour St W1, ℗ (020) 7402 5401. Named after the nonsense-verse writer. Small hotel with a homey feel. Informal but efficient. £70.

∞∞ **Fielding**, 4 Broad Ct, Bow St WC2, ℗ (020) 7836 8305. A pretty good deal for central London, right opposite the Opera House. Smallish rooms and a tiny reception area: a parrot greets you on your way in. £85.

∞∞ **Georgian House Hotel**, 87 Gloucester Place W1, ℗ (020) 7935 2211. Spacious rooms with personality; quietly high standards and good prices. Great discounts on 'student' rooms up 3 or 4 flights of stairs. £90.

∞∞ **Hallam Hotel**, 12 Hallam St W1, ℗ (020) 7580 1166. Quiet, businesslike hotel just around the corner from the BBC. Some rooms have views of the Telecom Tower. £102.50.

∞∞ **Hart House Hotel**, 51 Gloucester Place W1, ℗ (020) 7935 2288. Superbly run hotel in a Georgian mansion overlooking Portman Square, with remarkably large rooms for the area. £95.

∞ **Parkwood**, 4 Stanhope Place W2, ✆ (020) 7402 2241. Family-run hotel with slightly worn furniture but attractive prices. Charming Georgian mansion near Hyde Park. £87.50.

Bloomsbury

∞∞∞ **Bonnington**, 92 Southampton Row WC1, ✆ (020) 7242 2828. Renovated Edwardian establishment with bland furniture but warm management. Plenty of beds, relatively easy to book. £75–140.

∞∞∞ **Russell**, Russell Square WC1, ✆ (020) 7837 6470. Extravagant Gothic Revival architecture and an atmosphere to match. A renovated ballroom. Friendly service. £185.

∞ **Academy**, 17–21 Gower St WC1, ✆ (020) 7631 4115. Enjoy the atmosphere of a Georgian townhouse. Cosy library and small paved garden. An antique charm. £125.

∞ **Crescent**, 49–50 Cartwright Gardens WC1, ✆ (020) 7387 1515. Use of the garden and tennis courts a big plus here, as is family atmosphere. Old-fashioned and good value. £80 inc breakfast and tax.

∞ **Harlingford**, 61–3 Cartwright Gardens WC1, ✆ (020) 7387 1551. Floral-print wallpaper adorns the simple rooms. Access to tennis courts possible. £82 all inclusive.

∞ **Mabledon Court**, 10–11 Mabledon Place WC1, ✆ (020) 7388 3866. Clean but unexciting hotel near King's Cross with reasonable rates. £75.

∞ **Morgan**, 24 Bloomsbury St WC1, ✆ (020) 7636 3735. Beautifully furnished bed and breakfast style hotel, with warm atmosphere and excellent breakfast. Near British Museum. £78.

∞ **St Margaret's**, 26 Bedford Place WC1, ✆ (020) 7636 4277. Clean, fresh hotel with a plant-filled dining room and a wide variety of large, well-proportioned rooms. £58.50 all inclusive.

∞ **Tavistock**, Tavistock Square WC1, ✆ (020) 7278 7871. Large rooms, a good location, Art Deco finishes but impersonal atmosphere

and tour-group clientele. Views over Tavistock Square garden a plus. £75.

◊ **Arran House**, 77–9 Gower St WC1, ✆ (020) 7636 2186. Wonky floors and a lovely rose garden add charm to this otherwise no-frills guest house. In-house laundry and use of kitchen including microwave. £50.

◊ **Avalon**, 46–7 Cartwright Gardens WC1, ✆ (020) 7387 2366. Bright, old-fashioned Georgian house in a beautiful crescent packed with similar establishments. Drying and ironing facilities. £58.

◊ **Celtic**, 61–3 Guildford St WC1, ✆ (020) 7837 9258. Simple, unexciting family-run bed and breakfast. No private bathrooms but cheap at around £50.50. Street rooms can be noisy.

◊ **Elmwood**, 19 Argyle Square WC1, ✆ (020) 7837 9361. Basic but very cheap, in a lovely square near the new British Library. Not far from King's Cross. £40, discount for three-day stays.

Bayswater, Notting Hill

∞∞∞∞∞ **Hempel**, 31–5 Craven Hill Gardens W2, ✆ (020) 7298 9000. luxury hotel designed by Anoushka Hempel. Takes minimalism to its logical, most exotic extreme. Pure white blank foyer interrupted only by otherworldly flames and Thai ox-carts. £235–1200 + VAT.

∞∞∞∞ **Halcyon**, 81 Holland Park, W11, ✆ (020) 7727 7288. Modern but traditional, in a large, renovated Holland Park mansion house. Popular with showbiz and media people. Rated restaurant and bars. £270 inc. VAT.

∞∞∞ **Pembridge Court**, 34 Pembridge Gardens W2, ✆ (020) 7229 9977. Elegant Victorian townhouse, fastidiously deconstructed; but flourishing vegetation and an interesting collection of Victoriana in frames. Next to Portobello market. £270.

∞∞∞ **Whites**, 90 Lancaster Gate W2, ✆ (020) 7262 2711. Stucco palace overlooking

Kensington Gardens. Rebuilt behind the façade for modern tastes in traditional guise. Deferential service. £245 inc VAT. Breakfast is extra.

∞ **Portobello**, 22 Stanley Gardens W11, ✆ (020) 7727 2777. Victorian Gothic furniture conceals all-mod-cons comfort including a health club. Idiosyncratic rooms. A touch poky. £155–260 inc VAT and breakfast.

∞ **Ashley**, 15–17 Norfolk Square W2, ✆ (020) 7723 9966. Maniacally clean and quiet hotel, ideal for families or business people looking for peace. Party animals stay away. Bulletin board has hints on sightseeing. £58–69.

∞ **Byron**, 36–8 Queensborough Terrace W2, ✆ (020) 7243 0987 (toll-free number in US ✆ 1-800-448 8355). Young, friendly atmosphere in this smart hotel full of sunshine and flowers, just a stone's throw from Kensington Gardens. £96.

∞ **Delmere**, 130 Sussex Gardens W2, ✆ (020) 7706 3344. Smart building on an otherwise miserable street of hotels. Some tiny rooms, but others are spacious and comfortable. £98 inc VAT and breakfast.

∞ **Gate,** 6 Portobello Rd W11, ✆ (020) 7221 0707. Well-appointed, flower-bedecked no-nonsense hotel in plum location among the antique shops of Portobello Rd. £80–85.

∞ **Kensington Gardens**, 9 Kensington Gardens Square W2, ✆ (020) 7221 7790. Attractive rooms, good bath facilities and a light, pleasant breakfast room make this a good mid-range choice. £80 inc breakfast and VAT.

◊ **Abbey House**, 11 Vicarage Gate W8, ✆ (020) 7727 2594. Simple, spacious rooms in this delightful Victorian town house in a quiet square. Preserves many original features. Cheap at around £60.

◊ **Border**, 14 Norfolk Square W2, ✆ (020) 7723 2968. No-nonsense hotel with simple, cheap facilities, in a square full of other similar hotels. £59.

◊ **Garden Court**, 30–31 Kensington Gardens Square W2, ✆ (020) 7229 2553. Simple bed and breakfast with nice views over the square

at the front and gardens at the back. Well located next to Queensway and not far from Portobello. £52 inc VAT and breakfast.

◊ **Lancaster Hall (German YMCA)**, 35 Craven Terrace W2, ✆ (020) 7723 9276. Sounds grim and looks awfully generic, but the rooms are clean, the location excellent. £72 (twins only).

◊ **Mornington**, 12 Lancaster Gate W2, ✆ (020) 7262 7361 (toll-free number in US 1-800-528 1234). Scandinavian-run hotel with serious but professional staff. Nice library. Next to the Football Association, so lots of soccer types around. £120.

◊ **Ravna Gora**, 29 Holland Park Avenue W11, ✆ (020) 7727 7725. Palatial Holland Park mansion turned slightly dilapidated bed and breakfast, with a talkative Serbian owner. £54.

South Kensington

∞∞∞∞ **Blakes**, 33 Roland Gardens SW7, ✆ (020) 7370 6701. Richly decorated hotel with four-poster beds and antique lacquered chests. Birdcages and carved giraffes to boot. £220–310 + VAT.

∞∞∞∞ **The Gore**, 189 Queen's Gate SW7, ✆ (020) 7584 6601 (toll free in USA ✆ 1-800-528 1234). Gothic and Edwardian décor, plus hundreds of old prints, make this an atmospheric stopover. £165 + VAT.

∞∞∞∞ **Number Sixteen**, 16 Sumner Place SW7, ✆ (020) 7589 5232. Charming Victorian house with a garden and fountains, plus large reception areas and rooms with balconies. Posh B&B. £160.

∞∞∞ **Aster House**, 3 Sumner Place SW7, ✆ (020) 7581 5888. Silk-wall décor and lots of flowers all over this award-winning hotel. Light breakfast alternatives to the usual bangers, bacon and egg. £125–45.

∞∞∞ **Claverly**, 13–14 Beaufort Gardens SW3, ✆ (020) 7589 8541. Lovingly detailed and award-winning hotel, with attractive rooms and an imaginative breakfast featuring waffles and fresh juices as well as bacon and eggs. £130.

∞ **Cranley**, 10–12 Bina Gardens SW5, ☎ (020) 7373 0123 (toll free in US ☎ 1-800-553 2582). American-run hotel converted from three elegant town houses. Style, great attention to detail thanks to antiques and designer fabrics, and a view from the top of the pinnacle of St Paul's. £150.

∞ **Five Sumner Place**, 5 Sumner Place SW7, ☎ (020) 7584 7586. The feel of a country home in the heart of London, with a stunning conservatory-style breakfast room. Smart but unpretentious. Quiet. £120 + VAT.

∞ **Hotel 167**, 167 Old Brompton Rd SW5, ☎ (020) 7373 0672. Attractively decorated Victorian corner house with young clientele. £99 inc breakfast + VAT.

Knightsbridge

∞∞∞∞∞ **Hyatt Carlton Tower**, 2 Cadogan Place SW1, ☎ (020) 7235 1234. De luxe mod cons, marble bathrooms, a stone's throw from Harrods, with a well-equipped health club, swimming pool and spacious rooms. £270 + VAT.

∞∞∞ **Diplomat**, 2 Chesham St SW1, ☎ (020) 7235 1544. Elegant rooms and suites up and down a glass-domed stairwell. Copious buffet breakfast and just a short walk to Beauchamp Place and Harrods. £125 inc breakfast + VAT.

∞∞ **Wilbraham**, 1 Wilbraham Place, Sloane St SW1, ☎ (020) 7730 8296. Very English establishment just off Sloane Square, with Victorian décor and attractive wood panelling. £106 inc VAT.

Victoria/Pimlico

∞∞∞ **Ebury Court**, 28 Ebury St SW1, ☎ (020) 7730 8147. Labyrinthine corridors connect the beautifully laid out rooms in this long-established neighbourhood favourite. £140 inc breakfast + VAT.

∞∞ **Collin House**, 104 Ebury St SW1, ☎ (020) 7730 8031. Clean, hospitable bed and breakfast behind Victoria station. Homey but fresh. £62–73.

◇ **Enrico**, 77–9 Warwick Way SW1, ☎ (020) 7834 9538. Basic but comfortable hotel in Pimlico. £40.

◇ **Oak House**, 29 Hugh St SW1, ☎ (020) 7834 7151. Small rooms with basic catering facilities for only £35. Breakfast is in your room. No advance booking, so roll up early.

Earl's Court/Fulham

∞∞ **Hogarth**, 35–7 Hogarth Rd SW5, ☎ (020) 7370 6831 (toll free in US ☎ 1-800-528 1234). Part of Best Western chain, a hotel with full amenities near Earl's Court Exhibition Centre. Busy but friendly. £110–130.

◇ **Beaver**, 57–9 Philbeach Gardens SW5, ☎ (020) 7373 4553. Simple, attractive establishment, pool table and cheap car parking. Plush lounge with polished wooden floors. Lovely street. £80 inc breakfast + VAT.

◇ **Pippa Pop-Ins**, 430 Fulham Rd SW10, ☎ (020) 7385 2458. A real oddity: a hotel for children aged 2–12. Leave them here and they will play to their heart's content. Available also for daytime child minding. £50 per child. (Max stay: 3 days.)

Elsewhere

∞∞∞∞ **Tower Thistle**, St Katharine's Way E1, ☎ (020) 7481 2575. Not a great beauty, but ideally placed next to the Tower overlooking the river. Ultra-modern fittings and every conceivable comfort (including meeting rooms). £185.

∞∞∞ **Clarendon**, 8–16 Montpelier Row, Blackheath SE3, ☎ (020) 8318 4321. A bit of a way out, but a comfortable Georgian hotel with all mod cons including free parking and a beautiful view over Blackheath and Greenwich Park. £79 inc breakfast + VAT.

∞∞∞ **Dorset Square**, 39–40 Dorset Square NW1, ☎ (020) 7723 7874 (toll free in US ☎ 1-800-543 4138). Restored Regency building between Madame Tussaud's and Regent's Park with beautiful furniture and a strong cricket theme because of the nearby Lord's ground. £130 + VAT.

La Gaffe, 107 Heath St, Hampstead NW3, ℘ (020) 7435 4941. Charming bed and breakfast above an Italian restaurant in a former shepherd's cottage. Bedrooms reached via a precipitous stairway. £85 inc breakfast + VAT.

Swiss Cottage, 4 Adamson Rd NW3, ℘ (020) 7722 2281. Olde worlde atmosphere with lots of antiques, reproduction furniture and even a grand piano. Good location near Hampstead and Camden. £100 inc breakfast + VAT.

Hampstead Village Guesthouse, 2 Kemplay Rd NW3, ℘ (020) 7435 8679. Family household just a step away from Hampstead Heath. Lots of books and pot plants, plus fridges in your rooms. £60–100.

Bed and Breakfast

The bed and breakfast is a British (and Irish) tourist institution: you get to stay in someone's house, enjoy their company and eat a slap-up breakfast for a fraction of the cost of a hotel. In London the system works less freely than in the rest of the country, and you will have noticed that some of the hotels listed above have a distinctly B'n'B flavour to them. The least certain way of finding a B'n'B is by going to one of the tourist offices listed at the top of this chapter. A safer bet is to go through one of the following agencies:

Bulldog Club, 15 Roland Gdns SW7, ℘ (020) 7341 9495. Will fix you up in palatial surroundings in the city or the country—at a price of course.

Uptown Reservations, 50 Christchurch St SW3, ℘ (020) 7351 3445. Offers homes in Knightsbridge, Chelsea and similar neighbourhoods.

Host and Guest Service, 103 Dawes Rd SW6, ℘ (020) 7385 9922. Agency with 3000 homes on its books all over London. £18 per person per night.

London Homes, 6 Hyde Park Mansions, Flat G, Cabbell St NW1, ℘ (020) 7262 0900. A wide range to choose from, for as little as £18 per person.

London Homestead Services, Coombe Wood Rd, Kingston, Surrey, ℘ (020) 8949 4455. Minimum stay three nights for as little as £15 per person. Book early.

Stayaway Abroad, 71 Fellows Rd, Hampstead NW3, ℘ (020) 7586 2768. Slightly more expensive, but a classier service as a result.

Student Halls of Residence

A number of university halls of residence throw open their doors to foreign visitors during the long summer holiday from July to September and can be excellent value (£25 for a double room per night). Conditions are obviously a bit spartan, and you won't be able to cancel bookings very easily, but try the following addresses:

King's College Campus Vacation Bureau, 552 King's Rd SW6, ℘ (020) 7928 3777. Agency for seven halls of residence all over London.

John Adams Hall, 15–23 Endsleigh St WC1, ℘ (020) 7387 4086.

Walter Sickert Hall, 29 Graham St N1, ℘ (020) 7477 8822.

Ramsey Hall, 20 Maple St W1, ℘ (020) 7387 4537.

International Students House 229 Great Portland St W1, ℘ (020) 7631 8300. Strictly for students only, but excellent value for money, with access to a whole range of student amenities.

Youth Hostels

Not necessarily much cheaper than the cheapest B'n'Bs. You can get a full list of addresses from the **YHA Shop** in Covent Garden (14 Southampton St, ✆ (020) 7836 1036).

The most scenic locations are without doubt **Holland House**, ✆ (020) 7937 0748, slap bang in the middle of Holland Park in a converted Jacobean mansion, and **Highgate Village** (84 Highgate West Hill, ✆ (020) 8340 1831).

Self-Catering

Only really worth it if you are numerous, or if you are staying for several weeks. Try the following agencies:

Aston's, 39 Rosary Gardens, South Kensington, SW7 ✆ (020) 7370 0737.

Kensbridge Hotel Group Flat Rentals, ✆ (020) 7589 2923. Flats all over South Kensington.

Butlers Wharf Residence, Gainsford St, ✆ (020) 7407 7164. A chance to stay in one of the luxury flats built in the failed Docklands property boom of the 1980s. Very close to Tower Bridge and bang next to the Design Museum.

London: Entertainment and Nightlife

The indispensable guide to the week's events is the listings magazine *Time Out*, which appears on Tuesday afternoon or Wednesday morning; it provides addresses, descriptions and reviews of everything that moves or is scheduled to move over the following seven days. The magazine isn't perfect, tending to overhype celebrities and the latest fashion fads, but it has no serious competition.

Most of the West End theatres, as well as a good smattering of cinemas and nightclubs, are clustered around Soho and Shaftesbury Avenue. Some of the most interesting nightlife, however, takes place well away from the centre of town: jazz and fringe theatre in Islington, nightclubs in North Kensington or Brixton, comedy way up north in Crouch End or down south in Clapham. If you venture far afield, or if you have a long way to get home, you'll need to think carefully about transport. The Underground system dries up soon after midnight, and taxis can be hard to find in more remote parts of London. Night buses head to and from Trafalgar Square. If these aren't convenient, you may have to resort to a minicab. Don't let yourself be cajoled into taking a minicab off the street; not only is it illegal for drivers to solicit business this way, it may not be safe either. *See* p.7 for some safe compromises.

Theatre

Foreign visitors will find the cast lists of plays showing in London disconcertingly familiar: it looks as though the villains and eccentrics of Hollywood have mounted a takeover. In fact, the London stage is where actors like Anthony Hopkins, Ralph Fiennes and Alan Rickman come home to roost when they are not making megabucks in the movies. Those Californian casting directors know very well that London boasts the best serious stage acting anywhere, a reputation it has built up meticulously over several centuries. Its playwrights have pioneered no theatrical movements—England boasts no equivalent of Pirandello or Brecht—but have nevertheless turned out compelling and challenging dramas of a quality not seen in any other European city. Likewise, West End actors have rarely become major international stars, but still command enormous respect on Broadway and in Hollywood.

What to See and Where to Go

The major commercial theatre companies are concentrated in the West End, just as the main New York stages are grouped together on Broadway. Two distinct traditions are forever jostling for attention, the straight play and the musical. Shakespeare is of course a perennial favourite, along with Chekhov, Shaw and Noel Coward, but in pure terms of seat numbers the darling of the British musical, Andrew Lloyd Webber, is way ahead in the popularity ratings. Lloyd Webber's shows, from *Joseph and the Amazing Technicolour Dreamcoat* through to *Phantom of the Opera*, have been running without interruption in London for the past quarter century. Lloyd Webber's flagship theatre, the Palace on Cambridge Circus, has for the past few years been showing a musical he did not write himself, the smash hit *Les Misérables*. Just across the road at the St Martin's is the longest-running show in London, Agatha Christie's *The Mousetrap*, which has been on in one theatre or another since 1952. Longevity is no guarantee of quality, and you'd do well to give this wooden and outdated tourist attraction a wide berth.

Established playwrights, such as Tom Stoppard, David Hare, Harold Pinter, Tony Kushner and David Mamet, are increasingly turning to the off-West End theatre companies to stage their work. The most consistent and reliable of these is the three-stage **Royal National Theatre** on the South Bank, which puts on superb versions of the classics as well as showcasing high-quality new writing. The RNT is followed closely by the **Royal Shakespeare Company**, based at the Barbican, which concentrates mainly on the Bard and his contemporaries. The **Royal Court** in Sloane Square and **Lyric** in Hammersmith are excellent venues for new work, while experimental shows and reworkings of established plays are the hallmark of the **Almeida** in Islington, the **Hampstead Theatre** or the **Donmar Warehouse** in Covent Garden.

The **fringe** is always active, and occasionally you can find first-rate shows in draughty halls or upstairs rooms in pubs. If you are in London during the summer, don't forget about open-air venues like the **Globe Theatre**, **Regent's Park**, **Holland Park** and the garden of the **Royal Observatory** in Greenwich, where you can enjoy Shakespeare (particularly *A Midsummer Night's Dream*) and lively modern comedies.

Practical Details

Most performances start at 7.30 or 8.00pm, with matinées usually scheduled on Wednesdays and Saturdays. By far the best way to book is through the theatre itself. At most places you can pay by credit card over the phone, then pick up the tickets just before the curtain goes up. **Ticket agents** charge stinging commissions, usually 22 per cent, although they can be a necessary evil to get into the big musicals (try Ticketmaster on ✆ (020) 7344 4444 or First Call on ✆ (020) 7420 0000). The Royal National Theatre offers a limited number of cheap tickets from 10am on the day of the performance (get there early as there are often long queues), and the Society of London Theatre has a ticket booth in Leicester Square (*open 2.30–6.30pm, or noon–6pm on matinée days*) with half-price tickets for West End shows that night. If all else fails, you can try for returns in the hour before the performance starts; students can get a hefty discount this way.

A Few Addresses

There's not a lot of point recommending individual theatres, as the quality of each production cannot be guaranteed, but the following addresses—most outside the West End—should give you some pointers. The telephone numbers are for the box office.

Royal National Theatre, South Bank, ✆ (020) 7452 3000. The National has three stages—the large apron of the Olivier, the conventional proscenium at the Lyttleton and the smaller, cosier Cottesloe. An evening here not only guarantees top-notch theatre; you can enjoy foyer concerts, browse through the bookshops and linger in the cafés with views out over the Thames. Highly recommended.

Barbican Arts Centre, Silk St, Barbican, ✆ (020) 7638 8891. The Royal Shakespeare Company, based both in London and in Shakespeare's birthplace, Stratford-upon-Avon, has two stages here, the conventional Barbican Theatre and the more experimental Pit. Standards are excellent and well worth the byzantine complications of finding the venue in the first place (*see* p.61). The RSC tours the country Mar–Oct and you'll need to go to Stratford to see them in summer.

Royal Court, Sloane Square, ✆ (020) 7565 5000. The major venue for experimental or countercultural writing, made famous by Shaw and Granville-Barker in the 1920s and kept prominent by the likes of Edward Bond, Caryl Churchill, Howard Brenton and Hanif Kureishi. The Theatre Upstairs on the first floor is one of the better fringe venues in town.

Old Vic, Waterloo Rd, ✆ (020) 7928 7616. The former home of the National Theatre has come down in the world a bit, but still puts on good productions. Recently refurbished. Peter O'Toole caused a sensation here in the early 1980s by playing Macbeth for laughs in a near-incoherent drunken slur. The theatre was packed out every night, but the management was scandalized.

Wyndham's, Charing Cross Rd, ✆ (020) 7369 1736. One of the more reliable West End addresses, with plenty of serious productions that attract big-name foreign actors like John Malkovich and Dustin Hoffman.

Theatre Royal Haymarket, Haymarket, ✆ (020) 7930 8800. Unadventurous choice of plays, but impeccable production and acting standards in this early 19th-century theatre built by John Nash. Maggie Smith, Vanessa Redgrave and Ian McKellen are regular stars here.

Donmar Warehouse, Earlham St, Covent Garden, ✆ (020) 7369 1732. Excellent venue where many distinguished young directors have cut their teeth.

Lyric Hammersmith, King St, ✆ (020) 8741 2311. Hosts many regional and foreign theatre companies. Home also to the smaller, experimental Studio, ✆ (020) 8741 8701.

Hampstead Theatre, Avenue Road, ✆ (020) 7722 9301. Actors and audiences often mingle in the bar after the show at this friendly neighbourhood theatre, which is often a springboard for prestigious West End productions.

Theatre Royal Stratford East, Gerry Raffles Square, Stratford, ✆ (020) 8534 0310. High-quality drama in a Victorian palace in the midst of grey tower blocks. (*Currently closed for refurbishment.*)

King's Head, 115 Upper St, Islington, ✆ (020) 7226 1916. Eccentric pub (*see* 'Food and Drink', p.160) with popular theatrical tradition in a charming back room. Serves a 3-course dinner in the theatre just before the curtain rises (metaphorically speaking, because there is no curtain).

Almeida, Almeida St, Islington, ✆ (020) 7359 4404. A fringe theatre that has acquired a formidable reputation. Stages different productions every six or seven weeks. Often produces its own plays but also reworks classical pieces.

The Gate, 11 Pembridge Road, Notting Hill, ✆ (020) 7229 0706, *gate@gatetheatre. freeserve.co.uk.* Excellent pub theatre that features new plays as well as ambitious reworkings of the classics, including Greek tragedy.

BAC (Battersea Arts Centre), 176 Lavender Hill, ✆ (020) 7223 2223. Lively theatre venue south of the river.

Shakespeare's Globe, 21 New Globe Walk, ✆ (020) 7401 9919. Opened for business in 1997, this lovingly reconstructed version of Shakespeare's original London theatre puts on three or four Elizabethan productions each year, most of them by the Bard, in a season that lasts from May until September. It's proving popular, so book early (box-office opens around January once the programme has been fixed). Lots of audience participation and period high jinks (like jesters with firecrackers attached to their feet). Watch out for rain and cold, though, as the theatre is open to the skies (*see* p.33 for more on the theatre itself).

Regent's Park Open Air Theatre, Inner Circle, Regent's Park, ✆ (020) 7486 2431. Open-air theatre from May to September. Bring a blanket and umbrella to keep the worst of the English summer at bay.

Holland Park Theatre, Holland Park, ✆ (020) 7602 7856. Has a shorter open-air season, from June to August, but puts on all manner of productions. *See* p.113.

Opera and Classical Music

London has classical music coming out of its ears: two major opera companies, five world-class orchestras, lunch time concerts, summer festival concerts, open-air concerts. For generations, classical music in Britain was tinged with class prejudice, being a pursuit of the educated upper-middle classes who turned up their noses at the philistine hordes who couldn't tell their Handel from their Haydn. You'll still find the snobs lurking in the foyers of the Festival Hall and on the rarefied airwaves of the BBC's classical station Radio 3. But you'll also find a wealth of unpretentious, dedicated young performers and audiences, especially in smaller concert venues like Wigmore Hall. London's weakness is undoubtedly in contemporary and avant-garde music; programmers tend to play very safe, with a preponderance of Mozart, Beethoven and Brahms.

The following addresses are for the main concert and opera venues; again, you should check *Time Out* to see what is playing.

Royal Opera House, Covent Garden, ✆ (020) 7304 4000. Britain's leading opera venue is right up there with the Met, the Staatsoper and La Scala, but constant financial and political problems have not only pushed up prices almost as high as the top C in the Queen of the Night's bravura aria from Mozart's *Magic Flute*, they have put the very future of the theatre in doubt at times: the House's financial deficit meant that for a time it produced no opera during the summer for a time but after an exciting and long overdue renovation it reopened in December 1999. *See* p.64.

London Coliseum, St Martin's Lane, ✆ (020) 7632 8300. Home to the English National Opera, which performs in English to high musical standards and with infectious enthusiasm. Much cheaper (from £5, top price around £50) and far less pretentious than Covent Garden. *See* p.65.

South Bank Centre, South Bank, Belvedere Rd, ✆ (020) 7960 4242. Three first-rate concert halls under the same roof: the Royal Festival Hall, boasting its own organ and room for as many musicians and singers as any musical work might demand; the Queen Elizabeth Hall, which is smaller and a little more adventurous in its programming; and the Purcell Room, for chamber music only. The larger halls also host occasional jazz, rock, dance and even small-scale opera performances. *See* p.82.

Barbican Centre, Silk St, ✆ (020) 7638 8891. Home to the London Symphony Orchestra and English Chamber Orchestra. Excellent acoustics make up for the out-of-the-way venue. *See* p.61.

Royal Albert Hall, Kensington Gore, ✆ (020) 7589 8212. Hosts the Promenade concerts, or Proms, which run every year from July until early September. The Proms are an eclectic platform for music old and new, and for unknown as well as established performers. The seats are removed from the area in front of the stage, leaving an open space in which people either stand or sit on the floor for as little as £3 per person. Queues form in the hours before the performance begins; bring a cushion to soften the bum-numbing effects of the Kensington pavements. You can also book conventional seating in advance, at regular concert prices (up to around £30). The Last Night of the Proms is a raucous affair at which the all-English orchestra plays all-English music, and the all-English audience sings along to the national anthem and 'Rule Britannia'. *See* p.28.

Wigmore Hall, 36 Wigmore St, ✆ (020) 7935 2141. An intimate venue with excellent acoustics that attracts solo performers like guitarist Julian Bream or prima donna Jessye Norman. The tickets are very cheap—between £6 and £20—and sell out very fast.

Sadler's Wells, Rosebery Ave, ✆ (020) 7278 8916. A somewhat unfashionable venue for all kinds of music, including the infectious if supremely silly late Victorian operettas of Gilbert and Sullivan performed by the D'Oyly Carte company in April and May.

St John's Smith Square, Smith Square, Westminster, ✆ (020) 7222 1061. This fine Baroque church is one of the best lunch time concert spots in town. Other good church venues, whether for lunchtime or evening concerts, include St James Piccadilly (usually on Mondays at 1pm); St Martin-in-the-Fields in Trafalgar Square (which boasts its own excellent chamber orchestra); St Bride in Fleet St; St Michael's Cornhill (organ recitals); St Anne and St Agnes, Gresham St; St Giles Cripplegate, Silk St; St Sepulchre-without-Newgate (mainly piano recitals on Fridays); the magnificently restored St Helen's, Bishopsgate; and St John's Waterloo. Some concerts charge admission, others are free but ask for donations.

Kenwood House, Hampstead Lane, ✆ (020) 7413 1443. From June to September, enjoy idyllic outdoor concerts beside a lake at the top of Hampstead Heath. Highly recommended. Other open-air summer venues include Hampton Court and Marble Hill House in Twickenham (Sunday evenings only). *See* p.103.

Holland Park Theatre, Holland Park, ✆ (020) 7602 7856. Open-air season, from June to August, with all manner of productions including opera.

Dance

London puts on everything from classical ballet to performance art. Covent Garden (*see* above) is home to the highly accomplished Royal Ballet, which is cheaper and much less snooty than the Royal Opera in the same building; while the London Coliseum (*see* above) hosts the English National Ballet, at least for now. Sadler's Wells (*see* above) used to have its own ballet company too, but it decamped to Birmingham in 1990; the theatre nevertheless puts on an eclectic dance programme that has recently included both the mime artist Lindsay Kemp and the National Ballet of Cambodia. Two other addresses worth knowing about are the **ICA** on the Mall (✆ (020) 7930 3647), arguably the most avant-garde address in town; and **The Place Theatre** (17 Duke's Rd, Bloomsbury, ✆ (020) 7380 1268), in The Place building, which is also home to the London Contemporary Dance School. Every autumn, from mid-October to early December, London stages a festival called Dance Umbrella, which provides a showcase for performers from around the world.

Jazz

Jazz came to London in the 1950s, largely thanks to the effort of the late Ronnie Scott and his excellent club in Soho, and it has gone from strength to strength ever since. Venues used to be poky, smoky and cheap; now they are smartening up, perhaps a shade too much since they are starting to offer fancy food and drink at extraordinarily high prices. The music has not suffered yet, however, and continues to flow until the not-so-early hours of the morning. Check *Time Out* for jazz concerts in pubs and foyers of the larger theatres. Note that many clubs charge a (usually nominal) membership fee. You may find it hard to book for the more popular shows at Ronnie Scott's, for example, if you are not already a member.

Ronnie Scott's, 47 Frith St, W1, ✆ (020) 7439 0747 (*closed Sun*). The prime jazz venue in town, with a steady flow of big names and a suitably low-key, laid-back atmosphere. Book if you have time, and get there early (around 9pm) to ensure a decent seat. Admission is £15 Mon–Thurs, £20 Fri–Sat, or more for a very big name band.

100 Club, 100 Oxford St, W1, ✆ (020) 7636 0933. Lively basement venue with an eclectic mix of trad and modern jazz, as well as blues, swing and rockabilly. The Sex Pistols gave one of their first performances here in the mid-1970s.

606 Club, 90 Lots Rd, Fulham, ✆ (020) 7352 5953. Seven-nights-a-week basement club featuring many local musicians, with emphasis on contemporary jazz. Late-night restaurant licence and good modern food. 8.30–2am.

Jazz After Dark, 9 Greek St, Soho, ✆ (020) 7734 0545. Jazz, Latin jazz and salsa, with a bar and restaurant (licensed to 2am, 3am at weekends). Admission free before 11pm on weekdays.

Jazz Café, 5 Parkway, Camden, ✆ (020) 7344 0044. Typical of the new-style jazz club, a slick venue with plush dinner-table seating (food optional). The music is first-rate.

Bull's Head, 373 Lonsdale Rd, Barnes, SW13, ✆ (020) 8876 5241. Top-notch bands in a riverside setting.

Vortex, Stoke Newington Church St, ✆ (020) 7254 6516. Friendly first-floor jazz bar featuring many local north London bands.

Pizza Express, 10 Dean St, Soho, ✆ (020) 7439 8722. Be-bop to accompany your pizza; an unlikely setting, but a congenial one which boasts its own resident band as well as many prestigious visitors. Branch at **Pizza on the Park**, 11 Knightsbridge, off Hyde Park Corner, ✆ (020) 7235 5273.

Soho Pizzeria, 16–18 Beak St, ✆ (020) 7434 2480. Another pizza place with live music as you eat; no extra charge and the pizza is good too.

By and large, the big Madonna/Michael Jackson venues like Wembley Stadium are impersonal and have terrible acoustics, while smaller, more specialized clubs like the Africa Centre or the Mean Fiddler are infinitely more rewarding and cheaper too. Posters and press adverts will tell you how to buy tickets. You'll probably have to go through a ticket agency (*see* Theatre section above) for the bigger acts, otherwise go directly to the venue. Once again, *Time Out* will have all the details, including reliable recommendations on the week's best shows.

Wembley Stadium, Empire Way, Wembley, ✆ (020) 8902 0902. Appalling views, appalling acoustics, appalling transport links. If the big acts insist on coming here, it is mainly because of the seating capacity (up to 100,000); but as Madonna would be the first to tell you, size isn't everything. Only the Live Aid concert of 1985 and the Free Nelson Mandela bash of 1988 generated something approaching atmosphere. Otherwise, only the sledgehammer lyricism of U2 or Bruce Springsteen can ever get through to audiences. Bring a telescope.

Wembley Arena, same address as above. The indoor neighbour of the stadium, with all of its problems but with a seating capacity of only 13,000.

Royal Albert Hall, Kensington Gore, ✆ (020) 7589 8212. The iffy acoustics and somewhat grandiose Victorian architecture are more than compensated for by intelligent programming—folk-rock and R'n'B by the likes of Bonnie Raitt, Eric Clapton etc.

Brixton Academy, 211 Stockwell Rd, Brixton, ✆ (020) 7771 2000. Much more like it. Raw, raucous music in a crumbling Art Deco setting. Sweaty but exhilarating.

Forum, 9–17 Highgate Rd, Kentish Town, ✆ (020) 7344 0044. Formerly known as the Town and Country Club and arguably the best rock venue in town; an excellent blend of high-quality facilities and first-rate bands.

Shepherds Bush Empire, Shepherds Bush Green, ✆ (020) 7771 2000. Similar-sized venue to the Forum, with seats upstairs. Attracts big names; great atmosphere.

The Grand, Clapham Junction, St John's Hill, ✆ (0800) 783 7485. Newish rock venue with great view of the stage from the bar.

Subterania, 12 Acklam Rd, Ladbroke Grove, ✆ (020) 8960 4590. Funk, jazz, soul and rap, interspersed with new songwriter nights, make this one of the more unpredictable and enjoyable spots in west London. Hot rubber rooms.

The Rock Garden, 6–7 The Piazza, Covent Garden, ✆ (020) 7836 4052. Restaurant venue with live music. the night will have a theme (indie rock, pop/funk, new bands). No big names, but can be good, if expensive.

Africa Centre, 38 King St, Covent Garden, ✆ (020) 7836 1973. Groovy atmosphere and infectious African music. Cheap and great fun.

Camden Palace, 1a Camden Rd, ✆ (020) 7387 0428. Tuesday night features new indie bands. Dancing the other nights of the week.

Dingwalls, Camden Lock, ✆ (020) 7267 1577. Decent if grubby venue featuring a variety of bands, from rock to country.

Hammersmith Apollo, Queen Caroline St, ✆ (020) 7416 6080. A big-name venue, which puts on stage shows as well. Excellent sound and good views of the stage.

The Mean Fiddler, 24–8a High St, Harlesden, ✆ (020) 8963 0940. Ace setting for Irish folk and new country artists. Well worth the schlepp out to northwest London.

The Venue, 2a Clifton Rise, New Cross, ✆ (020) 8692 4077 (*open Fri, Sat*). Specializes in indie music, with dancing late into the night.

Comedy has been all the rage in London since the early 1980s, and clubs have been sprouting with amazing speed all over town. Traditionally, stand-up comedy was restricted to music halls or to working-men's clubs in the industrial towns of northern England. Performers were generally fat and male, and cracked jokes in dubious taste about blacks, big tits and mothers-in-law. The only 'sophisticated' comedy was the zany brand pioneered by the Footlights revue at Cambridge University and developed by the likes of Peter Cook, Dudley Moore and Monty Python. These were middle-class, well-educated performers who despite a strong anti-estab-lishment streak appealed mostly to their own kind. Comedy, like everything else in Britain, was divided along class lines.

All that changed with the advent of the Thatcher government in 1979. A new counter-culture of politically aware comedy sprang up, making what jokes it could out of industrial decline, growing gulfs between rich and poor and the 1980s culture of greed and self-advancement. Performers from a broader social and racial spectrum, including Lenny Henry, Rowan Atkinson, Harry Enfield, Ben Elton, Rik Mayall and Jo Brand, soon became established stars, both on television and in some cases in feature films too. All of them started out in London's comedy clubs, particularly the Comedy Store in Leicester Square (since transferred to new premises) which opened in 1979, the year of Thatcher's election. The comedy club circuit has expanded considerably since then, and established performers mingle easily with new talent in more than 20 major venues. Sit in the front rows at your peril, as you are likely to be roped into the act and insulted or humiliated. Some of the humour is a bit parochial, revolving around British adverts and television programmes, but many acts are truly inspired. Usually several artists will contribute to a single evening, so if you don't like one there's not long to wait for something better. Look out for hilarious Boothby Graffoe, political radical Mark Thomas, Al Murray's Pub Landlord and very funny Rob Newman; but going to a good club to see acts you've never heard of can be just as rewarding as following the big names.

Comedy Store, 1a Oxendon St, ✆ (020) 7344 0234. Improv on Wed and Sun by the Comedy Store Players, otherwise stand-up. The most famous comedy club of them all has got a bit slick for its own good and the hefty admission fee (£8/12) reflects that. The standard remains very high, however.

Bound and Gagged, Tufnell Park Tavern, Tufnell Park Road, ✆ (020) 7483 3456. Saturday night above-pub club with unusual, interesting acts.

Jongleurs, Battersea, The Cornet, 49 Lavender Gardens, Clapham; Bow Wharf, 221 Grove Rd; Camden Lock, Dingwalls Bldg, Middle Yard, Chalk Farm Rd. All ✆ (020) 7564 2500. Top acts on Fri/Sat nights. Book in advance.

Meccano Club, Finnegan's Wake, 2 Essex Rd, ✆ (020) 7813 4478. This intimate, sweaty cellar bar is one of the great London clubs, always worth a visit.

Hackney Empire, 291 Mare St, Hackney, ✆ (020) 8985 2424. Comedy with a political edge in a fine Victorian theatre.

East Dulwich Cabaret, East Dulwich Tavern, 1 Lordship Lane, Thurs–Sat, ✆ (020) 8299 4138. Pub venue.

Downstairs at the King's Head, 2 Crouch End Hill, ✆ (020) 8340 1028. Warm atmosphere encouraged by the very funny compères. Open Sat, Sun.

Red Rose Comedy Club, 129 Seven Sisters Rd, Finsbury Park, ✆ (020) 7281 3051. Top acts at knock-down prices in a slightly iffy area. Open Fri, Sat.

London cinemas are a bit like the British film industry—bursting with potential, forever on the verge of a real breakthrough, but poorly looked after and often disappointing. The mainstream cinemas are on the whole unfriendly and very expensive (£7 or more for a ticket, regardless of whether the venue is a plush auditorium with THX Dolby sound or a cramped backroom with polystyrene walls). The multiplex has hit London in a big way, for example at the Warner and Empire in Leicester Square or at Whiteleys in Queensway. For no discernible good reason seats tend to be numbered, which means confusion breaks out just as the main feature is starting, and the audience rarely settles down until 10 minutes into the first reel. There has been a flurry of interest in new British and independent cinema in recent years, thanks to *Four Weddings and a Funeral, The Full Monty* and the darkly humorous work of the Scottish director Danny Boyle (*Shallow Grave, Trainspotting,* etc.). But Hollywood blockbusters still grab more than their fair share of the market, and the work of some of the most challenging British directors— Mike Leigh, Nicolas Roeg or Ken Loach—might not make a first-run cinema at all.

On the plus side, the arthouse and repertory sector is reasonably healthy, showing subtitled foreign-language films as well as the classics of American and British cinema. Prices are lower than first-run cinemas—£4–5 is normal—and can be lower still if you pay a membership fee and return regularly. The National Film Theatre offers the broadest range, while clubs like the Everyman attract a fiercely loyal clientele.

Film censorship in general is very strict, and in some cases the British Board of Film Classification cuts out footage it finds offensive without alerting the audience. Films are graded U (family films), PG (parental guidance recommended), 12 (nobody under that age), 15 (ditto) or 18 (ditto). The system is governed by crazy pseudo-puritanical rules that border on para- noia—the very first film to be censored in Britain, back in 1898, was a close-up of a piece of Stilton cheese. Don't ask why. Steven Spielberg's dinosaur thriller *Jurassic Park* was given a PG rating despite its self-evidently disturbing effect on children, while an intelligent classic like Robert Altman's *McCabe and Mrs Miller* is lumped along with pornography and kung fu in the 18 bracket.

Odeon Leicester Square, Leicester Square, ✆ (0870) 5050 007. London's plushest venue, which premières major Hollywood productions, often with royals and film stars in tow. Even more expensive than the average mainstream cinema, with interminable adverts before the main feature.

Prince Charles, Leicester Place, ✆ (020) 7437 8181. This former soft-porn cinema has smartened up its act and shows a constantly changing schedule of cult classics at £3.50 a seat. Surely this can't go on... take advantage while you can.

Curzon Mayfair, 38 Curzon St, ✆ (020) 7369 1720. Cinema showing art or foreign films. A more relaxed venue is its sister-cinema, the **Curzon Soho** at 93 Shaftesbury Ave, ✆ (020) 7439 4805.

Metro, 11 Rupert St, ✆ (020) 7437 0757. Two- screen cinema that shuns Hollywood fare in favour of independent productions.

Renoir, Brunswick Centre, Brunswick Square, ✆ (020) 7837 8402. The most adventurous of central London's cinemas, showing lots of foreign films and the best of British and American independents.

Screen on the Hill, 230 Haverstock Hill, Belsize Park, ✆ (020) 7435 3366. Popular first-run and art cinema with excellent coffee at the bar. Affiliated cinemas include the rather cramped **Screen on Baker Street** (96 Baker St, ✆ (020) 7486 0036) and the more commercial **Screen on the Green** (83 Upper St, Islington, ✆ (020) 7226 3520).

Gate, 87 Notting Hill Gate. ℘ (020) 7727 4043. Classy west London cinema with lively Sunday matinée line-ups. First-run films and classic revivals.

National Film Theatre, South Bank, ℘ (020) 7928 3232. The mecca of London's film junkies and main venue for the annual London Film Festival each November. Lots of old and new films always showing in rep, with special seasons, for instance of Iranian cinema.

Pullman Everyman, Hollybush Vale, Hampstead, ℘ (0845) 606 2345. The oldest rep cinema in London with an excellent bar. Lots of old favourites and a dedicated, studenty audience.

ICA Cinemathèque, Carlton House Terrace, The Mall, ℘ (020) 7930 3647. The wackiest film selection in town, with the emphasis on the avant-garde, especially feminist and gay cinema.

Clapham Picture House, Venn St, ℘ (020) 7498 3323. Cheap and appealing cinema showing intelligent recent releases. A rare cinematic high spot south of the river.

Phoenix, 52 High Rd, East Finchley, ℘ (020) 8444 6789. Rather out of the way but very lovable old rep cinema, showing interesting double-bills.

French Institute, 17 Queensberry Place, South Kensington, ℘ (020) 7838 2144. A good place to catch up on Gabin, Godard *et compagnie*.

Goethe Institute, 50 Princes Gate, Exhibition Rd, ℘ (020) 7596 4000. Shows a broad range of German-language cinema, sometimes without subtitles.

Nightclubs and Discos

From the hot and sweaty to the cool and sophisticated, London has about 150 clubs and discos providing anything from big-band swing to rap and techno. The London club scene always used to be hampered by the strict licensing laws. Now you should be able to drink alcohol until 3am at most establishments and carry on dancing until dawn or beyond. (There is a chance that 24-hour drinking may be legalized in or after 2000, but nothing is certain.) The main handicap is price: it usually costs around £10 to get into a club, and £2 or £3 more to buy a drink. Some clubs have dress codes, which may mean no jeans or trainers.

Things change fast in clubland: the following venues are all long lasting but opening nights and music may change. Check a listings magazine.

Bar Rumba, 36 Shaftesbury Ave, ℘ (020) 7287 2715 (*open 10pm–3am*). Lively bar and club. Latin nights Mon and Tues, soul and R'n'B Sun, funk and house music other nights.

Bagleys Studios, Kings Cross Freight Depot, off York Way, ℘ (020) 7278 2777. This busy multiplex offers trancy techno on Fri, funky house and disco on Sat.

Café de Paris, 3 Coventry St, ℘ (020) 7734 7700 (*open Fri, Sat only 10pm–6am*). Club music all night in this 1920s ballroom. Very glamorous, with lots of red velvet and jacuzzis, but expensive.

Camden Palace, 1a Camden High St, ℘ (020) 7387 0428. Huge main floor and balcony offering space for a loyal, young crowd to dance to garage and techno.

The Complex, 1–5 Parkfield St, Islington, ℘ (020) 7288 1986. A must for the inexhaustible: it has a 24-hour party licence. A multi-level venue offering mainly funk, hip-hop and soul; gay nights with disco/80s/Motown.

The Cross, Goods Way Depot, off York Way, ℘ (020) 7837 0828. Low brick arches add to the hot, sweaty atmosphere. Three bars and a chill-out garden. Friendly crowd, but no jeans or trainers at Serious, the Friday night bash.

The End, 16a West Central St, ℘ (020) 7419 9199. Classic house party tunes at this central venue. *Open Thurs–Sat.*

The Fridge, Town Hall Parade, Brixton Hill, ℘ (020) 7326 5100 (*open Tues–Sat*). Funky music and a packed dance floor. Mainy gay nights, but open to all.

The Gardening Club, 4 The Piazza, Covent Garden, ☎ (020) 7497 3154 (*closed Sun*). Varied music during the week; house dominates at weekends.

Gossips, 69 Dean St, ☎ (020) 7434 4480 (*closed Sun*). Atmospheric dark cellar with wide range of music. Cheap entry (£5–7).

Heaven, Under the Arches, Craven St, ☎ (020) 7930 2020. Excellent club with multiple bars, dancefloors, laser shows and crazy lighting. The biggest gay club in Europe, but most nights very cool about anyone who wants to come.

Hippodrome, Cranbourn St, ☎ (020) 7437 4311 (*closed Sun*). Vastly popular club attracting a large crowd of non-Londoners. Trapeze artists and fire-eaters.

The Leisure Lounge, 121 Holborn, ☎ (020) 7242 1345. Packed for soul, funk and disco on Fridays with a 20–40s crowd. House on Sat, with R'n'B and swing in the more chilled second room.

Legends, 29 Old Burlington St, ☎ (020) 7437 9933 (*open Wed–Sat*). Cool-paced, elegantly designed club which livens up at weekends with house music.

Limelight, 136 Shaftesbury Ave, ☎ (020) 7434 0572 (*closed Sun*). A converted church blasting out all kinds of music, especially heavy rock.

Madame Jo Jo's, 8–10 Brewer St, ☎ (020) 7734 2473 (*closed Sun*). Outrageous transvestite cabaret. Camp and colourful but a bit touristy.

Ministry of Sound, 103 Gaunt St, Elephant and Castle, ☎ (020) 7378 6528 (*open all night Fri and Sat only*). Expensive (£15), but very trendy and always packed. A New York-style club with lots of garage and house music. Expect long queues.

The Scala, 278 Pentonville Rd, ☎ (020) 7833 2022 4480. Excellent club/live music venue. Far East monthly on Friday offers a dose of jazz to tech house.

Stringfellow's, 16 Upper St Martin's Lane, ☎ (020) 7240 5534 (*open Mon–Sat 9.30pm–3am*). Glamour models and footballers come here, as do lots of tourists dressed up in their smartest togs for this pricey yet somewhat tawdry night spot. Decent food.

Subteranea, 12 Acklam Rd (under Westway), ☎ (020) 8960 4590. Reggae and dub on Wed, funk, jazz and hip-hop on Fri, house on Sat.

Turnmills, 63 Clerkenwell Rd, ☎ (020) 7250 3409 (*open Fri, Sat*). Everything from funky jazz to house and techno at the home of Trade, London's original gay late-nighter (Sat).

Wag Club, 35 Wardour St, ☎ (020) 7437 5534 (*closed Sun*). Everything from live rock to funk and hip hop. A young, fairly trendy club spread over two floors.

Gay Bars

London's main drag centres on Old Compton St and adjoining streets in Soho, where passing media suits mingle freely with shaven headed, body-pierced fashion queens. Past squabbles between restaurateurs and Westminster Council over tables thrust onto wobbly narrow footpaths may have been resolved; the result is an untidy but lively compromise. The tidal pink pound has seen the rise and demise of many places to be seen in; what follows is a snapshot of the current scene. For gay clubs, *see* above.

The Admiral Duncan, 54 Old Compton St (*open Mon–Sat 12–11, Sun 12–10.30*). Traditional gay pub in the heart of Soho. Bombed by a bigot in 1999, it has acquired a certain iconic status as a symbol of resistance to prejudice.

BarCode, 3–4 Archer St, Soho (*open 12 noon–11 daily*). Busy, fun-loving cruise and dance bar on two levels, with pool tables and fruit machines.

The Black Cap, 171 Camden High St (*open Mon–Fri noon–2am, Sat noon–3am, Sun noon–midnight*). Gay disco and cabaret bar famous for its drag shows, with terrace and late licence.

The Box, 32–4 Monmouth St, Covent Garden (*open Mon–Sat 11–11, Sun 12–10.30*). Café by day and lively bar by night, attracting a young, trendy, mixed crowd and some celebs.

The Candy Bar, 4 Carlisle St (*open Mon–Thurs 5pm–midnight, Fri 5–2am, Sat 2–2, Sun 1–11*). Bustling, friendly, vibrant gay women's bar. Cocktails upstairs, dancing downstairs. Men welcome as guests.

The Edge, 11 Soho Square (*open Mon–Sat noon–1am, Sun 1–10.30*). Relaxed, mixed crowd in this four-floor bar.

First Out Café Bar, 52 St Giles High Street, Covent Garden (*open 10am–11pm*). Great veggie food served at this café bar, the first of its type in the West End. Women only on Fri eve.

Freedom, 60–66 Wardour St, Soho (*open 11am–3am*). Large café bar serving good food and cocktails to a trendy mixed crowd posing in designer gear. Downstairs club open until 3am.

Ku Bar, 75 Charing Cross Road, Soho (*open Mon–Sat noon–11pm, Sun 1–10.30*). Popular with young, scene-loving crowd.

Kudos, 10 Adelaide St, Covent Garden (*open Mon–Sat 11–11, Sun 12–10.30*). Brasserie and bar, popular with smart or after-work crowd. Big video screen downstairs.

The Retro Bar, 2 George Court, off Strand, Covent Garden (*open Mon–Sat 12–11, Sun 12–10.30*). Karaoke, '70s and '80s music and regular DJs in this friendly, unpretentious, traditional gay bar.

Rupert Street, 50 Rupert St (*open Mon–Sat 12–11, Sun 12–10.30*). Large, stylish, trendy bar, with similarly stylish and upmarket clientele of all ages and both sexes.

The Village, 81 Wardour St, Soho (*open Mon–Sat 2pm–1am, Sun 2pm–10.30 summer, 4pm–10.30 winter*). Stylish bar on two floors.

The Yard, 57 Rupert Street, Soho. Good food and cabaret attracting mixed stylish crowd. Outdoor courtyard a bonus in summer.

You're walking late at night along the Amstel. A frill of gables ends abruptly against the hard lines of the vast new opera house that cut across the evening skyline. A lone junkie in ragged red jeans and a flat Spanish hat sways and dances to a frail tune that no one else can hear. A young woman stands up to pedal her heavy black bicycle over a hump-backed bridge, her toddler asleep in a custom-built wicker carrier on the back. Just ahead, an ancient wearing a chauffeur's cap manoeuvres a along the uneven pavement. Its incumb dame swathed in black fur, nods as th gracious 'Goedenavond'. In Amsterda of life continually interweave: remi wealthy Golden Age trading city d Calvinist families, the sleaz hippie mecca of the 1960s

Amsterdam: Introduction

As a visitor you'll find Amsterdam at once familiar and curious. It has an edge and verve that will keep you on your toes. As Henry James wrote after a visit to the Netherlands in the 1870s, it will 'at least give one's regular habits of thought the stimulus of a little confusion'. You'll be daily launched into a farrago of sleek business people, droves of tourists, scruffs, bohemians and persons of decidedly ill repute. Yet everyone seems to get on remarkably well together, and the chance encounters with people here will be one of the lasting pleasures of your visit.

In the 1980s Amsterdam re-established its importance as a world finance centre. The 1990s saw a burgeoning of traffic through the harbour and Schiphol airport. Copywriters began to overuse the 'Gateway to Europe' epithet, as big-name computer companies and other industries reliant on speedy distribution networks arrived in town. Amsterdam's kernel of job-eager foreign residents, and the locals' facility with languages, made it an ideal location for freefone call-centres—next time your computer is on the blink and you call the number in the handbook, chances are (if you're phoning from within Europe) that you're speaking to someone in Amsterdam, however perfectly they speak your mother tongue. Today the Netherlands has one of the strongest economies in the EU, and the prosperity shows. Brazen, glittering business parks have sprouted on the outskirts of town, though thankfully the centre remains sacrosanct. Soon the entire inner city is to be placed on the World Heritage List of protected monuments, alongside such architectural stalwarts as the Great Wall of China.

Now that Amsterdam has notched up higher status in the business world, it seems anxious to become a little more respectable. Politics are becoming more conservative, police are clearing out junkies and dealers from the more squalid areas of the red-light district, and restaurants and galleries are appearing in their wake. But Amsterdam will never lose its alternative tang. It has a long tradition of liberal tolerance and is, after all, a port, with a port's rough edge. For centuries its heretics, whores and disruptive politicians have nudged and needled other Amsterdammers away from any tendency to complacency. Today you will still find a relaxed and tolerant city. Same-sex couples kiss in the street, whiffs of marijuana waft from psychedelic coffeeshops, clinics and crisis centres exist to help addicts with more severe drug habits. People seem aware of the environment, and in their spotless city are more often to be seen cycling and walking than whizzing about in cars.

This guide shows you Amsterdam in its diversity. It doesn't balk at the darker sides, and delights in the treasures. From grand museums to quiet, leafy squares; from the the tiny rooms where Anne Frank and her family hid from Nazi persecution to the red-light district—this is Amsterdam. Yet apart from the must-see sights, the town's greatest attractions are still its simplest pleasures: strolls along the canals, time spent in front of a painting that takes your breath away and long conversations in quiet cafés where centuries of tobacco smoke have turned the walls quite brown.

Amsterdam: Practical A–Z

Houses on the main canals are numbered from west to east, even numbers on the outer circumference. The Dutch write the house number *after* the street name, and follow it by Roman numerals indicating the storey: Bloemstraat 56 II would be an apartment two floors above street level at No.56 Bloemstraat. An apartment at street level is shown by the letters 'hs' (*huis*, house).

Amsterdammers seem to have run out of imagination when naming their streets. If they think they've hit on a good name they'll use it again and again—so you get not only Eerste/1e (1st) Helmersstraat but also Tweede/2e (2nd) Helmersstraat and Derde/3e (3rd) Helmersstraat. Transverse streets get the epithet '*dwars*', and also appear in multiples, so Tweede Egelantiersdwarsstraat will be the second street off Egelantiersstraat. The Oudezijd (old side of the city, east of Damrak) and the Nieuwezijd (new side, west of Damrak) are abbreviated in addresses to OZ and NZ—Oudezijds Voorburgwal, for example, is usually written OZ Voorburgwal. Postcodes are written *before* the word 'Amsterdam'. (Postcode directories are available in post offices.)

Amsterdam is a diminutive city, perfectly tailored to a small person's needs. Parents don't have to go to extraordinary expense or exercise great feats of imagination to give children a good time. Cycle lanes make bicycling quite safe, a pedalo on the canal can while away hours, even a ride on a clanging tram can be an event. If trams prove to be a hit, try one of the antique trolleys that go to the **Amsterdamse Bos**, a woody parkland where the children can ride horses, eat pancakes, swim and run about to their hearts' content. Trains leave every 20 minutes from Haarlemmermeer Station in west Amsterdam.

The **Zoo**, Plantage Kerklaan 40, © 523 3400 (*open 9–5 daily; entrance adults f25, under-12s f17.50*) is a good place to take chidren. It's green and quite attractive, as zoos go, with some interesting outcrops of 19th-century architecture. The complex includes a planetarium and an aquarium. There's also a museum and a children's farm, where you can stroke various animals (*open same times as zoo; entrance to both included in the zoo ticket*). There's another **city farm** (De Uylenburg, Staalmeesterlaan 420; *open Mon–Fri 9–5, Sat and Sun 10–5; adm free;* © *618 5235*) in the Rembrandtpark, with free horse rides and a playground. For running about, try the **Vondelpark**, a large and fascinating expanse of greenery near the major museums (*see* pp.226–7).

Some museums have special children's facilities. The **New Metropolis Center of Science and Technology,** Prins Hendrikkade, at the entrance to the IJ tunnel, is a paradise for young computer enthusiasts. All the high-tech displays have explanations in English. Most invite fiddling fingers. At the other end of the scale is the **Kindermuseum** (Children's Museum) at the Tropenmuseum (Tropical Museum), Linnaeusstraat 2, © 568 8300 (*open Wed for tours at 1.45 and 3.30, Sat and Sun at noon, 1.45, 3.30; special events some Saturdays; adm children f7.50 adults f12.50; children's programme lasts 1½ hours, adults join children after 1 hour. Children between 6 and 12 years old only; reservation recommended*). The staff, who have all had experience of a third world country, create a village-like environment where kids can learn first-hand about aspects of another culture—such as drumming, rice-making or dancing.

You can get hold of vetted and reliable **babysitters** from Oppascentrale Kriterion (© 624 5848; *open 24 hours*). Prices start at about ƒ7 an hour and you're expected to provide drinks, food for long sessions and the cost of transport home after midnight. Over weekends there is a minimum charge of ƒ20.

Consulates and Embassies

Australia, Carnegielaan 12, The Hague, © (070) 310 8200
Canada, Sophialaan 7, The Hague, © (070) 361 4111
Great Britain, Koningslaan 44, © 676 4343
New Zealand, Mauristkade 25, The Hague, © (070) 346 9324
USA, Museumplein 19, © 575 5309

For the telephone numbers of other consulates consult the Amsterdam Tourist Board (*see* 'Tourist Information', p.192), or one of the listings magazines.

Crime, Drugs and Police

As far as big cities go, Amsterdam is comfortably safe. You need have little fear of serious street crime at any time of day or night (though women walking alone would be well advised to avoid red-light districts after midnight). At one time the area around Zeedijk in the city centre prickled with drug dealers and junkies and was quite creepy to walk through. A massive police clean-up has made the area safer, but despite council efforts to encourage shops and galleries to move there, it can still seem seedy and tense.

Contrary to received opinion, **soft drugs** are not legal in Holland, though an official blind eye is turned to the possession of under 28g (1oz) of cannabis. The tolerance goes as far as allowing some coffeeshops to sell cannabis over the counter (*see* **Food and Drink**, p.245); here people smoke marijuana on the premises. This is not true of all coffeeshops. Anyone found in possession of hard drugs, such as heroin or cocaine, can expect swift prosecution.

Bicycle theft, **theft from cars** and **pickpocketing** are something of a problem. You'll often see quite abusive signs on car windows informing all who might be tempted that there is nothing at all inside to steal. A favourite trick of pickpockets is to sidle up close and offer to sell you something illicit while at the same time gently lifting your wallet. Sensible vigilance is the only way to avoid these petty crimes: don't leave valuables in your car, always lock your bike securely and don't carry a wallet in your back pocket or leave it on top of a shop counter when paying. Keep traveller's cheques and stubs separate and don't carry large amounts of money in one pocket.

Amsterdam's police generally keep a low profile and are a relaxed and sympathetic lot. If you do need them, the **emergency number is** © 112. Main **police stations** are at Elandsgracht 117 and Warmoesstraat 44. Report any theft immediately, and get a written statement for your insurance claim. The Amsterdam Tourist Assistance Service (ATAS, NZ Voorburgwal 114/8, © 625 3246) offers **victim support**, should you have been shaken up by your experience, or feel at a loss as to what to do. If, on the other hand, you find yourself in trouble with the police, phone your consulate as soon as you can (but remember that Dutch police are under no legal obligation to allow you a phone call, and can detain you without charge for up to 24 hours).

Disabled Travellers

Amsterdam's cobbled streets and tiny houses with narrow doorways and steep stairs pose problems for those with limited mobility. Older **trams** have high steps, and are not accessible at all, though newer models are more wheelchair-friendly. There is, however, a special **taxi service** for wheelchair users (✆ 613 4134) and the **metro** is accessible. The **Netherlands Railways** publishes timetables in Braille and a detailed booklet on Rail Travel for the Disabled, available at Centraal Station, or through their London office (✆ (01962) 773646).

Nearly all museums, cinemas and churches have wheelchair access and many have facilities for the visually impaired and hard of hearing. The **Amsterdam Tourist Board** (near Centraal Station (*see* p.192) or the London branch of the **Netherlands Board of Tourism** (18 Buckingham Gate, SW1, ✆ (020) 7828 7900) has lists of accommodation, restaurants, museums and tourist attractions with facilities for the disabled.

Discount Cards

The **Amsterdam Culture & Leisure Pass** entitles you to all sorts of discounts on museums and restaurants. It costs ƒ39.50—though it can pay for itself within a few days. It's available from the Amsterdam Tourist Board (*see* 'Tourist Information', p.192).

Electricity

The **voltage** in the Netherlands is 220 AC, which is compatible with the UK, but you'll need a transformer for American electrical equipment. Wall sockets take two-pronged plugs.

Festivals and Events

February	Though it's more a southern, Roman Catholic tradition, Amsterdammers (always in the market for a party) have also taken to the traditional dressing up and last-minute boozing before Lent at the February **Carnival**.
25	**Commemoration of the February Strike**—a solemn gathering at the Dokwerker statue on J. D. Meijerplein.
March	The **Stille Omgang** (Silent Procession) takes place at night on the Sunday closest to the 15 March. Roman Catholics from all over the world walk in silence along the Heiligeweg and up to Sint Nicolaaskerk to celebrate Amsterdam's 'Miracle' (*see* p.231).
April	**National Museum Weekend** is usually the third weekend in April. All museums allow free entry and get very crowded. Unless you're exceptionally hard-up, this is a date to avoid.
30	**Koninginnedag** (Queen's Day—a national holiday to celebrate the Queen's birthday). Amsterdam declares a 'free market'. Anyone can sell anything anywhere and all bar and restaurant takings are tax-free. The whole city turns into a cross between a carnival and a flea-market.
	An internationally respected **World Press Photo Exhibition** displays the pick of newspaper and magazine photography from the preceding year. (In the Nieuwe Kerk, mid-April–mid-May.)

Watch out also for **GRAP Day** at De Melkweg (*see* p.268, **Entertainment and Nightlife**), when Amsterdam's best new bands blast away well into the night.

May 4/5   **Herdenkingsdag** (Remembrance Day) and **Bevrijdingsdag** (Liberation Day) are not the pompous, jingoistic affairs such occasions often become. Queen Beatrix lays a wreath at the National Monument at 8pm on Remembrance Day and the whole city observes a moving two-minute silence. The next day erupts in street parties and live music.

June   The **Holland Festival** runs for the whole month of June. This is Amsterdam's answer to the Edinburgh Festival, with an impressive constellation of international performers booked into opera, dance and theatre venues around the city.

2nd Sunday   Around the beginning of the month (or at the end of May) the RAI Congress Centre plays host to **Kunst RAI**, an international contemporary art fair.

July   If the Holland Festival sounds too staid for your tastes, try the **July Summer Festival**—a bonanza of the avant-garde that goes on all over town (sometimes in the strangest places).

August   For most of August the Martin Luther King Park, beside the Amstel on the southern outskirts of town, is the scene of **De Parade**, a 'theatre funfair'.

The **Uitmarkt** (Entertainment Market) takes place in the last week of August. Groups from all over the Netherlands offer snippets of what the coming cultural season has to offer.

More open-air music is played during the three-day-long **Grachtenfestival** (Canal Festival)—this time from boats opposite the Pulitzer Hotel (Prinsengracht 315–31; also in the last week of August).

September   **Bloemen Corso** (Flower Parade) is a parade of floats from Aalsmeer ('the flower capital') to Amsterdam on the first Saturday of the month. Check with the Amsterdam Tourist Board (*see* 'Tourist Information', p.192) for details of the route and arrival times.

The **Jordaan Festival** is the liveliest of a series of neighbourhood street parties. All over the Jordaan, residents come out to booze, barbecue and try their luck in the often unabashedly dire local talent contests.

One weekend in September is given over to **Monumentendag** (Monument Day), when notable buildings that are not usually open to the public allow in streams of curious visitors.

November   In mid-November **St Nicholas (Sinterklaas/Santa Claus)** arrives by steamboat at Centraal Station (supposedly from his home in Spain). He parades through the city on a white horse.

December 5   **Pakjesavond** (Parcel Evening) is the traditional Dutch time to give presents—rather than Christmas Day.

Oudejaarsavond (New Year's Eve) is the perfect excuse for more partying. People take to the streets with bottles of champagne, some bars stay open all night and there are fireworks everywhere.

Ambulance, ☎ 112

The most useful place to ring if you are ill or need a dentist is the **Central Medical Service** on ☎ (0900) 503 2042. This 24-hour service will refer you to a duty practitioner. The most central **hospital** with an outpatients department is Onze Lieve Vrouwe Gasthuis, Eerste Oosterparkstraat 179, ☎ 599 9111. **Chemists** (*drogisterij*) sell non-prescription drugs and toiletries. If you need a prescription made up you should go to an *apotheek*. The Central Medical Service can also advise you on this. If you've crushed your contact lenses or dropped your specs in a canal, try **York Optiek**, Heiligeweg 8, ☎ 623 3295 (*open Mon–Fri 9.30–6, Sat 9.30–5; appointment advisable, major credit cards accepted*). If your dentures take a crunch try **Accident**, Amstelveenseweg 51, ☎ 664 4380 (*open 24 hours*).

It is advisable to take out **travel insurance** before any trip—and to do so as soon as you buy your tickets. Specially tailored travel insurance packages cover medical expenses, lost luggage and theft, and also offer compensation for cancellation and delayed departure. That said, EU nations are entitled to receive free or reduced-charge medical treatment in the Netherlands: British visitors will need a **form E111** (fill in application form SA30, available from DSS branches or post offices). Theoretically you should organize this two weeks before you leave, though you can usually do it in one visit. The E111 does not insure personal belongings.

Lost Property

There are **lost property offices** at Centraal Station, GVB Head Office, Prins Hendrikkade 108–114 (*open Mon–Fri 9–4; for items lost on public transport*), and at Waterlooplein 11 (*open Mon–Fri 11–3.30; for items lost in parks and on the streets*). Allow a day or two for your property to filter through the system before trying to reclaim it.

Maps

A few moments studying a good map will help you find you way round. Practically every free tourist leaflet has some sort of streetplan of Amsterdam. By far the clearest of all the commercially produced maps is the colour 3-D one published by Carto Studio, available at souvenir shops and book stores. If you need more detail, Falk publish a variety of maps ranging from simple fold-outs to the origami-inspired 'patent-folded' version.

Money

The unit of Dutch currency is the **guilder**, which is abbreviated as ƒ, f, fl (for the old Dutch term florin) or NLG (in business and banking contexts). On price tags, 'guilders' is often written as /-. A guilder is divided into 100 **cents** (shortened to 'c'). There are around ƒ3 to the pound sterling, and about ƒ1.66 to the US dollar. The notes are said to be the prettiest in Europe, and come in ƒ10, ƒ25, ƒ50, ƒ100, ƒ250, ƒ500 and ƒ1000 denominations (though you seldom see notes above ƒ100, and may have trouble finding shops that accept larger denominations). There are six types of coin: a **stuiver** (5c, copper); the **dubbeltje** (10c), **kwartje** (25c), ƒ1 and **rijksdaalder** (ƒ2.50)—all silver-coloured; and the ƒ5 (gold-coloured). All prices are rounded up to multiples of five.

Credit cards are not as widely accepted as you might expect. It's always a good policy to double check. A number of shops will charge you extra if you pay by credit card. Eurocheques and traveller's cheques are a better idea. If you have appropriate identification, many establishments will accept them direct. Nowadays hole-in-the-wall cash dispensers are the most convenient way of getting money. Check that your bank card is programmed for overseas withdrawals, and that your bank doesn't charge for the service. You can usually withdraw up to ƒ300 a day.

Lost or stolen credit cards can be reported on the following numbers: American Express, stolen cheques ✆ (0800) 022 0100, stolen cards ✆ 504 8000/504 8666 after 6pm; Diners Club ✆ 557 3407; Mastercard/Access ✆ (0800) 022 5821; Visa ✆ 660 0611.

The Postbank (at post offices) and GWK (Grens Wissel Kantoor—official *bureaux de change*) are the best places to change your money. Banks are open 9am to 4 or 5pm, Monday to Friday. (Some stay open until 7pm on Thursdays.)

There are *bureaux de change* open until midnight on Leidsestraat. The GWK exchanges at Centraal Station and Schiphol (both open 24 hours daily) are a better bet than the deals offered by hotel receptions, and even many banks.

You'll find offices of American Express at Amsteldijk 166, Damrak 66 (with 24-hour cash dispenser for cardholders and automatic traveller's cheque refund service) and Van Baerlestraat 39; and Thomas Cook at Dam 23–5, Damrak 1–5 (*open Mon–Sat 8–8 and Sun 9–8*), and at Leidseplein 31a.

Post Offices

The main post office is at Singel 250 (*open Mon–Fri 9–6, Sat 10–1.30; late opening Thurs until 8;* ✆ *556 3311*) and, as well as the usual facilities, it has phones, photocopiers, a gift shop and a philately counter. Parcels can be sent only through this office, or the sorting office (Oosterdokskade 3, near Centraal Station; *open Mon–Fri 8.30–9, Sat 9–12 noon;* ✆ *622 8272*). Stamps (*postzegels*) can also be bought from tobacconists. At the time of writing it costs ƒ1 to send a postcard to the UK, ƒ1 to send an airmail letter to the UK or a postcard to the USA and ƒ1.30 to send an airmail letter to the USA (prices for letters under 20g). The slot for overseas mail on post boxes is marked *Overige*.

Public Holidays

New Year's Day, Good Friday, Easter Sunday and Monday, Queen's Day (30 April), Ascension Day, Whit Sunday and Monday, Christmas Day and Boxing Day. On these days most things close, and Amsterdam can be very quiet indeed.

Sports and Activities

spectator sports

The most popular national sport is football. The Dutch team have not had many resounding international successes, but the local Amsterdam team, Ajax, has a vociferous and enthusiastic following. Ajax won European Cups three times in the 1970s, and managed again in 1995. If you want to see the team for yourself, head for their flashy new home, the Amsterdam Arena, ✆ 311 1333, next to the Bijlmer metro station in Amsterdam South East. Hockey (field hockey), on the other hand, is a sport in which both the men's and the women's national teams have been world champions. Many national home matches and some good club games are played at the Hockey en Cricket VVV, Aanloop 2, ℂ 640 2464, south of Amstelpark.

do-it-yourself

Among the numerous well-equipped gyms and **fitness centres** around town are: A Bigger Splash, Looiersgracht 26–30, ℂ 624 8404 (*open daily 7am–midnight; weights, machines, sauna, steam, massage and aerobics; f35 per day/f87.50 per week/f140 per month all inclusive*) and Garden Gym, Jodenbreestraat 158, ℂ 626 8772 (*open Mon, Wed, Fri 9–11, Tues and Thurs 12–11, Sat 11–6.30 and Sun 10–7 mainly, though not exclusively, for women; weights, dance, sauna, solarium, massage, self-defence; day pass f16, with sauna/shower f23.50, sauna only f18.50*). Sauna Deco, Herengracht 115, ℂ 623 8215 (*open Mon–Sat 11–11, Sun 12–6 adm f17.50 before 2pm, or f25 per day*) is an exhilarating experience. You sweat away those extra inches in a stylish Art Deco interior rescued from a famous 1920s Parisian department store.

Swimming pools in Amsterdam are clean, well-maintained and supervised. The Marnixbad, Marnixplein 9, ℂ 625 4843 (*adm f4.75*) has waterslides and a whirlpool. The Mirandabad, De Mirandalaan 9, ℂ 642 8080 (*adm f7*) has tropical temperatures, a pebble beach and a wave machine. There's an outdoor pool for good weather and a slide and whirlpool.

You'll find **squash** and indoor **tennis** courts at the Frans Otten Stadion, Stadionstraat 10, ℂ 662 8767 (*open Mon–Fri 9–12, Sat 9–8, Sun 9–10; tennis f45 per hour/f52.50 after 5pm, squash f37.50 per hour; racket hire f5*). There are 42 tennis courts, most of them outdoor, at the Amstelpark, Koenenkade 8, ℂ 301 0700 (*open daily 8am–11pm; indoor and outdoor courts f35 per hour*).

Telephones

Amsterdam's telephone boxes are green, with a white *ptt telecom* logo. **Payphones** take 25c, f1, f2.50 and coins. Increasingly, **cardphones** are taking the place of payphones. Many accept credit cards, and all operate with phonecards, which you can buy at post offices, railway stations and newsagents. Don't be confused by the local ringing tone—a long continuous sound rather like the British 'engaged' signal. All numbers given in this section which are not preceded by a bracketed code are Amsterdam numbers. Numbers preceded by 06 are either free, or charged at a special rate, usually between 50c and f1 a minute.

> **Directory Enquiries**: ℂ (0900) 8008
> **International Operator** (also for collect calls): ℂ (0800) 0410
> **International Directory Enquiries**: ℂ (0900) 8418

International direct dialling codes:

> From Amsterdam to USA: ℂ (00 1) + area code without 0
> From USA to Amsterdam: ℂ (011 31) 20
> From Amsterdam to UK: ℂ (00 44) + area code without 0
> From UK to Amsterdam: ℂ (00 31) 20

International calls are cheaper between 8pm and 8am, but calls to other European countries don't count as international.

Time

Amsterdam is two hours ahead of Greenwich Mean Time in the spring and summer, and one hour ahead in winter and autumn.

Tipping, Etiquette and Service

Restaurant and bar bills in Holland are inclusive of tax and service, so a tip isn't really necessary. It's customary, though, to round the amount up to the nearest guilder (or ƒ5 for a big bill). If the service has been exceptional, it's quite acceptable to add a little more. Taxi drivers expect 10 per cent—especially if they've helped with luggage.

Queuing at supermarket delicatessens, some banks and public institutions is controlled by an electronic ticketing system. You tear off a ticket as you enter and wait for your number to flash up on a screen. At cash machines and bank and post office counters, the rest of the queue keeps a polite metre or so's distance from the person transacting business. Sometimes there's a boundary line painted on the floor. Step over this mark (visible or otherwise) and the atmosphere turns icy.

English is spoken almost as a second mother tongue in Amsterdam. Some Hollanders seem to resent this, but many (especially those working in restaurants, bars and shops) seem insulted if you ask 'Do you speak English?' One way round this is to open with a cheery dag! ('darhg'—good day) and then speak English. 'Dag'—called out with a friendly upward lilt in the voice—is used at all times of day or night, entering and leaving shops, when speaking to barmen, policemen, cabbies and tram drivers. When you meet a Dutch person for the first time, it's polite to shake hands and say your name clearly.

If you are used to slick New York **service**, or even to the slightly less brisk British style, then you are in for a sad surprise when you visit Amsterdam. Bring a bottle of Valium to help keep calm and a pack of cards to while away the time, or you will find your holiday intensely frustrating. It is not unknown for customers to sit for twenty minutes to half an hour in a café before there is even a whiff of a waiter, though when they do come they are so full of shiny-eyed friendliness that it is difficult to be angry. Expect to wait at least half an hour to forty minutes for your dinner to arrive once you have ordered it.

Toilets

Amsterdam is dotted with rather attractive, but foul-smelling, curved green metal **urinoirs**. These are right on the pavement, and blot out only the mid-torso from public gaze. All passers-by see is a pair of feet and a face trying desperately to look nonchalant. Apart from those at railway stations, there are still no normal public toilets in Amsterdam. For women, or men who balk at the idea of peeing *al fresco*, the best option is to duck into a café. This is perfectly acceptable practice, though bars in some of the busier tourist areas discourage it. The better hotel foyers provide classier options, but this takes a certain amount of poise, as you have to stroll through the lobby as if you're a resident, all the time darting your eyes about for the relevant sign—not easy if you're caught in a last-minute dash. Station loos—and sometimes those in larger cafés—are guarded by fierce women, who require you to drop at least 25c into a saucer before passing.

The **Amsterdam Tourist Board** has English-speaking staff who can change money and (for a ƒ3.50 fee) arrange hotel and theatre bookings. They sell a range of maps and brochures and can suggest tours and walks. The main Amsterdam branch is opposite Centraal Station at Stationsplein 10. There is another, less busy branch at Leidseplein 1, a small branch in Centraal Station and one in the south of town on the corner of Stadionplein and Van Tuyll van Serooskerkenweg (*all open Mon–Sat 9 to 5*). During the high season some offices may extend their hours, and open on Sunday. There is a **central information telephone number**: ℂ (0900) 400 4040, but it costs ƒ1 a minute and you are usually kept for ages in an electronic queue. There is also a nationwide tourist office at the airport, **Holland Tourist Information** (HTI, Schiphol Plaza, *open Mon–Sun 7am–10pm*). You can get information on the Internet at two official websites: *www.nbt.nl/nbt-amst-index.html* and *www.amsterdam.nl.*

Information about public transport is given by the **GVB** (Amsterdam Municipal Transport Authority), Stationsplein 15 (*open Mon–Fri 7–7, Sat and Sun 8–7*).

The AUB Uitburo (Leidseplein 26; ℂ 621 1211; *open Mon–Sat 10–6*) gives information and sells advance tickets (booking fee ƒ2) for the city's theatres and concert halls and for many other cultural events. It also distributes leaflets and listings magazines. **Entertainment info** is also at the end of a phone line: Uitlijn ℂ (0900) 0191.

The **Netherlands Board of Tourism** offices can give you details of hotels and events:

UK: 25–8 Buckingham Gate, London SW1E 6LB
            ℂ (020) 7828 7900, ℂ (0891) 717 777 (recorded information)

USA: 355 Lexington Av, 21st Floor, New York, NY 10017
            ℂ (212) 370 7360

            225 N. Michigan Av, Suite 1854, Chicago, IL 60601
            ℂ (312) 819 1500

            605 Market Street, Room 401, San Francisco, CA 94105
            ℂ (415) 543 6772

Canada: 25 Adelaide Street E., Suite 710, Toronto, Ontario, M5C 1Y2
            ℂ (416) 363 1577

Amsterdam: Essential Sights

Anne Frank Huis

Prinsengracht, 263. ✆ 556 7100

Open Sept–May Mon–Sat 9–5, Sun 10–5; June–Aug Mon–Sat 9–7, Sun 10–7; adm ƒ10, under 18s ƒ5, under 10s free.

Anne Frank, the second daughter of German-Jewish immigrants living in Amsterdam, got her diary for her thirteenth birthday on 12 June 1942. Three weeks later her family were '*onderduikers*' ('divers')—in hiding from the Nazi occupying forces. They lived for two years in a small suite of rooms at the back of Anne's father's herb and spice business on the Prinsengracht. The windows had always been painted over to protect the herbs previously stored there, the entrance was hidden behind a hinged bookcase and, apart from four trusted office workers who supplied them with food, nobody knew they were there. Later they were joined by a dentist Fritz Pfeffer (whom Anne calls 'Dussel') and the Van Pelses ('Van Daans') and their son Peter. For two years they were cooped up in what became known as the Annexe, and Anne wrote in her diaries about life with the petulant and demanding Mrs Van Daan and her hen-pecked spouse, of the tiresomely childish Dussel, and of moments of joy and desperation within her own family. No one knows who betrayed them, but in August 1944 German police barged into the offices, walked straight up to the bookcase and demanded entry. All the hideaways, except Anne's father, died in concentration camps in Germany. The office cleaner found the diary in which Anne had written with astonishing lucidity about life in the Annexe and about growing up. When it was given to her father, he found that she'd already began to edit it for publication. It appeared in 1947 with the title *The Annexe*, the one Anne herself had chosen. Now it is printed in over fifty languages and an estimated thirteen million copies have been sold to date.

Well over half a million people visit the Anne Frank Huis annually. The house has been restored to its pre-war condition, giving a moving impression of what life was like for the families who hid there. In new premises next door you'll find an exhibition on Jews in Amsterdam and racial oppression.

Canals

Amsterdam's Canals are as much a part of the city's life as its coffee houses and cafés. Visitors to the city can walk beside them, cycle down them and take a variety of water-borne means of transport along them. The top five to see are Herengracht, Keizersgracht, Prinsengracht, Brouwersgracht and Reguliersgracht. The first three stretch out in ever increasing circles, marking the strands of Amsterdam's distinctive cobweb layout (*see* p.219–23). Brouwersgracht (Brewer's Canal) is quintessential Amsterdam. Though once upon a time it reeked of fish and beer, today its neat gabled houses, humped bridges and shady towpaths feature in almost every brochure intended to lure you to the city. Yet the crowds that tramp up and down the grand canals seem to pass it by. There are no neon lights or noisy cafés. It's a quiet residential canal for the hopeless romantic. With its quiet gables and bridges, Reguliersgracht is possibly the most picturesque of them all. It was to have been filled in until public protest saved it. On a clear day one of Amsterdam's best views is to be had from the very top of the canal at Thorbeckeplein: no fewer than seven parallel bridges stretching away into the distance.

Flower Market

Flowers are everywhere in Amsterdam. The tattiest houses sprout window boxes, you'll see neat little posies on the counters of bars and fetching bouquets on bank clerks' desks. People give flowers for the flimsiest reasons. Bunches hurriedly bought from canal-side barrows pass between friends like pecks on the cheek. Everyone has favourite blooms and nose-curling aversions, and to forget your loved-ones' floral preferences is like not remembering whether they take milk in their coffee. This adoration of flowers goes right to the top and the reigning monarch has to emerge on her birthday to accept thousands of posies and shake the hands of her subjects as they file past.

This makes it all the more surprising that after all the fuss that's made about it in the travel brochures, Amsterdam's floating flower market next to Muntplein can come as a bit of a disappointment for the first-time visitor. It's not very long, not all that cheap, you can't tell from the street that it's floating, and it's full of confused tourists clutching maps and asking each other: 'Is this it?' Even so, it is always crowded and the buckets of cut flowers and rows of potted plants are pretty to look at. On hot days the mingling scents of the flowers fill the whole passage and it is a pleasant spot to sit with a coffee and watch the world pass by. If you're a keen gardener there's a tempting variety of seeds and bulbs that can be posted home (but *see* **Travel**, 'Passports, Visas and Border Formalities', p.5). Spring is a good time for a visit when you can hardly move for the tulips which come in a huge variety of colours and shades. Homely, surburban and pure—they have, alongside clogs, cheese and blue and white china, become a classic part of the nation's iconography.

Red-Light District

Known to the Amsterdammers as 'de walletjes' (the little walls), the city's red-light district stretches across the canals that mark the edge of old Amsterdam, Oudezijds Voorburgwal and Oudezijds Achterburgwal. The prostitution here is one of the major city sights and has been a part of the area's life for hundreds of years. A 1629 law closed all taverns between St Annenstraat and the Oude Kerk because of the 'great acts of insolence and wantonness' going on there. The taverns have since reopened, though little else has changed. In those days the women nailed up romanticized portraits of themselves outside the doors. Nowadays they display themselves live, barely clad and deeply bored, perched on bar stools in the windows. Catch someone's eye and immediately there's a bright smile and a sparkle which disappears the moment you look away. If business is bad, or if you walk with eyes downcast, you'll hear the windows being rapped noisily. The rooms are functional cubicles, though from time to time you'll see one decked out in lace, knick-knacks and potted plants—a quaint parody of a Dutch bourgeois sitting room. In the mornings the little alleys, some narrower than a doorway, are inhabited only by the desperate (on both sides of the glass) and the area has a feeling of secrecy and expectancy, rather like an empty theatre. Off-duty prostitutes join friends to go out shopping, or wander off in groups to the clinic for a check-up. In the afternoons it all seems too blatant and seedy, but later a wild festivity sets in as the lanes fill with the merry, the lecherous and the plain curious. Phalanxes of Japanese businessmen troop about aching to take photographs, drunken schoolboys gawp and try to pluck up courage and tight clutches of Dutch families from the provinces 'ooh' and 'aah' and snicker at all the wickedness.

Stadhouderskade 42. © 674 4700. Open daily 10–5; adm f15, under-18s f7.50.

Take tram 6, 7 or 10 to Weteringschans. (If there is a long queue at the ticket office, nip around the back to the entrance to the new South Wing, where there is usually hardly anyone waiting at all.) There is an excellent guided tour to the museum on CD-ROM, obtainable on the shop level for f7.50. Walk around at your own pace, punching in codes to learn more about individual paintings.

Like the Centraal Station on the other side of town, the Rijksmuseum (National Museum, pronounced *reyks-museum*) was designed as a grand entrance to the city. (When it was built there were only fields beyond it.) A walkway through the middle of the building has bright bathroom acoustics that attract anything from opera-singing accordionists to steel bands. Because of this tunnel, the museum's important halls are on the first floor.

The Rijksmuseum was completed in 1885 to house the national collection of paintings and sculpture. The collection has evolved from a hoard of 200 paintings confiscated from the exiled Prince William V in 1798. First they had been gathered in the Huis ten Bosch palace in The Hague, and later were brought to the Trip brothers' 17th-century mansion in Amsterdam. By the 1860s it was clear that the Trippenhuis was going to be too small for the growing collection. The quest for a new temple for the nation's art sparked off a conflagration of chauvinism, in-fighting and intrigue that would have impressed the Borgias. When the winners of an anonymous competition for a new museum design turned out to be German, the plan was rejected as 'non-Dutch'. Once a suitable Dutch architect was found in P. J. H. Cuypers (of Centraal Station fame) a new scandal emerged. The architect, project co-ordinator, government advisor and decorator were all Roman Catholics. Protestant Holland scented nepotism and popery. The building Cuypers produced was thought altogether too extravagant, too churchy and too foreign to house the treasures of Dutch culture. What made it worse was that Cuypers, having had a more sober Romanesque plan accepted, managed, while building was in progress, to slip in more fantastical bits of a previously rejected Gothic plan. Good patriotic Calvinists found this mishmash of foreign styles deplorable. One critic railed: 'For two million guilders we now have the most sorry spectacle of a building that anyone could have thought to call a museum.' In response to the gilding and plethora of sculptures, portraits and tiling depicting Dutch artists that adorns the outside walls, another critic compared the museum to 'a garishly decorated house of a rich parvenu'. Even the king pleaded a prior engagement on the day of the opening ceremony.

Gallery of Honour

If your time is really tight, this is the one place to visit. It gives a good introduction to Golden Age painting, and houses the Rembrandt for which the museum is famous. At the far end, taking up the full wall, is Rembrandt's **Night Watch**. The *Night Watch* was commissioned in 1642 by the militiamen of the Kloveniersdoelen (the Arquebusiers' Guildhall) to hang in their banqueting room alongside five other portraits of companies of the civic guard. It's officially called *The Company of Captain Frans Banning Cocq and Lieutenant Willem van Ruytenburch* and got its present title in the 19th century because ageing layers of varnish made it dim and murky. For years it's had the reputation of being the work that signalled Rembrandt's decline. This is ill-deserved—he still had some of his most important commissions ahead of him. It is true though, that the 17th-century public didn't like it very much, and when it was moved to the Town Hall in 1715 the city fathers thought nothing of lopping a bit off the left-hand side so that it would fit on the wall: two of Captain Cocq's militiamen disappeared forever.

Today, together with *The Syndics*, it is considered the prize of the Rijksmuseum's collection. It was usual to paint group portraits in fairly static compositions, giving each member equal prominence. Rembrandt, however, paints the company in a flurry of movement, as if about to set off on a march. Rich clothes and a wonderful collection of plumed and pointed hats all add to the sense of grandeur and motion (this is all pure invention—the guards' uniforms were in reality rather dull, and they never marched). A little girl in a luminous gold dress, possibly the company mascot, looks bewildered by all the activity. (The rather surreal touch of a dead chicken tied to her waist is an allusion to the militia's coat of arms.) The captain and his lieutenant, in fine clothes, dominate the scene. The rest of the company look far less important—which is possibly why the painting was initially unpopular: they had after all each paid their ƒ100, and deserved the same billing.

When the controllers of the Drapers' Guild (the 'Staalmeesters', or 'Syndics') commissioned Rembrandt to paint their portrait in 1662, they were determined not to make a similar mistake, and stipulated a more traditional composition. Rembrandt obeyed, yet still managed to create a work that brims with life. The Syndics look up from their table, and the viewer has the odd sensation of having just walked into the room and disturbed them at work. It's one of the finest group portraits ever painted—Kenneth Clark goes as far as acclaiming it 'one of the summits of European painting'—and seems to be the image picture librarians most reach for to evoke old Holland.

As you wander through the Gallery of Honour, keep an eye open for three more of Rembrandt's paintings: *The Jewish Bride* (1667), a glowing, tender portrait of a couple, no longer all that youthful, but very much in love; a rather depressed, world-weary *Self-portrait as the Apostle Paul* (1661); and *St Peter's Denial* (1660), showing a very troubled, down-to-earth apostle. Other paintings in the Gallery of Honour may change from time to time, but you can probably see Nicholas Maes's delicately detailed *Old Woman at Prayer* and work by one of Rembrandt's better-known pupils—Ferdinand Bol. Massive *penschilderijen* ('pen paintings', rather like etchings) of naval battle scenes by Willem van de Velde I are also on show.

Rooms 207–236

Rooms 207–236 are filled with paintings from the 17th century, the 'Golden Age' not only of Dutch art but of the Netherlands' political and economic might. Intense realism and the naturalistic rendering of domestic and everyday life are the hallmarks of the Golden Age. There are precise, calm interiors, minutely detailed still lifes, wild taverns and salacious brothel scenes. Homely Dutch mothers and their *onnozele schaapjes* (innocent lambs) take the place of the Madonna and Child, and you'll see businessmen and civic guards rather than generals and fantastical battle scenes. As you walk around the collection you'll see more of Rembrandt and his pupils, but there are a number of other artists particularly worth searching out.

Frans Hals' happy and rather cheeky-looking *Wedding Portrait of Isaac Abrahamsz. Massa and Beatrix van der Laen* (1622), and the florid *Merry Drinker* (1628–30), seemingly dashed off with swift brushstrokes and scratches in the wet paint, testify to his greatness as a portrait-painter. Pieter Saenredam's church interiors are so still, and he pays such close attention to architectural shapes, that they seem almost abstract. Pieter de Hooch—especially in *Woman and Child in a Pantry* (1658) and *Women beside a Linen Chest* (1663)—is a master of quiet family scenes. Light from the busy outside world streams in through a door or window in the background, while in the spotless rooms with their symmetrical black and white floor tiles all is order and calm—though the impish children seem just on the verge of disrupting it.

A somewhat sadder *schaapje* can be seen in Gabriel Metsu's touching, yet unsentimental *Sick Child*. Jan Steen gives quite another idea of family life. He used his experiences as a tavern-keeper to create scenes of such jolly domestic upheaval—as in *The Merry Family* (1670)—that the Dutch still use the expression 'a Jan Steen household' for any chaotic but cheerful home. You'll also find still lifes which, at the beginning of the century, are sober arrangements of herring, bread and cheese, but later overflow with ornate tableware, full-blown flowers and juicy fruit at its *toppunt* (literally: top-point)—the last moment of perfection before decay. Abraham van Beyeren's 1665 painting shows fat peaches, seafood, leaking melons and a toppled silver candlestick in meticulous detail. Look out also for Gerard ter Borch's exquisite fabrics—poor little Helena van der Schalke (1648) is weighed down by her fine silk dress and in *Gallant Conversation* the young woman's silver gown shimmers. (The conversation wasn't really that gallant—the man holding up his hand in gentle admonition was originally offering her a coin. A pious owner painted it out.)

Skim as fast as you like through the rest of the collection, but don't miss the **Vermeers** (Room 221a). Only thirty works by Johannes Vermeer (1632–75) exist; the Rijksmuseum has four of them. He had a passion for light and his paintings seem translucent. Light from a window reflects off a white wall, a jug, or softly glowing fabric. The tranquil *Kitchen Maid* (1658) and *Woman Reading a Letter* (1662/3) are totally without stylistic artifice, yet come close to perfection. In quiet, everyday scenes, Vermeer captures a sense of eternity.

The Golden Age

France has shown a great deal of inventive genius, but little real faculty for painting. Holland has not imagined anything, but it has painted miraculously well.

Eugène Fromentin, art critic, writing in 1875

In 1565 mobs stormed through the Netherlands breaking church windows and destroying religious art. In their enthusiasm to eliminate idolatry, these iconoclasts wiped out much of the country's heritage. The austere Calvinists who took control of the northern provinces after 1579 whitewashed the insides of churches and had no time for papish decoration. Italy and its art went out of fashion. The rising merchant classes seemed suspicious of unprofitable aristocratic foibles like patronage of the arts. Artists were in a dilemma: what *were* they to paint, and who would pay them for it? Their answer was set about painting 'the portrait of Holland, its external image, faithful, exact, complete, life-like, without any adornment'. In the Golden Age that followed, you find few flamboyant devotional paintings. Instead, you are given portraits of merchants, town squares, street scenes, glimpses of daily life, breakfast tables, brothels, taverns, the countryside, or moments in history. No other nation has managed a more intimate and beautifully executed chronicle of its life and times.

Rembrandt

Rembrandt Harmensz. van Rijn (1606–69) was the son of a Leiden miller. When the poet Constantijn Huygens visited Leiden in 1628, he went into raptures over Rembrandt's paintings. A few years later Rembrandt upped sticks for the big city where wealthy burghers, trades guilds and companies of the civic guard all spent handsome sums to be painted by the fashionable young artist. In 1634, already a rich and celebrated painter, he married heiress Saskia van Uylenburgh and five years later felt confident about paying a swinging ƒ13,000 for a house in the Jewish quarter.

Saskia died in 1642, having just changed her will to leave all to their infant son Titus, with the estate to be held by Rembrandt so long as he didn't remarry. The painter got round this condition by having an affair with Titus' nurse, Geertghe Dircx. Then, in 1649, he fell in love with a younger servant, Hendrickje Stoffels. Geertghe sued successfully for breach of contract. This came at a bad time. Rembrandt was receiving fewer commissions now and in 1656 the artist was declared bankrupt. The property that had been his home for some 20 years was sold, and he moved out to live on the Rozengracht with Hendrickje and Titus. Rembrandt was so hard up that he had to sell Saskia's tomb to pay for Hendrickje's funeral. When he died, he was buried in an unmarked grave in the Westerkerk.

Sculpture and Applied Art

The museum's collection of sculpture and applied art includes ceramics, china, glass, furniture, costumes, lace, tapestries, jewellery and silver from the Middle Ages to the 20th century, and can be utterly overwhelming. On a first visit the best idea is to give yourself a gentle overview. In the rooms leading off the entrance hall (Rooms 238–42), you'll find some of the best pieces in the collection. Ten 15th-century bronze figures, poised in graceful attitudes of mourning, have been filched from the tomb of Isabella de Bourbon in Antwerp. There's a tiny portable altar, carved in gold and encrusted with enamel, that some lucky nun used for her private devotion in the Abbey de Chocques in France in the 16th century. Look out also for Adriaen van Wesel's busy and energetic oak carving of *The Meeting of the Three Magi* (1475–7). A little further on, in Room 245, you can see Late Gothic German carvings of *Christ and the Last Supper*, still with some original polychrome and gilding.

If you have a taste for camp, head straight for Room 251a and Wenzel Jamnitzer's extraordinary *Table Ornament*, made for the city of Nuremberg in 1549. Mother Earth stands, one hip cocked, in a rockery of flowers, lizards and shrimps (all silver casts of real specimens) and supports on her head an enormous birdbath of cherubs rampant, scrolls, snakes and more flowers. All this is surmounted by yet another posy of enamelled silver foliage.

The collection of Delftware (Rooms 255–57) has some prize polychrome as well as more traditional blue and white pieces. The people of Delft started making cheaper imitations of the Chinese porcelain brought back by the Dutch East India Company in the 17th century. (Things have turned full circle. Now souvenir shops sell imitation Delftware made in Taiwan.) Among the usual plates and cups you can see a functioning Delftware violin and towering tulip pagodas with space for forty stems (which, in the 17th century, would have cost a fortune to fill).

The South Wing

The restored South Wing houses a small but carefully selected costume and textile collection (in Room 15, near the door to the walkway) and 18th- and 19th-century art, including bright, ethereal pastels by the Swiss artist Jean-Etienne Liotard (1702–89)—mostly of aristocrats and socialites. The best 19th-century work is by painters of two movements from the second half of the century. The three Maris brothers were leading artists of the Hague School (nicknamed the 'grey' school after its heavy, cloudy skies). Jacob painted beaches and townscapes, Matthijs portrayed romantic fairy-tale scenes and Willem seemed preoccupied with ducks. Anton Mauve's pearly grey *Morning Ride along a Beach* (1876) is characteristic of the movement. The Amsterdam Impressionists are well represented by George Breitner, who liked to paint Amsterdam in the rain, and Isaac Israels, whose brighter pictures are closer to the work of the French Impressionists.

Downstairs you'll find The Asiatic Art Collection. Three hundred years of Dutch trade connections have resulted in a glittering stash of treasures from the East. You can see lacquerwork, ceramics and textiles from Japan, Javanese sculptures, and religious works from China and India. A small, bronze dancing Lord Shiva (the Hindu god of creation) from the 12th century and an elegantly relaxed Chinese Buddhist saint, the Bodhisattva Avalokitesharva, from the same period, make the trip across to the South Wing worthwhile.

Stedelijk Museum

Paulus Potterstraat 13. © 573 2911. Open daily 11–5; adm ƒ9, under-17s ƒ4.50.

Trams 2, 3, 5 and 12 will drop you at the corner of Van Baerlestraat and Paulus Potterstraat, right opposite. Tram 16 will drop you near the Concertgebouw, so you'll need to walk westwards up Van Baerlestraat to the museum.

The Stedelijk Museum is a solid 19th-century red brick building with fussy plaster decorations and spiky gables. A row of rather haughty architects stares down at you from niches on the first floor. The widened entrance and glass box extension at the back were part of a drive in the 1950s to make art more accessible: the guiding principle was that a museum loses its sense of mystery when works can also be viewed from the street. A good idea—if the blinds didn't have to be drawn every afternoon against the damaging sunlight.

Don't be deceived by appearances. It's a bright, lively museum of modern art. You'll find not only conventional paintings, but all sorts of applied art (designer chairs, feather hats and gaudy teapots) as well as work by less established artists.

The Museum's Founders

The museum owes its existence to two benefactors. Sophia Augusta de Bruyn, the eccentric dowager of Jonkheer (Lord) Lopez Suasso, spent as little as she could on clothes (scandalizing Amsterdam society by wearing the same dress more than once). Instead she amassed as many jewels, trinkets, curios (and especially clocks) as she could. When she died, she left everything to the City of Amsterdam. There was so much that the council felt obliged to build a museum to display it all. At the same time the wealthy Vereeniging tot het Vormen van eene Openbare Verzameling van Heedendaagsche Kunst (Society for the Formation of a Public Collection of Contemporary Art) or VvHK, was looking for a home. The city council and the 'society with the long name' (as it was understandably nicknamed) got together and the museum opened in 1895. It wasn't until the early 1970s that the last of Sophia Augusta's bric-a-brac was dispersed to specialist museums and the Stedelijk became devoted exclusively to modern art.

Successive directors have left their imprint on the collection, but it was the imagination, energy and skill of Willem Sandberg—'part poet, part artist, part designer, part administrator, part magician'—that between 1945 and 1963 established the Stedelijk as one of the world's leading modern art museums. He built up an important collection and held a series of notable, usually controversial, exhibitions. In 1949 there were fisticuffs in the foyer at the opening of the first COBRA exhibition. (COBRA was a group of artists from **Co**penhagen, **Br**ussels and **A**msterdam whose colourful, childlike painting was the first to provoke the response that 'a three-year-old could do better'.) Though that's not happened again, daring new acquisitions still spark off public uproars.

Space is limited here, so only a small portion of the collection is shown at any one time. Outside the summer months (May–September) you may even find that much of the museum is taken over by a special exhibition, though present museum policy is to show the core of the permanent collection on a more stable, long-term basis. A plan of what is currently on view is available from the information desk (to the left of the entrance). The catalogue (a survey of the entire collection, in English) is a bargain at ƒ35.

The Permanent Collection

The permanent collection can be found up the wide marble staircase, on the top floor. In 1972 the large Van Gogh collection, which had been kept at the Stedelijk, moved next door to its own museum (see below). Because Van Gogh is considered so important to modern art, a few paintings were left behind. La Berceuse (The Cradle) was inspired by a story Gauguin told Van Gogh about fishermen who pinned prints of their patron saint—Stella Maris (Maria, Star of the Sea)—to the cabin wall. Van Gogh felt that a portrait of Madame Roulin (a postman's wife), holding a cord for a rocking cradle, would be ideal for such a print. He imagined the seamen 'would feel the old sense of being rocked come over them and remember their own lullabies'. It's a pity that the painting isn't hung the way Van Gogh suggested—as a triptych with sunflower paintings on either side. Don't miss the paintings by George Breitner, Van Gogh's contemporary and drinking partner. In De Dam, a view of Dam square, he captures that special Amsterdam light in a way that makes the exact time of year, even the time of day, immediately recognizable. Keep an eye open also for his highly patterned, exotic Woman in a Red Kimono (in reality a hat shop assistant).

The museum has a good collection of modern art classics. You'll probably find Manet's picture of a barmaid, a study for his famous Bar at the Folies-Bergère. There are some gentle Cézanne landscapes and a range of Picassos—from bright early collages to nudes from his Blue Period. One wall is sure to be filled by Matisse's vast paper cut-out The Parakeet and the Mermaid, done towards the end of his life when his eyesight was too poor for painting, and painstakingly restored in 1996. You'll find at least one of Kandinsky's vivid Improvisations—paintings where he used colour to represent the sounds of various musical instruments—and some Chagalls. The 1960s are well represented by Warhol screen-prints, Roy Lichtenstein's comic strip blow-ups and Bruce Nauman's neon light installations, and the museum comes right up to date with works by some of the best living European and American arists.

The high point is the museum's collection of the Russian artist, Kazimir Malevich and the Dutch movement, *De Stijl*. Side by side, these two collections show how abstract art began and we see the gradual disappearance of any reference to outside reality. The visionary director of the museum, Willem Sandberg, was responsible for tracking down the Malevich collection, unearthing a treasury of works that had been forgotten in a cellar in Germany. Malevich had left the entire contents of an exhibition for safekeeping with a friend in Beieren, but was subsequently never allowed to leave Russia. He died in 1935, so there the cache remained (under a pile of rubble after the war) until Sandberg swooped down and bought it in the late 1950s. The museum has a complete range of his work, from early Impressionist pieces, through a Cubist period to the completely abstract—solid shapes of colour on a white background. Malevich composes these shapes at such angles that the paintings seem full of movement.

De Stijl

At around the same time (1917) *De Stijl* artists were coming up with very similar work. The best known is that of Piet Mondriaan (he dropped the last 'a' to appear French, but the Dutch prefer the original). His *Compositions* of vertical and horizontal black lines with blocks of primary colours, so shocking at the time, now appear on everything. When Theo van Doesburg (co-founder of *De Stijl*) after ten years of rectilinear painting produced a *Contra-composition*, in which he daringly tilted his lines through 45°, Piet left the movement in a huff. They were never reconciled, though Mondriaan later took up the challenge by tilting his *canvas* through 45° and keeping the lines vertical.

Halfway down the staircase you can find the **Print Room**. Here you could find anything from a Toulouse-Lautrec poster to Mapplethorpe's startling close-up photographs of male nudes. Keep an eye open for the innovative work of Dutch photographer Cas Oorthuys, and Roland Topor's blackly comic cartoons. Work not on display can be viewed by appointment in the study room.

Most of the ground floor is given over to **travelling exhibitions** and **applied art**. The small door to the left of the ticket office leads to rooms of odd-shaped furniture, gaudy ceramics and lumpy mats. There's a video art room under the stairs, and the glass box extension at the back of the building occasionally displays work (often dire) by an assortment of contemporary Amsterdam artists. Two installations on the ground floor shouldn't be missed. The *Appelbar* (through a door to the right of the information desk), adorned with murals of colourful birds, fish and children, is the work of the COBRA artist Karel Appel. It was used as a café until the opening of the present restaurant in 1956. The commission was offered to Appel as a palliative after a debacle at the Town Hall in 1951: a mural in the canteen, commissioned by the Building Department, had to be boarded over when the Catering Department insisted that it would put people off their food.

Edward Kienholz's *Beanery* is a near life-sized version of a poky Los Angeles bar. You can wander about in the dim light, examining the bric-a-brac. Rusty music scratches away in the jukebox. There's a murmur of conversation. A couple sit at the bar. Someone has passed out in the corner. A waitress clears the remnants of a disgusting meal. But all the faces of the figures are clock-faces, and as you're the only thing that moves it is a surreal and rather disorientating experience. Luckily, the real bar (bright and airy) is just across the corridor. (Unlike the *Appelbar*, the *Beanery* is not a permanent installation, so sometimes disappears on tour.)

Paulus Potterstraat 7, © 570 5200. Open daily 10–6; adm f12.50, under-18s f5.

If you've arrived on Tram 2, 3, 5 or 12, walk down Paulus Potterstraat—the Van Gogh Museum is halfway down, on the right. If you've taken Tram 6, 7 or 10, then you'll need to cross the Singelgracht and Stadhouderskade and walk through the walkway under the Rijksmuseum. This brings you to Museumplein. A walk up the right-hand side of Museumplein will bring you to the museum.

The Rijksmuseum Vincent Van Gogh has really cornered the Van Gogh market with 200 paintings, 500 drawings, a collection of works by Van Gogh's contemporaries, the letters from Vincent to his brother Theo, Vincent's collections of Japanese woodcuts and 19th-century engravings, a press archive dating from 1899—and publishing copyright for the lot. The museum was completed in 1973 and is based on an initial drawing by the influential Dutch architect, Gerrit Rietveld, who died before working the plan through. Brave efforts by later architects to realize his rather sketchy ideas produced a hard-edged and unsympathetic building. But in 1999, a new wing by renowned Japanese architect Kisho Kurokawa gave the museum the sort of proud architectural profile it deserves.

Works from the permanent collection are displayed in the old part of the museum, the Kurokawa wing is used for temporary exhibitions and houses the darkened **Print Room**, where you can find Van Gogh's drawings and studies, and trace some of his influences—sketches by friends, pictures he copied and his collection of Japanese prints and magazine engravings. The selection on display changes frequently, but you can usually follow his development through some rather conventional Dutch landscapes, with all the expected perspectives, and studies of gnarled hands and heavily jowled peasant faces to the wild movement of *Women Dancing* (1885). Millet's *Labours of the Field* and woodcuts by Hiroshige and Kesai Yeisen clearly had an influence on some of Van Gogh's better known oils. The museum has an exceptionally good library, where you can view photographs of Vincent's letters to Theo. Training courses, and all sorts of activities to help working artists, are held regularly. (*Details from the museum.*)

Van Gogh's Early Life

Vincent van Gogh was born in 1853 in the tiny village of Zundert, near the Belgian border. We have an image of him as a wild, schizophrenic bohemian; a simpleton, out of touch with the world and reliant on his younger brother's handouts. This isn't the full truth. He came from an old Dutch family of clerics, naval officers and gallery owners. Though he was constantly at odds with his relations, and offended almost everyone he met, he was in many ways part of the Establishment. He spoke three languages fluently, had a wide knowledge of European art and had the connections needed to organize two exhibitions of friends' work in Paris. He signed himself 'Vincent' because he thought his surname, difficult for foreigners to pronouce, would be bad salesmanship. (You say it with two guttural 'gs'—'fun HGoHG'). Yet all his life he was desperately lonely, dogged by a sense of failure and frustrated by how few people appreciated his art. Towards the end he was beset by bouts of madness, which left him exhausted and depressed. He was acutely sensitive to his surroundings. The colours, people, light or weather in one environment would become loathsome to him and the need to move would become consuming. Suddenly he'd up sticks and go—to the sun, to the city, to the country. These moves were often reflected in a change in his work.

Vincent's first job, at the age of 16, was as an assistant with the art dealer Goupil & Cie in The Hague. In 1873 he went to work at the London branch and was impressed by Constable, Turner and especially the Pre-Raphaelite John Everett Millais. An unhappy love affair made him grumpy at work. He began to be rude to customers about their taste, was shuttled between London and Paris and, finally, dismissed. Still obsessed by his English rose, he returned to Britain as a teacher, but was soundly rebuffed. He went back to Holland to work in a bookshop, but still didn't know what he wanted to do with his life.

But in May 1877 it all suddenly seemed clear: following in his father's footsteps, he set off for Amsterdam to study theology. Greek, Latin and algebra proved an uphill struggle, and after less than a year he went to a crammer for evangelists in Brussels. But he couldn't preach either. Yet again the family pulled strings. The Brussels Evangelist Committee sent him to work among the coalminers of the Borinage in south Belgium, but he was soon dismissed for over-zealous involvement with the poor.

He stayed on in a hovel for another year, almost starving to death, and began to draw. He was 26 and had found his direction. His younger brother, Theo, rescued him and started to pay him the monthly allowance that was to be Vincent's only income for the rest of his life.

Life as a Painter

Van Gogh was largely self-taught, though he spent a brief period studying perspective and anatomy in Brussels in 1880. The following year he fell in love with his widowed cousin, Kee Vos. He stormed into her father's house on the Keizersgracht and held his hand over a candle yelling, 'Let me see her for as long as I can hold my hand in the flame.' But Kee had fled. He was thrown out of home and went to The Hague, where he met members of the Hague School of painting, a movement characterized by muddy colours and gloomy skies. He was given lessons by one of its leading members, Anton Mauve (a cousin by marriage), and was also much influenced by Jozef Israëls' earthy studies of peasants. He was especially friendly with George Breitner, who later became known as one of the best Amsterdam Impressionists. They discovered a mutual interest in Zola and together drew the street life in the seedier parts of town. An uncle who had commissioned twelve views of the city was horrified by Vincent's unconventional approach and refused to pay up. The relationship with Mauve grew tense when Van Gogh began to reject the older painter's advice, and family relations soured on a wider scale when it became known that he was living with the prostitute Sien Hoornik 'in order to reform her'.

In September 1883 Van Gogh suddenly left The Hague for the countryside of Drenthe in the north of Holland. He had begun to paint in oils, but still with a muddy Dutch palette. The good people of Drenthe thought him a dangerous lunatic and a tramp, and refused to pose for him—so this became a period of landscapes with small figures in the distance. After a few months, loneliness drove him to a reconciliation with his parents and he went back south to live with them in Nuenen. Weavers and peasants in the surrounding Brabant farmland were his dominant motif. The period culminated in the dim glow and gravy browns of *The Potato Eaters* (1885). Van Gogh loved this 'real peasant picture'—he felt you could smell the bacon, smoke and potato steam.

In *The Old Church Tower at Nuenen*, the tower stands crooked and solitary in a flat, empty churchyard, crows flutter against the overcast sky. Van Gogh painted it in May 1885, a few months after his father, an unpopular preacher in a declining sect had been buried there, and just before it was demolished and all the wood—including the graveyard crosses—sold to peasants. *Open Bible, Extinguished Candle and Book* (1885) has been seen as Vincent's homage to their difficult relationship.

Margot Begemann, a neighbour, took poison after her family had refused permission for her to marry Vincent. She survived, but Vincent got the blame and the village turned against him. He went to Antwerp, studied Rubens, covered his walls with Japanese prints and enrolled in the academy—which he left a few months later without ever learning of the academy's decision to demote him to the beginners' class. He then went to Paris, and moved in with his brother, Theo. The first few canvases in Paris (such as *View over Paris*, 1886) still use the Dutch browns and greys. But when Theo introduced him to a few Impressionist friends, the shock of their fresh, bright canvases changed Vincent for life. At first the colour creeps in gradually (*Woman Sitting in the Café du Tambourin*, 1887) but soon he is copying the flat colours of the Japanese prints and painting some of the familiar bright self-portraits. He began to long for harder light and a less hectic milieu than Paris could offer. Writing to his sister Wil about *Self-portrait at the Easel* (1888), he draws her attention to his sad expression. He's had enough of Paris and wants the sun.

Van Gogh and Gauguin

On 20 February 1888 Vincent escaped to the Mediterranean warmth of Arles in the south of France. Here in the famous 'Yellow House', which he shared for a while with Gauguin, his best known works were painted. It is hard to believe that the raucous yellows and bright reds and blues of *Harvest at La Crau* were painted only three years after *The Potato Eaters*. Look closely at one of the versions of *Sunflowers*. Between the greens and yellows are bright streaks of ice blues, mauves and reds—colours you never notice in the reproductions. Portraits of the postman, Roulin, and his wife are drenched in sun and colour. Even the *Night Café* has a bright, steamy heat. The solitary *Sower at Arles* works under an enormous yellow orb in a green and pink sky. The most ordinary things around him evoke intense response. Vincent's *Bedroom at Arles* is filled with a brilliant light but the smooth paintwork, the mauves and blues of the walls have a calming effect.

Van Gogh was very excited by Gauguin's arrival on 20 October 1888 and went to great pains to furnish his room comfortably. The money to do this, of course, came from Theo. *Gauguin's Chair* shows a piece Vincent bought for his friend (elaborate in comparison with his own). On the seat are novels intended to indicate Gauguin's spirituality and modernism. A candle burns as well as the gas light, to suggest Gauguin's fiery nature. Together they visited nearby towns such as Les Saintes-Maries-de-la-Mer, where Vincent painted *Boats on the Beach*. The small red, green and blue boats had reminded him of flowers.

Gauguin's stay was not a happy one. The two artists had tempestuous arguments. After a particularly violent dispute on Christmas Eve, Vincent threatened Gauguin with a razor, then slashed off his own right ear and presented it to a prostitute who had complimented it. Gauguin left for Paris. Another nervous crisis followed Van Gogh's recuperation, and he was voluntarily admitted to the asylum of St-Paul-de-Mausole at Saint-Rémy. Paintings from this period—usually of fields around the asylum, the hospital garden or of individual trees and flowers—are in softer hues. In February 1890 Vincent painted *Branches of an Almond Tree in Blossom* for Theo's newly born son—blossom-laden branches stand out against an eggshell-blue background.

The Final Days

By May he felt well enough to leave the asylum, though he could only bear Paris for three days. He travelled to Auvers-sur-Oise where an eccentric art-lover, Dr Gachet, promised to keep an eye on him. But Vincent became more and more overwrought: his colours became harder, brush strokes more violent. In *Crows in the Wheatfields* (July 1890) it seems difficult for the birds to fly into the thick, dark sky. A path curves and goes nowhere. One of his last paintings, *Roots and Tree Trunks*, has even more disorientating perspectives and thick layers of paint in unexpected colours. The painter seems completely self-engrossed, and the viewer is quite alienated.

On 27 July Vincent went into the fields and shot himself, but he bungled even this. He staggered back to the inn where he was staying and died on 29 July, in Theo's arms. After a short illness, Theo himself died six months later, at the age of 32. The brothers are buried side by side in the churchyard at Auvers-sur-Oise.

Dedication, or desperation, drove Theo's widow—Johanna van Gogh-Bonger—to promote the works stacked all over her apartment. The art world began to take notice. In 1891 there was an exhibition in Brussels, followed by numerous others all over the Netherlands and in Paris. After Johanna's death in 1925 her son, Vincent's namesake, took over the collection and in 1931 put it on permanent exhibition in the Stedelijk Museum. To prevent the break-up of the collection after his death, the Van Gogh Foundation was formed in 1960 and set about building the present museum. With three members of the Van Gogh family on the board of the foundation, there's a feeling that it's still very much a family concern—and Vincent, once the black sheep, is again part of the Establishment.

Amsterdam: *Kwartiers*

The original settlement of Amsterdam grew up in the early 13th century along Kerkstraat (Church Street, later renamed Warmoesstraat) on the left (east) side of the river. Warmoesstraat, which runs parallel to Damrak, is the oldest street in the city. Towards the end of the next century the village expanded along Windmolenstraat (Windmill Street) on the right (west) bank. The Church Side and the Windmill Side soon became known as Oude Zijd (Old Side) and Nieuwe Zijd (New Side) and the corresponding sides of Damrak are still called that today. The Old Side still has its canals, the Oudezijds Voorburgwal and Oudezijds Achterburgwal and remains the city's heart, spilling over with energy, life, shops, cafés, markets and museums, as well as the brazen strip of porn shops, video booths and peep shows which make up the city's infamous red-light district (*see* p.195).

Lunch and Cafés

Het Karbeel, Warmoesstraat 58. An up-market café on the edge of the red-light district. It started life in 1534 as an inn and is still connected to the Damrak by a secret smugglers' passage. Good sandwiches, snacks and fondues.

Lunchlokaal, Pijlsteeg 35. Tucked behind the Hotel Krasnapolsky, and reached through a narrow alley, is a quiet courtyard garden. Chairs are set out between the trees and you can enjoy sandwiches and home-made soup (*around ƒ6*) in calm obliviousness of the seething Dam.

Ricky's Koffiehuis, Oudezijds Voorburgwal 206, in the red-light district. Starts early as a workers' café and changes clientele as the day progresses. Accordions hang from the walls, sugar is served from zinc buckets and there's a large, cheery communal table in a nook at the back.

Crea Café, Grimburgwal, at the end of Oudezijds Voorburgwal. Spacious student café with tatty pool tables, earnest groups arguing in corners and tired-eyed academics.

Upstairs Pannekoekhuis, Grimburgwal 2 (*open Tues–Sun 11–7*). Home-made pancakes up an almost vertical stairway, in a tiny room overhanging the street, with space for about ten customers. The owner's collection of teapots outnumbers clients 10:1. Pancakes around ƒ10.

Kaptein Zeppos, Gebed Zonder End 5 (*open Mon–Fri 11–1am, Sat and Sun 4pm–2pm*). The street-name means 'prayer without end'—the narrow alley used to wind through ten different cloisters and was always crammed with muttering clerics. The restaurant serves simple, well-prepared food in an airy, relaxed environment. On some afternoons you'll find a gipsy violinist or jazz band.

Hotel Krasnapolsky Winter Garden, Dam 9. Careful redecoration in the early 1990s gave the Krasnapolsky back some of the old elegance that an insensitive 1970s job had destroyed. In the Winter Garden you can sit surrounded by palms and enjoy a genteel lunch. Breakfast (*6.30–10.30*) ƒ30, buffet lunch (*12–2*) ƒ42.50.

Oude Kerk

Open summer Mon–Sat 11–5, Sun 1–5; entrance ƒ5.

Only the tower of the Oude Kerk actually dates from 1300. The original basilica disappeared behind an increasingly haphazard outgrowth of side chapels, transepts and clerestories. Most of what you see today is lofty early 16th-century Renaissance, but even that has a crust of warden's offices, choir rooms and houses, built over a period of three centuries. The interior has survived frequent bouts of heavy-handed restoration, an engulfing coat of Prussian blue paint in the 18th century and violent attacks by iconoclasts. In August 1566, roused by the sight of fragments of statuary from smashed-up churches in Antwerp, Protestant mobs stormed the church, breaking windows and destroying all graven images. A local girl, Lange Weyn, threw her shoe at a picture of the Virgin Mary in the excitement, and was later drowned in a barrel on the Dam for the outrage.

After what is discreetly called the 'Alteration' of 1578, when the Protestants finally took control of the city, the new Calvinist city fathers stripped the church of its dedication to St Nicholas (patron saint of sailors and so, aptly, of Amsterdam) and the popular title of Oude Kerk became official. They also set about turning it into a more sombre place of worship.

It had become a hearty communal gathering place. Dossers and travellers slept in the corners, pedlars set up stalls in the aisles, merchants clinched deals on the square outside and dog-owners crowded the entrance. (Only certain classes of Amsterdam society were allowed big dogs, and if your mutt couldn't squeeze through the special iron hoop at the church door, its days were numbered.) These days the church plays host to travelling exhibitions and the occasional concert.

Inside you can see the tomb of Rembrandt's wife, Saskia van Uylenburgh (near the Weitkoperskapel on the north side); some beautifully restored and remade stained glass (especially the windows depicting the Annunciation in the Mariakapel); and the secret door (once covered by plaster, 5m above the ground in St Sebastiaan- skapel) to the IJzeren Kapel (Iron Chapel), a hiding place for important city documents until 1892.

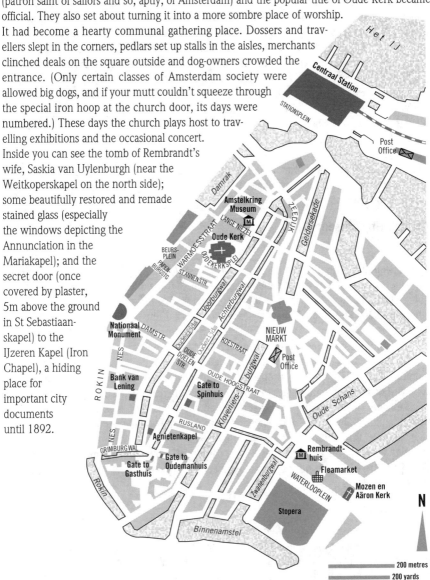

Warmoesstraat

Warmoesstraat is Amsterdam's oldest street. Originally a cluster of wattle and daub cottages, it was by the 16th century a row of prosperous merchants' houses and powerful banks. The Duke of Alva lived here in 1574 during his reign of terror (the rest of the street was understandably empty at the time) and left without paying his rent. Vondel (the 'Dutch Shakespeare') had a small hosiery business at the Dam end before he became a famous poet (*see* p.226); and Sir Thomas Nugent, a seasoned 17th-century traveller, recommended it as the only street where you'd find English inns and so avoid being cheated by wily Dutchmen. In 1766 Mozart senior held court in the tavern of De Goude Leeuw and sold tickets for his son's recitals at *f*2 apiece; and a century later Karl Marx pondered and scribbled away in the inn next door. These days Warmoesstraat is the first layer of the red-light district, and a strange mixture of past respectability and the seediness that lies beyond. You arrive directly opposite the Condomerie (condom as consumer item—everything you could imagine). Next door is W139, an enormous gallery, set up by squatters, where you're sure to catch the very latest (though not always the best) of what's going on in Amsterdam art. Further up, past a string of leather fetish bars, you'll find Amsterdam's best tea and coffee specialists (Geels & Co at No.67). Just around the corner a butcher's shop lays out its trays of chops and drumsticks right next door to a display of enormous dildos and little plain-covered books with titles like 'Pent-up Pleasure' and 'Mom's Donkey Urge'. It's a grubby, dishevelled street, but no one seems to take it seriously enough for it to be sordid.

Amstelkring Museum

Open Mon–Sat 10–5, Sun 1–5; adm f7.50.

The Amstelkring Museum, also known as *Ons Lieve Heer op Solder* (Our Lord in the Attic), was once a '*schuilkerk*'—or clandestine church. During the 17th and 18th centuries Roman Catholic services were illegal, but ever-tolerant Amsterdam turned a blind eye to what was going on behind domestic façades. The attic of the little spout-gabled house joins up with two others in the houses behind and was consecrated as a church in 1663. Inside the museum you can wander about an 18th-century reception room, into a classic 17th-century Dutch '*sael*' (living-room) with symmetrical black and white marble flooring and a monumentally grand walnut fireplace, up through bedrooms with quaint box-shaped cupboard beds, higher and higher to a small wooden staircase. Turn the corner at the top of the stairs and suddenly you're in what seems an enormous church with two galleries, light streaming in, an abundance of carving and painting and a voluptuous organ that *must* have been audible throughout the neighbourhood. The church is filled with treasures and mementoes of oppressed Catholicism (you can get an explanatory pamphlet downstairs). Try to get there early in the day, when you can appreciate the dream-like atmosphere in relative solitude.

Nieuwmarkt

Nieuwmarkt is an open, brick-paved square that connects some of the more sinister alleys of the red-light district. Furtive men pop out of side streets, blink uncertainly in the bright light, then slip quietly away. The police have cleared out the junkies and dealers who used to hang about the square, and it's been given a facelift. Now that the underworld is banished,

Nieuwmarkt has moved into limbo. Cafés are opening in the area, and the once barren square is beginning to fill up with terraces and regain some of its old liveliness, but it retains an edge of seediness. On Sundays in the summer months there's a bustling antiques market and on feast days you can sometimes find a fairground or one of the old Dutch travelling dance halls.

Bank van Lening

Halfway down the Oudezijds Voorburgwal the sleaze shops suddenly come to an end and you find yourself in a leafy nook of old Amsterdam. At No.300 is the Municipal Pawn Broker—the Bank van Lening, euphemized as '*Ome Jan*' (Uncle John's). For the past three hundred years it has been a more sympathetic alternative to professional moneylenders—interest is fixed at a rate that corresponds to your ability to pay. The poet Vondel, bankrupted by his playboy son, spent his septuagenarian years here as a clerk, going to work each day through a gateway that had one of his own poems inscribed in the arch. (It's still there, advising the rich to hurry past, as they have no business inside.)

Gasthuis, Oudemanhuis and Spinhuis

A little way along from the Bank van Lening can be found three former almhouses. Most of the buildings in this area are now part of the University of Amsterdam but once upon a time they were (in the words of a 17th-century visitor) a collection of 'almshouses which look like princes' houses, hospitals for fools and houses where beggars, frequenters of taphouses, women who feign great bellies and men who pretend they have been taken by Turks' were confined and set to hard work.

These institutions, clustered round the **Huis op de Drie Grachten** (House of the Three Canals—the only one in the city with this qualification), are a product of prosperous and Calvinistic Amsterdam, and were considered far-sighted and revolutionary by the rest of Europe. The gateway on the corner, copied from a Michelangelo design, led to the **Gasthuis** (hospital). A little further down you come to another elaborate arch, the entrance to the **Oudemanhuis**, an old men's almshouse. These days glass doors slide back as you approach and you find yourself in a dim arcade of second-hand bookstalls with medieval-looking proprietors. A shaft of light halfway along comes from a door that leads to the elegant almshouse courtyard. It's a private court belonging to the university, but nobody will stop you if you want to have a look. Further on down Oudezijds Achterburgwal you can turn right into Spinhuissteeg. On the left is the entrance to the **Spinhuis**.

The Spinhuis was a place where 'incorrigible and lewd women' were made to spin cloth for the poor. A rather alarming relief above the door shows the poor women being whipped with a cat-o'-nine-tails. Underneath is the not entirely convincing inscription:

> *Schrik niet, ik wreek geen quaat maar dwing tot goet.*
> *Straf is mijn hand, maar Lieflijk mijn gemoed.*

> Cry not for I exact no vengeance for wrong, but force you to be good.
> My hand is stern but my heart is kind.

The altruism of successive custodians seems to have been directed more towards passing gentlemen. For a small fee they were given access to the wicked inmates.

Rembrandthuis

Open Mon–Sat 10–5, Sun and hols 1–5; adm f7.50.

Rembrandt lived at Jodenbreestraat 4–6 for nearly twenty years (*see* p.199) and his old house is now a museum. It has been carefully restored to its original state, using old plans and descriptions to ensure authenticity. In the adjoining modern wing, you can see the pick of Rembrandt's etchings, including a series of tiny self-portraits of the painter pulling funny faces. Rembrandt used himself as a model more than any other 17th-century painter. He even slips into crowd scenes on some of his larger canvases. There's a slide-show on Rembrandt's life, in English, in the basement (hourly on the hour until 3pm).

Waterlooplein Fleamarket

Open Mon–Sat approx. 10–4.

There's a wonderful lack of logic in its layout and a pervasive air of bargain-hunting and money-making. Antiquarian booksellers rub shoulders with purveyors of used porn. Lines of Peruvians, Balinese and Indonesians sell bright national clothing and jewellery. There are heaps of mildewy second-hand overcoats and racks of precision-selected designer classics, tables of used kitchenware and haphazard conglomerations of expensive antiques. The rows of oddities and exotica are punctuated by more down-to-earth stalls selling bicycle parts, underwear or cleaning equipment. A fringe of derelicts gathers around the edge of the market, returning day after day with little spreads of unwanted (and sometimes unidentifiable) bric-a-brac. In one corner a muttering clump of old men surreptitiously flash watches and bits of gold to each other. A relentless stream of collectors, tourists, Amsterdammers looking for bargains and the openly curious flows up and down between the stalls.

The near end of the market is dominated by the **Mozes en Aäron Kerk**. In 1649 it was a clandestine Roman Catholic church, named after the gable stones (one depicting Moses and the other Aaron) on the two house-fronts that hid it. The present heavy-looking neoclassical church (with wooden towers painted to look like sandstone) was built in the 19th century, but you can still see the original gable stones round the back. The church was famous for its choir and even the local Jews would come in for the music on Christmas night. The Jewish philosopher Spinoza lived in the house next door to the original church. The Sephardic community excommunicated him for his secular beliefs, but regretted their haste when he went on to become one of the most lauded intellectuals of his time.

Stopera

Despite Amsterdam's strong Calvanistic past, Opera has been a popular passion for Amsterdammers since the 17th century. Yet it was not until after the Second World War that there were murmurings in the corridors of power about the need for a national opera house. Plans for a building on the Museumplein, and for one further to the south on Allbéplein (where a Hilton hotel was later built), were abandoned when someone suggested Frederiksplein. This large site, closer to the city centre than the other two, had been derelict since Amsterdam's Crystal Palace—the glittering *Paleis voor Volksvlijt* or Palace of Industry, built to house international exhibitions—had burned down in 1929.

At just the same time, the council committee responsible for the building of a new city hall was also attracted to the idea of Frederiksplein. There followed a sort of architectural musical chairs, during which opera house and city hall pursued each other about Amsterdam, claiming for themselves in turn the few choice sites and preventing each other's plans from materializing.

By 1969 the council had decided to build the new city hall on Waterlooplein. An Austrian architect, Wilhelm Holzbauer, won the competition to design the new *Stadhuis*, but in 1972 the provincial authority vetoed the funding because his building was going to be too expensive to run. One afternoon in 1979, with the authorities still locked in negotiation, Holzbauer was standing on the Blue Bridge, looking glumly over Waterlooplein, when he had the brilliant idea of *combining* the *Stadhuis* and opera house into one complex. This seemed to solve everyone's problems. Within weeks the Prime Minister had approved a 230 million guilder budget and a combined plan by Holzbauer and local architect Cees Dam had been passed. But the idea caused a furore among the burghers of Amsterdam.

Many of the objections seemed to follow the old Calvinist pattern. Opera was unnecessary. Amsterdam didn't need an opera house, especially not in the centre of town. Those who really felt the urge could indulge themselves in theatres on the outskirts. But it was the choice of the site that caused the greatest ill feeling. Waterlooplein had been the heart of Amsterdam's large Jewish neighbourhood, and had been a sad and derelict scar since the Nazis had all but obliterated the Jewish population. Many people thought an opera house to be an inappropriate building to occupy a location with such poignant associations. The few people still living on Waterlooplein after the war had already been evicted in the 1960s to make way for the proposed *Stadhuis*; they had then looked on as their empty homes were occupied by squatters while the council dithered over the cost of the proposals. When plans for the combined *Stadhuis* and *Muziektheater* were mooted, the by then long-established squatter communities had no intention of giving up their homes to what they saw as a temple of élitist entertainment. The complex was nicknamed the Stopera (from *St*adhuis and *opera*) and a vociferous 'Stop the Stopera' campaign erupted. Police attempts to evict squatters met with the strongest public resistance the city had seen since the street fighting of the 1960s and 1970s. Opposition raged, with little success, right up until the day the *Muziektheater* opened in 1986. (At the opening ceremony Queen Beatrix and Prince Claus had to be smuggled in through the stage door to avoid the angry throngs around the main entrance.)

Today the dust has settled, and though few people like the austere, bland *Stadhuis*, most Amsterdammers will grudgingly admit to the beauty of the *Muziektheater*. Its glass walls, sweeping stairways, soft pink colour scheme and marble coliseum-like shell look their best in the early evening. As the light fades, the whole building seems to glow. The artists themselves are delighted with the state-of-the-art equipment and huge dressing rooms. But acoustics experts from around the world haven't been able to solve the (severe) problems in the auditorium and there have been some massive and incredible architectural blunders backstage—the ballet rehearsal rooms have ceilings so low that dancers can't practise lifts, the orchestra doesn't have a rehearsal room at all and the scenery lifts are at the opposite end of the building from the loading entrances. Both the Netherlands Ballet and Opera are resident, and the programme is varied, with many international visitors.

Also see: the **Red-Light District**, p.195.

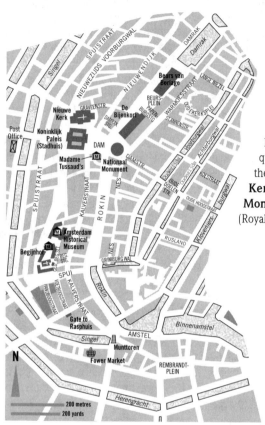

To the right of Damrak is the New Side of the old centre. The New Side is only slightly newer than the Old Side but nevertheless has its own distinct character with quiet, leafy squares and some of Amsterdam's grander hotels. At its heart is **Dam Square** which isn't quiet at all but is home to three of the city's main attractions: the **Niewe Kerk** (New Church), the **National Monument** and the **Koninklijk Paleis** (Royal Palace).

Lunch and Cafés

't Nieuwe Café Restaurant, Eggertstraat 8, next door to the Nieuwe Kerk. A noisy terrace, but quiet interior. Set breakfasts, snacks and fuller meals.

De Drie Fleschjes, Gravenstraat 18. *Proeflokaal* behind the Nieuwe Kerk that dates from 1650.

Café Esprit, Spui 10 (*closed Sun*). Trendy aluminium-box café on the Spui.

Lasalle, Spui 15. At the sharp end of Amsterdam dining chic, and good for lunches too. Waiters with epaulettes, like stewards on a 1930s liner.

Café Luxembourg, Spui 22–4. Grand café that becomes crammed with young professionals on the way home from work.

Café Hoppe, Spui 18–20. Dates from 1670, also popular with local office workers. On summer evenings there's standing room only on the terrace, and it looks a bit like a cocktail party.

Beurs van Berlage

Open Tues–Sun 10–4; basic adm f6, includes visit to tower.

Halfway up Damrak, on the left-hand side is the Beurs van Berlage museum. The first Beurs (Exchange) was built by the prolific 17th-century architect Hendrick de Keyser in 1608. The city council thought it necessary to confine all the outdoor wheeling and dealing that took place along Damrak and around the Oude Kerk to one (warmer and drier) venue. The result was deafening. As international trade expanded, Turks, Indians and Hungarians joined the locals packed around the pillars and arcades of the small hall on the Rokin, bargaining madly for silks, shares, tobacco and tulips—or anything the boats brought in. De Keyser's Beurs held out for two hundred years. The building that replaced it (on the site of the present Bijenkorf department store) was universally unpopular and in 1874 the city held a competition for a new design. When it was revealed that the winner had cribbed the façade from a French town hall, H. P. Berlage (who had come third) smartened up his original plans and landed the prize. Many revisions later (he was still at the drawing board while the builders were at work), he came up with a building that has become an Amsterdam landmark and earned him the reputation of being the father of modern Dutch architecture.

The Beurs van Berlage (completed in 1903) is all clean lines and functional shapes. Berlage allows himself some gently patterned brickwork, but there's not one extraneous twirly bit nor a glimmer of 19th-century gothic fantasy. The pillars and arcades inside are an echo of the original Beurs. The clock tower (also a quote from De Keyser's building) displays the mottoes '*Duur uw uur*' and '*Beidt uw tijd*' ('Last your hour' and 'Bide your time'), apt maxims given the seven years Berlage took to come up with a final design. These days part of the Beurs is used for concerts, while the rest is a museum (comprising a modest display on the history and design of the building) and exhibition hall. A visit to the museum gives you access to the clock tower and a view over the oldest part of town. In the smaller of two concert halls you sit and listen to the music in an enormous glass box which has solved the problem of abysmal acoustics without defacing the original interior. You can get a glimpse inside without buying a concert or a museum ticket by popping into the café at the south end.

Nieuwe Kerk

Open daily 11–5.

The construction of the Nieuwe Kerk (New Church) actually began nearly 600 years ago. It's a soaring Gothic heap without a steeple. (In the 17th century, Oude Kerk parishioners, who had always been jealous of the flash rival church, were delighted when the city council stopped construction of the tower because it was going to be higher than the town hall.) Until 1890 all the city's clocks were set weekly by the church's sundial. Like most of Amsterdam's large churches, the Nieuwe Kerk is now used mainly for exhibitions and concerts. Even if you can't catch a recital on the sumptuous Great Organ, the instrument itself, fluttering with angels and cherubs and surrounded by soft-painted shutters, is worth a visit. Admiral de Ruyter, the Dutch naval hero, is buried in the choir. (His invasion of the River Medway in England caused Sir William Batten, Surveyor of the British Navy, to explode to Samuel Pepys: 'I think the devil shits Dutchmen.') There's a memorial to the poet Vondel near the west door. Before you leave, have a look also at the richly carved pulpit and ornate copper choir screen.

Koninklijk Paleis

Opening times vary, in summer generally daily 11–5.30, sometimes closed for state functions; information on ✆ 620 4060.

The Koninklijk Paleis (Royal Palace) was the Stadhuis (City Hall) until Louis Bonaparte decided he wanted to live there in 1808. It's been a royal palace ever since, though Queen Beatrix prefers the leafier groves of Huis ten Bosch in The Hague and never spends the night here. The area in front of the Stadhuis was a favourite spot for theatrical public executions. On the right, above the entrance arches, you can still see the blocks where the scaffold slotted into the wall. The ornate street lamps along the front were commissioned by King Willem Frederik in 1840. They were the city's first gas lamps, but were so expensive to run that the council secretly turned them off whenever the king was out of town.

When the Stadhuis was built in the mid-17th century, only St Peter's, the Escorial and Venice's Palazzo Ducale rivalled it in grandeur. The poet Constantijn Huygens dubbed it 'the eighth wonder of the world', and a passing Englishman wrote of 'a most neat and splendid pile of a building'. But Sir William Temple, the British Ambassador to the Netherlands, harrumphed that it was '*una gran piccola cosa*' ('a big little thing'—he was quoting someone else's remark about the Louvre).

The architect, Jacob van Campen (designer of the ill-fated Nieuwe Kerk tower), had produced a grandiose celebration of Amsterdam's mercantile supremacy and civic might—a classicist heap of windows, pilasters and relief carving. On the front pediment, collected water deities worship an allegorical Maid of Amsterdam; at the back of the building the trading nations of the world grovel to her. Peace stands high under the dumpy dome (a cornucopia overflowing at her feet) holding not only an olive branch, but also Mercury's staff (a symbol of commerce). Atlas buckles under a copper globe so heavy that it needs iron rods to prop it up. Despite all this confident symbolism, there's no grand entrance (the eight little arches along the front look more like tradesmen's gates or the way into the stables) and nowadays you are more likely to agree with Sir William Temple than Constantijn Huygens: the rather grimy palace in a busy city centre has as much architectural impact as a main post office or magistrates court.

However, if you're passing during the rather restricted opening hours, don't miss the chance of popping inside to be dazzled by the Burgerzaal (Citizens' Hall). It's a vast space encrusted with marble carving that glints in the light pouring in from all sides. Rows of chandeliers drip from the distant ceiling, and brass inlaid maps on the floor show the heavenly and terrestrial worlds (with Amsterdam very much at the centre of things and the enthroned maid of Amsterdam proudly surveying it all). The few chairs around the edges, even a grand piano for the inevitable recital, look like doll's house furniture. Scattered throughout the building are delicate and often witty marble reliefs (Icarus takes a tumble outside the Bankrupts' Court, caryatids look bored with holding up the crossbeams). Most of them are by Artus Quellinus, the noted Golden Age sculptor who also carved the pediments outside. The city fathers, however, blundered when it came to commissioning the wall paintings: they sent Rembrandt packing after he had presented his preliminary sketches.

The Empire furniture dispersed around the building was left behind by Louis Bonaparte. When he took over the Stadhuis he carpeted the marble floors, boarded up the galleries, turned the virtually empty upper storey into living accommodation and also had the weighing house on

Amsterdam—Centre of the Universe

A map worked into the floor of the *Stadhuis* places the city at the centre of the universe—and for much of the 17th century that must have seemed true. Goods flowed into the port from around the world, guilds flourished, and even the lowliest workers earned nearly twice as much as their English counterparts. The **Bours** (Exchange) thronged with merchants from countries as far away as India and Turkey. Isaac le Maire had the idea of trading *in blanco*—dealing on paper with goods he didn't yet own—and the first futures market was begun. In 1609 the city council founded the **Amsterdam Wisselbank** (Bank of Exchange). It drew up bank drafts to replace coins (which could be clipped, melted down or stolen), gave quick mortgages and lent at a good rate of interest (an encouraging 3½–4 per cent).

the Dam demolished because it spoiled his view. When the bored and wayward Queen Hortens granted a royal pension to a foundling abandoned at the palace door, he forestalled an inundation of hapless infants by surrounding the entrance with cobble stones and appointing guards to prevent anyone from stepping on them. His wooden-partitioned upstairs apartments lasted well into this century and were such a fire risk that whenever Queen Wilhelmina used the palace everyone was instructed not to smoke and to sleep with the doors open. A fireman in gym shoes would creep about at night to catch offenders.

National Monument

The eastern end of Dam Square is dominated by the towering National Monument, erected in 1956 as a memorial to the people killed in the Second World War. In the 1960s it became a sort of hippie totem pole and hundreds of people would sleep around it in the summer. Police attempts to put a stop to this (such as washing it down with firehoses) led to protest riots, but in 1970 a marauding group of off-duty marines chased away the campers forever.

Begijnhof

The Begijnhof has the atmosphere of a quiet village square. You can hardly believe, in the leafy calm walled in by its neat gables, that the busiest parts of the city are only a few metres away. The Béguines were an order of lay nuns, founded in the 15th century, who, through self-effacement and powerful family connections, remained undisturbed by the religious upheavals of the following centuries. Sister Antonia, the last of the order, died in the house at No.26 in 1971. The small mound near the gate (covered by flowers in the spring) is the grave of another Béguine, Sister Cornelia Arens. When she died in 1654 she was buried, at her own request, in the gutter. Most of the houses were rebuilt in the 17th and 18th centuries, but at No.34 you can see the last remaining original façade, one of only two medieval wooden houses left in Amsterdam. Next door is an old clandestine church, which still holds weekly mass. The church across the pathway was the original **Begijnkerk**, consecrated in 1419 and the only medieval church in the city with the tower in its original state. After a period of disuse during the Reformation, it was offered to Protestant dissenters fleeing England in 1607 and became known as the English Church. A plaque on the tower and stained glass in the chancel commemorate the fact that this group formed the core of the Pilgrim Fathers who sailed for America in 1620.

Spui

At the southern end of Spui is the diminutive statue of *Het Lieverdje* ('The Little Darling', an impish Amsterdam rascal), which was the focal point of provocative 'happenings' in the 1960s when the **Provos** (from *provocatie*—provocation) protested against (among other things) capitalism, traffic and tobacco and demanded free bicycles and free sex for all. If you nip down Voetboogstraat, look out for the outrageous gate of the old **Rasphuis**, the male equivalent of the Spinhuis, where men had to saw wood into a fine powder used for dye.

Rembrandtplein

Rembrandtplein was a butter market until the mid-19th century when a group of worthy burghers plonked a statue (Amsterdam's first) in the middle and grew some grass around it. Cafés sprang up. Variety artists from the halls along the Amstel would meet their agents at the posh Café Kroon, then retreat across the square to the darker recesses of the Hotel Schiller where they felt more at home among the artists, writers and other friends of proprietor Frits Schiller (whose paintings still decorate the walls). Nowadays the square is a favourite after-work stopover and a magnet to tourists, who come for the relaxed Amsterdam conviviality. Traffic is banished from most of the square but buskers keep the noise level high. When the sun sets, things get even livelier. The cafés change gear as the night staff come on duty. Music systems are turned on full, jazz from one corner, Dutch singalong from another. Congas of drunken Dutchmen snake out of pubs and around bemused policemen.

Tuschinski Cinema

Abraham Tuschinski, a Jewish refugee from Poland, saw his first film in 1910 and immediately wanted to own a cinema. His first 'bioscope' opened in 1911 in a disused seamen's church with a converted outside lavatory as the box office. But Tuschinski wanted a cinema where his 'guests' could lose themselves in another world. In 1921 he was wealthy enough to achieve his dream. You walk through a soaring Art Deco façade with flagpoles, camp statuary and curly iron lamps into an interior that lurches between heady luxury and high kitsch. It's a stylistic cocktail of five different colours of marble, Persian carpets, and thousands of electric lights. You can go on a guided tour (*Sun and Mon during July and Aug, 10.30am; f10*), or come back later and see a film. Ask for a balcony ticket in the main cinema. On the first Sunday of each month during the winter, there's a special morning screening of a silent movie, with musical accompaniment and sound effects from the original Wurlitzer organ.

Munttoren

The Munttoren (Mint Tower), a solitary clock tower with a polygonal base, is yet another steeple by Hendrick de Keyser—a verticomaniac responsible for nearly every spike on Amsterdam's skyline. The base dates from 1490 and was part of Regulierspoort, one of the gates in the old city wall. The structure gets its name because the guard house was briefly used as a mint in 1672–3, when the French were occupying much of the rest of the Netherlands and the Amsterdam merchants couldn't get at their usual source of Rijksdollars and ducatoons.

Also see: the **Flower Market**, p.195.

Amsterdam's population increased tenfold between 1550 and 1650. In the early 17th century the far-sighted city fathers were already planning to push the city boundaries outwards with three grand concentric canals. The Prinsengracht (Princes' Canal), Keizersgracht (Emperor's Canal) and Herengracht (Gentlemen's Canal, rather than Kings', a nice move by bourgeois Amsterdam) encircle the old city and give Amsterdam its distinctive cobweb layout. These canals were intended for rentiers and rich merchants who wanted to live away from the smells and noise of the harbour. Today the canals, and the narrow houses with their winding stairways, which stretch along their banks are one of the city's landmark sights. Gently flowing and unmistakably Dutch, they look their best in the early evening. On summer nights the stateliest stretches are floodlit, and the bridges twinkle with fairy lights.

Lunch and Cafés

Café Aas van Bokalen, Keizersgracht 335. Good brown café with an arty crowd and a restaurant-sized menu.

De Admiraal, Herengracht 319. *Proeflokaal* for Amsterdam's last remaining independent distillery, De Ooievaar. Here you will find soft sofas, and also potent liqueurs like 'Hempje ligt op' and 'Pruimpje prik in' (the names translate obscenely).

Backstage Boutique, Utrechtsedwarsstraat 65–7 (*closes 6pm*). Teas, coffee and home-made cakes in a coffeeshop that doubles as a boutique for fluorescent knitwear, tarot-reading and local gossip.

Beiaard, Herengracht 90. Reproduction Art Deco lamps, snooker tables and numerous varieties of Belgian beer.

De Belhamel, Brouwersgracht 60 (*open daily 12–12; lunch served 12–2.30*). Art Nouveau café/restaurant on Amsterdam's most photographed canal.

Café Chris, Bloemstraat 42, across the canal from the Westerkerk. A taphouse since 1624, it predates the bar that calls itself 'Amsterdam's oldest' by five years. The workers who built the Westerkerk received (and spent) their wages here. It's so small there's no room for a cistern in the men's loo; you flush it from a handle on the wall once you're back in the bar. On Sunday afternoons and evenings the café reverberates, in traditional Jordaan style, to a rousing opera sing-along.

Huyschkamer, Utrechtsestraat 137. The name means 'living room', but there's little sign of comfy sofas or cosy firesides here, nor of the building's dubious past as a male brothel. Instead you find a tastefully designed and studiously hip café that sells good food.

Café/Restaurant Kort, Amstelveld 2, tucked behind the Amstelkerk. Sleek and modern with one of the few terraces in central Amsterdam where the traffic doesn't hurtle between you and the canal.

Winkel Lunchcafé, Noordermarkt 43, opposite Noorderkerk. Good salads. Gets its produce (much of it organic) fresh from the farm.

The Pancake Bakery, Prinsengracht 191, near the Anne Frank Huis. A low-beamed cellar that boasts the best pancakes in town.

Café 't Papeneiland, Prinsengracht 2, just up from the Noorderkerk. Full of pink-faced old men. A 17th-century café with a shady past. It was originally a funeral parlour that sold beer on the side. There's an unexplained secret passage running from the cellar to the house over the canal.

Pompadour, Huidenstraat 5. A chocolaterie and pâtisserie. The interior—hardly bigger than an average kitchen—somehow incorporates carved oak panels, a staircase and a balustrade from an 18th-century town hall near Liège.

De Prins, Prinsengracht 124. Trendy café with a sunny canalside terrace.

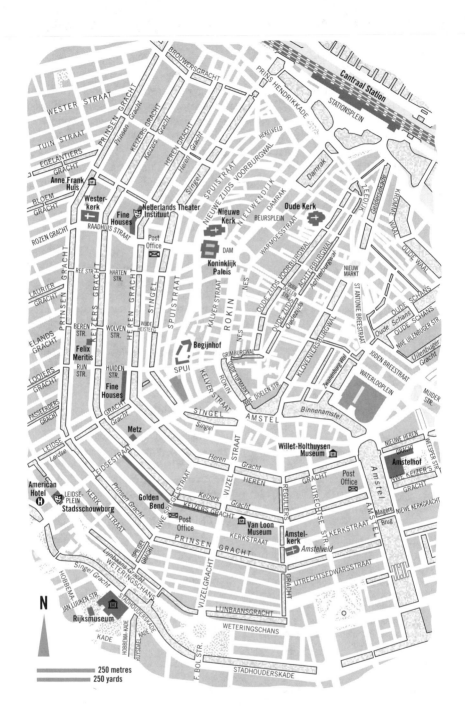

The Herengracht

Fashion has claimed each canal, at one time or another, as Amsterdam's best address, but it was the Herengracht that was really built to impress. It's more grand than pretty, a little ravaged by centuries of ostentation. Subsequent occupiers have (until recently) thought nothing of pulling down old buildings to make way for bigger and better displays of wealth, but the survivors have an endearing panache. Some extraordinary gables poke up out of the trees that line the canal. Monumental sandstone frontages seem to push aside the traditional dainty gabled brick façades. Cornices curled with acanthus leaves, strung with garlands and surmounted by urns lord it over the modest step-gables, though the odd defiant bell or neck-gable might reply with an extravagant claw-piece.

At No.120 you can see one of the few smaller 17th-century houses to have kept its façade free of later additions and amendments. Farther along, at Nos.170–2 is the Bartolotti House, built in 1617 by Hendrick de Keyser (who designed most of Amsterdam's spiky towers) for West India Company director Van den Heuvel. (It was paid for by Van den Heuvel's mother-in-law who stipulated the house be called after her late husband.) Its enormous neck-gable is all but invisible under the encrustation of pilasters, pinnacles and decorative reliefs. These days part of it houses the **Nederlands Theater Instituut** (*open Tues–Fri 11–5, Sat and Sun 1–5; adm f7.50. See* p.242).

The white sandstone house next door (known as the White House), built in 1668, was the first by the later famous 17th-century domestic architect, Philips Vingboons. The dignified row of four houses (Nos.364–70) farther down the canal, with clean lines, stately neck-gables and quiet decoration are also by Vongboons. No.380–2 is an outrageous confection—a late 19th-century imitation of a French Renaissance château scrunched down to city mansion size. Just up the canal is a pretty little 17th-century house with a simple festooned neck-gable (No.394), and across the way, No.401 manages to lean in three different directions at once.

The bit of the canal between Vijzelstraat and Leidsestraat is known as the **Golden Bend**, perhaps more for the wealth of the inhabitants than the refinement of the architecture. There are two clusters of more gorgeous and more graceful dwellings further up the canal that better deserve the epithet, though the elegant Louis XIV building with curved balustrades at No.475 does have the reputation of being Amsterdam's most beautiful house.

In the Beginning...

The first houses in Amsterdam were made of wood, but after fires nearly destroyed the city (in 1421 and 1452), people began building in brick. At first this only applied to the lower walls; the gables (which formed the outer walls of attics and were often shaped to give more interesting definition to steep triangular roofs) were still wooden. The shapes of early brick gables, called **spout gables**, are a direct reflection of their wooden ancestry. Wooden constructions were built with each successive storey sticking out a little further than the previous one, so that rainwater would drip on to the street and not seep back into the body of the building. Early brick gables leant over for the same reason, which is another contributing factor to Amsterdam's cityscape of tilting façades.

Amsterdam burgemeesters have been officially resident at No.502 since 1927, and next door (Nos.504–10) is a little stretch of wildly decorative claw-pieces. Tigers, dolphins and seagods curl about the gables and for once upstage the grander buildings.

Willet-Holthuysen Museum

Open Mon–Fri 10–5, Sat and Sun 11–5; adm f7.50.

At No.605, you'll come to the Willet-Holthuysen Museum, a 17th-century canal house. For two centuries it was occupied by a succession of Amsterdam glitterati. The last, Sandrina Holthuysen, had spent most of her life married to Abraham Willet, an avid collector of paintings, art books, glass, ceramics and silver. When she died in 1895, alone, riddled with cancer and surrounded by cats, she left the house and contents to Amsterdam as a museum. The city then filled it with pickings from a number of similar bequests. Most of the rooms are now reconstructed as 18th-century period pieces, with the different collections scattered about the house, mainly in rather stiff salons and boudoirs; there's also a crisp formal garden. Everything seems in its Sunday best—including the surreal headless mannequins that stand strategically about, sporting 18th-century costume. It's a good place to get an insider's view of one of the more stately canal houses.

The Keizersgracht

Less ostentatious than the Herengracht, the Keizersgracht nevertheless offers some architectural gems. At No.319 you can see the first house (built in 1639) in which architect Philips Vingboons combined classic elements (the Doric pilasters) with the traditional Dutch style. Nearby is the imposing classicist **Felix Meritis** building (No.324 on the left-hand side; open daily 5pm-midnight). It was built in 1778 to house an arts and scientific society founded in the spirit of Voltaire and Rousseau. With an observatory, library, laboratories and a small concert hall, the Felix Meritis Foundation became the cultural centre of the Dutch Enlightenment. When Napoleon made his triumphal entry to Amsterdam, he was punted up the canal and ushered with pride into the building. He got no further than the foyer, spat on the floor, said the place stank of tobacco smoke, and strutted back to the boat. Towards the end of the 19th century the society went into terminal decline. The building was later used as the Communist Party headquarters, but won back its cultural prominence in the 1970s when it housed the Shaffy Theatre, in the forefront of the European avant-garde. The theatre lost some of its significance and impact during the 1980s, but the Felix Meritis Society has been revived. As an arts complex and the home of Amsterdam's Summer University, the building is once again playing host to artists and intellectuals from around the world.

A wander farther along the canal reveals more architectural delights. The startlingly large windows of No.440 (built 1897) originally lit a clothing design studio and factory. It must have been the world's most gracious sweatshop. The bank at No.452 was once a private residence. Designed by Outshoorn in 1860 it is one of the last of a series of grand canal houses, influenced by French and Italian architecture, that were built by the three great domestic architects—Vingboons, van Campen and Outshoorn—over a period of 200 years. At No.546 nothing of the façade, except the windows, has changed since it was built in 1760. The bell-gable is a good example of the playful cake-icing Louis XV decoration. The ornately decorated building that cuts the corner with Leidsestraat is German inspired—the Dutch were more into solid right angles at corners. A frieze of fat naked babies, lurking in shrubberies and grumpily pushing carts and canoes, runs around the wall. The bust commemorates the 17th-century poet Pieter Cornelisz Hooft. The pompous building on the opposite corner was built on the site of Van Gogh's uncle's art shop for an insurance company in the late 19th century, but is now the refined Metz department store. Inside, you can mount stairs, passing racks of tasteful kitchenware and mounds of Liberty prints. As you climb, the atmosphere becomes increasingly rarefied and the floors emptier and emptier. By the time you're nearing the top, there's hardly anything for sale at all. The few pieces of designer furniture scattered about look more like museum pieces than anything you could put in the dining room. At the top is a café designed by Gerrit Rietveld. Gazing through its glass cupola, you have a rare opportunity to view Amsterdam's spider's web from on high. Back down on ground level, try to get to the **Van Loon Museum** at Keizersgracht 672 (open Fri–Mon 11–5; adm f7.50). The house still belongs to the Van Loon family (who live in a small apartment next door) and offers the best example of all of Amsterdam patrician home life.

The Prinsengracht

The Prinsengracht is the site of one of the most enduring symbols of Amsterdam—the spire of the **Westerkerk**. The Westerkerk (West Church) was consecrated in 1631. Its sober Protestant interior is brightened by large painted organ shutters showing a dancing King David and a voluptuous Queen of Sheba laden with gifts for Solomon. Rembrandt was buried here, but no one knows where the body is. There's a flutter of academic excitement every time old bones are found, but it's most likely that his were crunched up during the digging of an underground car park. A memorial plaque has been put up near his son Titus's grave. The church tower, known as the **Westertoren**, built by (you guessed it) Hendrick de Keyser, is Amsterdam's highest (85m) and contains its heaviest bell (7500kg). The Westertoren has something of the significance to Amsterdammers as St Paul's has to Londoners. Sentimental songs are addressed to it, and you can only be a true Jordaaner (*see* below) if you were born in its shadow. In the 1940s a fervent engineer climbed out on to the top of the tower during a violent storm and, with the help of a theodolite, worked out that it swayed all of 3cm. During the summer months you can climb up rather more sedately for a rare view of Amsterdam from high up (*open April–Sept, Mon–Sat 10–4; adm f3*).

If you walk around the outside of the church you can see the house where Descartes lived when he was in Amsterdam (Westermarkt 6); the pink marble triangles of the Homomonument which commemorates gays killed in the concentration camps; and a sad little statue of Anne Frank, who wrote her diary just around the corner.

Towards the eastern end of the Prinsengracht you'll find Amstelveld, a secluded square with a white wooden church and small Monday flower market, tucked away from the bustle. The recently restored 17th-century Amstelkerk has a popular left-wing preacher and is the one of the few churches in central Amsterdam that packs in a congregation. It isn't continuously open to the public, but sometimes stages chamber recitals. In front of the church, crossing the Prinsengracht, runs the Reguliersgracht, held by many to be the prettiest canal in town.

Also see: the **Anne Frank Huis**, p.194.

Onwards to: Shopping along **De Negen Straatjes**, p.238.

Amsterdam broadens out in the area containing its museums. The city's (if not the nation's) greatest cultural institutions border Museumplein, a large grassy space in the centre of town. The Rijksmuseum and Concertgebouw at either end and the Van Gogh and Stedelijk Museums up one side are world-class institutions exhibiting work by the Dutch masters of the Golden Age through to modern masterpieces and the latest in conceptual art. Until recently Museumplein was bisected by a busy road nicknamed 'Europe's shortest motorway', and was windswept, deserted and nasty. But dramatic relandscaping in the late 1990s created a green and stylish spot with a long pool, a café and underground garages that suck up all the cars and coaches. A short walk away is the Vondelpark, a large irregular mass of lakes and ponds, lawns, canals, ornate bridges, trees and gardens. There are even a few cows and sheep. At the weekends, Amsterdammers flock here to stroll around, picnic and enjoy the theatre performances, buskers and assorted summer festivities which stretch into the night.

The Concertgebouw

The Concertgebouw at the southern end of the square was designed by A. L. van Gendt (one of the collaborators on the Centraal Station design) and completed in 1888. It is solid Dutch neo-Renaissance; no French frivolity here—indeed, the few urns and obelisks he included in the design either never went up for lack of funds, or have fallen off through lack of funds. The twin staircase towers are intended to harmonize with Cuypers' Rijksmuseum across the way (more out of toadyism than artistic integrity—Cuypers headed the committee that chose the design). Busts of Beethoven, Bach and Sweelinck (Holland's one claim to musical fame) grace the

Lunch and Cafés

Café Américain, American Hotel, Leidseplein. Art Nouveau grand Café. Once the hangout of Amsterdam's literati, it's now visited mainly by tourists, but is just the right environment for a pot of fresh coffee and an extravagantly gooey cake. It also serves snacks and fuller meals.

The Bulldog, Leidseplein. One of the first places allowed to sell marijuana on the premises. It's now a slick commercial enterprise with alcohol upstairs, dope downstairs and even a souvenir shop.

Café Cox, beneath the Stadsschouwburg. Named after the theatre's erstwhile director Cox Habbema. It serves scrumptious salads and light meals.

Hollandse Manege Café, Vondelstraat 140, overlooks the arena of the elegant 19th-century riding school. It's a quiet place to sip coffee and watch the horses, though there are occasional invasions of groups of 11-year-olds in jodhpurs.

't Ronde Blauwe Theehuis, Vondelpark. 'The Round Blue Teahouse' is an odd piece of 1930s New Functionalist architecture in the middle of the Vondelpark. After years of mediocrity as a café, it has taken on a new life as a trendy watering hole.

Stedelijk Museum Café is the best café on the museum circuit. You can lounge about in basket chairs reading art magazines, or sit in the sun and look out at the sculptures.

Café Vertigo is in the cellar of the Film Museum and spills out into the park in good weather. The cuisine surpasses that of any museum restaurant in town; even has appropriate theme menus during film festivals.

Café Welling, J. W. Brouwersstraat 32, behind the Concertgebouw (*open daily from 3pm*). A traditional brown café. The main door is always locked—the entrance is around the side.

façade. The gilded lyre on top is a 1960s replacement of the original (which fell off). The entrance is no longer through the front, but through a shiny glass extension built in 1988 as part of a complete renovation of the building, which had been subsiding dangerously. It certainly meets the general manager's stipulation that if there was to be a new front door, he didn't want to have to hang an 'Entrance around the Corner' notice on the old one.

In the 1870s Amsterdam, a city with metropolitan aspirations, found itself without a concert hall and with Brahms's admonition ringing in its ears: '*Ihr seid liebe Leute aber schlechte Musikanten*' (You are lovely people but awful musicians). The government maintained that art was not its business, so it was a committee of private citizens that raised the money, bought some cheap land outside the city limits next to an evil-smelling candle factory and commissioned Van Gendt (more for his figures than his design). Van Gendt prided himself on being a salesman rather than an artist and was completely unmusical. It is ironic that he should have produced a concert hall with possibly the best acoustics in the world.

Under the baton of conductors like Mengelberg (who was sacked for his Nazi sympathies in 1945 after 50 years of service) and Haitink, the resident Royal Concertgebouw Orchestra has become world-famous. If you're passing on a Wednesday, pop in for a free 'lunch concert' (*12.30pm, though it's a good idea to be there by 12*). These are usually recitals given in the Kleine Zaal (Small Hall—a chamber music room upstairs), but if you're lucky you might catch the RCO itself in open rehearsal in the Grote Zaal (Big Hall)—the main auditorium.

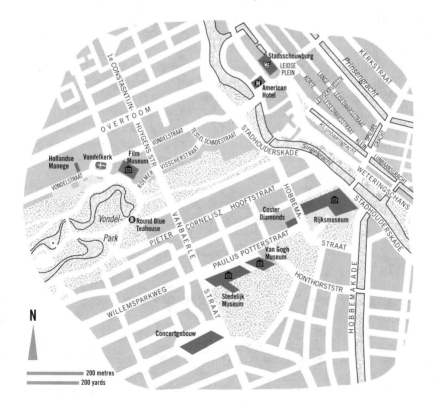

Leidseplein

Leidseplein is Amsterdam's tourist vortex with more than the usual complement of British boys in Union Jack shorts learning the strength of Dutch lager. Fire-eaters and itinerant musicians busk while your pockets are picked, though at night the atmosphere improves a little as the square becomes the festive hub of late-night transport. As a 17th-century traveller cautioned, 'Here be sure to furnish yourself with money.' The neon alleys leading off the square are lined with expensive and nasty restaurants and nightclubs with names like 'Cash'. **Leidsestraat**, the northern exit, is clogged wtih pedestrians and bicycles travelling on no particular side until, bells clanging, a yellow tram hurtles down the central rails scattering all. Mainly airline offices, 24-hour bureaux de change and shops selling clogs and Taiwan Delft, Leidsestraat is happily avoided.

American Hotel

The jutting balconies and odd protruding windows are a Dutch interpretation of an original Art Nouveau design. The architect, W. Kromhout, is considered a forerunner of the fanciful Amsterdam School. The writers and artists who used the **Café Américain** (*open daily 10am–midnight*) for most of this century have fled the tourist armies of the Leidseplein, but it's still worth a visit for the glass Japanese parasol lampshades and patterned windows that filter the hard Amsterdam light into a soft and playful kaleidoscope.

Vondelpark

Joost van Vondel (1582–1674; pronounced in the way an old English army officer might say 'fondle') is proclaimed as the Dutch answer to Shakespeare. He excelled in ornate poems in celebration of public events, clocking up over a thousand lines for the opening of the Town Hall alone. The lack of action in his dramas is notorious: he went in for static pictorial representations accompanied by long flowery descriptions of anything exciting. His play *Gijsbrecht van Amstel* is a Dutch literary classic. It's said that one of the scenes inspired Rembrandt's *Night Watch*. By all accounts the Master would have had quite enough time to paint it during the performance. From humble beginnings in his father's busy hosiery shop on the edge of the red-light district, Vondel built up a considerable reputation and small fortune. The former counted for little in mercantile Amsterdam when his son squandered the latter. At the age of 70 he had to go back to work in the city pawnbrokers. He was sacked after 10 years' service for writing poetry in office hours and finally, in his eighties, was granted a state pension. He died at 92 of hypothermia, and suggested his own epitaph:

> *Hier ligt Vondel zonder Rouw,*
> *Hij is gestorven van de kou.*

> Here lies Vondel, without regret [or unmourned],
> He was killed by the cold.

During the so-called 'Second Golden Age' at the end of the 19th century, when the butter market was turned into Rembrandtplein and the neighbourhood around the museums was being developed as an upmarket residental area, some local burghers got together to commemorate the poet by creating the Vondelpark. It's a large park by Amsterdam standards and J. D.

Kocher's informal English landscaping gives it calm, graceful lines and wide perspectives. Curved tree-lined avenues, irregularly shaped lakes and ponds, little furrow-like paths through shrubberies, hidden gardens and wide stretches of lawn attract Amsterdammers from all over the city—especially at weekends. A lone accordionist sits on a bench and plays for the ducks. Refugee guitarists from South America play heartrending tunes, homesick for a stronger sunlight. Jugglers meet to learn, practise and show off. There's a party atmosphere whenever the sun shines, and in the summer the festivities go on well into the night with concerts, theatre performances and an open-air cinema. On holidays (especially Queen's Day) enjoyment reaches carnival pitch.

There are dainty bridges, a few sculptural surprises and some odd architecture to catch your eye. Entering the park, you can see, across the pond, one of the more attractive examples of Nieuwe Zakelijkheid (Functionalist) architecture: H. J. Baanders' **'t Ronde Blauwe Theehuis** (Round Blue Teahouse), a cross between a pagoda and a flying saucer that seems to hover over the water. Across the way Vondel himself, in badly fitting laurels, looks gouty, prosperous and entirely oblivious of the Muses playing at his ankles. His ornate pedestal was made in 1867 by P. J. H. Cuypers (architect of the Centraal Station and Rijksmuseum).

Netherlands Film Museum

Open Tues–Fri 10–5, Sat 11–5; adm free.

The pavilion that houses the Netherlands Film Museum was designed in 1881 by P. J. and W. Harner. There is no exhibition as such, but the museum shows films from the archive, details of which are published in the listings magazines. The first director, Jan de Vaal, was a voracious but secretive collector. He hoarded his treasures and seemed wary of the outside world. The result was that no one bothered about the film museum until the dynamic duo—director Hoos Blotkamp and film buff Eric de Kuyper—took over in the late 1980s and discovered an archive of world significance. Funding was secured, the building was revamped, the long process of cataloguing begun (unearthing such gems as hand-coloured silent movies) and the occasional screenings were boosted to three times a day.

There are all sorts of special events and films are shown in the original language. On summer Saturdays there are free screenings on the terrace (*around 10pm*), when you can buy a beer and giggle at Charlie Chaplin or Abbott and Costello. The main hall is worth a peek. Its interior is from Amsterdam's first cinema, the Cinema Parisien built in 1910. The Parisien had declined ungracefully into a porn pit when the daughter of the orginal owner heard, in 1987, that it was about to be gutted by the hotel next door. Armed with coffee flask and screwdriver she went to rescue the interior (still intact after a 1930s redecoration) and, aided by the Monuments Trust, the old atmosphere was bottled and transferred to the Film Museum. The library, with a good selection of magazines and reference works and a stash of posters and publicity material, is in the building alongside the pavilion.

Also see: the **Rijksmuseum**, pp.196–200; the **Stedelijk Museum**, pp.200–202 and the **Van Gogh Museum** pp.203–06.

Onwards to: **chic shopping**, on P. C. Hoofstraat and Van Baerlestraat, p.237.

The inviting side streets, alleys and intimate canals of the Jordaan are lined with cosy cafés, curious shops and good restaurants, all luring you to ferret about in your own way. Jordaan comes from the French '*jardin*', but during the housing crisis in the 19th century this 'garden' on the outskirts of the city disappeared under rows of working-class housing. The houses were small, dark and close together and all the smellier industries (such as tanning) were banished to the Jordaan from the posher areas of town. Naming the streets after flowers didn't cheer things up much. Conditions were appalling, but the Jordaaners developed a pride and a culture akin to London's cockneys. The true Jordaaner is born in the small patch bound by Prinsengracht, Brouwersgracht, Lijnbaansgracht and Looiersgracht, in the shadow of the Westertoren. The church tower is the symbol of the Jordaan. Jordaaners have their own accent and are renowned for a wry sense of humour and for being adept pigeon-fanciers. Everyone over the age of forty is known as '*ome*' or '*tante*'—uncle or aunt. (Until a decade or so ago, you could still be woken by Ome Hein, a professional 'waker-up', as he made his early morning rounds with a pet goat.) They're a rebellious lot. There have been a number of historical riots, including one in 1886 when police tried to put a stop to the gory-sounding pastime of 'eel-jerking'; and another when the council threatened to reduce the dole in 1934. Recently, traditional Jordaan life has been given a new edge by an influx of artists and music students. You're quite likely to be accompanied on your walk by strains of Mozart and will probably encounter odd art objects suspended over the street.

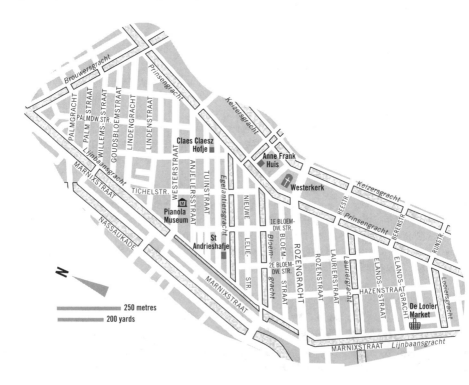

Lunch and Cafés

Café Chris, Bloemstraat 42, across the canal from the Westerkerk. A taphouse since 1624, it predates the bar that calls itself 'Amsterdam's oldest' by five years. The workers who built the Westerkerk received (and spent) their wages here. It's so small that there's no room for a cistern in the men's loo and you have to flush the toilet from the bar on the way out. On Sunday afternoons and evenings the café reverberates, in traditional Jordaan style, to a rousing opera sing-along.

De Prins, Prinsengracht 124. Trendy café with a sunny canalside terrace. Serves good sandwiches and snacks (*f*5–*f*20).

The Pancake Bakery, Prinsengracht 191, near the Anne Frank Huis. A low-beamed cellar that boasts the best pancakes in town. Sweet and savoury pancakes from *f*8.50 to *f*18.

Café 't Smalle, Egelantiersgracht 12. Restored *proeflokaal* of Pieter Hoppe's 18th-century liqueur distillery. These days sells a wider range of drinks and snacks.

Hofjes

At Egelantiersgracht 107–45 can be found one of several *hofjes* in the district, St Andrieshofje. Hofjes, the courts of almshouses, are magically quiet garden courts, often completely hidden from the street. You reach this one (built 1616) through a door that looks like any other front door along the canal and down a passage lined with Delft tiles. Most *hofjes* are private residences, but as long as you're sensitive to that, residents don't mind you popping in for a few calming moments.

Westerstraat

Westerstraat (once a canal) is too wide to be really attractive, but at No.67 there's a tiny shop full of good, old-fashioned, low-tech toys. Skipping ropes, bright-coloured balls, red wooden buses, pretty paper cut-outs are stacked on shelves and hanging from the walls and ceiling. There are boxes and boxes of all sorts of little things that will keep parents and kids digging about for ages.

Noordermarkt and Noorderkerk

The square is quiet, and usually empty, but if you come back early on a Monday morning you'll find a crush of trendies, students and down-and-outs at Amsterdam's cheapest clothes market. The Noorderkerk was Hendrick de Keyser's last church and, as befits an old man, is solemn and austere with only the teeniest of spires. If your legs need a rest, you can relax with a quiet coffee in one of the cafés around the square before plunging back into the Jordaan. Bloemgracht and Lindengracht are both very much worth a look. Lindengracht (Canal of Limes) is yet another filled in canal and hosts in own Saturday Market, as does the Bloemgracht. On the other side of the Prinsengracht are two more *hofjes*: 'De Ster' at Prinsengracht 89–133 (one of the best, though now closed to the public) and 'Zons Hofje' at Nos.159–71

Also see: the **Anne Frank Huis**, p.194.

Onwards to: the **Canals**, p.219; the **Netherlands Theater Instituut**, p.242; the **Pianola Museum**, p.242.

The old port and island neighbourhoods are redolent of the days when wooden ships bulging with corn, spices, silks and gold came from all over the world to fill the city's warehouses. Today the area is made up of crumbling warehouses, startling new apartment blocks and colourful houseboats. You can still see the city's old shipyards and step down into the bowels of a 17th-century sailing ship at the Maritime Museum. With its salty tang and fresh sea breezes, this is a good place to come for a Sunday walk to stretch your legs and blow away Saturday night's cobwebs.

Centraal Station

Built between 1884 and 1889 atop thousands of wooden piles on an artificial island, Centraal Station is such an elaborate and sustained exercise in 19th-century ornament that it can almost be forgiven for screening off Amsterdam's view of the old harbour. The architect P. J. H. Cuypers (also responsible for the Rijksmuseum) succumbed to every temptation to gild bits of his red-brick extravaganza, so that it sparkles in the sunlight like a Walt Disney palace. Its twin towers are adorned not only by a clock, but also by a wind-rose, a delightfully superfluous instrument that rotates languidly showing the frequency of winds blowing from the various leading points of the compass. The roof bristles with stone and iron spikes and the central section sports classically inspired reliefs showing allegories of sailing, trade and industry. There's a large section over the entrance depicting the peoples of the world paying homage to the maiden Amsterdam. The building seems very much in the tradition of the triumphal arch or elaborate city gate and is indeed a grand place to arrive in Amsterdam.

Sint Nicolaaskerk

Open April–Oct, Mon–Fri 11–4, Sat 2–4.

St Nicholas's Church is a sprucely restored 19th-century neo-Renaissance building with a murky interior. A small ship set above the door at the back is the only remainder that it was a seamen's church. Every March during the Stille Omgang (Silent Procession), Roman Catholics walk silently through the streets to the Sint Nicolaaskerk to commemorate Amsterdam's miracle. Paintings in the left-hand transept depict the story.

Lunch and Cafés

Café Karpershoek, Martelaarsgracht 2, opposite Centraal Station. Claims to be Amsterdam's oldest bar (dating from 1629—but *see* Café Chris, p.219). It was a popular seamen's tavern. It still has sand on the floor, as in the 17th century.

De Druif, Rapenburgstraat 83, at the gate to the Entrepotdok. Opened in 1631. A brown café with barrels to the ceiling and a rare antique *jenever* pump on the counter. Locals maintain that naval hero Piet Heyn was a regular visitor. His entrance would have caused a stir, as Heyn died in 1629.

Grand Café Restaurant I[e] **(Eerste) Klas**, Platform 2b, Centraal Station. Recently restored First Class dining room, now open to all. It's timeless railway camp. You wouldn't bat an eyelid if you saw women in cloche hats whispering in the corner or an Edwardian touring party march through the door. Coffee, snacks and also much grander meals (*from around f25 for a main course*).

Maritime Museum Café is a good place to sip coffee and look out over the harbour.

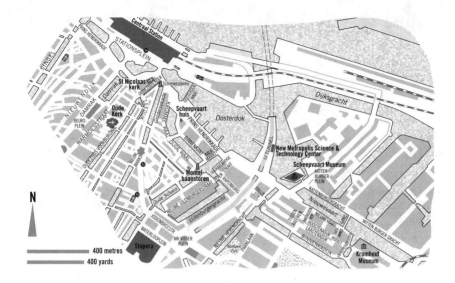

Scheepvaarthuis

At No.108 Prins Hendrikkade is the Shipping Building. The house was built in 1916 (on the site of the place where the first Dutch fleet set sail for the East Indies) as the offices for six big shipping companies. After serving as the headquarters of the municipal transport authority during the 1980s and most of the 1990s it was closed for renovation, and will probably reopen as an hotel. It was the first building designed by the team of architects (Van der Meij, Kramer and De Klerk) who became known as the Amsterdam School, a sort of fantastical Dutch Art Nouveau movement. Nothing escapes decoration. The building comes to a prow-like point crowned by a statue of Neptune. He waves his trident while his wife Salicia takes the wheel. Four female figures represent the points of the compass. The walls are encrusted with unflattering reliefs of sea heroes. Doors, stairs, window frames and any wall space left are patterned with appropriate images—wave forms, sea horses, dolphins, anchors, seals and ship's wheels. The roof line is a *cheval-de-frise* of moulded lead. It's as if you're viewing the building in a distorting mirror: there's hardly a smooth surface in sight. Inside, the maritime motifs continue with filigreed metalwork ornamentation, beautiful stained-glass skylights and windows and much of the original furniture (also designed by the architects). Door-knobs, lamps, wall-panels, floor patterns all reflect the theme.

Amsterdam's Miracle

In 1345 a dying man had vomited up the host after his last communion. It was thrown on a fire but didn't burn. Later it developed healing powers, and would transport itself overnight between churches. A chapel of its own seemed to make it stay in one place and, though this burnt down, the host survived. It became an object of worship, and is still honoured today in the **Stille Omgang** (Silent Procession) on the Sunday closest to the 15 March when Roman Catholics from all over the world walk in silence along the Heiligeweg and up to Sint Nicolaaskerk in celebration.

Nederlands Scheepvaart Museum

Open Tues–Sun 10–5; adm f14.50.

It's a wonder the Maritime Museum is still upright: in 1655 the workers were bribed with '*drinkgelt*' (drinking money) and finished what was to be an admiralty warehouse in an amazing nine months and fourteen days. The new warehouse had a system of cisterns and sprinklers to put out fires and an army of rat-catching cats with their own office and keeper. The museum's main attraction—a full size replica of the *Amsterdam*, one of the Dutch East India Company's ships—is moored outside (though occasionally it pays visits to other ports). You can swan about the captain's cabin, have a look at his tiny loo then descend into the ship's murky maw where up to 200 sailors would live for months at a stretch.

From the upper deck you can look across to the warehouses on the end of Prins Hendrikkade, or back over the water to the **New Metropolis Science & Technology Center** (*see* **Museums and Galleries**, p.242), designed by Renzo Piano, architect of the Pompidou Centre in Paris, to resemble the prow of a gigantic ship.

Back in the museum you can see a cutaway of an 1840s outrigger and the ostentatiously gilded (and rather uncomfortable) Royal Barge used for state occasions and for paddling visiting dignitaries around the canals. You can also climb up to the Second World War room to peer out at Amsterdam through a periscope. The rest of the museum comprises room after room of maps, navigational equipment from previous eras, and models and pictures of ships. Everything is informatively labelled in Dutch and English, giving you a good introduction to the history of Dutch seafaring. The 'Time Voyage' multimedia show takes you a step further, portraying—with smoke machines, movies, slide shows and special effects—how unjolly it was to be a tar in the 17th century.

Kromhout Museum

Open Mon–Fri 10–4; adm f3.50.

The Kromhout Shipyard, one of Amsterdam's oldest, was one of the few to survive the 19th-century decline in shipbuilding. It had a new lease of life in the 20th century when it produced the diesel engine used by most Dutch inland craft. In the 1960s it moved to larger premises and the yard became a museum. Some boat building and restoration still goes on, but rows of diesel engines form the bulk of the exhibits. It's very much a place for the enthusiast.

Amsterdam: Shopping

Amsterdam's markets, boutiques and eccentric speciality shops are still one of the city's greatest allures. The range of goods and oddity of the shops can keep you browsing for hours and the only barriers against your absolute financial ruin are the inconvenient opening hours. Calvinism wins over tourism—despite the recent relaxation of laws governing shop hours, you'll find very few places at all open on a Sunday. Amsterdammers enjoy their weekends, and the fun tends to overflow into Monday: many shops also stay closed on Monday mornings, if not for the whole day. However, most stay open late on Thursday nights. (Thursday, the night before the weekenders descend on the city, has a wild feeling of local festivity that dissipates under the influx of outsiders.)

Weekday **opening hours** are generally 9–6. On Saturdays shops close around 5. Some shops in the city centre now open from noon to 6 on Sundays. Many of the smaller shops can be quite idiosyncratic about when they open, but all have a little black and yellow timetable of opening hours posted on an outside window.

Dutch **sales tax** (BTW—17.5 per cent on most goods) is included in the marked price, though many stores offer **tax-free shopping** to non-EU tourists. Most will help with the paperwork as well.

Old Amsterdam

The old centre is home to Amsterdam's red-light district but it is not just sex that is on sale here. This is quintessential Amsterdam: compact, vibrant and full of contradictions. While it may not be the best part of the city in which to go shopping, there are a few shops worth seeking out. The area also contains the capital's largest concentration of markets, including the famous Waterlooplein.

Allert de Lange, Damrak 62. Good, well-stocked and established bookshop.

Arxhoek, Damstraat 19. Farm cheeses.

De Bijenkorf, Dam 1. In the heart of Amsterdam, 'The Beehive' is aptly named. Bustling shop with a wide range of good quality merchandise, and no pretensions to being Harrods.

Book Exchange, Kloveniersburgwal 58. This huge, dark and rather dingy second-hand book shop is essential in this town of outrageous prices for low-cost books.

Clubwear House, Herengracht 265. Clubwear for the brave and the beautiful.

Condomerie, Warmoesstraat 141. Condom as consumer item. Every size, colour, shape and flavour to suit all budgets and tastes.

The Head Shop, Kloveniersburgwal 39. Accessories for dope devotees.

Joe's Vliegerwinkel, Nieuwe Hoogstraat 19. Kites weird and wonderful.

De Klompenboer, Nieuwezijds Voorburgwal 20. Clogs and other wooden goodies carved on the premises. Also pewter and lace.

Nieuwmarkt, *May–Sept, Sun 10–5.* Good quality antiques in the shadow of a medieval city gate and weighing house.

Oudemanhuis Book Market, Oudemanhuispoort, *Mon–Sat 10–4.* A dim alley smelling of musty binding and yellowing paper.

Stamp Market, near Nova Hotel, Nieuwezijds Voorburgwal 276; *Wed, Sat 11–4.* Grizzled collectors swap stamps, currency, medals and esoteric philatelic-related jokes.

A Taste of Ireland, Herengracht 228. Irish and British provisions for the homesick.

Waterlooplein, *Mon–Sat 10–4.* The city's best-known fleamarket sells just about everything whether saleable or not. The rows of oddities and exotica, jewellery and clothes, are punctuated by more down-to-earth stalls selling everything from bicycle parts to cleaning equipment (*see* p.212).

Around the Flower Market

The area around the Flower Market is good for books and designer clothes and, of course, flowers. It gets pretty busy round here but there are plenty of cafés in which to take a breather and in spring, when people flock to see the huge variety of tulips on offer, there are few more pleasant places to visit.

a la Carte, Utrechtsestraat 110–12. Maps, street-plans and guide books.

Atheneum, Spui 14–16. Stamping ground of the city's intelligentsia. Good selection of magazines and English non-fiction.

Baltus, Vijzelstraat 127. Late-night grocery store. Open until 1am.

De Beestenwinkel (The Animal Shop), Staalstraat 11. Stuffed bunnies, tiger puppets and teddy bears to put your pyjamas in.

Big Bananas, Leidsestraat 76. Late-night opening grocery store. Big price tags. Rude assistants.

Bloemenmarkt (Flower Market), Singel, between Muntplein and Koningsplein, *Mon–Sat 9–6*. Amsterdam's famous floating flower market (*see* p.195).

Body Sox, Leidsestraat 12. All manner of socks, tights and stockings to suit every conceivable taste.

Cora Kemperman, Leidsestraat 72. Slightly off-the-wall yet supremely stylish fashion outlet.

Kenneth Cole, Leidsestraat 20. Groovy yet well-made boots.

Lambiek, Kerkstraat 78. Cheery comic shop. Collectors' pieces and cartoon gallery.

Plantenmarkt, Amsteveld. Good for plants and flower pots, plus a small selection of flowers.

Shoebaloo, Koningsplein 7–9. Glitz, ruffs and teetering heels for the oddly shod (unisex).

Sissy Boy, Leidsestraat 15. Sartorial elegance at fast-lane prices.

Vlieger, Amstel 34. Pencils, pigments and piles of inspiring paper.

High Street Amsterdam

Just like any other city the world over, Amsterdam has its high-street shopping opportunities. The mainstream fashion and department stores can be found along the Kalverstraat and the Niewwendijk leading to Dam Square as well as the major book and magazine stores. If you have run out of underwear, there is even a Marks and Spencer. Just across the road from Nieuwezijds Voorburgwal is the Magna Plaza, Amsterdam's old post office, which is now a huge shopping mall.

Akkerman, Kalverstraat 149. Huge number of pens and other writing paraphernalia.

American Book Center, Kalverstraat 185. After W.H. Smith's, this has the best stock in town of English fiction and non-fiction, magazines and children's books.

Bam Bam, Magna Plaza, Nieuwezijds Voorburgwal 182. Clothes for trendy toddlers.

De Bierkoning, Paleisstraat 125. Cosy shop behind the palace. Glasses of all shapes and around 750 brands of bottled beer.

Brillenwinkel, Gasthuismolensteeg 7. All kind of

classic spectacle frames, from Mahatma Gandhi to Dame Edna.

Candy Corson, St Luciensteeg 19. Stylish leather bags and belts.

Christmas World, Nieuwesijds Voorburgwal 137–9. Everything you could possibly want (and many things that you probably won't) in order to decorate your home for Christmas.

Freelance Shoes, Rokin 88. Good range of designer shoes.

Frozen Fountain, Prinsengracht 629. Ultra-modern household design store.

Galerie KIS, Paleisstraat 107. Plenty of furniture, lighting and other household objects produced by independent designers and architects.

Hema, Kalvertoren, Kalverstraat (and all around town). The Dutch Woolworth's or five-and-dime—but all in good taste. An excellent one-stop shop to stock up on essentials.

Marks & Spencer, Kalverstraat 66. All that you'd expect from this once great giant of the high street.

Maison de Bonneterie, Rokin 140. Good building with a central dome. By appointment to Her Majesty and rather on the pricey side.

Metz & Co., Keizersgracht 455. Liberty prints, stylish kitchenware and design-museum furniture. Superb view from the café on the top floor.

P. G. C. Hajenius, Rokin 92–6. Long-established tobacconist with famed house-brand cigars plus assorted smoking paraphernalia.

Puk and Hans, Rokin 66. Popular outlet for designer clothes.

Rokin Diamonds, Rokin 12.

De Slegte, Kalverstraat 48–52. Discount and anti-quarian megastore.

Tothem, Nieuwezijds Voorburgwal 149. Swimsuits and sexy underwear for men.

Waterstones, Kalverstraat 152. Large well-stocked branch of the British bookshop chain.

W.H. Smith, Kalverstraat 152. Branch of the UK book and magazine chain over four floors.

Jordaan

The inviting side streets, alleys and intimate canals of the Jordaan are lined with cosy cafés, curious shops and good restaurants, all luring you to ferret about in your own way. This is where many local artists ply their wares. You can find individual items of genuine interest as well as more specialized and adventurous clothes shops.

Architectura & Natura, Leliegracht 44. Just what it says, with an impressive collection of books on Amsterdam.

Boerenmarkt, Noordermarkt, *Sat 10–3*. Organic produce, ethnic crafts.

Big Shoe, Leliegracht 12. Unisex shoe shop.

Fever, Prinsengracht 192. Nifty fashion store. Hot little numbers for hot little people.

Kitsch Kitchen, 1e Bloemdwarsstraat 21. Gaudy plastic goodies, brightly patterned enamel bowls and curious implements.

Lapjesmarkt, Westerstraat, *Mon 7.30–1*. Bargain clothes and spectacular fabrics.

Lindengracht, *Sat 9–4*. Small general market, but the best.

Noordermarkt, *Mon 7.30–1.30*. Pile upon pile of junk. Get there early for a treasure hunt.

Pas-destoel, Westerstraat 260. Trendy household furniture, aimed especially at children as well as toys and fabrics.

Petticoat, Lindengracht 99. Fifties retro, hats, shawls, cufflinks and zooty underwear.

Rinascimento Gallerie d'Arte, Prinsengracht 170. Old and new Delftware (the real thing, not souvenir shop tat). Watch the designs being painted on by hand.

Spiegelkwartier

The Spiegelkwartier has gone up-market in recent years—these days even museums buy here for their collections—but it hasn't lost its charm, and the prices are still lower than in most other major cities. Here you'll find shops crammed with elaborate clocks, solemn rows of carved wooden dressers and ornate gilded furniture. Enormous chandeliers hang at eye-level, and gold, silver and colourful gems shine at you from all sides. Tucked amongst all this grandeur, you can still find idiosyncratic little shops, obviously the domain of a single collector.

Aalderink, Prinsengracht 15. Sparse but expertly selected range of oriental pieces and Africana.

Anneke Schat, Prinsengracht 20a. Delicate, sculpted jewellery inspired by spiders' webs and butterflies and much favoured by Dutch glitterati and the royal family.

Ariëns Kappers/van der Peet, Nieuwe Spiegelstraat 32. Antique maps and Japanese prints.

Blitz, Nieuwe Spiegelstraat 37a. Quality ceramics, mostly Chinese.

Van Dreven & Toebosch, Nieuwe Spiegelstraat 33. Antique clocks and music boxes.

Elisabeth Hendriks, Nieuwe Spiegelstraat 61. If you're after snuffboxes, this is the place to come.

Hart's Wijnhandel, Vijszelgracht 3. Wide range of wines and spirits.

C. O. Hotkamp, Vijzelgracht 15. Mouth-watering edible goodies close to the town centre.

Jan Beekhuizen, Nieuwe Spiegelstraat 49. Antique European pewter.

Kramers, Nieuwe Spiegelstraat 64. Tangles of old jewellery and trinkets, barrels of clay pipe bowls and a roomful of Delft tiles ranging from 15th to 20th centuries.

Lankamp & Brinkman, Spiegelgracht 19. Children's books in English.

Roel Houwink, Nieuwe Spiegelstraat 57. Everything from musical boxes to escutcheons.

The Museum Area

Close to the major museums are P. C. Hoofstraat and Van Baerlestraat—one of the few places in the city where you can confidently window-shop without stepping in something nasty. These and the surrounding streets are the corridors of high fashion and the top designers where even a pair of socks might set you back a week's wages. There are a few exotic delis, certified Delft porcelain and some elegant, if rather dull, cafés. Mostly it's clothes though, whether it be shops for the hip toddler or the fashion-anxious adolescent. All the favourite names can be found from Armani to Gucci to Hamnett. And for something with a more local flavour, P. C. Hoofsraat and Van Baerlestraat are also home to some of the better Dutch designers such as Edgar Vos and Sissy Boy.

Coster Diamonds, Paulus Potterstraat 2–6. One of the biggest and most famous diamond shops in the city, selling here at far less than you'd pay in either London or New York.

La Culotte, P. C. Hooftstraat 111. Pricey, sensuous silk lingerie.

Edgar Vos, P. C. Hooftstraat 134. Nifty suits for high-powered businesswomen.

Focke & Meltzer, P. C. Hooftstraat 65. Certified Delft porcelain.

Hans en Grietje, Overtoom 255. Ethnic and colonial bits and bobs.

Henrikse, Overtoom 472. Tarts and cream cakes fit for Queen Beatrix.

Hobbits, Van Baerlestraat 34. Pricey but reasonable selection of men's and women's clothes.

Intertaal, Van Baerlestraat 76. Every kind of book you need to learn Dutch or teach English.

't Mannetje, Frans Halsstraat 35. Tandems, three-wheelers and other curious cycle designs for sale, as well as repairs.

Natuurwinkel, Weteringschans 133, and all around town. Everything from organic vegetables to vitmins and tofu-burgers.

Oilily, P. C. Hooftstraat 133. Clothes for tiny tots whose mums and dads have big pockets.

Pasteuning Deliwijn, Willemsparkweg 11. A traditional Italian deli with a good selection of wines and cheeses.

Raymond Linhard, Van Baerlestraat 50. Reasonable prices for brght and breezy separates.

Robert Premsela, Van Baerlestraat 78. Art books a cut above the museum shops.

Sissy Boy, Van Baerlestraat 15. Dutch designer which offers middle-of-the-road elegance but at fast-lane prices.

De Negen Straatjes

Amsterdam abounds in idiosyncratic specialists shops: old family businesses, and outlets for the fantasies of quixotic visionaries. These are dotted all around the city but the short streets leading off from both sides of the three bridges beyond the Leidsegracht, known as De Negen Straatjes 'The Nine Alleys' have more than their fair share. These alleys offer some of the best of Amsterdam's more off-the-wall shopping. Keep a steady progress up the Keizersgracht, ducking down each in turn, only as far as the next canal.

Animation Art, Berenstraat 19. Original drawings as well as cels (the acetate originals from which cartoons are made) of everyone from Winnie the Pooh to Betty Boop.

Boekie Woekie, Berenstraat 16. Books by and about Dutch artists and designers.

Comendium, Hartenstraat 14. All kinds of games, from the old fashioned to the ultra hi-tech.

English Bookshop, Lauriergracht 71. Carefully selected range of English-language books, some second-hand.

Gerda's, Runstraat 16. One of Amsterdam's more unusual flower shops.

Hangmatten Maranón, Singel 488–90. Bright and breezy hammocks from around the world.

Klamboe Imports, Prinsengracht 232. Mosquito nets—the best way to ward off the pests.

Knopenwinkel, Wolvenstraat 14. Buttons of all shapes and periods, some in such shapes and sizes that their function is hardly recognizable.

Kramer, Reestraat 20. Candles and candlesticks—ethnic to high altar.

Lady Day, Hartenstraat 9. Reasonably priced second-hand fashionware.

De Looier Indoor Antiques Market, Elandsgracht, *Mon–Thurs 11–5, Sat 9–5*. Mid-price antique market.

Olivaria, Hazenstraat 2a. Entirely devoted to olive oil; there's even a tasting bar.

Poppendokter, Reestraat 20. Dolls and parts of dolls with a disconcerting catalogue of dolls' faces hanging from the walls.

Rob & Rik, Runstraat 30. Leatherwear from functional to fetish.

Rommelmarkt, Looiersgracht 38. An indoor flea-market that seems almost subterranean with piles of old toys, tea caddies, zippo lighters 1960s records and magazines.

Second Best, Wolvenstraat 18. Good selection of top-notch second hand clobber.

Witte Tanden Winkel, Reestraat 5. For nothing but the tooth—psychedelic and electric toothbrushes, pastes galore, curious aids and sound clinical advice.

Amsterdam: Museums and Galleries

Amsterdam has over 40 museums. You can admire world art treasures, or poke about in back rooms crammed with one hoarder's booty. Most museums (except the Rijksmuseum, Van Gogh and Stedelijk) are closed Mondays, and swarm with schoolchildren on Wednesday afternoons. Many keep Sunday hours on public holidays, but some close entirely.

All but seven of the museums are privately owned and nearly all charge an entrance fee. Most offer discounts to children, but not all offer reductions to students. If you intend visiting more than one or two, the **Annual Museum Card** or **CJP** (youth pass) is a must (*see* **Practical A–Z**, 'Discount Cards', p.186).

A **Museum Boat** will chug you pleasantly along the canals between 16 of Amsterdam's museums. Tickets valid for a day (*f*25) also entitle you to discounts on some admissions. Boats leave every 45 minutes, 10–3.15 daily, from one of six stops: Centraal Station (main boarding point and office, © 622 2181); Prinsengracht/Egelantiersgracht (Anne Frank Huis); Singelgracht (Van Gogh, Stedelijk, Rijksmuseum); Herengracht/Leidsegracht (Bijbels, Fodor, Amsterdams Historisch, Allard Pierson); Amstel/Zwanenburgwal (Rembrandthuis, Jewish Historical); Oosterdok/Kattenburgergracht (Tropenmuseum, Kromhout).

Public Museums and Galleries

Agnietenkapel, Oudezijds Voorburgwal 231, © 525 3339 (*open Mon–Fri 9–5, though phone first to check; adm f3.50*). A 15th-century convent church that houses a specialized and not particularly captivating collection of prints, photographs and ephemera centering on Amsterdam university life. The 15th-century chapel is infinitely more interesting than the collection it houses.

Ajax Museum, Arena Boulevard 3, © 311 1333 (*open daily 9–6; adm f12.50, under-13s f10*). Ephemera relating to Amsterdam's most famous sports team.

Allard Pierson Museum, Oude Turfmarkt 127, © 525 2556 (*open Tues–Fri 10–5 and Sat, Sun 1–5; adm f9.50, children f3*). Superb archaeological collection, poorly presented. Few English texts, but children like the Roman chariot.

Amsterdams Historisch Museum, Kalverstraat 92, © 523 1822 (*open Mon–Fri 10–5, Sat and Sun 11–5; adm f11, under-16s f5.50*). The exhibition is arranged chronologically from Amsterdam's foundation right up to the 20th century and, armed with a file of English explanations of all the exhibits (free from the ticket desk), you can skim round quickly or stop to pick up details about periods that interest you. A map on the ground floor lights up in sections showing different phases of Amsterdam's growth. There's a sudden expansion in the Golden Age and an even

bigger one in the late 20th century, after which all the lights go out with an alarming thud. You can get a bird's-eye view of early Amsterdam from a medieval painting (quite a feat of imagination for an artist who had never been higher than the top of the Oude Kerk tower); see a collection of the surprisingly basic navigational instruments that guided the Dutch East Indiamen all over the world; and push buttons that make period music come out from behind models and paintings. There's a whole room of paintings, banners and relics connected with Amsterdam's 'miracle' (*see* p.231). Up a spiral staircase at the top of the building you can listen to recordings of the city's various carillons and even have a go at playing the one taken from the medieval Munttoren (*see* p.218)—though if you get too carried away an attendant clambers up to glower at you. The museum also stages excellent temporary exhibitions on specialist aspects of Amsterdam's history.

Anne Frank Huis, Prinsengracht 263, © 556 7100 (*open Sept–May Mon–Sat 9–5, Sun 10–5; June–Aug Mon–Sat 9–7, Sun 10–7; adm f10, under-18s f5, under-10s free*). See p.194.

Artis Museum (Zoo Museum), Plantage Kerklaan 38–40, © 523 3400 (*open daily 9–5; adm included in zoo ticket: f23.50, children f15.50*). Slides and stuffed animals in a corner of the zoo.

Aviodome, Schiphol Centre, Schiphol Airport, ✆ 406 8000 (*open Oct–March Tues–Fri 10–5, Sat and Sun noon–5; April–Sept daily 10–5; adm f12.50, under-13s f10*). Aeronautics and space travel. Models from a flimsy 1903 Wright Flyer to American Mercury capsules—some open to clamber in.

Beurs van Berlage Museum, Damrak 277, ✆ 530 4141 (*museum open Tues–Sun 10–4; adm varies*). Berlage's epoch-marking Stock Exchange houses a small display on the history of the building and larger travelling exhibitions. See p.215.

Bijbels Museum (Bible Museum), Herengracht 366, ✆ 624 2436 (*open Mon–Sat 10–5, Sun 1–5; adm f5, under-16s f3.50*). Worth a visit only if you are interested in models of Solomon's temple and the history of the Dutch Bible over the past millennium—though the interior does preserve ceiling paintings by the 18th-century design supremo Jacob de Wit.

COBRA Museum, Sandbergplein 1–3 Amstelveen, Tram 5, 51; ✆ 547 5050 (*open Tues–Sun 11–5; adm f7.50, under-16s f3.50*). Permanent displays and temporary exhibitions focusing on one of the most important modern Dutch art movements (*see* p.201).

Dutch Press Museum, International Institute for Social History, Cruquiusweg 31, ✆ 668 5866 (*open Mon–Fri 9–5, Sat 9.30–1; adm free*). History of the Dutch press through newspapers, leaflets and political literature. Fairly specialized interest.

Elektrische Museumtramlijn (Electric Tramline Museum), Amstelveenseweg 264, ✆ 673 7538 (*open April–Oct Sun 10–6; July–Aug, Tues–Sat 1–4; adm f5 (return), f3 (single), under-12s half-price*). A museum on the move. Antique trams rattle along a 20-minute ride to the Amsterdam Forest.

Geels & Co. Museum, Warmoesstraat 67, ✆ 624 0683 (*open Tue 2–4, Fri and Sat 2–4.30*). Displays devoted to coffee and tea above a shop that sells them both.

Hash & Marijuana Museum, Oudezijds Achterburgwal 148, ✆ 623 5961 (*open daily 11am–10pm; adm f6*). History of dope and dope smoking—every now and again the exhibits are confiscated by the authorities.

Heineken Brewery Museum, Stadhouderskade 78, ✆ 523 9666 (*guided tours only: Mon–Fri 9.30 and 11am; 1 June–15 Sept also at 1 and 2.30pm; Saturdays in July and August also noon and 2pm; adm f2. Tours may be booked out in advance in high season—phone to check*). This is the birthplace of Heineken beer. The brewery, established here in 1867, stopped production on this site only a few years ago when Amsterdam began to drink more than the brewery could produce. Now smart guides lead you through the stables (old dray horses *in situ*) and past huge copper vats. The real purpose of the visit, however, seems to be the free beer at the end of the tour.

Holland Experience, Jodenbreestraat 6, ✆ 422 2233 (*open daily 9am–10pm; adm f17.50 adults, under-12s f15*). A multimedia show that offers 'scent and sound effects' not to mention 80,000 litres of water crashing towards you as a simulated dyke collapses.

Joods Historisch Museum (Jewish Historical Museum), Jonas Daniël Meyerplein 2–4, ✆ 625 4229 (*open daily 11–5, closed Yom Kippur; adm f8, under-18s f3.50, under-10s free*). The Museum's displays do not dwell on gruesome images of the Holocaust and tales of woe, but are a combination of works of art, memorabilia and artefacts aimed at explaining Jewish life. Naturally it is moving to see one of the yellow stars Jews had to wear during the war, but the museum also diffuses a positive energy from the delicately embroidered prayershawls, photographs of barmitzvahs and overwhelmingly extravagant silverware also on show. The 'Jewish identity' displays in the New Synagogue explain aspects of tradition, Zionism and the reaction to persecution. Most of the Great Synagogue is given over to expositions of the religion itself—the rituals, festivals and rites of passage. You can see the original Mikveh (ritual bath) unearthed during the renovations, a cute circumcision set and some stylish modern temple silverware. In the galleries of the Great Synagogue paintings and old documents illustrate the history of Jews in Amsterdam. The connecting walkways house temporary exhibitions and work by Jewish artists (look for Jaap Kaas's fierce, funny bronze monkeys). The museum also has a library and media centre, a kosher café and a good bookshop.

Kattenkabinet (Cat Museum), Herengracht 497, ✆ 626 5378 (*open Mon–Fri 10–2, Sat and Sun 1–5; adm ƒ10*). Art with a feline theme in a restored canal house.

Madame Tussaud's, Peek & Cloppenburg Building, Dam 20, ✆ 622 9949 (*open daily 10–5.30, July and Aug 10–7.30; adm ƒ17.50, under-15s ƒ15, under-5s free, family ticket ƒ57.50*). Here you can see some rather good reconstructions of 17th-century life and a perfectly horrible personified Europe (in a frock made of national flags) who rises from the centre of a tulip to the strains of Beethoven's 'Ode to Joy'. Madame Tussaud disdainfully floats away from it all on a painted cloud.

Max Euwe Centrum, Max Euweplein 30, ✆ 625 7017 (*open Tues–Fri and first Sat of the month 10.30–4; adm free*). Chess memorabilia and the chance to play the game with live people or be beaten by clever computers.

Museum Amstelkring ('Our Lord in the Attic'), Oudezijds Voorburgwal 40, ✆ 624 6604 (*open Mon–Sat 10–5, Sun 1–5; adm ƒ7.50*). *See* p.210.

Museum van Loon, Keizersgracht 672, ✆ 624 5255 (*open Fri–Mon 11–5; adm ƒ7.50*). The most charming of the canal house museums, with a cosy, lived-in atmosphere.

Museum Willet-Holthuysen, Herengracht 605, ✆ 523 1870 (*open Mon–Fri 10–5, Sat and Sun 11–5; adm ƒ7.50, children ƒ3.75*). *See* p.222.

Nationaal Vakbondsmuseum (Trade Unions Museum), Henri Polaklaan 9, ✆ 624 1166 (*open Tues–Fri 11–5, Sat and Sun 1–5; adm ƒ5*). The father of modern Dutch architecture, H. P. Berlage, designed the building in 1900 for Holland's first trade union, the mainly Jewish General Netherlands Diamond Workers' Union (ANDB). Wedding-cake layers of brick arches create a light and airy entrance hall. An ornate *Jugendstil* lamp hangs through the depth of two storeys in the centre of the room. Upstairs there is a cosy panelled boardroom with more metal lanterns, and murals by the Dutch Impressionist Roland Holst. However, you'll have to be severely interested in the Dutch labour movement to appreciate the small exhibitions of photographs, clippings and documents (all in Dutch) in the other room.

Nederlands Filmmuseum, Vondelpark 3, ✆ 589 1400 (*Library open Tues–Fri 10–5, Sat 11–5; adm free*). *See* p.227.

Nederlands Scheepvaart Museum, Kattenburgerplein 1, ✆ 523 2222 (*open Tues–Sun 10–5; adm ƒ14.50, under-18s ƒ8*). The museum shop is well provisioned with books on ships, and is a treasure chest of maritime flotsam and jetsam. In an unmarked room in the cellar a man sells model kits of awesome complexity (*Thurs–Sat only*). *See* p.231 for further details.

Nederlands Theater Instituut, Herengracht 168, ✆ 551 3300 (*open Tues–Fri 11–5, Sat and Sun 1–5; adm ƒ7.50, under-17s ƒ4, under 7s free*). The Nederlands Theater Instituut is in a beautiful canal house (18th-century ceiling paintings by Jacob de Wit) with enticingly presented costumes, scenery and backstage equipment. It always has good exhibitions, usually of the sort where you push buttons or pull levers and make things happen. If there are three of you, you can raise a storm with the wind, thunder and lightning machines on the ground floor.

New Metropolis Science & Technology Center, Oosterdok 2, ✆ (0900) 919 1100 (*open Tues–Sun 10–6, Sat open until 9pm; adm ƒ24, after 4pm ƒ14, under-17s ƒ16*). All sorts of interactive equipment in a giant ship-shaped museum designed by Renzo Piano.

Open Haven Museum, KNSMlaan 311, ✆ 418 5522; bus 32 (*open Wed–Fri 1–5; adm ƒ5*). Journals, uniforms and seafaring paraphernalia celebrating the age of steamship travel.

Pianola Museum, Westerstraat 106, ✆ 627 9624 (*open Sun 1–5 only; adm ƒ7.50*). Pianolas and player-pianos demonstrated using part of a massive hoard of music rolls.

Rembrandthuis, Jodenbreestraat 4–6, ✆ 520 0400 (*open Mon–Sat 10–5, Sun 1–5; adm ƒ7.50, under-17s ƒ5, under-10s free*). *See* p.212.

Rijksmuseum, Stadhouderskade 42, ✆ 674 4700 (*open daily 10–5; adm ƒ15, under-18s ƒ7.50*). *See* p.196.

Sex Museum, Damrak 18, ✆ 622 8376 (*open daily 10am–11.30pm; adm ƒ3.95*). Lurid evidence that the pornographer's imagination has changed remarkably little over the centuries.

Stedelijk Museum, Paulus Potterstraat 13, ☎ 573 2911 (*open daily 11–5; adm ƒ9, under-17s ƒ4.50*). *See* p.200.

Tattoo Museum, Oudezijds Achterburgwal 130, ☎ 625 1565 (*open Tues–Sun noon–6; adm ƒ6*). The Tattoo Museum is not as tacky and sensationalist as one might expect, but a genuinely well-researched survey of the history of tattooing and body art in a variety of cultures.

Tropenmuseum (Tropical Museum), Linnaesusstraat 2, ☎ 568 8200 (*open Mon–Fri 10–5, Sat and Sun noon–5; adm ƒ12.50, under-18s ƒ7.50*). Tapes, models and life-sized installations evoke the atmosphere of what is is like to live in the Third World. This splendid 1920s building also houses exhibits of ethnic musical instruments as well as fascinating reminders of Holland's colonial past.

Van Gogh Museum, Paulus Potterstraat 7, ☎ 570 5200 (*open daily 10–6; adm ƒ12.50, under-18s ƒ5*). *See* p.203.

Verzetsmuseum (Museum of the Resistance), Plantage Kerklaan 61a, ☎ 620 2535 (*open Tues–Fri 10–5, Sat and Sun 1–5; adm ƒ8, under-18s ƒ4*). Newspaper clippings, photographs, tape recordings and makeshift secret equipment give intimate insight into the Resistance movement from the 1940s .

Kromhout (Shipyard Museum), Hoogte Kadijk 147, ☎ 627 6777 (*open Mon–Fri 10–4; adm ƒ3.50, under-12s ƒ1.50*). *See* p.232.

Woonbootmuseum (Houseboat Museum), Prinsengracht opp. 296, ☎ 427 0750 (*open Tues–Sun 10–5; adm ƒ3.75, children under 152 cm ƒ2.50*). A glimpse of the nitty-gritty of life in a houseboat.

Commercial Galleries

There are over 140 commercial art galleries in Amsterdam. They're scattered all over town, though you'll find a number of the more established ones along the Keizersgracht as well as in the Spiegelkwartier.

The listings magazine *What's On in Amsterdam* (ƒ3.50 from the Amsterdam Tourist Board, newsagents and hotels) will guide you to mainstream exhibitions.

For a fuller picture, pick up a copy of *Alert* (ƒ4 from most galleries), the monthly Amsterdam gallery diary. Although this is in Dutch, the pages of photographs, clear symbolic coding and detailed maps give you a good idea of what's showing around town and where to find it.

Look out also for 'Open Atelier' posters—artists working in one neighbourhood will open their studios for a day, and you can wander in for a chat, a look and possibly (they no doubt hope) a happy purchase.

'Open Ateliers' are also listed on the Gallery pages ('Beeldende Kunst') of the *Uitkrant* (a 'what's-on' freebie available at cafés and from the Uit Buro).

Contemporary Art Galleries

Carla Koch, Prinsengracht 510 (*open Wed–Sat noon–6*). Top of the list for arty glass and ceramics.

De Appel, Nieuwe Spiegelstraat 10 (*open Tues–Sun noon–5*). Innovative gallery that shows anything from artsy chairs to artsy videos, from a spectrum that runs from lesser-known artists to famous names.

Galerie Atelier Amsterdam, Weteringschans 221 (*open Mon–Sat 10–5*). Bright and imaginative art from a group of people with mental disabilities, who also have their studio on the premises.

Mokum, Oudezijds Voorburgwal 334 (*open Wed–Sat 11–6*). Dutch realistic art—a good place to find work by Magic Realists.

Rob Jurka, Singel 28 (*open Wed–Sat 1–6*). One-time establishment-rattler Rob Jurka has linked up with go-getting digger-out of new talent Barbara Farber to make one of the most respected galleries on the Amsterdam scene.

SBK Kunstuitleen, Nieuwe Herengracht 23 (*open Tues, Thurs 1–8, Fri 1–5, Sat 9–5*). Art library that hires out original work by Amsterdam artists from ƒ25 per month—and you get the option to buy.

Stedelijk Museum Bureau Amsterdam, Rozenstraat 59 (*open Tues–Sun 11–5*). An offshoot of the museum (*see* p.200) that exhibits and sells work by challenging up-and-coming artists on the international scene.

Swart, Van Breestraat 23 (*open Wed–Sat 3–6*). Swart is run by the queen of the city's art scene. She rules with a rod of iron and her exhibitions seldom fail to excite.

Torch, Lauriergracht 94 (*open Thurs–Sat 2–6*). Torch specializes in video and photography, but it has recently become a leading light in other art forms as well.

W 139, Warmoesstraat 139 (*open Wed–Sun 1–6*). Cavernous space used by fledgling artists. Sometimes the work is dire, sometimes plain curious—but occasionally you'll find a gem, and will seldom be bored. (At present W 139 is *undergoing extensive rebuilding, so not all of the gallery will be open.*)

Some Specialists

ABK (Amsterdam Sculptors' Collective) (*open Thurs–Sun 12–5*). The sixty members (some of the city's best young sculptors among them) keep the gallery well supplied. Exhibitions change frequently. Most work is on sale and not all of it is of a size to preclude taking it home in your overnight bag.

Animation Art, Berenstraat 19 (*open Tues–Fri 11–6, Sat 10–5*). Original drawings of everyone from Popeye to Betty Boop.

The Frozen Fountain, Prinsengracht 629 (*open Mon 1–6, Tues–Fri 10–6, Sat 11–5, Thurs open until 9pm*). Household items from wastepaper baskets to sofas elevated to high art.

Amsterdam: Food and Drink

Erasmus, the great 16th-century Dutch humanist and man of letters, was pleased to note that his fellow countrymen were not given to much wild or ferocious behaviour, treachery or deceit, indeed were 'not prone to any serious vices except, that is, a little given to pleasure, especially to feasting'. Two centuries later the national ability to tuck in and drink up was still impressive enough to shock the British—themselves no mean feasters. In 1703 the seven or so deacons of the Arnhem guild of surgeons dispatched, at one sitting, 14lb of beef, 8lb of veal, six fowl, stuffed cabbages, apples, pears, bread, pretzels, assorted nuts, 20 bottles of red wine, 12 bottles of white wine and some jugs of coffee. Today, eating is still a supreme Dutch enthusiasm, and one in which any visitor can happily join.

Paradoxically, native Dutch cuisine is not all that inspiring. The Dutch culinary clichés are *hutspot* ('hotchpotch'), a well-boiled stew that was much appreciated by starving citizens after the siege of Leiden and to be enjoyed still requires a similar state of ravenousness; and *erwtensoep*, a porridgy pea soup which comes (vegetarians beware) with bits of sausage floating in it and a side dish of bread and raw bacon. The quality of *erwtensoep* is judged by testing whether or not your spoon will stand up on its own in the middle of the bowl. These are the staples of many a 'tourist menu', but (like the English) the Dutch have recently begun to explore more exciting avenues in their local cuisine—with game and fish especially. Other palatable traditional foods include *pannekoeken* (pancakes) with sweet or savoury fillings, and *haring* (herring) eaten raw by tossing your head back and dropping a whole fillet down your throat. If you can stomach it, this is a marvellous cure for a hangover. *Belegde broodjes* are crusty rolls filled with a delicious variety of fillings—travellers' tales of sliced beef layered on buttered bread predated anecdotes about Lord Sandwich's invention by about a century. Waffles, dripping with syrup or smothered with fruit and cream, are sold on the streets and are treacherously gooey and unmanageable, but quite irresistible. Cones of *frites* (potato chips), usually with a large dollop of mayonnaise, are ubiquitous. They're normally cooked with good-quality potatoes in clean oil.

In the absence of a stimulating local tradition, Dutch chefs have looked further afield. French cuisine first came into fashion during the Napoleonic occupation, and remains the cornerstone of many of the best kitchens. Nowadays most menus are tantalizingly eclectic, showing influences from Japan, Indonesia, Surinam and Turkey. This makes for some curious—but usually delicious—combinations. Don't be surprised to find peanut sauce, saffron pasta and oysters on the same menu. The Dutch were enjoying 'fusion cuisine' years before trendy London and New York chefs could distinguish lemon grass from lime leaves.

Ingredients are usually market-fresh and microwave cookers are pleasingly thin on the ground. Food is cooked to order in most restaurants, so expect an unhurried meal. The Dutch eat early in the evening—between 7 and 9pm—and many kitchens are closed by 10 or 11pm.

Specialist ethnic restaurants are well represented. Reasonable Indian and Italian food is to be had all over town, with Thai and Japanese restaurants an increasingly popular alternative. It's the culinary heritage of Holland's imperial past, however, that makes for the best ethnic binge. Treat yourself to an Indonesian *rijsttafel*—a personal banquet of rice or noodles with myriad spicy side dishes.

Vegetarians will have a difficult time. The Dutch are great carnivores, and if you enquire about vegetarian dishes you're often offered *kabeljauw* (cod). However, in the 1970s the tastes of the hippies spawned a few vegetarian restaurants and more have opened recently. Chefs in better kitchens are beginning to be more imaginative with their vegetarian options, and most restaurants will have at least one vegetarian meal on the menu.

Budget eating is easy, and needn't be boring. Many restaurants offer a three-course 'Tourist Menu' for under ƒ30, but you're generally better off looking out for signs advertising a *dagschotel* (dish of the day). For this, you will usually end up with an oversized white plate with some well-prepared meat and a constellation of pickles and salads. Many cafés serve food—menus change daily and often offer the best value of all (*see* 'Cafés', below). Best bet budget restaurants: **Axum** (Central), **Keuken van 1870** (Central), **La Place** (Central), **Moeders Pot** (Central).

Takeaway foodstalls punctuate markets and shopping streets all over town. As well as *frites*, *haring* and waffles you can sample all sorts of foreign delights: Turkish kebabs, Israeli falafel, Japanese sushi and spicy nibbles from Surinam and Indonesia. Under signs flashing *Automatiek* you can select a deep-fried croquette from a row of tiny windows displaying this and similar wares: drop in your ƒ1.50, pull a lever and collect your reward. 'Snack' was originally a Dutch word. Snack Bars are the Amsterdam equivalent of street food. At worst they sell pre-prepared mushy croquettes, but at best they are tiny family-run establishments that hover in the middle ground between restaurant and takeaway. Often run by immigrants, they have simple décor, a scattering of tables and some of the best foreign food in town. Try **Bird** (Thai; Zeedijk 77), **Kismet** (Turkish; Albert Cuypstraat 64), **Maoz** (Israeli falafel; Reguliersbreestraat 45), **Riaz** (Surinam; Bilderdijkstraat 193).

Amsterdam is very much a cash city. Many smaller restaurants don't accept credit cards, and there's an air of reluctance about those that do. Even some of the larger establishments don't like plastic—so it's always a good idea to check in advance. Feasting Amsterdammers and hungry tourists fill up most good restaurants pretty quickly, so it is also a good policy to reserve a table by telephone.

restaurant prices

The restaurants below are all graded according to the approximate price of a three-course meal, without wine. You'll find eating out cheaper than in most large cities.

∞∞	**expensive**	over ƒ80 (though seldom more than ƒ175)
∞	**moderate**	ƒ45–ƒ80
◊	**cheap**	under ƒ45

The bill will include tax and a 15% service charge—though if you feel you've been well looked after you can leave a little extra. It's usual to leave behind any small change (or round up larger bills to the nearest ƒ5). It's worth checking out expensive restaurants, even if they seem above your budget, as many offer special three- or four-course meals for between ƒ45 and ƒ75.

Restaurants

The following list is a very personal selection from the hundreds of good restaurants Amsterdam has to offer. An exploratory wander around the Jordaan, through the alleys that crisscross the canals (from Reestraat to Huidenstraat), or along Utrechtsestraat will reveal even more. Restaurants are listed in three areas. 'Central' refers to the semi-circle bounded by the three main canals; the Jordaan is the area in the west of the city, just beyond the canals. Restaurants in the north, south and east will be found under 'Further Afield'.

Breitner, Amstel 212, ✆ 627 7879 (*open till midnight; closed Sun, Mon*). An even more sublime view than from the Excelsior, with a menu that is perhaps even more imaginative. The relaxedly chic atmosphere and excellent cuisine are a great attraction to artistes from the Opera House. *f*95.

Excelsior, Hotel l'Europe, Nieuwe Doelenstraat 2–8, ✆ 531 1705. Grand without being pompous. Waiters in tails bring you haute cuisine classics or the very best in new Dutch cooking, and there's a superb view over the Amstel. *f*110. Dress: jacket and tie.

Sichuan Food, Reguliersdwarsstraat 35, ✆ 626 9327. Proud possessor of the first Michelin star awarded to a Chinese restaurant in the Netherlands. Aperitifs made from flowers, sautéed oysters with tangy sauces; local western restaurants are beginning to imitate the seafood dishes. *f*90.

De Silveren Spiegel, Kattengat 4–6, ✆ 624 6589. The building is all Delft tiles and cosy corners and dates from 1614. The visionary chef comes up with such dishes as guinea fowl with rose petal sauce, and uses prime local ingredients, such as lamb from the North Sea island of Texel (where the creatures frolic freely and eat wild herbs). Service is personal and friendly. *f*80.

't Swarte Schaep, Korte Leidsedwarsstraat 24, ✆ 622 3021. Up a steep staircase in a 300-year-old building with oak beams, antiques, superb wines, an eclectic cuisine. More than likely you might pass a member of the Dutch royal family here. *f*90.

De Utrechtsedwarstafel, Utrechtsedwarsstraat 107, 625 4189 (*closed Sun, Mon*). There's no menu, just a grid offering three, four or five courses, at a simple, medium or gourmet level. Wine is included in the price. You pick your level, tell them if there is anything you prefer not to eat, and wait to see what you get. Tailor-making choices as you go along. On a matrix, from *f*60 to *f*180, with wines included.

Van Harte, Hartenstraat 24, ✆ 625 8500. Modest, yet excellent kitchen. Berries and wild mushrooms in the sauces, tender meats and charming service. *f*75.

Vasso, Rozenboomsteeg 12–14, ✆ 626 0158. Fresh pasta and fine Italian food in a restaurant that has the lively atmosphere of the kitchens of a faded palazzo. *f*75.

D'Vijff Vlieghen (The Five Flies), Spuistraat 294–302, ✆ 624 8369. An intriguing conglomeration of antique-filled rooms in a wonky 17th-century inn. It gets its name from the original owner, Jan Vijff Vlieghen. In the 1950s and 1960s it was frequented by the likes of Orson Welles, Benjamin Britten, Jean Cocteau and Walt Disney. These days the restaurant rests on its laurels, and doesn't give good value for money. *f*90.

le Klas, Platform 2b, Centraal Station, ✆ 625 0131. Well-prepared (though not adventurous) Dutch fare in the beautifully restored First Class restaurant. *f*60.

Centra, Lange Niezel 29, ✆ 622 3050. Busy, garish, cafeteria-like atmosphere, and the best Spanish food in town. *f*40.

De Compagnon, Guldehandsteeg 17, ✆ 620 4225. Nip down an alley in the red-light district, pass through a green door and you will find a series of tiny rooms, perched on top of each other, filled with antique bric-à-brac, and with views across the little harbour on the Damrak. An unexpected find, romantic and intimate—but sadly the atmosphere outdoes the cuisine, which is run-of-the-mill Franco-Dutch. *f*75.

Hemelse Modder, Oude Waal 9, ✆ 624 3203 (*closed Mon*). Before you get to the divine chocolate mousse that gives the restaurant its name (Heavenly Mud), try some of the delicious fish or vegetarian dishes. *f*55.

Kort, Amstelveld 2, ✆ 626 1199. Freshly prepared food with simple sauces. Quiet terrace on the water's edge, and a coolly rational Wiener Werkstätte interior. *f*60.

∞ **Krua Thai**, Spuistraat 90a, ☎ 620 0623. After much audible campery in the kitchen, spectacular dishes issue forth. The hot-and-spicy beef salad is unbeatable, and the stuffed chicken wings divine. ƒ60.

∞ **Maison Descartes**, Vijzelgracht 2, ☎ 622 4936. Excellent regional French cuisine in the depths of the French cultural institute, surrounded by the Delft tiles of a 17th-century Dutch kitchen. ƒ75.

∞ **Memories of India**, Reguliersdwarstraat 88, ☎ 623 5710. Top-class Indian cuisine in curious post-modern surrounds: copper palm trees and stubs of marble column. ƒ65.

∞ **Pier 10**, De Ruyterkade Steiger 10 (behind Centraal Station), ☎ 624 8276. A little wooden hut, once a shipping line office, on the end of a pier in the IJ. Watch the boats chug past as you devour scrumptious Dutch/French food. ƒ70.

∞ **Rose's Cantina**, Reguliersdwarsstraat 38, ☎ 625 9797. Crowds of Bright Young Things, tasty Tex-Mex food and lethal margaritas. ƒ50.

∞ **Saturnino**, Reguliersdwarsstraat 5h, ☎ 639 0102. Italian restaurant on Amsterdam's main gay street. The atmopshere is glitzy, but the food has a wholesome home-made touch. ƒ50.

∞ **Sluizer Visrestaurant**, Utrechtsestraat 45; and **Sluizer**, Utrechtsestraat 41–3, ☎ 622 6376. Two adjacent trendy restaurants, evocative of the thirties with marble-topped tables and fringed lamps. The fish restaurant especially has a good reputation. ƒ65.

∞ **d'Theeboom**, Singel 210, ☎ 623 8420. Georges Thubert scorns rip-off prices and culinary pretension. He runs his restaurant, in a converted canalside warehouse, in classic French style, and offers excellent value and fine cooking. ƒ50.

∞ **Tujuh Maret**, Utrechtsestraat 73, ☎ 427 9865 Treat yourself to a flavoursome feast of Indonesian *rijsttafel*. The *soto ayam* (chicken broth) has a fine bouillon base, and the different chicken and meat dishes are just that—different. ƒ60.

∞ **Turquoise**, Wolvenstraat 22–4, ☎ 624 2026. A bizarre combination of wood-panelled Art Nouveau décor and Turkish cuisine. Under

Tiffany lamps, beside cherubs rampant, you can tuck into a feast made up of different starters or try such main courses as chicken breast with cheese and garlic. Warm, friendly service. ƒ55.

∞ **Le zinc...et les dames**, Prinsengracht 999, ☎ 622 9044 (*closed Mon*). Converted 17th-century warehouse adorned with portraits of women. The clientele may all seem under 25 and on their first date, but the French cuisine is robust and tasty, with dishes from various regions and wines by the glass to match. ƒ75.

∞ **Zuid Zeeland**, Herengracht 413, ☎ 624 3154 (*closed Sat and Sun*). Specializes in fish dishes from Belgium and the south of Holland, but also meat dishes with a French and Japanese influence. ƒ65.

◇ **Anda Nugraha**, Waterlooplein 339, ☎ 626 6046. Tasty home-cooked Indonesian food. *Rijsttafel* ƒ45 for 2 people.

◇ **Axum**, Utrechtsedwarsstraat 85–7, ☎ 622 8389. Authentic Ethiopian cuisine—a giant communal pancake and a few sizzling pots of stew and curry. Add salad and yoghurt sauce, and a spoon of stew, and roll up mouth-sized bites with your fingers. Appropriately ethnic décor and utterly charming service. ƒ35.

◇ **Balthazar's Keuken**, Elandsgracht 108, ☎ 420 2114 (*open Wed–Fri*). The kitchen takes up a third of the room, and diners crowd around a few small wooden tables. Starters are usually *meze*-style: cockles with ginger and parsley or red-pepper salad with anise pepperoni. There's a fish-or-flesh choice for the main course. ƒ45.

◇ **De Blauwe Hollander**, Leidsekruisstraat 28, ☎ 623 3014. Cheap and cheerful, if heavy, Dutch cooking. ƒ30.

◇ **Bird**, Zeedijk 77, ☎ 420 6289. Tiny Thai snack bar with a kitchen one end, a trendy crowd and tantalizing Thai cuisine. ƒ25.

◇ **Casa di David**, Singel 426, ☎ 624 5093. Pizzeria with wooden beams and canalside charm. The food is good too—pasta made on the premises, excellent antipasti, and fragrant, crusty pizzas cooked in a wood-burning oven. Pizzas around ƒ20.

Et Alors, Nes 35, ℗ 421 6056. Run by two sisters smack in the heart of the alternative theatre district. The small restaurant is decorated with a comfortable clutter of old furniture picked up on their treks through France and all of it is for sale. The cuisine is unpretentious French fare, with a cared-for, home-cooked touch. ƒ40

Goodies, Huidenstraat 9, ℗ 625 6122. Arty hangout that sells good sandwiches and salads by day, and pasta by night. ƒ30.

Haesje Claes, Spuistraat 273–5, ℗ 624 9998. Touristy, but unhurried. Folksy Old Dutch interior, solid tasty Dutch food, including plenty of salad and vegetables. Tourist menu ƒ30.

Keuken van 1870, Spuistraat 4, ℗ 624 8965 (*kitchen closes 8pm weekdays, 9pm Sat, Sun*). This began as a soup kitchen way back in 1870. Today punks, pensioners and passing backpackers come in for huge, tastily cooked meals for under ƒ17.

Pancake Bakery, Prinsengracht 191, ℗ 625 1333. The best pancakes in town. Sweet and savoury pancakes from ƒ8.50.

La Place, Rokin 162, ℗ 620 2364. A great salad bar, fresh pastas and grilled meats cooked while you wait. Most of the ingredients are organic, you sit in one of a honeycomb of rooms in an atmospheric 17th-century building—and it's cheap. ƒ30.

Song Kwae, Kloveniersburgwal 14, ℗ 624 2568. The place to go for Thai food when you can't squeeze into Bird (*see* above). Lots more space, and good food too. ƒ30.

Surinam Express, Halvemaansteeg 18, ℗ 622 7405. Tiny sandwich shop off Rembrandtplein with searingly authentic Surinamese food—spicy vegetable and tangy curry fillings. Eat fuller meals too, at a counter along the wall. ƒ25.

Upstairs Pannekoekhuis, Grimburgwal 2, ℗ 626 5603. Teeny pancake parlour suspended above a bustling lane. From ƒ10.

Woeste Walmen, Singel 46, ℗ 638 0765 (*open Sat and Sun only*). Decorated with quirky flair and run by squatters who come up with food that they have obviously enjoyed cooking. Usually one meat and one non-meat option for the main course. ƒ30.

Jordaan

Christophe, Leliegracht 46, ℗ 625 0807. Superb French cuisine enlivened by zesty north-African flavours. A little stuffy. ƒ100.

Caramba, Lindengracht 342, ℗ 627 1188. Lively South American restaurant where an arty crowd consumes tortilla and vicious margaritas. ƒ45.

De Eettuin, 2ᵉ Tuindwarsstraat 10, ℗ 623 7706. Forests of greenery, generous Dutch portions and a modest salad bar. ƒ30.

De Luwte, Leliegracht 26, ℗ 625 8548. Romantic candlelit restaurant overlooking a small canal. Delicious meals made with fresh (often organic) ingredients. ƒ55.

Pathum, Willemsstraat 16, ℗ 624 4936 (*closed Tues*). Inexpensive Thai place with cheerful atmosphere. ƒ40.

Speciaal, Nieuwe Leliestraat 142, ℗ 624 9706. Reputedly the best Indonesian in town. *Rijsttafel* ƒ50.

Stoop, 1ᵉ Anjeliersdwarsstraat 4, ℗ 639 2480. Small, busy restaurant: pastrami salad with ginger and yoghurt dressing, Peking duck with a chutney of aubergines and dried figs. ƒ55.

Ristorante Toscanini, Lindengracht 75, ℗ 623 2813 (*closed Tues*). Cavernous, rowdy and very Italian. A gastric and sensual delight, but service is exceeding slow. ƒ50.

Moeders Pot (Mother's Cooking), Vinkenstraat 119, ℗ 623 7643. A one-person affair run by a huge hairy man. Meat and ten veg for under ƒ20.

∞∞ **Beddington's**, Roelof Hartstraat 6–8, ℗ 676 5201 (*closed Mon*). Austere décor, but sumptuous meals by a chef with culinary experience from Derbyshire, the Far East and the summits of French *haute cuisine*. *f*95.

∞∞ **Ciel Bleu**, Okura Hotel, Ferdinand Bolstraat 333, ℗ 678 7111. On the 23rd floor with wonderful views. The cuisine is appropriately haut. *f*120. Dress: jacket and tie.

∞∞ **De Gouden Reael**, Zandhoek 14, ℗ 623 3883. A 17th-century house on a quayside in the Western Islands. Renowned for its French provincial cuisine—a different area every three months. *f*75.

∞∞ **De Groene Lanteerne**, Haarlemmerstraat 43, ℗ 624 1952. The narrowest restaurant in the world, run by a couple who are renowned for their hearty French fare. *f*75.

∞∞ **De Knijp**, Van Baerlestraat 134, ℗ 671 4248 (*open till midnight*). Fresh oysters are a speciality. *f*75.

∞∞ **Vis aan de Schelde**, Scheldeplein 4, ℗ 675 1583. Minimalist décor. Fish comes perfectly cooked: marinated salmon with asparagus steeped in vanilla and orange, tuna with just a tinge of pink, meltingly soft monkfish, excellent *bouillabaisse*, tuna in a red-wine and flageolet bean sauce. *f*100.

∞∞ **Yamazato**, Hotel Okura, Ferdinand Bolstraat 333, ℗ 678 7111. Superb Japanese cuisine, exquisitely presented. *f*110.

∞∞ **Yoichi**, Weteringschans 128, ℗ 622 6829. Amsterdam's oldest Japanese restaurant, and still one of the best. Traditional food, high prices. *f*80.

∞ **Basak**, Frans Halsstraat 89, ℗ 664 9534. Unassuming Turkish restaurant serving tasty casseroles and grills accompanied by heaps of salad. *f*45.

∞ **La Brasa**, Haarlemmerdijk 16, ℗ 625 4438. One of the more intimate of the Argentinian grills. Cow-hide seats and juicy beef on a wood grill. *f*55.

∞ **Griet Manshande**, Keerpunt 10, ℗ 622 8194. The daily selection includes anything from *coq au vin* to roast skate with *beurre noir*. Friendly service and skilled cooking. *f*55.

∞ **Bodega Keyzer**, Van Baerlestraat 96, ℗ 671 1441 (*closed Sun; open till midnight*). Next to the Concertgebouw. Writers and musicians have been coming here for nearly a century to eat smoked eel and fresh sole. *f*55.

∞ **Kilimanjaro**, Rapenburgerplein 6, ℗ 622 3485. Fish soup from Guinea, crocodile from Senegal, Tanzanian red snapper curry and Castle lager from South Africa, home-made ginger beer or hibiscus and baobab cocktail. *f*50.

∞ **The Movies**, Haarlemmerdijk 159, ℗ 626 7069. Crowded restaurant attached to an old Art Deco cinema offers challenging concoctions such as red bass with kumquats. *f*50.

∞ **De Ondeugd**, Ferdinand Bolstraat 15, ℗ 672 0651. Just minutes from the Albert Cuyp market: the fish and vegetables are alarmingly fresh. *f*50.

∞ **Sparks**, Willemsparkweg 87, ℗ 676 0700. Friendly neighbourhood brasserie, with a small garden courtyard, understated décor, and inspired Mediterranean cooking. *f*75.

∞ **De Vrolijke Abrikoos** (The Jolly Apricot), Weteringschans 76, ℗ 624 4672 (*closed Tues*). Pastel shades, pine tables and bio-dynamic ingredients combined with subtlety and flair: giant roast mushroom with a creamy sauce, delicate oriental soups, or bass with a robust tomato sauce. There are tables outside in the garden. *f*45.

∞ **De Witte Uyl**, Frans Halsstraat 26, ℗ 670 0458. Big tables, comfortable chairs, a carefully chosen wine list, and a menu of imaginative medium-sized dishes. *f*80.

∞ **Witteveen**, Ceintuurbaan 256–8, ℗ 662 4368. Vast red, black and gilt interior, dressed-up waiters, and tables smothered with white linen. Formal setting for some of the best traditional Dutch cooking in town. *f*70.

Zabars, Van Baerlestraat 49, 679 8888. It doesn't look much from the outside, but inside you'll find a cheery crowd enjoying wonderfully flavourful Mediterranean food: Moroccan lamb casserole or crunchy Greek halva. *f*80.

Arena, 's Gravesandestraat 51, *Ø* 694 7444. Budget travellers chomp their way through stews and other tummy-filling fare in café-like surrounds. The occasional cloud of hashish smoke wafts by. *f*20.

Kong Kha, Rijnstraat 87, *Ø* 661 2578. Small, bustling restaurant and takeaway, with authentic Thai home cooking. Well worth a short ride on the number 4 tram. The fishcakes are delicious, and the chicken and coconut soup sweet and soothing. *f*25.

Riaz, Bilderdijkstraat 193, *Ø* 683 6453. Great Surinamese curries, eaten with rice or *roti*—a pancake in which you roll up your food, then eat it with your fingers. *f*30.

Waroeng Asje, Jan Pieter Heijestraat 180, *Ø* 616 6589. Surinamese/Indonesian takeaway with a few tables close to the Vondelpark. The *soto soep* (spicy meat-and-veg soup with a bowl of rice alongside, *f*7) is great value and a meal in itself. *f*25.

Vegetarian

Zest, Prinsenstraat 10, *Ø* 428 2455. Trendy with good vegetarian choices: Thai risotto with sugarsnap peas and mushrooms. *f*55.

Bolhoed, Prinsengracht 60, *Ø* 626 1803. Exotic Thai statues, quirky lamps, bright colours (soft lighting). The cuisine has a Mexican touch, and is imaginative and tasty. There are vegan dishes available, fish too, and the daily special three-course menu (*f*30) is excellent value. *f*35.

Golden Temple, Utrechtsestraat 126, *Ø* 626 8560. With simple décor and tasty Indian food, this has more going for it that the usual Amsterdam veggie. Vegan options. *f*30.

Sisters, Nes 102. *Ø* 626 3970. Close to the Historial Museum, this is a busy and extremely popular restaurant, serving budget vegetarian food. *f*25.

De Vliegende Schotel (The Flying Saucer) Nieuwe Leliestraat 162. *Ø* 625 2041. The Flying Saucer is one of the best budget restaurants in the city. Plenty of space and large portions to match. *f*25.

De Waaghals, Frans Halsstraat 29, *Ø* 679 9609. Vegetarian cuisine with organic ingredients and international influences: Tunisian bean casserole, coconut and aubergine soup. Flavours sometimes rather bland. *f*45.

Restaurants that put special effort and imagination into the vegetarian options on the menu are: **Hemelse Modder** (Central); **Woeste Walmen** (Central); **De Luwte** (Jordaan); **De Vrolijke Abrikoos** (Further Afield); **Griet Manshande** (Further Afield).

Late Night

Some of these restaurants stay open until midnight: Further Afield: **Bodega Keyser** and **De Knijp**; Central: **Koriander**, **Sluizer** and **Saturnino**.

The downstairs Diner at the **Holland Casino** is open until 2am and serves good food. You don't need a ticket to get in here, either. **Bojo**, Lange Leidsedwarsstraat 51, is an Indonesian restaurant open until 2am (weekdays) and 5.30am (Fri and Sat). Be prepared to wait, though, as the service is not exactly what you would call zippy. **Maoz**, Reguliersbreestraat, near Tuschinski Cinema, serves scrumptious *falafel* and salads all through the night. **Gary's Late-Nite Bagel Shop**, Reguliersdwarsstraat 53, sells genuine New York bagels, cheesecake and muffins until the wee hours.

Cafés are at the centre of an Amsterdammer's social life. Wooden floors and furniture, and walls stained by years of cigarette smoke, have inspired the name 'brown café'. Here you can have a drink or just a coffee, nibble snacks or plough through hefty meals. But most of all you sit and talk, or while away the time leafing through the day's papers or glossy magazines. There's seldom any grating background music—though in friendly neighbourhood bars the clientele may burst into song.

The term 'café' covers a wide range of establishments. At one end of the spectrum are the poky bars, where you go to knock back a few beers (with the odd *jenever* chaser); you might also be able to buy bread rolls, *tostis* (pale toasted sandwiches) or *bitterballen* (balls of meat purée, coated in breadcrumbs and deep-fried). At the other end you'll find enormous, airy **grand cafés** and places that offer such sumptuous fare that they're really indistinguishable from small restaurants. These often call themselves *eetcafés* (literally 'eating cafés') or even *petit restaurant cafés*. Some rather startling newcomers made an appearance during the 1980s: the **designer bars** are the complete antithesis of the brown café—hard metal furniture, bright light and colours and loud music—but are now part of the Amsterdam scene.

Most Amsterdammers drink beer. Ordering *een Pils* at the bar will get you a small glass of lager topped with a finger or two of froth. Or you might prefer a *jenever* (Dutch gin—oilier and weaker than its British counterpart, with a whiff of juniper berries). In this case ask for a *borrel*. You can have either *oud* (old—more mellow) or *jong* (young—sharper). *Jenever* may also be flavoured: *citroenjenever* (lemon) or *besenjenever* (blackberry) are popular. Ask for a *kamelenrug* (camel's back) and your glass will be filled to the rim. Traditionally, you knock back all of your *jenever* with a single gulp. Should you require both beer and gin simultaneously, request a *kopstoot* (literally 'knock on the head'). On freezing winter's days a quick visit to a *proeflokaal* will warm your blood. These were once free tasting-houses attached to spirit-merchants and taphouses. These days you have to pay, but the procedure is much the same: walk in, drink up, walk out.

Coffeeshops serve tea, coffee and wonderful cakes and pastries. Sometimes they serve snacks and fuller meals, but never alcohol. Tea is seldom served with milk, unless you ask for it. Coffee will come black or with strange processed *koffiemelk*, unless you order *koffieverkeerd* (literally 'coffee wrong'), in which case you'll get a delicious 50:50 mixture with fresh milk. Since the 1970s some coffeeshops (the so-called **smoking coffeeshops**) have openly sold marijuana. These are easily distinguishable at first glance/sniff. They are painted psychedelic colours, often have leaf designs on the windows and emit loud music and fazed customers.

Café-crawling is one of the best ways to discover Amsterdam: between museum visits, on rainy afternoons, on long, hot summer evenings. There are nearly 1,500 cafés, and you're sure to rootle out a few favourites for yourself. Most cafés close at 1 or 2am at weekends. They begin opening their doors around 11am, though some don't get it together until 3 or 4pm. An asterisk (*) indicates cafés particularly recommended for their food. The letters in the margins are there to give you some indication of where the café is: **C**—the central area bounded by the main canals; **J**—the Jordaan and northwestern Amsterdam; **S**—south and southeast of the centre.

(C) **In't Aepjen**, Zeedijk 1. A 'rariteitencafé', crammed with antiques.

(C) ***AmTricain***, American Hotel, Leidseplein. Splendid Art Deco grand café.

(C) ***Aas van Bokalen***, Keizersgracht 335. Arty brown café.

(J) ***Belhamel***, Brouwersgracht 60. Art Nouveau décor on a pretty canal.

(C) ***Eetcafé Van Beeren***, Koningsstraat 54, ✆ 622 2329. Quiet neighbourhood café with an imaginative chef.

(J) **De Blaffende Vis**, Westerstraat 118. Cheery café on the Westerstraat.

(C) **Cul de Sac**, Oudezijds Voorburgwal 99. Down a side alley—one of the few good bars in the red-light district.

(C) **Dantzig**, Zwanenburgwal 15. Attractive corner of the ugly Stadhuis. A grand café that frequently fills with wedding parties.

(C) **De Druif**, Rapenburg 83 (near the Maritime Museum). Dates from 1631.

(J) **Dulac**, Haarlemmerstraat 118. Fantasy grand café, inspired by the French fairy-tale illustrator Edmund Dulac.

(S) ***De Duvel***, 1ᵉ van der Helststraat 59–61. Busy café with a large terrace near the Albert Cuyp market.

(C) ***1ᵉ Klas*** (First Class), Platform 2b, Centraal Station. Lose yourself here in the great age of rail travel.

(C) **Eik en Linde**, Plantage Middenlaan 22 (near Zoo). Brown café with mixed, arty crowd.

(C) **Eland**, Prinsengracht 296. Traditional old brown café.

(C) ***Engelbewaarder***, Kloveniersburgwal 59. Writers gulp down pasta and scribble away on wooden tables. Heated discussions about art and life echo from the corners.

(J) **De Gijs**, Lindengracht 249. Tiny eccentric two-tier bar.

(C) **Gollem**, Raamsteeg 4. Home of a hundred (or more) beers.

(S) ***De Groene Olifant*** (The Green Elephant), Sarphatistraat 510. Cosy bar flooded with light. The folk are friendly and the food delicious.

(C) **Het Hok**, Lange Leidsedwarsstraat 134. A refuge from the hordes, filled with quiet people playing chess.

(S) **Hollandse Manege Café**, Vondelstraat 140. Overlooks an exquisite 19th-century riding school arena.

(C) **Hoppe**, Spui 18–20. Dates from 1670. Busy after work.

(C) ***Huyschkamer***, Utrechtsestraat 137. Trendy café in a former male brothel.

(S) **De IJsbreker**, Weesperzijde 23. Attached to the contemporary music venue. Tranquil riverside terrace.

(C) ***De Jaren***, Nieuwe Doelenstraat 20. Light and airy grand café. Home of the arts and media set.

(C) **Karpershoek**, Martelaarsgracht 2. Claims to be Amsterdam's oldest café.

(J) **De Kat in de Wijngaert**, Lindengracht 160. Quiet and friendly.

(J) **Koophandel**, Bloemgracht 49. Converted warehouse that fills up around midnight and throbs till dawn.

(C) ***Kort***, Amstelveld 2. Modern café with a quiet canalside terrace.

(C) **De Kroon Royal Café**, Rembrandtplein 17. Historic meeting place of variety artistes and agents, with a view over Rembrandtplein.

(C) **Luxembourg**, Spui 22–4. Grand café that attracts well-heeled office workers.

(C) ***Het Molenpad***, Prinsengracht 653. A brown café that sometimes crams a live jazz band into one corner. A smoky, dreamy place to while away a Sunday afternoon.

(J) **Nol**, Westerstraat 109. Outrageously kitsch bar. Locals, gangsters and visitors get swept into singsongs.

(C) **L'Opera**, Rembrandtplein 19. Sedate Art Deco café on a bustling square.

(C) **Papeneiland**, Prinsengracht 2. Built in 1642, with a secret passage across the canal.

(C) **De Prins**, Prinsengracht 124. Pretty canalside pub popular with students.

(C) ***Van Puffelen**, Prinsengracht 377. Sawdust on the floor, and cherubs on the ceiling. A good restaurant at the back, a terrace on a barge on the canal in front. Smart clientele.

(J) **Rooie Nelis**, Laurierstraat 101. A Jordaan institution. Bursting with locals and visitors having a good time.

(J) ***Rosereijn**, Haarlemmerdijk 52. Cosy brown café with a good selection of magazines and cheap, tasty food.

(C) ***Schiller**, Rembrandtplein 26. Cosy Art Deco bar tucked away from the rumpus of Rembrandtplein. Excellent cuisine.

(J) **'t Smalle**, Egelantiersgracht 12. An 18th-century *proeflokaal* converted into brown café. Gets packed most evenings.

(J) **De Tuin**, 2e Tuindwarsstraat 13. Dim light, plenty of board games and more than just a twinge of eccentricity. An unpretentious classic brown café.

(C) **Twee Prinsen**, Prinsenstraat 27. The Twee Prinsen has a heated terrace and a friendly, alternative crowd who profess great rivalry with the 'yuppies' at the **Vergulde Gaper** on the opposite corner.

(C) **Twee Zwaantjes**, Prinsengracht 114. You can get electric organ music here as well as unforgettable big ladies with even bigger voices from the Jordaan.

(S) ***Vertigo**, Vondelpark 3. Wonderful terrace on Vondelpark as well as a cosy cellar underneath the Film Museum.

(C) ***De Waag**, in the old weighing house on Nieuwemarkt. Vast candlelit café, decorated with medieval austerity.

(C) **Welling**, J. W. Brouwerstraat 32. Traditional brown café which is convenient for the Concertgebouw.

(C) **De Wetering**, Weteringstraat 37. A real log fire in winter and an ancient television for crucial football matches.

(S) **Wildschut**, Roelof Hartplein 1–3. Art Deco interior with a noisy and smoky, but none the less popular, terrace.

Designer Bars

(C) **Esprit**, Spui 10. Aluminium and plateglass for the trendy.

(S) **Krull**, Corner of 1e van der Helststraat and 1e Jan Steenstraat. Friendly café near the Albert Cuyp market.

(C) ***Morlang**, Keizersgracht 451. Brittle, trendier-than-thou atmosphere, but good food.

(C) ***Het Land van Walem**, Keizersgracht 449. Friendlier than the Morlang next door, with a bigger terrace and a garden at the back.

(C) **Schuim**, Spuistraat 189. Shop-window café full of students during the day, and artsy types at night who admire their friends' paintings.

(C) **Seymour Likely Lounge**, Nieuwezijds Voorburgwal 250. Real creation of a fictitious artist, and one of the trendiest spots in town.

Proeflokaalen

On freezing winter's days there are no better places to visit to warm your blood before continuing on with your journey.

(C) **De Admiraal**, Herengracht 319. Enormous, with comfy chairs.

(C) **De Drie Fleschjes**, Gravenstraat 18. More traditional *proeflokaal*. Some nearby offices have their own marked barrels.

(C) **Het Proeflokaal**, Pijlsteeg 31. Delightfully cramped and crooked old *proeflokaal* with a range of flavoured *jenevers* and sticky liqueurs.

Coffeeshops

(C) **Backstage Boutique**, Utrechtsedwarsstraat 65–7. Run by former cabaret performers,the Backstage is one of the zaniest coffeeshops in the city.

(C) **Greenwoods**, Singel 103. Real home-made English afternoon tea.

(S) **Granny**, 1^e van der Helststraat 45. Near Albert Cuyp market. Some of the best *appelgebak* in town.

(C) **Pompadour**, Huidenstraat 12. Refined hand-made chocolates in a splendid setting.

(C) **Puccini**, Staalstraat 17. Irresistible cakes and outrageous chocolates near the Waterlooplein fleamarket.

(J) **Reibach**, Brouwersgracht 139. German specialities, such as wickedly alcoholic fruit from the *Rumtopf* jar, and a view over a beautiful canal.

Smoking Coffeeshops

(C) **The Bulldog**, Leidseplein 13–17/ Oudezijds Voorburgwal 90. Oldest and most commercial. Housed in a former police station, it also has a large cocktail bar.

(C) **Prix d'Ami**, Haringpakkersteeg 5. Deeply respectable-looking branch of a chain of coffeeshops.

(C) **Rusland**, Rusland 16. One of the first coffeeshops. Privately owned, intimate and relaxedly scruffy. Strangely, for a coffeeshop, it has 43 different kinds of tea.

(C) **Pink Poffertje**, moored at southern end of Oude Schans. Cosy boat that even sells marijuana beer.

Dutch specialities

amandelbroodje	sweet roll with almond-paste filling
appelgebak	world-famous apple pie
appelmoes	apple sauce (with everything)
belegd broodje	bread roll with variety of fillings
bitterbal	ball of meat purée covered in breadcrumbs and deep-fried
blinde vink	slice of veal rolled around stuffing
boerenomelet	omelette with vegetables and bacon
drie-in-de-pan	fluffy pancake with currants
erwtensoep	thick pea soup with sausages in it
frikandel	meatballs
hete bliksem	potatoes, bacon and apples cooked in butter, salt and sugar
Hollandse nieuwe	freshly caught filleted herring
hutspot	hotchpotch (beef and vegetable stew)
kroket	croquette (with any filling imaginable)
pannekoek	pancake
poffertjes	mini doughnut-like pancakes
rolpens	fried slices of beef and tripe with apple
speculaas	spiced almond biscuit
uitsmijter	bread, ham and fried eggs (and variations)
vla	custard, served with everything that doesn't have *appelmoes* (q.v.)
Vlaamse karbonade	braised beef and onions—usually with beer
wentelteefje	bread fried in egg batter, then sprinkled with cinnamon and sugar

Amsterdam: Where to Stay

To really relish Amsterdam you need to stay right in the centre, preferably on a canal, and to do that you should make sure you **book a hotel room well in advance**—two to three weeks at least, more in the summer or over holiday weekends. There is, of course, always the chance of catching a cancellation, and some hotels do keep back a room or two until the last minute. Reservations can be made, once you're in the country, through the VVV (*see* **Practical A–Z**, 'Tourist Information'. p.192). They charge a ƒ5 booking fee and a ƒ10 room deposit, which is later deducted from your bill. The Netherlands Board of Tourism in your home country can give you a list of hotels, but unfortunately can't make bookings.

If you cannot book in advance, try calling the hotel direct just before noon—the witching hour between check-out and check-in—and try your luck. Because accommodation is at such a premium, you'll find that most hotels will ask for a deposit or the security of a credit card number. Some simply won't accept weekend reservations unless you book, or at least pay for, Friday, Saturday *and* Sunday.

Hotels are graded by the Benelux star system (one to five stars), though this isn't a particularly useful guide as it is based on an inventory of facilities and tells you nothing about location, service or ambience. Facilities vary in direct relation to price—you get what you pay for. Around the top end of the moderate range (ƒ220—280) you should be assured of at least a TV and telephone in your room. Beyond that lies the world of minibars, *en suite* jacuzzis and telephones in the loo.

As Amsterdam is such a compact city, hotels in this list are graded by price rather than area. Nearly all of them are within easy walking distance of the main tourist sites and museums, and have been chosen because of their pleasant atmosphere, location or historical significance.

The hotels in the 'expensive' range tend to be business hotels. Here you're paying for facilities like fax machines and meeting rooms. Such places are briskly efficient, but are often soulless and used to expense-account customers. You can be just as comfortable, and will probably be far happier, in one of the more idiosyncratic hotels from the top of the 'moderate' range. Price ranges given in this guide are as follows:

An asterisk (★) indicates hotels that are especially recommended.

∞∞∞	luxury	ƒ450 and over
∞∞∞	expensive	ƒ280–ƒ450
∞∞	moderate	ƒ175–ƒ280
∞	cheap	under ƒ180

These prices are for a double room with bath or shower *en suite* in season, and include services and taxes and (unless otherwise stated) Dutch breakfast. For prices of single rooms deduct 15–20 per cent. The addresses given below include the Amsterdam postcode.

American Hotel, Leidsekade 97, 1017 PN, ☎ 556 3000, ✆ 625 3236. An Art Deco extravaganza of a hotel overlooking the thronging Leidseplein. The café downstairs was once the meeting place for Amsterdam's literati. From ƒ475; breakfast ƒ32.50.

Amsterdam Hilton, Apollolaan 138–40, 1077 BG, ☎ 710 6005, ✆ 710 6000. Modern building in the south of the city, not in the centre. Weekdays ƒ450 excl. breakfast, weekends from ƒ415.

*Amstel Hotel Intercontinental, Professor Tulpplein 1, 1018 GX, ☎ 622 6060, ✆ 622 5808. A gracious and sedate hotel on the banks of the Amstel. If you're stuck for transport you can use the hotel's motor yacht or limousine. ƒ850; breakfast ƒ42.50.

Blakes, Keizersgracht 384, 1016 GB, ☎ 530 2010, ✆ 530 2030. Style diva Anouska Hempel brings her touch from London to a grand canal house. Bedrooms range from voluptous to Buddhist minimalist. Guests are rich and famous. Well, rich anyway. From ƒ550.

*Hotel de l'Europe, Nieuwe Doelenstraat 2–8, 1012 CP, ☎ 531 1777, ✆ 531 1778. An elegant 19th-century hotel in the grand old style. Knocks spots off the Doelen down the road. From ƒ630; breakfast ƒ35.

The Grand Amsterdam, Oudezijds Voorburgwal 197, 1001 EX, ☎ 555 3111, ✆ 555 3222. The Grand Amsterdam was built as an inn in 1578 before being used as Admirality Headquarters, and finally serving as Amsterdam's city hall (from 1808 to 1988). This hotel has many fine 1920s interior fittings remaining (including the Wedding Room in which Queen Beatrix plighted her troth). A few visitors, however, may be put off by the close proximity of the red-light district. ƒ730 excl. breakfast.

Grand Hotel Krasnapolsky, Dam 9, 1012 JS, ☎ 554 9111, ✆ 626 1570. Excellent position, right in the centre of town. Very grand from the outside, and inside a mix of period charm and all mod cons. From ƒ620; breakfast ƒ37.50.

*Hotel Pulitzer, Prinsengracht 315–31, 1016 GZ, ☎ 523 5235, ✆ 627 6753. Twenty-four canal houses linked up to form a warren of oak-beamed rooms. The hotel has a peaceful garden and a magnificent 18th-century restaurant. From ƒ650; breakfast ƒ37.50.

Hilton International Schiphol, Herbergierstraat, 1118 ZK, ☎ 710 4000, ✆ 710 4080. Part of Schiphol complex around the airport. Shuttle bus from airport. From ƒ640 excl. breakfast; breakfast ƒ42.50.

Seven One Seven, Prinsengracht 717, 1017 JW, ☎ 427 0717, ✆ 423 0717. Superb, antique-filled suites on one of the smartest canals in town. The owners have aimed at creating a cosy atmosphere— which is extremely chic and well appointed. From ƒ550; weekend rates from ƒ450. Price includes breakfast, afternoon coffee and drinks from the bar in the evening.

Hotel Ambassade, Herengracht 335–353, 1016 AZ, ☎ 626 2333, ✆ 624 5321. Eight converted houses, dotted about with antiques and with a magnificent breakfast-room overlooking the canal. ƒ335; breakfast ƒ22.50.

*Dikker & Thijs Fenice Hotel, Prinsengracht 444, 1017 KE, ☎ 626 7721, ✆ 625 8986. Plum in the middle, in a lively area of town. Modern furnishings in a 100-year-old shell. From ƒ415.

Golden Tulip Doelen Hotel, Nieuwe Doelenstraat 24, 1012 CP, ☎ 554 0600, ✆ 622 1084, telex 14399. One of Amsterdam's oldest hotels, though fading in grandeur. Rembrandt painted the *Night Watch* here in 1642. ƒ420.

Jan Luyken Hotel, Jan Luykenstraat 58, 1071 CS, ✆ 573 0730, ✉ 676 3841. Smart, efficient business hotel in quiet area near the Concertgebouw. From ƒ370.

★Schiller Karena Hotel, Rembrandt-plein 26–36, 1017 CV, ✆ 554 0700, ✉ 626 6381. The Schiller Karena is decorated with the paintings of its 19th-century owner, the downstairs café was at one time the meeting place of actors and artists. The hotel itself is smart and comfortable, and overlooks a lively square. From ƒ420; breakfast ƒ32.50.

Acca International, Van de Veldestraat 3a, 1071 CW, ✆ 662 5262, ✉ 679 9361. This is a modern, functional hotel which benefits from being close to the main museums. From ƒ195; breakfast ƒ10.

Hotel Acro, Jan Luykenstraat 44, 1071 CR, ✆ 662 0526, ✉ 675 0811. Sparkling, simple, if a little soulless. Set in the quiet museum district. ƒ175.

Hotel Agora, Singel 462, 1017 AW, ✆ 627 2200, ✉ 627 2202. The owner of the Agora is interested in fine furniture—and it shows. Rooms overlooking the canal or back garden are the best. Good value from ƒ215.

Hotel Amsterdam Prinsengracht, Prinsengracht 1015, 1017 KN, ✆ 623 7779, ✉ 623 8926. Friendly staff, all mod cons and canal views, though the décor is a little bland. From ƒ190.

Hotel Belga, Hartenstraat 8, 1016 CB, ✆ 624 9080/623 6862. Unpretentious, family-run hotel in a quaint shopping alley. ƒ190 (ƒ160 without shower).

★Het Canal House, Keizersgracht 148, 1015 CX, ✆ 622 5182, ✉ 624 1317. Stunning converted canal house, filled to the brim with the owner's carefully chosen antiques. The breakfast room has a piano and a drippingly beautiful crystal chande-lier. The hotel has the feel of a tastefully (if somewhat grandly) decorated private home, and it even has a lift (quite a rarity in these historic houses). From ƒ265 to ƒ345.

★La Casaló, Amsteldijk 862, 1079 LN, ✆ 642 3680, ✉ 644 7409. Romantic houseboat with a waterside terrace and just four rooms, all individually decorated. It's on the outskirts of town, so a car or bicycle is a good idea. From ƒ235 to ƒ275.

★Hotel De Filosoof, Anna Vondelstraat 6, 1054 GZ, ✆ 683 3013, ✉ 685 3750. Each room is named after a well-known thinker, and decorated accordingly. The hotel can arrange consultations with one of Holland's practising philosophers, many of whom frequent the bar. From ƒ195.

Hotel Orlando, Prinsengracht 1099, 1017 JH, ✆ 638 6915, ✉ 625 2123. Canalside house with just five rooms, indi-vidually decorated in a modern style. Need to book well in advance. ƒ160 to ƒ260.

Owl Hotel, Roemer Visscherstraat 1–3, 1054 EV, ✆ 618 9486, ✉ 618 9491. Smart family hotel with large garden. In the museum neighbourhood. ƒ210.

★Quentin Hotel, Leidsekade 89, 1017 PN, ✆ 626 2187, ✉ 622 0121. Popular with musicians playing at De Melkweg around the corner. Posters of past (now famous) residents adorn the walls. Spotless, tastefully decorated and good views over the canal. From ƒ220.50 excl. breakfast.

★Hotel Seven Bridges, Reguliersgracht 31, 1017 LK, ✆ 623 1329. No fax. The most charming small hotel in Amsterdam. Beautifully decorated rooms—and breakfast served in bed. ƒ200 to ƒ340.

Hotel Toren, Keizersgracht 164, 1015 CZ, ✆ 622 6033, ✉ 626 9705. Seventeenth-century canal house with high moulded ceilings, and antiques scattered among the modern furniture. From ƒ225, breakfast ƒ17.50.

Hotel Washington, Frans van Mierisstraat 10, 1071 RS, ✆ 679 6754, ✉ 673 4435. Large 19th-century house on an avenue near the Concertgebouw. Room furnishings are simple but tasteful, and there's a back garden. Much appreciated by visiting concert musicians. From ƒ185.

∞ ***Hotel Wiechmann**, Prinsengracht 328–30, 1016 HX, ✆ 626 3321, ✉ 626 8962. Carefully converted canal houses with an air of old world charm, and a noble breakfast-room. From ƒ200.

○ **Hotel De Admiraal**, Herengracht 563, 1017 CD, ✆ 626 2150, ✉ 623 4625. Friendly owner, views over *two* canals, and a good breakfast. Around ƒ165 (ƒ110 without private bathroom); breakfast costs an extra ƒ7.50.

○ **Hotel Adolesce**, Nieuwe Keizersgracht 26, 1018 DS, ✆ 626 3959, ✉ 627 4249. Cheerful, simple hotel with a sunny breakfast room. A good one if you have children, as it is one of the few establishments that genuinely welcomes them. From ƒ125–150, some rooms come without a bathroom.

○ **Hans Brinker**, Kerkstraat 136, 1017 GR, ✆ 622 0687, ✉ 638 2060. Hans Brinker prides itself on its no-frills good value and central situation. ƒ145.

○ **Hotel Brouwer**, Singel 83, ✆ 624 6358, ✉ 520 6264. This is a real gem. A canal house with rooms tastefully done up and with lovely old furniture. Most also have a good view. ƒ154.

○ **Hotel Engeland**, Roemer Vischerstraat 30, 1054 EZ, ✆ 689 2323, ✉ 685 3148. English representative in a quaint row of 19th-century houses built to show seven different national architectural styles. From ƒ175 (breakfast extra).

○ **Hotel de Harmonie**, Prinsengracht 816, 1017 JL, ✆ 625 0174, ✉ 622 8021. Bright, jolly, family-run hotel. ƒ130 (without bathroom) to ƒ140.

○ **Hotel Hoksbergen**, Singel 301, ✆ 626 6043. ✉ 638 3479. No-nonsense knotty pine, some canal views, clean rooms, friendly management.

○ **Hotel Impala**, Leidsekade 77, 1017 PM, ✆ 623 4706, ✉ 638 9274. Clean, laid-back hotel with young crowd. From ƒ130–140.

○ **Hotel Prinsenhof**, Prinsengracht 810, 1017 JL, ✆ 623 1772, ✉ 638 3368. Quiet, thoughtfully decorated hotel with friendly management thrown in. ƒ165 (ƒ125 without bathroom).

○ **Hotel de Westertoren**, Raadhuisstraat 35b, 1016 DC, ✆/✉ 624 4639. Well kept, if a little noisy. From ƒ140.

Bed & Breakfast

In the main, Amsterdammers do not seem much taken by B&B. When you do find private accommodation, it probably won't be all that much cheaper than (or very different from) a room in a small hotel.

Bed and Breakfast Holland, Theophile de Bockstraat 3, 1058 TV, ✆ 615 7527, ✉ 669 1573. Has a number of B&Bs on its books. Prices range from ƒ95 for a minimum 2-night stay and there is a ƒ20 booking fee per reservation. Advance bookings only.

Hostels

The two official International Youth Hostel Federation hostels are:

Vondelpark, Zandpad 5, 1054 GA, ✆ 589 8999, ✉ 589 8955.

Stadsdoelen, Kloveniersburgwal 97, 1011 KB, ✆ 624 6832, ✉ 639 1035. Members ƒ28 per person (including breakfast); non-members ƒ33; sheet hire ƒ6.25.

A number of other non-federation hostels are worth trying. These include:

Arena, 's Gravesandestraat 51, 1092 AA, ✆ 694 7444, ☎ 663 2649. Erstwhile seedy hippy Sleep-In, which has now been considerably smartened up and attracts a very friendly crowd of backpackers. Double room *f*135, dormitories from *f*27.50, bedding *f*5.

*Eben Haezer Christian Youth Hostel, Bloemstraat 179, 1016 LA, ✆ 624 4717, ☎ 627 6137. Spotless, not oppressively religious and the best value of the lot. *f*27.50, including breakfast and bed linen. No membership required. Lockers are available.

The Flying Pig Park, Vossiusstraat 46, 1071 AJ, ✆ 400 4187, ☎ 470 5159. The Flying Pig Park has a friendly crowd, clean dorms, free lockers and a cosy café beside the Vondelpark. Dorm beds from *f*26.50 per person, double room *f*120.

Camp Sites

A good number of camp sites are close to Amsterdam. Some are more geared towards youth while others are designated as 'family camp sites' and are considerably quieter.

Het Amsterdamse Bos, Kleine Noorddijk 1, 1432 CC, Aalsmeer, ✆ 641 6868 (open April–Oct). Bus 171 from Centraal Station, 169 from Schiphol. Good facilities but far out. *f*8.75 per person, *f*4.75 per car, *f*6.75 caravans; *f*4 per night electricity charge for camper vans and caravans. Suitable for families or those seeking a quiet time.

Vliegenbos, Meeuwenlaan 138, 1022 AM, ✆ 636 8855 (*open April–Sept*). Bus 32 (10 minutes from Centraal Station). 'Youth Camp site'—all ages welcome but be prepared for late-night high spirits. From *f*10 per person, cars *f*5.50, electricity *f*5.

Apartments

Amsterdam Apartments, Kromme Waal, 1011 BV, ✆ 626 5930, ☎ 626 9544. Privately owned flats around town—usually let by holidaying Amsterdammers—from *f*700 per week.

GIS Apartments, Keizersgracht 33, 1015 CD, ✆ 625 0071, ☎ 638 0475. From the simple to the luxurious. From *f*2,000 per month, minimum three months.

Global Home Network, Suite 205, 110-D Elden Street, Herndon, Virginia, USA, ✆ +1 703 318 7081, ☎ +1 703 318 7086, have a number of canalside apartments on their books, for short- and medium-term lease. Prices on application.

Amsterdam: Entertainment and Nightlife

Amsdam's nightlife centres on cafés. They offer everything from a quiet evening over the backgammon board to jolly singsongs in just about any language you choose. There are even some cafés where you can dance, though a handful of good nightclubs serve those who really like to bounce and sweat. The more genteel spectator entertainments are accessible to foreigners. Films are usually shown in their original language, with Dutch subtitles; there's a strong tradition of visual theatre, and many performances in English; the new Muziektheater provides a venue for touring opera and dance companies, and Amsterdam has high international status in the various music worlds. Up and coming British rock bands test the water here before facing jaded audiences at home; there are some good jazz festivals, and recent immigration has upped the quality of salsa and Latin American music. The acoustically superb Concertgebouw attracts leading classical artists and conductors, and there's a healthy contemporary music scene.

Information

The tourist office publishes a monthly *What's On In Amsterdam* (*f*4, available from the Amsterdam Tourist Board (ATB) and around town). The free monthly *Uitkrant* (from the ATB, libraries, museums and theatres) is more comprehensive and, although it's in Dutch, fairly easy to follow. An even better bet (also in Dutch) is the PS Weekend supplement to *Het Parool*. *Queer Fish* (*f*2.50 from larger newsagents) is a twice-monthly guide to trendy Amsterdam, focussing mainly on clubs and with a strong gay slant. *Oor* (from newsagents) is the Dutch equivalent of *NME*, the British rock music newspaper. Both the Amsterdam Tourist Board and the AUB booking office (*see* **Practical A–Z**, 'Tourist Information' p.192) can reserve tickets. The AUB also has an up-to-the-minute What's On notice board (good for pop music) and masses of leaflets. *www.aub.nl* has up-to-the-minute information on shows and exhibitions, and a bookings service too. (Also *see* **Practical A–Z**, 'Festivals and Events', p.186).

Film

You'll find most of the multi-screened **commercial cinemas** in the area around Leidseplein, where they offer pretty standard fare. The six-screen Tuschinski (*see* p.218) must be a hot contender for the most beautiful cinema in the world. Cinema **prices** range from *f*10–15 and there are often discounts on week nights. In the rare cases where an English film has been dubbed over you'll see the words *Nederlands Gesproken* on the publicity.

art houses

Desmet, Plantage Middenlaan 4, © 627 3434. Ornate Art Deco cinema used by a Jewish cabaret company during the early years of the Second World War.

Netherlands Film Museum, Vondelpark 3, © 589 1400. Frequent changes of programme, usually with something from the museum's archive—such as tinted silent movies (*see* p.227).

Kriterion, Roeterstraat 170, © 623 1708. Cult American movies and erotic French late-nights.

The Movies, Haarlemmerdijk 161, © 638 6016. Some of the programming verges on the mainstream, but the 1920s interior is a delight and there's a vibrant café/restaurant.

Rialto, Ceintuurbaan 338, © 675 3994. Good on retrospectives, Sci-Fi and children's films.

De Uitkijk, Prinsengracht 452, © 623 7460. Amsterdam's oldest cinema, squashed into an even older canal house. Features a white grand piano that has long since tinkled its last notes.

Theatre

There is no national theatre company; the chief mainstream company is the rather stolid **Toneelgroep Amsterdam**, resident at the Westergasfabriek. Two local English-speaking companies compete with foreign touring productions for the Amsterdam audience. The In Theatre presents small-scale productions, usually upstairs in a converted prop room at the Stadsschouwburg, and Boom Chicago offers improvised comedy in their own supper theatre next door. The Nes (off Damstraat) and the banks of the Amstel are traditionally theatreland, but these days no old warehouse, factory or stable is safe from troupes of eager actors.

The best thing to do is check the listings magazines for touring companies—and here's a short list of venues where you're likely to find good work in English.

't Fijnhout Theater, Jacob van Lennepkade 334, ✆ 685 3755. A popular theatre with English-language touring companies.

Koninklijk Theater Carré, Amstel 115-25, ✆ 622 5225. Built for a circus—a function it still performs over the Christmas period. The home of most big Amsterdam musicals.

Felix Meritis, Felix Meritis Building, Keizersgracht 324, ✆ 626 2321. A descendant of the Shaffy, which was at the forefront of the avant-garde during the 1970s and 1980s, and housed in a building with a rich cultural past. Still a place to catch exciting new work (*see* p.222).

De Stadsschouwburg, Leidseplein 26, ✆ 624 2311. Amsterdam's municipal theatre. A wide range of national productions and visiting international companies. There's a good **theatre bookshop** near the main entrance.

Dance

The Nederlands Dans Theater keeps up a salvo of fine ballet and modern dance. Look out also for work by **Djazzex** (jazz dance) and **Dansgroep Krisztina de Chatel** (vivid theatrical style). Once again the listings magazines will tell you what's on, but the following venues are worth checking out:

Bellevue, Leidsekade 90, ✆ 624 7248. Modern dance touring companies.

Frascati, Nes 63, ✆ 626 6866. More established modern dance companies.

Muziektheater (Stopera), Waterlooplein 22, ✆ 625 5455. If you want to see something in this new opera house, ballet may be the best choice as the acoustics are a little iffy (*see* p.212–13).

Music

Classical and Opera

Baroque and period instrument orchestras are reaching particularly high standards (try to catch the **Amsterdam Baroque Orchestra** or the **Orchestra of the 18th Century**). The Nederlandse Opera repeatedly comes up with sharp, adventurous productions, often of 20th-century works, and the contemporary music scene is very lively (look out for pieces by Louis Andriessen and performances by the refreshingly unorthodox Ricciotti Ensemble). **Tickets** will seem cheap if you're used to London or New York prices, but they sell out quickly. You can try for returns half an hour before a performance, but there are no last-minute discounts, and systems of selling return tickets (especially at the Muziektheater) can be disorganized.

Churches are favourite venues for concerts and recitals: the Oude Kerk, the Nieuwe Kerk, the Engelse Kerk and the Waalse Kerk. Other venues include:

AGA Zaal and Yakult Zaal, Damrak 213, ✆ 627 0466. Home to the Netherlands Chamber Orchestra and the Netherlands Philharmonic respectively. Beautifully converted concert halls in the old Beurs van Berlage (*see* p.215).

Concertgebouw, Concertgebouwplein 2–6, ✆ 671 8345. The Grote Zaal (Large Hall) has perfect acoustics and is used for orchestral concerts and visiting pop stars and jazz bands. Nervous students from the Sweelinck Conservatorium across the road make their professional debuts in the Kleine Zaal (Small Hall). Free lunch-time concerts on Wednesdays (*see* p.224).

De IJsbreker, Weesperzijde 23, ✆ 693 9093. A deservedly famous centre for contemporary music which offers a stimulating programme of local and international composers and improvisers.

Muziektheater (Stopera), Waterlooplein 22, ✆ 625 5455. Home to the national ballet and opera companies, but subject of one of the biggest architectural and property development controversies of the century (*see* p.212–13). There are backstage tours (*Wed and Sat 4pm; f8.50; book in advance on ✆ 551 8103 for English guide*).

De Rode Hoed, Keizersgracht 102, ✆ 638 5606. Varied programmes in a converted church.

Rock and Pop

Chart-busters and stadium-packers like Madonna and Prince used to give Amsterdam a miss and head for the larger venues of Rotterdam. But in 1996 Amsterdam gained a state of the art sports and entertainment stadium. The **Amsterdam Arena** looks like a giant spaceship, hovering on the southeast outskirts of the city. It opened with concerts by Tina Turner and Michael Jackson, and has been packing in the audiences ever since. Keep an eye out also for Dutch stars who have made it internationally—such as Mathilde Santing, Eton Crop and the not-so-gently ageing Golden Earring—who have a loyalty to the old town and come back for a gig or two at venues in the centre.

Young British bands (who see Amsterdam as the penultimate ring on the ladder to fame and glory) are often the best bet if you're looking for good rock. Many of these head for **Paradiso** or **De Melkweg**, though they often also strain the sound systems of smaller venues around town such as a new dance and concert hall called (confusingly) Arena. Many bands who have since made it big also have a soft spot for Paradiso and De Melkweg. In 1995 The Rolling Stones popped in for an unscheduled 'unplugged' concert in Paradiso before a first-come-first-served audience of just 500. The listings magazines are your best guide to what's on. Prices range from free entrance to around *f*20 and starting times are usually between 9 and 11pm.

Akhnaton, Nieuwezijds Kolk 25, ✆ 624 3396. Recording studios, rehearsal facilities and a forum for much of the liveliest new music, hip-hop, Latin and ethnic bands.

Amsterdam Arena, Arenaboulevard 1, ✆ 311 1333. The venue for visiting megastars.

Arena, 's Gravesandestraat 51, ✆ 694 7444. The old hippy Sleep-In is now one of the trendiest music and dance venues in town.

Cruise Inn, Zeeburgerdijk 272, ✆ 692 7188. Shake, rattle and roll in an old wooden clubhouse.

Korsakoff, Lijnbaansgracht 161, ✆ 625 7854. A venue for headbanging post-punks..

Paradiso, Weteringschans 6–8, ✆ 626 4521. A bright and buzzing venue for good music—anything from big rock names to jazz, African, Latin and even contemporary classical.

See also **De Melkweg**, p.268.

The mellow tones of jazz seem to suit the atmosphere of the brown cafés, and many have a live band on a Saturday night or Sunday afternoon. There are often special gigs around the same time as the Holland Festival (*see* **Practical A–Z**, p.187). Surinamese and other South American immigrants crowd out a number of vibrant drinking and dancing venues around town. Bars and cafés with live music often don't charge entrance, but have more expensive drinks.

Jazzcafé Alto, Korte Leidsedwarsstraat 115, ✆ 626 3249. Live jazz every night in a cosy brown café in a brash touristy street.

De Badcuyp, 1ᵉ Sweelinckstraat 10, ✆ 675 9669. Neighbourhood café-cum-arts centre in an old bathhouse. A lively venue for jazz and salsa.

Bimhuis, Oudeschans 73, ✆ 623 1361. Major jazz venue. Visiting artists and the best locals; free sessions Mon and Wed.

Brasil Music Bar, Lange Leidsedwarsstraat 70, ✆ 626 1500. Live Samba and a gyrating throng of Latin expatriates.

Casablanca, Zeedijk 26, ✆ 625 5685. Café hosting mainstream and standard bands, with the occasional jam session.

Jazz Cruise, ✆ 623 9886, starts at Rijksmuseum (*April–Nov Sat 8 and 10pm*). An hour-and-a-half of jazz on a canal boat, with beer, wine and cheese thrown in.

Maloe Melo, Lijnbaansgracht 163, ✆ 420 4592. Enduring, rather poky, blues café.

Meander, Voetboogstraat 3, ✆ 625 8430. Lively café where student types swing to salsa, bop to funk and chill out to jazz.

Mulligan's, Amstel 100, ✆ 622 1330. Rousing Irish singalongs.

Odeon Jazz Kelder, Singel 460, ✆ 624 9711. Trad jazz in an intimate atmosphere.

Rembrandt Bar, Rembrandtplein 3, ✆ 623 0688. Dutch folk music.

Rum Runners, Prinsengracht 277, ✆ 627 4079. Live Latin bands (Sun pm and early evening).

Soeterijn, Linnaeusstraat 2, ✆ 568 8500. The top venue for music from Africa, Indonesia, Eastern Europe and the Middle East.

For a real knees-up and noisy accordion visit **Café Nol** or **De Twee Zwaantjes** (*see* **Food and Drink**, 'Cafés').

Nightclubs and Dancing

Entrance prices for nightclubs are low enough—and the city small enough—for you to wander from one club to the next. The mood is carefree and unpretentious—late-night clubbing seems just an extension of early evening café life.

The *Queer Fish* booklet (on sale at larger bookstores) is a good source of information about one-nighters or parties. The **commercial discos** (chart music, plastic palm trees, expensive drinks and posses of drunken men) cluster around Leidseplein. What follows is a list of places for those with rather different tastes. Most venues close at 4am (5am over weekends). You should tip the doorman as you leave (about ƒ5), and avoid using cabs cruising outside. Legal cabs will be found at a nearby rank—or the club may phone for you.

Dansen bij Jansen, Handboogstraat 11, ✆ 620 1779. A bit like a Students' Union bop. You usually need to prove membership of a college or university to get in. Frequent theme and fancy-dress nights.

Escape, Rembrandtsplein 11, ✆ 622 1111. A cavern of a place that's a hyper-trendy club, complete with shops and even a hairdresser.

Mazzo, Rozengracht 114, ✆ 626 7500. Comfortable club with a good atmosphere and an excellent range of music, often live, with local bands playing.

Odeon, Singel 460, ✆ 624 9711. Multi-roomed venue in a converted canal house; often overpopulated by adolescent tourists.

See also **De Melkweg**, below.

Scandals Lounge, Reguliersdwarsstraat 13, ☎ 422 6220. Glitzy hip and garage.

Sinners in Heaven, Wagenstraat 3, ☎ 620 1375. Weird 'n' wonderful décor; with world-famous-in-Holland clientele.

Soul Kitchen, Amstelstraat 32, ☎ 620 2333. The sort of music that 30-somethings can dance to, in a friendly refreshingly untrendy atmosphere. No under-25s.

Trance Buddha, Oudezijds Voorburgwal 216, ☎ 422 8233. Young New Age crowd with appropriate soundtrack.

West Pacific, Haarlemmerweg 8, ☎ 488 7778. Fun, hip dance-café that is part of an arts complex in an old gasworks.

Arts Centres

De Brakke Ground, Nes 45, ☎ 626 6866. Attractive venue for Flemish art and performance. Excellent dance programmes.

De Meervaart Centrum, Meer en Vaart 1, ☎ 610 7498. A good variety of film, theatre, dance and music (classical and jazz).

De Melkweg (Milky Way), Lijnbaansgracht 234a, ☎ 624 1777. A vibrant centre for the arts converted in the 1960s from an old dairy. The theatre hosts companies from around the world (often in English) with extraordinarily imaginative plays. The small cinema shows a range of films from mainstream to cult. The concert hall stages excellent African and South American bands, and acts as a try-out venue for up-and-coming rock groups. At weekends an alternative disco takes over. The coffeeshop was one of the first where the sale of marijuana was tolerated by the authorities. Consider taking out membership (ƒ15, valid three months) which gives you considerable discounts.

Amsterdam RAI, Europaplein 12, ☎ 549 1212. A business congress centre which houses large concerts and touring musicals. Venue for KunstRAI, an annual contemporary art fair.

Westergasfabriek, Haarlemmerweg 8–10, ☎ 681 3068. Newest arts centre, in a converted gasworks. Home to the Toneelgroep Amsterdam (see above) and European base for the Cirque du Soleil. Visiting shows are usually experimental. Every night after 11pm customers bop until late.

Amsterdam: Gay Amsterdam

In the heady social upheaval of the 1960s and 70s, when pixie-hatted members of the Gnome Party held protest meetings on the Dam and troupes of hippies camped out in the Vondelpark, Amsterdam's lesbians and gays joined in the frolic. Homosexuality had been decriminalized in 1811, but the gay community wanted a city free of the petty prejudices and subtle discrimination they ran up against in day-to-day life. In many ways they succeeded. Today Amsterdam is known as the Gay Capital of Europe. Gay bars and cafés, though often in clusters, aren't in ghettos. Nobody bats an eyelid if two men kiss or hold hands in public. The city was quick off the mark in coping constructively with AIDS, the council housing department gives gay couples the same status as married heterosexuals, and in 1987 the world's first memorial to persecuted lesbians and gays, the Homomonument, was unveiled (the three triangles of pink granite between the Westerkerk and the Keizersgracht are the focal point of many a party, protest or commemoration service).

There are gay bars, clubs, hotels, bookshops and restaurants all over town. You'll find most of the heavier leather bars lurking up the north end of **Warmoesstraat**, ribbons of coffeeshops, restaurants and bars along **Kerkstraat** and **Reguliersdwarsstraat**, a jolly throb of clubs and pubs along the **Amstel** off Rembrandtplein, and scores of local neighbourhood cafés. Despite accusations that the Amsterdam gay scene is stagnating, gay tourists flock to the city. Many Amsterdammers respond to this invasion by staying at home, venturing out on Thursdays and Sundays when the occupying forces are thinner on the ground.

The atmosphere, though, is friendly and welcoming. Most gay venues distribute free **maps of gay Amsterdam**, leaflets and free magazines (such as *Rainbow*) giving you an idea of what's on about town; but as people are so open and chatty, word of mouth is often the best way to find out what the evening might have in store.

Here is an idiosyncratic selection of places to go; some are well known but others are quirky, local establishments, out of the tourist maelstrom.

Cafés, Coffeeshops and Restaurants

Backstage Boutique (a.k.a. The Twins), Utrechtsedwarsstraat 75; *open Mon–Sat 10am–6pm*. The Boutique is not exclusively gay, but has an atmosphere of stratospheric camp that shouldn't be missed.

Café Secret, Kerkstraat 346; *open Sun–Thurs 9pm–3am, Fri–Sat 9–4*. Cosy café that sometimes has live entertainment.

COC, Rozenstraat 14; *coffeeshop open Wed–Sat 1–5pm*. Spartan but amiable haven in Amsterdam's lesbian and gay 'culture centre'.

Downtown, Reguliersdwarsstraat 31; *open daily 10–8*. A friendly daytime coffeeshop, popular with tourists and locals, in one of Amsterdam's gay streets. It serves food and has a sprawl of pavement tables on sunny days.

Getto, Warmoesstraat 51; restaurant/café *open Wed–Sat noon to 1am, Sun noon–midnight; closed Mon and Tues*. A young, friendly crowd and good food make this one of the most popular recent additions to the gay scene.

Le Monde, Rembrandtplein 6; *open daily 8am–midnight*. Tiny, cheery snack café with a terrace on Rembrandtplein. The sister restaurant along the square does good Dutch food.

Reibach, Brouwersgracht 139; *open daily 10–8, but closes 6pm Oct–Mar*. Trendy café with a Germanic edge and a pleasant, small terrace on one of Amsterdam's most tranquil canals.

La Strada, Nieuwezijds Voorburgwal 93; *open daily noon–1am*. Brown café with good food and friendly staff, popular with local lesbians.

Amstel Taveerne, Amstel 54; *open daily 3pm–1am, to 2am at weekends.* Beer mugs and bric-a-brac hang everywhere. Dutch reproductions on the walls. Dutch originals around the bar. A provincial pub in the middle of the city with sing-alongs and good cheer (all Dutch).

April, Reguliersdwarsstraat 37; *open daily 2pm–1am.* More than double its previous size (and more attractively designed) after a 1996 renovation. Popular with young Amsterdammers during the week. Over the weekend tourists swell numbers until the bar bursts into a street party.

Argos, Warmoesstraat 95; *open Mon–Thurs 9pm–3am, to 4am at weekends.* Amsterdam's oldest leather bar sweats with bikers' jackets, cowboy chaps and denim. As you wander into the dimmer recesses, what gay guides coyly term 'action' becomes quite lively.

Havana, Reguliersdwarsstraat 17; *open daily 4pm–1am, to 2am at weekends.* Comfortable café/bar with an exhausting constellation of beautiful people. There's a small dance floor upstairs.

Casa Maria, Warmoesstraat 60; *open Sun–Thurs noon–1am, Fri–Sat noon–2am.* In the heart of the red-light district. A jukebox full of uproarious kitsch, a gregarious Spanish owner, and a picture window that offers the best people-watching possibilities in town.

Montmartre, Halvemaansteeg 17; *open daily 4pm–1am, to 2am on Fri and Sat.* Dancing barmen, original 1920s décor, loud music and a tight squeeze.

Le Shako, 's Gravenlandseveer 2; *open daily 9pm–2am, to 3am at weekends.* A miniscule bar that attracts students, writers, academics and a good load of local scruffs.

De Trut, Bilderdijkstraat 165; open Sun 11pm–4am. A trendy, but relaxed and pose-free club with a wide range of music, a (mainly) young crowd and a mix of lesbians and gay men. The Trut is in the cellar of what was once one of Amsterdam's biggest squats. The entrance is unmarked, but if you turn up between 11 and midnight, you'll see where to go. Often the club gets so full you have to wait for someone to leave before you're allowed in.

COC, Rozenstraat 14. Amsterdam's Gay Centre runs a disco every Friday night (10pm–2am) which attracts a local crowd as well as ingénues from the provinces.

C'ring (or Cockring), Warmoesstraat 96; open daily 11pm–4am, to 5am on Fri and Sat. Steamy, sweaty, swarming venue.

Exit, Reguliersdwarsstraat 42. April's busy disco-sister (*see* above).

Lesbians are not as well catered for as gay men in Amsterdam, but there's a lively, friendly scene in places such as:

Sarah's Grannies, Kerkstraat 176; *Mon–Sat 9am–6pm.* Offers good Dutch meals in a relaxed atmosphere. Not exclusively gay, but popular with local women.

Café Saarein, Elandsstraat 119; *open Mon 8pm–1am, Tues–Thurs and Sun 3pm–1am, Fri and Sat 3pm–2am.* A cosy local café, currently the citadel of Amsterdam's lesbian life.

Café Vive-la-Vie, Amstelstraat 5; *open daily noon–1am, to 2am at weekends.* Sociable crowd

in a vaguely Art Deco bar with music that increases in volume as the night wears on.

COC (*see* under 'Clubs' above) holds a house-oriented women-only disco on Saturdays from 8pm–2am.

You II, Amstel 178, *open Thurs to Saturday 11pm to 5am; Sunday 4pm to 1am.* More of a disco than Vive-la-Vie, and less heavily house than COC. Much-needed hip, yet pretty, relaxed lesbian meeting place.

If the sun's shining, the place to be is **Zandvoort**, on Amsterdam's **gay beach**. Zandvoort is not the forgotten patch in the dunes that such places usually are, although it's a bit of a trek to reach it. There are two gay bars (**Eldorado** and **Sans Tout**) on the beach. Both are open from 8am until midnight. You can get there by train from Centraal Station (about 30mins, frequent trains right through the day). Once you get to the beach, walk south along the promenade and then on past the '*Naakt Strand*' (nudist beach) for about 5km.

There's a **gay cinema** every Saturday and Sunday at Desmet, Plantage Middenlaan 4a, ✆ 627 3434. It shows a selection of popular and independent films and attracts a local crowd.

You can spend hours browsing around **gay bookshops** like Intermale, Spuistraat 251—mostly for men—or Boekhandel Vrolijk, Paleisstraat 135, which has a wide selection of literature, biographies and non-fiction of interest to lesbians and gay men. The American Discount Bookshop, Kalverstraat 185, has a good gay section.

Mandate, Prinsengracht 715 (*open Mon–Fri 11am–10pm, Sat noon–6pm, Sun 2–6pm; daily membership f18, six visits f63*) is a well-equipped **gay gym** with a busy coffee bar; and the notorious Amsterdam **saunas** are Thermos Day, Raamstraat 35 (*open Mon–Fri noon–11pm, Sat and Sun noon–10pm; adm f30*) and Thermos Night, Kerkstraat 60 (*open daily 11pm–8am; adm f30*).

Accommodation

Hotels are forbidden by law to discriminate against gay couples, but here's a selection of specifically gay places to stay. The prices are for a double room with shower in season, with breakfast included. (Addresses are given with the Amsterdam postcode.)

Amsterdam House Hotel, 's Gravelandseveer 3, 1011 KM, ✆ 624 6607, @ 624 1346. Friendly canalside hotel just minutes from gay hotspots. From f140.

International Travel Club/ITC, Prinsengracht 1051, 1017 JE, ✆ 623 0230. Quiet hotel overlooking one of Amsterdam's finest canals, popular with an older crowd. From f140.

Jordaan Canal House, Egelantiersgracht 23, 1015 RC, ✆ 620 1545, @ 638 5056. Beautifully situated, exclusively gay 17th-century canal house. From f170.

Hotel New York, Herengracht 13, 1015 BA, ✆ 624 3066. Swish hotel with all the mod cons, tucked away behind three 17th-century canal houses at a tranquil end of Amsterdam's grandest canal. From f250.

GIS Apartments, Keizersgracht 33, 1015 CD Amsterdam, ✆ 625 0071, offers furnished apartments from f150–250 per night.

Information

COC is Amsterdam's lesbian and gay social centre (Rozenstraat 14; ✆ office 626 3087/information ✆ 623 4079; *open Mon–Thurs 9am–5pm; for disco and coffeeshop hours, see* 'Clubs' *and* 'Lesbian Amsterdam' *above*).

Gay and Lesbian Switchboard (✆ 623 6565; *open 10am–10pm*) provides information and advice in English.

Dutch is not an easy language to grapple with. However, to a short-term visitor to Amsterdam this need present no problem, as nearly everyone you meet will speak such good English that you could almost consider it to be the city's second language. The list of words and phrases below will help the polite and adventurous who wish to master everyday courtesies.

Pronunciation

Pronunciation is a question of tackling some rather difficult vowel sounds. Happily, spelling is phonetic, so once you've learned the sounds you'll be able to make a pretty accurate stab at pronouncing anything you read. The stress in Dutch, as in English, generally falls on the first syllable of a word.

Consonants

Most consonants are pronounced the same as they would be in English. However, *ps*, *ts* and *k*s aren't aspirated (i.e. they're pronounced without the accompanying puff of air). Say *ch* and *g* as in the Scottish 'loch' (*g* is more strongly voiced in northern parts of the country). Good luck in getting your tongue around the combined *s* and *ch* sounds in words like *schip* (ship), *school* (school) or *schrijfter* (writer). You have a choice for *r*—you can roll it at the back of your mouth or trill it behind your teeth, but you must *always* pronounce it. Say *w* halfway between the English 'w' and 'v', except before *r*, when you pronounce it 'v'. The Dutch *v* is closer to English 'f'. Say *j* as English 'y'; *sj* as English 'sh' and *tj* as English 'ch'.

Vowels

Pronounce the basic *a, e, i, o, u* sounds the same as you would in English, but *much shorter* (*a* as in 'hard', but shorter). Say *ie* as in 'neat', *oo* as in 'boat' and *oe* as in 'pool', but make all the sounds shorter. *aa* is like the 'a' in 'cat', but longer and *ee* is similar to the vowel sound in 'hail'. Say *eu* to rhyme with 'err', but round your lips tightly, and say *uu* as English *oo* in 'hoot'. The combination *ij* is a distinct letter in the Dutch alphabet, and is pronounced 'ay', whether it begins a word like *ijs* (ice/ice cream), or comes in the middle, as in *wijn* (wine). The stretch of water north of Centraal Station is Het IJ, 'het ay'. The diphthong *ui* is a killer. In getting their tongues around the streetname Spui, Americans usually come up with 'Spew-ee' and the Brits manage 'Spow'. The Dutch sound is closer to the way a French person would say *œil*.

Amsterdam: Language

do you speak English?	*spreekt u Engels?*	where	*waar*
I don't understand	*Ik begrijp het niet*	what	*wat*
could you speak	*kunt u wat lang-*	when	*waneer*
more slowly?	*zamer spreken?*	which	*welk*
hello/goodbye	*dag*	who	*wie*
hi	*hoi* (grating to some ears)	why	*waarom*
'bye	*doei* (grating)	where is the lavatory?	*waar is het toilet?*
goodbye	*tot ziens*	may I	*mag ik*
see you later	*tot straks*	can you	*kunt u*
good morning/	*goede morgen/*	how much is	*hoeveel kost*
afternoon/night	*middag/nacht*	this/that?	*dit/dat?*
good evening	*goedenavond*	expensive	*duur*
yes/no/maybe	*ja/nee/misschien*	cheap	*goedkoop*
please	*alstublieft*	can you help me?	*kunt u mij helpen?*
thank you/thanks	*dank u wel/bedankt*	I'm hungry/thirsty	*ik heb honger/dorst*
don't mention it	*niets te danken*	I'm in a hurry	*ik heb haast*
there is/there are	*er is/er zijn*	I'm lost	*ik ben verdwaald*
there isn't/aren't	*er is/zijn geen*	call a doctor quickly	*roep vlug een*
I have	*ik heb*		*dokter*
I don't have any	*ik heb geen*	call the police/	*roep de politie/*
I'd like	*ik wil graag*	an ambulance	*een ambulance*
we'd like	*wij willen graag*	entrance/exit	*ingang/uitgang*
I like it	*ik vind het leuk*	push/pull	*duwen/trekken*
I don't like it	*ik vind het*	open/closed	*open/gesloten (dicht)*
	niet leuk		

Hotel

single room	*eenpersoonskamer*
double room	*tweepersoonskamer*
with private bath/shower/toilet	*met privé bad/douche/toilet*
may I see the room?	*mag ik de kamer zien?*
did anyone telephone for me?	*heeft er iemand voor mij gebeld?*
may I see the manager, please?	*mag ik de directeur spreken, alstublieft?*

Transport

airport	*luchthaven/vliegveld*	take me to this address	*breng me naar*
customs	*douane*		*dit adres*
railway station	*trein station*	I want to go to...	*ik wil naar...*
platform	*perron*	how can I get to...?	*hoe kom ik bij...?*
platform five	*spoor vijf*	where is...?	*waar is...?*
car	*auto*	the ticket office	*het loket*
bicycle	*fiets/rijwiel*	I'd like a ticket to...	*ik wil graag een*
ticket	*kaartje*		*kaartje naar...*
occupied/reserved	*bezet/gereserveerd*	single/return	*enkeltje/retourtje*
where can I get a taxi?	*waar kan ik een taxi*	when does the next/	*wanner vertrek de*
	krijgen?	first/last train leave?	*volgende/eerste/*
			laatste trein?
what's the fare to...?	*wat kost het naar...?*	how long does it take?	*hoe lang duurt het?*

Numbers

nought	*nul*	seventy	*zeventig*
one/two/three	*een/twee/drie*	eighty	*tachtig*
four/five/six	*vier/vijf/zes*	ninety	*negentig*
seven/eight/nine	*zeven/acht/negen*	hundred	*honderd*
ten/eleven/twelve	*tien/elf/twaalf*	two hundred and	*tweehonderd-*
thirteen, fourteen etc.	*dertien/veertien* etc.	twenty	*twintig*
twenty	*twintig*	thousand	*duizend*
twenty-one	*eenentwintig*	million	*een miljoen*
twenty-two	*tweeëntwintig* (etc.)	first/1st	*eerste/1^e*
thirty	*dertig*	second/2nd	*tweede/2e*
forty	*veertig*	third/3rd	*derde/3e*
fifty	*vijftig*	fourth/4th	*vierde/4e*
sixty	*zestig*	eighth/8th	*achtste/8e*

Time

what time is it?	*hoe laat is het?*	tomorrow	*morgen*
one o'clock	*een uur*	morning/afternoon	*morgen/middag*
a quarter past one	*kwart over één*	evening/night	*avond/nacht*
half past one	*half twee* [sic]	Monday	*maandag*
a quarter to two	*kwart voor twee*	Tuesday	*dinsdag*
ten to/past three	*tien voor/over drie*	Wednesday	*woensdag*
twenty past five	*tien voor half zes*	Thursday	*donderdag*
twenty-five to eight	*vijf over half acht*	Friday	*vrijdag*
I'll come at 2 o'clock	*ik kom om twee uur*	Saturday/Sunday	*zaterdag/zondag*
today	*vandaag*	day/week/month	*dag/week/maand*
yesterday	*gisteren*	year	*jaar*

Menu Guide

may I see the menu/wine list?	*mag ik de spijskaart/wijnkaart zien?*
bon appétit	*eet smakelijk*
it tastes good/bad	*het smaakt lekker/niet lekker*
may I have the bill, please?	*mag ik de rekening, alstublieft?*
waiter/waitress	*ober/serveerster*
service	*bediening*
starter	*voorgerecht*

Drinks

a beer, please	*een pils, alstublieft*	fizzy mineral water	*spa rood* (brand)
a bottle of wine	*een fles wijn*	still mineral water	*spa blauw*
red/white	*rode/witte*	coffee (with milk)	*koffie (verkeerd)*
sweet/dry	*zoete/droge*	tea	*thee*
fresh orange juice	*jus d'orange*	(with milk/lemon)	*(met melk/citroen)*
tomato juice	*tomatensap*		

Index

Numbers in **bold** indicate main references. Numbers in *italic* indicate maps.

LONDON

AMSTERDAM